Color Choreography

FOUNDATIONAL STUDIES, INVESTIGATIONS AND DISCOURSE IN COLOR THEORY FOURTH EDITION

Alan McManus Burner

CENGAGE
Learning™

Australia • Brazil • Japan • Korea • Mexico • Singapore • Spain • United Kingdom • United States

CENGAGE
Learning™

Color Choreography: Foundational Studies, Investigations and Discourse in Color Theory, Fourth Edition
Alan McManus Burner

V.P Product Development: Dreis Van Landuyt

Custom Editor: Jason Fremder

Marketing Manager: Rob Bloom

Custom Production Editor: Kim Fry

Permissions Specialist: Kalina Ingham Hintz

Manufacturing Manager: Donna M. Brown

Sr. Production Coordinator: Robin Richie

Copy Editor: OffCenter Concepts

Cover Design: DB Graphic Design Services and Alan Burner

Cover Image: Color Choreographed by Shijo. Choreographed to Camile Saint Saens' *Carnival of the Animals-Danse Macabre*

Compositor: International Typesetting and Composition

For product information and technology assistance, contact us at
Cengage Learning Customer & Sales Support, 1-800-354-9706

For permission to use material from this text or product, submit all requests online at **cengage.com/permissions**
Further permissions questions can be emailed to
permissionrequest@cengage.com

Library of Congress Control Number: 2007936015

ISBN-13: 978-1-426-62923-5

ISBN-10: 1-426-62923-0

Cengage Learning
5191 Natorp Blvd.
Mason, OH 45040
USA

Cengage Learning is a leading provider of customized learning solutions with office locations around the globe, including Singapore, the United Kingdom, Australia, Mexico, Brazil, and Japan. Locate your local office at:
international.cengage.com/region

Cengage Learning products are represented in Canada by Nelson Education, Ltd.

For your lifelong learning solutions, visit **custom.cengage.com**
Visit our corporate website at **cengage.com**

Printed in the United States of America
1 2 3 4 5 6 7 12 11 10 09 08

PREFACE

Color is all around us. It is an overwhelming factor of our daily lives, more than we even realize. Color appears in nature where it beautifies our world, in our homes where it comforts and welcomes our guests, in the supermarket where we identify corporate products and packages, and as direction, communication and emotion in our everyday experiences. Colors tells us when to stop the car to allow opposing traffic to flow, it helps organize our paperwork and filing systems, it is used in creating mood, feeling and style in artwork, environments and communications of all types. Different cultures in the world interpret color in different ways as do people perceive color differently. The depths of the information about color and its use are as vast as the colors that can be created. This manual is the source to find the answers to the questions asked about all aspects relating to color and color theory.

Use of color in the visual communications industries has been opened to new horizons with the introduction of new technologies. Gone are the days where the extreme costs associated with reproducing color were prohibited to the artist and designer. The color expressions required are more available than ever to express the unique needs of the communication intended. But, without an understanding of the meaning behind the use of color, confusion and misinterpretation could hinder the intended message.

To really understand color and its uses, this textbook identifies the areas that define the theory and use of all aspects of color—light and physics, pigment and digital processes, scientific and historic arenas, and cultural and physiological issues. Applications in all aspects of art and design, vocabulary, concepts and expressions are used to further define the all-encompassing world of color and how we use and apply it to our processes. Students of color need to understand and use color correctly to not only communicate effectively, but to stir the desired reaction in the viewer.

Melinda Lester
Dean of Academic Affairs
The Art Institute of California – Orange County

Wenceslas Square

Enjoying a warm August afternoon while the beautiful hues of architecture are subtly muted in the shadows.

AUTHOR'S PROLOGUE

While traveling with my companions in Europe during the summer, I realized why I had become so passionate about color. During a lifetime of travels through Europe I have seen many cities, which seemed beautiful beyond compare. It was not until I visited the city of Prague that I truly understood the breadth of color's transforming capabilities.

From 1939 to 1989, darkness and gloom prevailed over the city, with gray drab, colorless buildings, as the evil empires of Nazi Germany, and then later the Soviet Communists engulfed the country. For five decades Prague was under siege by foreign powers until the collapse of soviet communism in 1989. Since that time, the city has become one of the most profound examples of color in a variance of *period architectural styles* in Europe

I feel as though we are in a period of color liberation. The people of Prague have been bringing back the former glory of the city; restoring the beautiful colors of sandstone buildings underneath the time worn surfaces. One by one, each building is being restored and painted with various hues of reds, oranges, yellows, blues, blue-greens and greens; all topped with terra cotta and copper crowns. The subtlety of every kind of color has instead invaded the city of Prague. It is as a fantasy, or a dream, with every historical period of architecture in one city, it seems to be the quintessential Europe. Color becomes symbolical of the overwhelming response to freedom and national pride.

Here, in the heart of Prague, we pause to appreciate the wonder of the subtle and delicate nuances of color and architecture. Color transitions throughout the city, as the sun makes its trek across the sky, creates ever changing mood responses. Minute by minute, the light hues are transformed into deep and magnificent colors; just before the city sleeps, and then repeats its chorus of color dispositions again.

It is a grandiose city of color where it seems but for awhile, fantasies can come true. Prague is a place that is being transformed. In Wenceslas Square, we stop for a moment and sit tranquilly, at peace and enjoy the glory of color.

Alan Burner
Prague, 2007

St. Franciscus Seraphicus Monastery Church

The changing colors of Prague as the new colors of the church are contrasted against the centuries old patina on the Charles Bridge statues.

PHOTO BY THE AUTHOR.

ABOUT THE AUTHOR

Alan Burner is a graduate of the University of California. Having received his MFA degree, he has an additional background in Japanese Language and Literature at the University. Since that time, he has been extensively involved in the global art community. Alan has worked in various capacities as an artist, lecturer, educator and author. He has contributed his skills as and artist and educator in Johannesburg, South Africa; Paris, France; Yokohama, Japan; Thailand and throughout Southern California. His art form includes mediums in photography, painting, bronze sculpture, ceramics and video performances, and has been featured on televised presentations on PBS and gallery exhibitions.

As an avid traveler and color enthusiast, he has been involved with critical investigations about the nature and character of color, various theories, realities and cultural perspectives. His current primary research is in Europe and Thailand. Gothic architecture, Japanese literature and Thai elephants that paint with acrylic paint, demonstrates the span of his research interests in the world of color, and frequently serve as some of the most passionate examples for discussions about the theory of color today. A truly international artist, his choreographed painted performances seek to bring physical reality to color's chief attribute, which is emotional appeal, or the creation of mood. His visualizations of the mood component in music, as well as dance, are peppered with multi-cultural richness.

Botana in Prague, Aug 07

ACKNOWLEDGEMENTS

To Brad Janis, my good friend. Thank you to my colleagues at Paris University and the University of California for their thoughtful dialogues during the construction of this research. A debt of gratitude to Kayo Suzuki for *Japanese color connections,* Denis Ribouillault for discourse in *French perspectives,* and Christo and Jeanne-Claude for their counsel in respect to *The Valley Curtain* and *The Umbrellas.* I am deeply appreciative to Melinda Lester for her constant encouragement, Richard Ewing for his marvelous caricatures in the first chapter, and Bill Jaynes for his inspirational attitude. A very special thanks to Surachai Nimwat, for his efforts to make Thailand's elephant *rendez-vous* a reality. Of particular noteworthiness, is my *discourse of praise* to Narumol Sornkeaw for consistent devotion.

To Sharada and Kelly

The Prague Castle Wall Along the Old Castle Stairway — Prague, Czech Republic

This is the largest continuous castle complex in the world, which houses some of the greatest examples of the *glory of color*. Within these walls are the Coronation Jewels, a collection of renowned paintings from the 15th and 16th centuries, and some of the most extraordinary colored glass windows (St. Vitus' Cathedral) known to humankind.

TEXTBOOK COMPONENTS
A NEW APPROACH TO COLOR EDUCATION

This textbook offers some new and challenging approaches, as well as traditional approaches, to the instruction of color theory, both in content and methodology. In reality, it is a collection of *color investigations,* that take a serious look into the psychological, philosophical, and physiological effects of color. *Color Choreography* also covers conventional physics and the traditional characteristics of color. It is instructional discourse, which covers everything from the science of color to the emotional and spiritual nuances of color. The student will learn to integrate the visual and intellectual aspects of learning in a more comprehensive way through a series of *written analysis* and *color projects.*

The respected institution of color theory and those who preceded us—Aristotle, Sir Isaac Newton, Johannes Itten, and many others—have made critical color investigations, wrote extensively about their findings, and presented them to the world. In the case of Newton, certain key elements of the nature of light and color are the foundation for what we teach today. Out of these early findings emerged a conventional method for teaching color theory that we've subscribed to for many years. This foundation of color theory pioneered the discovery of color and its ramifications, and for that we owe it eternal loyalty and great respect.

Since Newton's time, we have discovered new and exciting aspects about color and methods for teaching it. When this textbook was conceived, it was my intention not to create yet another color theory book for the sake of writing a text. We don't need another book on the subject repeating the same approach. As we reach into the twenty-first century, we have discovered and enacted many new approaches to living our lives. Why then, shouldn't we make solid steps forward in the all-inclusive education of color theory?

Through the expertise of the color theory instructor, students will discover the mysteries of the color world. To enhance that discovery, this book offers a comprehensive arrangement of color investigations and a story of color from the physical to the spiritual attributes.

One of the components of the text that departs from traditional books on the subject is the suggested written analysis of color compositions, which is an important option in the student's education of color. Within any color theory course, as in this text, there are a collection of relevant hands-on projects. Accompanying these projects, whether selected from this text or the individual instructor's preferred repertoire of assignments, is written analysis for the sake of thoroughness. The student could, for example, write a summary or analysis on his or her finished project, or analyze an assigned color composition of the instructor's choice.

One of the problems of educating the serious student of color lies within the proper exercising of critical thinking skills. Certainly, the traditional approaches to color theory education are sound and encouraged in the conventional application of color project assignments. We have found, however, that incorporating the written analysis of various color compositions is a valuable tool in the deeper understanding and retention of color theory and science. This book encourages the development of critical color observation by project solutions, as well as written and oral analysis.

Studies show that a student's ability to absorb and retain information is most effective when writing as opposed to merely listening to lectures. Therefore, *class lecture notes, written assignments,* and *color analysis* serve to aid in a student's retention of what is taught. Preservation of learned material is typically 35–45 percent greater when putting the pen to paper in a lecture, or if writing about a particular research project. Writing helps not only to perfect the student's proclivity to retain information, but also in his or her ability to efficiently *communicate* about the subject. Our goal then is to develop the capability to demonstrate color proficiency by both written work and project assignments.

The students are provided with an opportunity to illustrate their development in critical thinking skills by researching selected artists work and making a thorough written analysis. For the analysis, the student is first asked to study and write about important historical information (short biography) concerning an assigned artist, linking the purposes of the artist to the work. Secondly, the student presents an effective written color analysis about the artwork itself.

MOOD AND EMOTION IN COLOR

Before we begin with the color analysis, it will be beneficial to briefly discuss the emotional issues of color. Every color scheme or harmony elicits a particular emotion or mood. The component of mood is clearly one of the most important functions of color. Everything that incorporates the use of color, whether applying pigments on a canvas, designing on a computer monitor, or perhaps planning the interior of a room, has the end result of creating very specific moods. In reality it is mood, created by color, that reaches the soul and stirs the emotions. It is therefore vital to develop an understanding of how color is part of that spiritual world—the inner being. During the course, mood will become an issue that gains greater momentum as the student learns more about color and its various functions.

Here then, is an explanation of the components of this textbook, beginning with the critical component of the *written analysis.* Consider the following work of George Inness and Frederic Leighton as two color-mood analysis examples.

In the case of the American painter George Inness, we find that he made critical choices about the use of color in his artwork. These choices are directly responsible for the

GEORGE INNESS, **Evening Landscape,** 1862, gift of Dr. and Mrs. William E. Boeing, from the Permanent Collection, Museum of Art/Washington State University, Pullman, WA.

creation of specific moods. Let's look at the colors incorporated into George Inness' *Evening Landscape.*

This painting sets up a striking contrast of complementary colors, or opposites, in terms of the *light, heavenly* red-orange sky, and the *weighty mass* of the blue-green terra firma. It is both complementary in terms of color and the representation of luminous space as opposed to solid heavy mass. The trees and the ground seem to consume the better part of the composition, with its dark and gloomy values.

It is the luminous, almost spiritual approach to painting the sky that focuses the eye on the earthiness of the environment and the toil of humankind. It is a revealing manifestation of color's effect on the human psyche. The mood is somber and respectful of both the human condition on earth and the earth itself. It speaks of the journey through life, both the bright spots and the burdens.

Inness shows us a world where God exists in a heavenly, spiritual realm, and humankind's existence is grounded and tangible. The mood and symbolic references are replete within the *Evening Landscape.*

"The wisest and best way to know
George Inness is to sit before his works,
to search them to their depths, to study
each item of composition, its bearing
upon the great mass, to find, if one may,
the law by which he constructed his proportions and placements, *to discover the reasons for color or tone choice, or that deeper significance,* the impulsive, artistic and religious, which created it."

ELLIOTT DAINGERFIELD

Leighton's *Flaming June* (next page) is one of the finest examples of eighteenth-century Victorian art today. Intensely feminine, the mood of this painting replicates a *tranquil* slumber, and yet it conveys a sensuous *energy.* The *calmness of mood* is reflected by the image itself, yet the various hues of orange expose a sensually *energized* composition. The painting illustrates the fine and subtle nuances of chromatic value, which change through the elegant, sheer drapery. The delicate hues of orange seem to invite a type of erotic expectation, if not in a dream.

In Leighton's painting, we again see contrasts; the tangible and the intangible. June's physical body, the warm passionate hues in the composition, contrasted to her dream state or spiritual existence perhaps seen by the delicate luminescence of the composition itself.

Frederic Leighton, *Flaming June*, 1895.

Written Analysis of Color

Consider how import it is to adequately explain a lovely village in Italy, for example, to clients in order to develop a central theme in their minds. One of the themes in this textbook relates to exactly how we are to develop a sensitivity to appropriate color descriptions. This scene may sound something like the following written analysis.

Tivoli (next page), with its typical small town "pottery village" atmosphere, creates an ambiance of beautiful simplicity and delicate color nuances. A subtle complementary color harmony of warm yellow-oranges and cool blue-violets dominate this street scene. The background apartment building bathes in the sun's intense light on a hot July summer day, while the foreground wall beckons the passer-by to a shady retreat from the heat of the day.

The plaza street's imagery, in a sense, becomes a painting, which is emphasized by high contrasting color and graceful variations of tints and shades. The monolithic architecture with its hot, radiant, yellow-orange surface is in direct opposition to the wall's cooling blue-violet shades. Values of violets and oranges exemplify the sense of mass and weight seen in the majestic vases on the wall. Their dull violet and deep orange patinas provide a transitional link of color gradations between the wall and the building.

Street Scene, Tivoli, Italy.

PHOTO BY THE AUTHOR.

The lack of saturated color on the architectural wall, as well as the dull shades of the concrete and wood partition, illustrates the extremes of high contrast with the more delicate transitions of value gradations, which are indicative of a hot summer day in Italy. The warm and cool contrasts of hue variations help to establish a certain power in the imagery itself. The chromatic value transitions of the large vases, the strong vertical thrust of the blue-violet textured wall, and the flat monolithic yellow-orange architecture controls the temperature of the space. As we feel the heat of the day, contrasted by a cooling shade, there is a very tranquil mood set specifically by the sedate sensibility on this quiet street in Tivoli.

Now we will discuss how important writing is by using specific examples of successful artists throughout history. If we can establish their success based on their need to write, then certainly we are beholden to consider the same for ourselves. Some of the greatest color artists throughout history understood that creative prowess cannot be achieved by simply responding to the medium based on physical response alone, but by very careful observation and investigation. Each of the following artists used writing to achieve a specific result, albeit not the same one, but they all achieved one thing in common—successful art.

Leonardo da Vinci of the high Renaissance knew something of the relationship between the written word and visual creation. Leonardo wrote extensively about art—in fact, some thought that perhaps he wrote too much and painted too little. Certainly, a great number of his journals contain both sketches and written observations. Da Vinci was a leader in the world of written investigations into art and color, as well as a *scientist* and inventor. He was both a *philosopher* and *scientist* on the subject of color.

Da Vinci understood the development of critical thinking skills and color prowess attained by the persistent use of the pen. The more he observed, the more he wrote; the more he wrote, the more proficient he became with color. How could he remember so many critical observations about color unless he was recording them? By doing so, he developed an intimate understanding about the use of color.

His written scientific annotations served him well in clarifying his color formulas accurately, and his recorded philosophical arguments among the painter (himself), the poet, and the musician also proved beneficial. His written discourse on their debates (as to whose medium was the most "excellent" in the creative process) cemented in his own mind the validity of *his* opinion and therefore, the difference and superiority of painting. We realize that his philosophy concerning superiority is subjective, and serves more to the benefit of the artist.

NATIONAL GALLERY OF ART, WASHINGTON.

Leonardo Da Vinci, *Ginevra de Benci,* 1474.

VINCENT VAN GOGH, *Harvest Landscape*, 1888.

It shouldn't be any wonder or secret then, after so many austere renderings and written observations about people and their sensibilities, that works such as the *Mona Lisa* and *Ginevra de Benci* are so accomplished. Da Vinci's strict execution of pigments is certainly due to his faithful records of observation. In this case, it would seem that observations from past records gave him the edge for the creation of *Lisa Gherardini,* because we have no records or notes about her specifically.

Vincent van Gogh was notorious for his written observations of life via his letters to his brother Theo. It has been reported that there are at least 800 known letters in which van Gogh discusses his personal needs and beliefs, hardships of life, his inability to work, and the reflections and memories that fill his "head and heart."

Van Gogh's approach to the recorded journal was decidedly different from the conventional notebook because he wrote letters, and yet they carried the tone of a diary read by his benefactor, Theo. Van Gogh worked through his observations about people—how they worked, labored, and the difficulty of life, for example—in his letters. Once he had reconciled their pains, he chose the subdued and shaded color schemes necessary to project that mood.

In his painting the *Potato Eaters,* he was fascinated with the idea of back-breaking work: planting, cultivating, digging the potatoes out of the ground, and harvesting them to sell and eat. All this was a product of the laborers' own hands. There were times when he would write and produce paintings about *Arles,* where he spent many

happy days as a young man. They were pleasant memories; paintings such as the *Harvest Landscape* (above), which is a ablaze with rich saturated color. They are brilliant color fields of yellows and oranges, paintings that allowed him to vicariously live out his life, for the moment, in peace and tranquility.

Van Gogh's letters reveal a highly intelligent man in spite of his psychological issues. He was one of the greatest master color experts throughout the history of art. His vast luminescent color fields of emotion create the precise mood of the artist and help us to understand the mind of van Gogh. Clearly, the success of his work depended on his evaluation of everyday life through writing letters to his brother Theo.

Paul Gauguin (next page), with his flat and often saturated color fields of paint, knew how important keeping a journal was to an artist. In his Tahitian journals, he records many personal feelings and accounts of island life away from his native France. As Gauguin moved more toward the abstract use of color, he began to write more frequently about the validity of his color theories. In a lesson to one of his young apprentices, he wrote, ". . . . How do you see these trees? They are yellow. Well then, put down yellow. And that shadow is rather blue. So, render it with pure ultramarine. Those red leaves? Use vermillion." He saw color in the trees and painted them with as much saturation as possible.

Often times painting *from memory*, he recorded the color exaggeration as he translated it in his mind. What he

PAUL GAUGUIN, *Ia Orana Maria* (Hail Mary), 1891.

committed to the written page was then cemented in his mind. Gauguin wrote extensively about his art concerns as well, often validating and sometimes inviting criticism. Like van Gogh, who occasionally received one of Gauguin's letters, Gauguin was a letter writer extraordinaire.

Wassily Kandinsky, the artist, intellectual, and profound writer about art concerns in the twentieth century, revealed his prowess in the spiritual realm of art. His writing about communicating the spiritual intangible into a physical concrete world are unparalleled. He presents his findings through the written word, a discourse on the subject few have managed to achieve. He has made critical observations about the ramifications of line and symbolism, and his revelations of exploratory missions in art take us deep into the spiritual world of color.

Kandinsky's precise and very meticulous observations give us a greater understanding of what he refers to as "external nature," expressed in linear color compositions, which are then contrasted to the "inner nature." Kandinsky declared that color in and of itself is capable of unfolding the spiritual realm if it is not assigned a certain predetermined shape or image.

Pablo Picasso (next page), one of history's most successful artists, is replete with artwork but seriously deficient in writing skills. (His focus was singular to a fault, as he depleted his female companions of their vigor.) He would use them for the sole purpose as art subjects, and discard

WASSILY KANDINSKY, *Yellow-Red-Blue*, 1925.

them after transfusing their energies into his work—the finished painting. However, Picasso fully understood the necessity for the written journal regarding art and its evaluation, so he surrounded himself with poets and writers. Francoise, his young lover, wrote that Picasso was able to discuss his artwork eloquently because of his friendships with poets and writers. After one of Pablo's gatherings with friends she wrote, "Afterwards Pablo, who—for things like that—was an extremely adaptable, supple person, always talked very perceptively about his painting because of his intimacy with those who had been able to discover the right words." f/n (p.136 of *Life with Picasso*)

Even a nonwriter like Picasso understood the extreme value of the written word. After all, how could he have been so articulate in his dialogues without some source that enabled him to clearly define what he accomplished in his work? Certainly, if he was unable to write for whatever reason, then his writer friends could. Here is an art form so full of expression and visual dynamic that it requires the descriptive force and sophistication only a writer can provide. Writers such as Max Jacob, Paul Eluard, Andre'

Breton, and Apollinaire were all key elements of his writing success.

How to Begin a Written Analysis of Color in a Composition

Often, the student of color will be asked to fine-tune his or her critical thinking skills by the careful analysis of a composition (in this case, a painting). Frequently, students are overwhelmed because they tend to look at the composite parts simultaneously, rather than singularly. The result is always "where do I start?" or "why can't I find much to write about?" Because mood is the chief characteristic of color, and the final result of most color analysis, first try to isolate the mood, and then validate that decision. In the second composition, we will cite the mood of the colors lastly, which is normally a more accurate method. Finally, there should be three phases to the analyzing of color in any composition. Look at the following two samples and notice how each area is observed and noted, piece by piece, section by section.

PABLO PICASSO, **Portrait of Dora Maar,** 1937.

Example One

ERICH LESSING/ART RESOURCE, NY.

FERRÉOL DE BONNEMAISON, ***Young Woman Surprised by a Thunderstorm.***

First Draft General Outline of Ferréol de Bonnemaison's Painting

1. Mood: Background is dark and fearful. Blue tones.
2. Shaded blue gradations. Background values.
3. Tree is centered. Foreground. Greens and yellows, some red tones.
4. Different value changes in the composition.
5. Red-orange and yellow-green bark.
6. Tree contrast.
7. Tree's texture.
8. Figure of a young girl. Clothing blowing off.
9. Intensity of the skin tones, seems luminous.
10. Contrast of figure with background.
11. Delicate vs. harshness.
12. Earth/foreground.

Second Draft with Specific Outline of Ferréol de Bonnemaison's Painting

1. Mood: Fearful, depressing, filled with gloom and despair. It is full of darkness contrasted by light.

2. Background: Beginning at the horizon and ascending to the top of the composition, the background of medium shaded blue to darkest blue, creates a smooth transition of chromatic values. It is the shaded blue gradations that seem to create the mystery, the darkness that overwhelms the center figure.

3. Large and slightly diagonal tree splits composition. Lighter shade of green foliage creates a marginal contrast between it and the darker background.

4. Tints and shades, or value changes from light to dark and back again, create the illusion of three dimensions as is the case throughout the painting.

5. The underneath layer of tree's bark is composed of a red-orange, ranging from an intense red-orange area over her head to a shaded red-orange. The outer layer of bark is a dull yellow-green.

6. The bark of the tree sets up a middle-range contrast between it and the background.

7. The rapid transitions of values or light to dark gradations of yellow-green in the bark create the illusion of rough texture.

8. The foreground is occupied by a young girl, whose clothing is being ripped from her body by the force of the wind. The mood is now validated, as we sense dark, stormy, dismal weather. The girl's expression matches the mood created by the colors in the composition.

9. The texture of her skin seems very soft, as very intense lightest orange values make the subtlest value gradations.

10. The intense light blue gown reveals the severity of the weather by its horizontal rippling. The resultant contrast of the lightest blue robe and the darkest blue background creates the illusion of space in the composition. The lightest orange hue of her skin helps to push her further into the foreground.

11. There is a symbolic contrast among the delicacy of the light orange skin, the lightest blue gown in the foreground, and the sturdy and harsh darker blues of the stormy environment around her.

12. Finally, the shaded or dulled green and orange hues of the foreground on which the girl stands lead the eye back to the horizon and up into the dark blue clouds.

Third and Final Draft of Ferréol de Bonnemaison's Painting (no longer an outline)

Beginning with the mood of the painting, we are drawn to several aspects of the composition; the figure, the tree, and the background. I want to cite the mood aspects of color in the painting first, and show why it is color that creates mood, more than the expression of the figure's face itself.

I am drawn to the background hues of shaded blue and violet values. As the eye moves from the horizon, the lighter shaded blues make a smooth transition upward, graduating into an extremely dark blue that is almost black in appearance. The background clouds create a darkness, a certain mystery about the weather and what is about to happen. The sky is depressing and the air heavy, as the intensity of the storm increases and begins to overwhelm the young girl.

The tree is particularly important because it sets up a gradual diagonal, splitting the composition and creating a tilt or certain instability about the composition. The light and dark values of dull green leaves blow with intensity, and seem to barely separate themselves from the dark sky. The value gradations in the green foliage seem to create a leaf that is forced into a cupped shape, further exaggerating the storm's ferocity. The leaves are convincingly three-dimensional, as is the entire composition, because of the variations of value changes.

The texture of the tree's bark is believably rough, thanks to a more severe or rapid change of value, or light to dark rendering. The underneath, newer bark exposing itself in selected patches, is shown by the red-orange to shaded red-orange hues, compared to the older higher intensity surface bark of yellow-greens. The bark now creates a middle-range contrast between the tree and the background. A definite depth of space is created as a result.

A young girl occupies the foreground, positioned close to the center of the composition, just ahead of the tree's trunk. Her clothing, rippling violently in the wind, is partially blown off of her body. The leaves on the tree seem to struggle to remain on the branches, as does her sheer gossamer robe to her body. At this point, we look up to her face, only to find the girl's expression validates the mood that the colors have already revealed.

The texture of her skin reflects a very intense lightest orange, making the most subtle of *sfumato* value gradations. Her skin is soft, delicate and contrasts against the harshness of the dull blues and violets in the background. Commensurately, the refined lightest blue fabric and darkest blue background creates the illusion of deep space by nature of the contrast itself. Her intense light orange skin assists to move her body into the foreground.

The shaded or dull green and orange hues of the foreground, by which the girl stands, leads the viewer's eye toward the background horizon again, and eventually ascends up into the darkness of the deep blue-violet clouds.

Finally, there also is a *symbolic contrast* between the delicacy of her light orange skin tones and her light blue gown, against the sturdy and harsh darker blues and blue-violets of the stormy environment around her. The red-oranges of the tree's bark and the red-orange hair draw the figure close to the tree, holding her safely against the trunk.

The emotion and energy of this painting in the totality of its composite parts, combine with the subtle dyad harmonies, (complements of blues and oranges) to create a dynamic composition reflecting the mood of terror in this impending storm.

Example Two

VINCENT VAN GOGH, *The Red Vineyard at Arles,* 1888.

First Draft General Outline
of Vincent van Gogh's Painting

1. Background light yellow sun.
2. Sky/horizon occupies very little space. Intense sky.
3. Saturated orange—background.
4. Saturated red/shaded red—middle-ground.
5. Dark foreground—blue-greens.
6. Curved road, like shimmering body of water: blue-greens and yellow-oranges.
7. Grape pickers.
8. Perspective by line and color. Larger analogous areas.
9. Lesser blue-green areas.
10. Black shade and line.
11. Light violet hills, under trees.
12. Mood is somber.

Second Draft Specific Outline of Vincent van Gogh's Painting

1. Background focal point illuminated by a very intensely lit light-yellow sun, surrounded by yellow-orange rays of light.

2. Horizon line to the top of the composition occupies only one-fifth of the uppermost composition. In that space the sun, a barn, and a row of blue-green trees exist. There is a green tint that radiates out from the trees, into the intensely lit, light-yellow sky.

3. Just below the horizon, still in the extreme background, lies a patch of fairly saturated orange, which takes the eye to the stretches of the vineyard.

4. Middle-ground area consists of saturated red hues, which move further into the foreground to create a darker shaded red area of vines.

5. Foreground is perceived to be light shaded greens to very dark shaded green, interspersed with splashes of shaded red-orange.

6. On the right side of the composition there is a road; it appears as a shimmering body of water, reflecting blue-greens and yellow-oranges.

7. The vineyard itself is peppered with field hands, or grape pickers who are harvesting the crop. End of day and tired from hard labor.

8. Strong sense of perspective is created by line and color. Foreground is dark and becomes lighter, or more intense as we move into the background. Red, orange, and yellow dominate, with red-orange and yellow-orange interspersed between those areas. A dominant *analogous* color harmony prevails throughout the largest part of the composition.

9. Blue-green dominates the remaining one-third of the painting.

10. Patches and lines of black accent the composition, creating shades under the trees as well as the floor of the vineyard and the grape stakes.

11. A slight amount of light violet shows up under the trees, the horizon's hills, and on fabrics worn by the workers.

12. Mood is somber, created not by the saturated colors, but by contrast of them to the very dull and shaded blue-greens. The darkness creates contrast to the saturation, and it seems as though the lesser area of that darkness is consuming the greater area of saturated space.

Third and Final Draft of Vincent van Gogh's Painting

The Red Vineyard exhibits a blazing light-yellow sun setting near the horizon line. Yellow-orange lines surround the sun's perimeter and radiate out from its edge into a sky of intense yellow. The circular lines of yellow-orange mix with the intense yellow of the sky to produce a saturated yellow field of color. The area that occupies the sky is no more than one-fifth of the overall composition, and yet it dominates as a focal point, in contrast to the bulk of colors in the painting. A blue-green tint radiates into the yellow sky. Working from the background of the painting, the row of blue-green trees seems to pull the eye from the horizon into the vineyard itself.

The immediate area or field below the horizon emits a soft glow of saturated orange, contrasting and drawing attention to the figure on the cart. Just below, in the middle-ground area, the vineyard becomes a very saturated red, which transforms it closer to the viewer's space, into a shaded red, or red-orange field. The foreground then becomes light shaded blue-greens and dark blue-greens, interspersed with splashes of shaded red-orange hues.

On the right side of the composition, the road almost appears to be a body of water as it glistens with its bright colors. The yellow-orange hues of the setting sun are mirrored, as the blues of a darkening sky create a cool quiet across the road and adjoining field.

The vineyard is peppered with people picking the grape crop, as the horse-drawn cart moves through the field to collect the harvest. They seem to be working slowly, weary at a day's end of hard labor. Darkness is settling over the field, and the colors of red begin to darken in the first half of the composition, sedating the picture.

A strong sense of deep space is created by line and color perspective. As the eye focuses on the foreground, it slowly moves into the background space, as the hues become lighter, or more intense. Red, orange, and yellow seem to control the predominately analogous composition, with hues of red-orange, and yellow-orange interspersed between those areas. The remaining one-third of the painting is dominated by blue-greens, with black patches in the foreground field, grape sticks, lines, and shadows under the trees. Additionally, there exists the smallest amount of light violet in the horizon's hills, and on some of the worker's clothing.

The mood is somber at this day's end, created not by the saturated colors themselves, but by the very nature of their contrast to the darker, dull, shaded blue-greens. The dullness of the blue-greens creates a type of saturated contrast with the more intense hues. It is as though the darkness of the lesser area consumes the greater area of saturated space. The rapidly changing chromatic values bring about the night quickly, as workers hurriedly pick the last remaining fruit.

The analysis of Ferréol de Bonnemaison and Vincent van Gogh's works are just two examples of breaking down the component parts of a color composition and identifying their specific functions. There are various other techniques for the accomplishment of analyzing a color composition, but this methodology seems to produce the best results for the average student. Looking at the entire painting can be intimidating, but by describing each color area of the composition, we are more careful to see everything in that quadrant. A color theorist is not merely concerned with identifying visual components alone, but also about learning to see color correctly—how it functions and manipulates mood.

In the first example, we began by identifying the mood immediately. When we analyzed the second image, however, mood may have been more difficult to identify, and so the emotional issue was the last attribute to be cited. Often the mood of a composition is apparent immediately; other times it is not. To validate why a color or a scheme of colors creates a particular mood, it's sometimes necessary to break down and identify each compositional element first. Afterward, the sum total of these components help us recognize the emotional factors. When we successfully analyze a work of art we essentially transform our critical thinking into concrete knowledge. The results are in, and what we learn must be calculated in the written word. This process of analysis has lasting results that the student actually carries out of the class and commits to memory.

I hope that the student realizes the significance of written color analysis. Artists and designers from all disciplines must possess the ability to effectively communicate and use appropriate color vocabulary whether in written or oral form.

STUDENT ARTWORK, **Reclining Nude.**

RACHAEL WUEST, **Chalk Drawing.** This student understands the value of her ability to analyze compositional color. The drawing demonstrates her knowledge of saturation, intensity, value, tints and shades, contrast, harmony, and emotional appeal.

STUDENT ARTWORK, *Three-Dimensional Color Study.* Ordinary objects are changed by color and texture differences. The emphasis was to analyze color mood transformations when altering the original colors.

PROJECT PROPOSALS

Undertaking a project is an equally important task for the student of color. What we know intellectually we also must put into practice. The next step is to transform knowledge into a demonstrated product. The application of colored pigments to a surface, the creation of color fields on a computer monitor, or the three-dimensional application of color harmonies of a designed interior all rely on physically manipulating color.

In the first chapter, you will be introduced to *saturation, intensity,* and *values.* In the next chapter we will continue our discussions about saturation and intensity issues, and then in the third and fourth chapters *contrast, tints,* and *shades* will be explored through a variety of possible projects. Chapter 5 will focus on *color harmony,*

and Chapters 7 and 8 investigate emotional factors of *color expression* and the *spiritual dimension* of color.

Chapters include a sample developed project, referred to as a *project proposal,* as one of many projects possible for the respective chapter. Projects can be in the form of physical paint or digital processes such as a camera or computer. *The purpose of the hands-on project is the* [*physical manifestation of your understanding of color, just as the written analysis evaluates your intellectual comprehension of the topic.*] Your assignment may come in various forms: the application of color pigments and various materials, arrangements of three-dimensional color objects, photographs, computer applications, and such, depending on the instructor's construction of the class.

It is important to note here that there are various suggested projects throughout the text. However, the instructor may select project assignments from his or her own repertoire of projects to better accommodate the structure of the particular class. The projects in this text are focused primarily on the hands-on approach, such as with pigments (paint) and film (photography). However, from time to time computer applications may become necessary as well.

There are many equally legitimate project methods and mediums for the instruction of color theory. Whatever the medium of choice, or selected project style, the basic information presented in this text is relevant for all applications of color theory education.

READING COMPLEMENTS

There are segments of guest and author lectures referred to as *Reading Complements,* which provide special emphasis on color related topics. These areas are considered complements to the learning process, rather than essential study components. Certainly, they serve as an additional

MICHELANGELO BUONARROTI, *The Creation of Adam,* 1510. This ceiling fresco is a small portion of a much larger rendition of Biblical stories, which many consider to be a visual record of events.

THE GALLERY COLLECTION/CORBIS.

PUBLIC DOMAIN.

SCALA/ART RESOURCE, NY.

Wall Fresco from a House Featuring a Banquet in Pompeii. (top) The triclinium, frescoed in the 3rd style, featured banqueting scenes in the centre of the walls; a complete glass table service resting on a three-legged wooden table is portrayed here, as if to flaunt the owner's standard of living. (left) In scene VIII, when the pleasure is over, the girl is whipped by a winged demon to the clash of cymbals played by two bacchantes.

source to provide supplementary research, and to illuminate and clarify lecture topics in their respective chapters. Additionally, the length of the course and instructor preference will be determinants as to which of these sectors are incorporated into the instruction.

HIGHLIGHTS

Highlights are short observations about color relationships in a variance of contexts. These additional indulgences of color include:

I. Colors of Temples—Thailand: Architectural Surfaces
II. Color in Sculpture—Japan: Art and Stained Glass
III. Colors in City Environments—Japan: Architecture
IV. Color in Paintings of Elephant Painters—Thailand: Art and Acrylic Paint
V. Color in Costume Design—Japan: Fashion and Fabrics

VI. Colors of Mozart—Europe: Music
VII. Colors of the Northern Lights—Aurora Borealis-Northern Hemisphere: Science
VIII. Color Matching and Moods in Nature—Thailand: Psychological

Highlights are representative of the textbook itself, in that there are many approaches to color. These serve as stimulus for further research, or simply as interesting anecdotes of information.

HISTORICAL ART EXAMPLES IN COLOR

Historical art examples in color exist throughout the book, both in separate illustrations, as well as in the *Color Equations* preamble to follow. It is important to observe and be able to analyze the applications and function of color through its historical chronology. Whether it be physical or digital color processes, the artist's and designer's

Details from the Law Window in the Nave—Washington National Cathedral.

prowess in color, is predicated on the knowledge of color's history. Basically, we want to make a case for the study of color in artwork, through art history.

We now have artworks and writings of artists from past centuries that contain valuable information about the history of the world. History is about written records of past human events; art history concerns *visual* records of past human events. It is one thing to read about past civilizations, but it is quite another to witness them through such things as pigmented frescoes and painted compositions.

It is profound that we knew so little about ancient Rome and their habits until the excavation of Pompeii's ruins, a popular vacation spot and luxurious city south of Rome. The excavation of the city of Pompeii was begun in 1748, and continued for the next 247 years to the end of the twentieth century (about 1995). These diggings proved to be one of the most significant discoveries in the history of art, revealing beautiful frescoes, often wall to wall, within the homes of the city's inhabitants.

In 79 A.D., after the area was plagued with a series of earthquakes, the nearby Mount Vesuvius erupted, spewing tons of volcanic ash into the air over Pompeii. As the ash settled over the city, intermittent rain storms quickly cooled and hardened the ash layer falling over the city. For more than 1,600 years, Pompeii lay buried and forgotten. These layers of ash sealed the city and protected it from nature's

punishment of time. As a result, the well-preserved pigmented walls of Pompeii have provided us with amazing detail and insight into the Roman culture. The frescoes are in such good condition, we know exactly which *colors* were important to the Romans and the significance of particular color schemes and harmonies in that culture.

The case for the study of color is particularly relevant both then and now. Every artist should be concerned with the study of art history and how colors of any particular period in history functioned, and why. One example is seen in the red and blue color schemes that typify many of the Gothic cathedral windows (see the law window above). Long before the Roman Empire, red was the predominant color of choice when dying fabrics. Red was plentiful, it came from an organic or plant-based (flora) dye, and it was much more resistant to fading than other colors. Red certainly was more vivid, and seemed to possess a majestic ambiance not seen in the remaining spectrum.

Red was so popular in the Roman world, it actually reigned as the color supreme through the midpoint of the Medieval period. As time progressed far beyond the Roman Empire, *blue* began to surface as the popular color, thanks to the availability of the woad plant, or leaf. Blue was no longer thought of as a commoner's color, and began to be worn and used more frequently during the eleven and twelfth centuries. By the thirteenth century, contrasting red and blue color schemes began to grace the Gothic cathedral windows. Soon enough, hues of blue became the color of choice over red, worn even by the highest of nobility.

Color choices throughout history have not been arbitrary. Color decisions incorporate symbolic, psychological, and spiritual aspects into any given situation, as well as a host of other specific and well-designed color functions. Anyone who has a career associated with color is beholden, then, to the importance of color proficiency.

Our brief studies of individual artists in the *lecture artists* section, therefore, will not be unlike the student's quest to color analyze a given work of art. The difference is that the lecture artist's section provides an opportunity for the student to see how the instructor methodically analyzes a color composition. The student is encouraged to take notes while the instructor discusses each composition. This will provide the student with an example of how the instructor wants the analysis to proceed.

Historically, colorists understood the importance of the *critical thinking* mind. Now, in the twenty-first century, the color-savvy professional artist or designer needs critical thinking skills more than ever. The great art masters of centuries past were awesome because of their intensive investigations into the dynasty of light.

Note: Colors referred to in the text may occasionally differ from the originals due to differences in various printing processes. Every effort is made to present colors as accurately as possible.

In this introduction section "*A New Approach to Color Education*," we discussed:

1. Color's foremost attributes, which are emotional appeal and mood. (marjor characteristic)

2. The importance of project and written assignments. In today's art and design world color studies are vital, and it is the development of critical thinking skills that makes one a successful problem solver. The emphasis here has been on the written analysis of color within a given composition.

3. Down-to-earth examples have been provided as a coaching tool for the understanding of how to write a creative analysis.

4. A word about the vital Reading Complements, or guest essays.

5. Historical references, which introduce the importance of history in color.

CHAPTER ONE

Figure 1-1 Thai Monk in the Bangkok Area of Thailand. Traditionally, wood from the jackfruit tree was responsible for the orange tones of fabric worn by Thai monks. The sawdust generated from the jackfruit wood was used as a dye for their robes. Results are a range of orange hues, from deep yellow-orange to a darker red-orange (brown). At one point, saffron was used as a yellow dye during the process as an accompaniment, but the high cost and availability of saffron became an issue. At the time of this printing, saffron prices average a little under $2,000.00 per pound. Today synthetics have made color more accessible or affordable, whether in the coloring industry or for the individual artist and painter.

1

COLOR EQUATIONS

A PREAMBLE TO COLOR
ASSOCIATIONS IN ART HISTORY

Before we begin our basic studies of color, color equations is offered as an introduction to the role of color throughout history.

When we say color *elements*, we refer to the specifics of color, such as *hue, value (tints and shades), intensity, saturation, contrast,* and *harmony.* The combined force of these elements are the factors that construct the color composition, and work together to create particular moods, or applications of emotional appeal.

Some of the best known art forms have been compiled chronologically in order to discuss the attributes of color in a historical context. It is a type of *history of color* seen through art's traditional sequential periods. Much is said during lectures about these art forms over the course of any given *Art History* class: the story of the painting, the artist's background, period, style, composition, culture, as well as a general accounting about the elements and principles of art (design) and so forth. This chapter, however, involves a brief discussion about specific attributes and pigments of color in a more isolated sense, which is to say that our *focus will be color.* The following brief *survey of color in history* is not meant to pose as standard lessons in art history, or to replace traditional art history instruction; rather it is a brief sampling of the philosophical, physiological, and psychological nature of color. Art history simply becomes the *vehicle* by which we can gain a broader understanding of color through historical visual applications.

Artwork examples are labeled accordingly:

1. *Title of the artwork* (and artist when known);
2. *origins of color pigments,* referring to specific colors and pigments used in each visual application;
3. *binders* used that are important for the longevity of the artwork; and
4. the *emphasis,* which refers to the particulars of a given style and/or time period

This chapter can serve as an introduction to color's physical, psychological, and symbolical characteristics, as well as historical *teasers* about the function of a given painting or artwork.

Significant elaboration on these issues will be approached throughout the following chapters. Our brief survey will begin in the ancient world, where colors from raw earth pigments and basic organic matter were realized as elements to use for recording a people's experience as a primitive culture.

From earliest known pigments in the caves of Lascaux, to 21st century digital color, this chapter in particular, attempts to lay the foundations of color throughout the ages. Whether we examine the prehistoric use of pigments applied with raw chunks of manganese, or the modern refined CMYK printer inks, it is significant to take a look at the use and development of color pigments throughout history.

THE ANCIENT WORLD

PREHISTORIC ART—PALEOLITHIC PERIOD
40,000–10,000 B.C.

Cave Paintings, c. 22,000–10,000 b.c. Lascaux, France.

Origins of Color Pigments: Red and yellow ochre-earth (iron oxide with varied degrees of crystallization), black (from charcoal), brown (manganese oxide), and white (ground bones and chalk)

Binder/s: Animal fat, vegetable oils, or water

Emphasis: Hunter/gatherers may have recorded their victories of the hunt, or these cave paintings may have been rendered prior to the hunt as good luck charms, for a successfully accomplished chase.

The early prehistoric colors were primarily limited to *manganese* based materials and *iron* in the form of hematite and goethite. The caves of Lascaux are situated in a region in France saturated with huge quantities of these natural pigments.

Raw pigments such as red and yellow ochres, which were typically ground into powder and then mixed with water, enhance the walls of the Paleolithic caves. Blowpipes of hollow bones and reeds were used to "spray" large painted areas that depict their daily hunt. This is the beginning of color, discovered through the use of pigment. Historically, pigments have been the foundation for the expression of color and can consist of various powders produced from organic substances such as animal and plant life. Alternatively, pigments have developed from inorganic matter such as various minerals and even semi-precious stones. Various binders have to be incorporated into the various pigments in order to *bind* the pigment particles. The cave paintings consisted of fats and oils as binding agents. This strengthened the paint and allowed for good adhesion to the surface.

The dull light of fire provided a yellow or yellow-orange light within the cave, which affected the outcome of hue and shading that we see today within the caves. The importance of this observation can be seen as the cave art is unfortunately flooded with intense, white, *artificial light* at the actual site. Optimally, to observe these cave paintings and accurately appreciate their color value would be to provide the same colors of light by which they were painted. Needless to say, that is not realistic. The beauty and immediate attraction to these paintings and reliefs can

Figure 1-2 ***The "Chinese Horse."*** Prehistoric Cave Painting. Lascaux Caves, Perigord, Dordogne, France.

be attributed to the earth colors and pigments, particularly when properly illuminated.

Various tints and shades of reds, oranges, and yellows dominate the cave dwellings, with contour-lined stampeding animals. The mood created by these wall paintings reflects the somber and respectful feeling of a people whose preoccupation was survival or the hunt. In many places, parts of the cave walls are coated with pigmented color. Additionally, the hues that represent the animal figures are commensurable with the natural coloring of the cave walls themselves. Paleolithic painters rendered either what would be the future hunt, perhaps as a good luck forecast, and/or a commemoration of their activities, which had already taken place.

The Paleolithic caves are found not only in France but also extend over the larger area of Europe. One of the oldest accounts of civilization left behind a visual record of its activities with a profound interest that its record also was a work of art. Why else would they have endeavored to create such beautiful ***color values*** and ***movement of line*** in this primitive gallery?

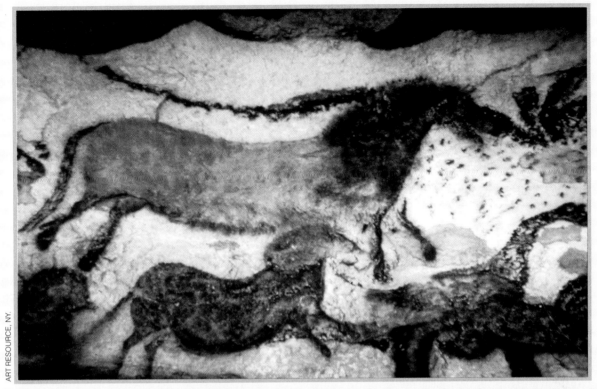

ART RESOURCE, NY.

Figure 1-3 *Herd of Horses.* Serigraph Transcription of Prehistoric Cave Painting. Lascaux Caves, Perigord, Dordogne, France.

ART RESOURCE, NY.

Figure 1-4 *The Crossed Bison.* Prehistoric Cave Painting. Lascaux Caves, Perigord, Dordogne, France.

EGYPTIAN ART

2,700–1,000 B.C.

Queen Nefertiti, c. 1360 b.c. Agyptisches Museum, Berlin.

Origins of Color Pigments: Pigmented color on limestone/white lead (lead carbonate), madder (red dye from madder root), malachite (green), lapis lazuli (blue), verdigris (blue-green), red and yellow ochre

Binder/s: Glue of boiled animal skins or egg whites

Emphasis: First Pharaoh Queen

Nebamun Hunting Birds, from the Tomb of Nebamun, c. 1400 b.c. British Museum, London.

Origins of Color Pigments: Pigmented color on dry plaster (fresco secco) Egyptian blue or Egyptian frit (Cuprorivaite), azurite and/or malachite (blue)

Binder/s: Glue of boiled animal skins or egg whites

Emphasis: The visual documentation of historical accounts. Figurative images and hieroglyphics communicated about a civilization, primarily royalty, such as the Pharaoh and his family.

The image of Queen Nefertiti, who was Pharaoh Akhenaten's wife, illustrates one of the most skilled executions of chromatic values from Egypt to date. Although incomplete, the bust of Nefertiti indicates a very accomplished work in progress. Her form is sophisticated and more realistic than the art of Egypt to which we are accustomed. The Egyptian canon of proportion, which typically illustrates the human form with the profile head

Figure 1-5(A) *Nefertiti.* Portrait Bust, Egypt, c. 1350 BC. Frontal view. Aegyptisches Museum, Staatliche Museen zu Berlin, Berlin, Germany.

Figure 1-5(B) *Nefertiti.* Portrait Bust, Egypt, c. 1340 BC. 3/4 Profile. Aegyptisches Museum, Staatliche Museen zu Berlin, Berlin, Germany.

but with *frontal shoulders and one frontal eye*, does not exist here. More important for our discussion, however, would be the evidence of surface quality on Nefertiti's face, which indicates that the artist was perhaps developing a more translucent effect. Certainly, the hues of facial pigments were in a stage of development, indicating a very naturalistic appearance.

When we look at the *Nebamun fresco*, the colored pigment application is very different in appearance than that seen on the face of Nefertiti. Egyptian pigmented *fresco secco* was typically rendered on dry plaster, giving the painted figures a very opaque appearance. Nefertiti's face is more translucent. It is only fair to point out that the difference of color opacity and translucence is, in part, due to light being fixed on a flat surface as opposed to that of a three-dimensional form. Nevertheless, there is a decided difference in the appearance between surface value gradations of chromatic values.

Egyptian blue, or Egyptian frit, is a pigment of one-part copper oxide, one-part calcium oxide (lime), and four-parts of silica (quartz). The minerals are chalk/limestone, malachite, and sand. These materials were blended and fired in a kiln to about 1,600 degrees Fahrenheit. After cooling, the substance is transformed into a very brittle opaque blue solid. It is then ground into a fine powder with a mortar and pestle. It is the **oldest synthetic pigment** known to humankind. Together, **gold and this rich blue compound represented royalty and power.**

Figure 1-6 Nebamun standing on a reed boat hunting birds in papyrus marshes. Nebamun's wife and daughter (who wears the "side lock of youth") look on. 18th dynasty, from the tomb of Nebamun. British Museum, London, Great Britain.

NEO-BABYLONIAN ART

612–539 B.C.

Ishtar Gate of Babylon, c. 575 b.c. Staatliche Museum, Berlin.

Origins of Color Pigments: Azurite [blue], aluminum oxide, silica; iron oxide and lead (yellows); blue glazed bricks

Binder/s: Heat (approximately 1,600 degrees Fahrenheit)

Emphasis: Main city gate to the great city of Babylon

The Ishtar Gate was the main entrance to ancient Babylon built by King Nebuchadnezzar. This gate has been painstakingly reconstructed at the Staatliche Museum in Berlin and is a testimony to the glory of the ancient city. The rich and sumptuous deep blue hue is a result of heating a copper mineral, such as Azurite, to a molten state. The blue glass-like copper glaze is transformed into this powerful blue color by heat. When melted at the appropriate temperature, the color transforms into a richer, darker blue. The molten state of the glaze then causes the glaze to adhere to the brick. As the brick cools, the blue glaze becomes one with the brick, a bond that is not easily separated.

Blue is very significant for Nebuchadnezzar's city gates. Historically, blue has been synonymous with trustworthiness (honesty), tranquility (peace and calm), and divinity (infinity)—all attributes of which a king would like to be known. A king has to be *trustworthy* and provide the sense of peace and *tranquility* that his subjects desire in order to keep the kingdom healthy and strong. Certainly, *divinity* or wanting to appear as god-like as possible had crossed the minds of more than just Nebuchadnezzar. Blue most certainly is a color that creates a feeling of strength, stability, and calm. All of the attributes that you would want an empire to retain remains within the symbolical references to blue. The yellow-orange (gold) and various blue hues create a strong complementary contrast with the figures and border trim of the structure. The blue hues associated with this gate are inviting and keep an otherwise threatening and overwhelming structure from becoming imposing. Instead it creates a feeling of power yet serenity for the citizens who entered the city.

Look again at the Ishtar Gate, and see if this is not the feeling or emotional response that comes from such a powerful structure.

Figure 1-7(A) Ishtar Gate. Neo-Babylonian c575 BC; Restored Glazed Brick. Pergamon Museum Berlin. Close-up.

Nebuchadnezzar, according to the Biblical record, built ancient Babylon and ultimately constructed an image of pure ***gold*** measuring 9 feet wide by 90 feet high (about seven stories). He then commanded that all citizens bow and worship the image when the city music played. Apparently, he had taken credit for the blessings that had been bestowed upon him, as he exhibited his arrogance for the accomplishment. Nebuchadnezzar was cast out of his own city for seven years, and at the end of that period confessed that it was God who had blessed him, and not he who should have taken the credit for Babylon's success. He was restored as king, with greater blessings than before because he had extolled God and not himself any longer.

Figure 1-7(B) Ishtar Gate through which ran processional road. One of eight fortified gates of Nebuchandrezzar's city of Babylon.It was decorated with dragons and young bulls in brick relief.

AEGEAN ART

MINOAN CIVILIZATION 3000–1500 B.C.

Toreador Fresco, c. 1500 b.c. Heraklion Museum.

Origins of Color Pigments:	Pigmented red and yellow ochre and malachite blue on wet lime plaster (Est. Buon Fresco)
Binders:	Animal fats
Emphasis:	Bullfights, popular game of Minos

The Queen's Megaron, Palace of Minos, c. 1500 b.c. Knossos, Crete.

Origins of Color:	Pigmented red and yellow ochres and malachite blue on wet lime plaster (Est. Buon Fresco)
Binders:	Animal fats
Emphasis:	Architectural/Color

We know that there are many Egyptian frescos that have survived fairly well, while a great percentage of original Minoan artwork has vanished. A number of frescos that have survived consist of large restorative segments in each piece. The Toreador fresco is a good example. Only the darkest areas that you see are original, so the *darker blue is original*, whereas the lighter blue is not. This is the general condition of the Minoan frescos throughout the area, with a few exceptions.

Most scholars believe that the fresco style rendered is Buon Fresco, which is wet pigment on wet plaster, as opposed to Egyptian Secco Fresco, which is wet pigment applied to dry plaster. While Egyptian examples of the inferior Secco Fresco technique are generally in better condition, they also were better protected with less moisture than Minoan frescos. To this day, it seems difficult to say for sure whether they are Buon or Secco frescos.

The Toreador Fresco is rigid, hard edged, geometric, and formal. It is full of red and yellow ochres, as well as malachite blues. The fresco colors are unique in that they are very dry and matte in appearance. We will see in later periods just how varied the appearance of the same blue pigment can be when egg or oil is added as a binder. The difference can be quite amazing. Light, as it is received onto the surface of a fresco, recognizes its specific molecular arrangement. In other words, the molecular constitution of a blue hue can be quite different than that of red or yellow. When the light floods over that fresco surface, the distribution of that light is such that it very simply illuminates exactly what is there: blue. Later, in the Renaissance period, we will see the difference that improved binders can make. For now, the frescos allow us to see the *implication* of how life was, but later the change in binders will demonstrate how color will create the *illusion* of life.

The Queen's Megaron, Palace of Minos, illustrates the complex and typical methods of incorporating color in the Minoan culture. Geometric patterns and flat figurative work are at the heart of the frescos, and tints and shades of blues and yellows are common. The more saturated red hues provide a serious contrast to the lower-keyed colors of blues and yellow. Saturation, as we will see later in the Renaissance, will achieve greater heights thanks to different pigments and binders.

Figure 1-8 La Parisienne from the Campstool Fresco.

ROGER WOOD/CORBIS.

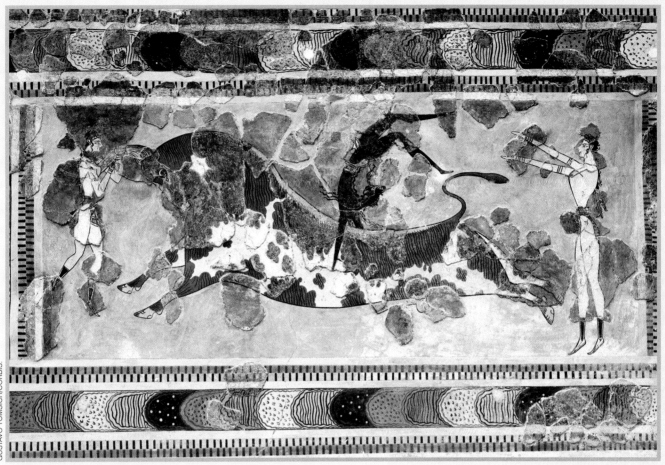

Figure 1-9 Minoan Toreador Fresco.

Figure 1-10 The Queen's Megaron, in the Palace of Minos at Knossos, is lit by a large light well. On the wall is a reproduction of the Dolphin Fresco. Crete, Greece, September 1965.

GREEK ART

ARCHAIC TO CLASSICAL c. 640–400 B.C.

EXEKIAS, *Amphora of Achilles and Ajax Playing a Board Game,* c. 540-530 b.c. Archaic-Classical Style—Black Figure Vase. Musei Vaticani, Rome.

Origins of Color Pigments:	Terra cotta clay with iron oxide and iron-rich ochre *clay slips* (paint): SiO_2, Al_2O_3, FeO, CaO, MgO, K_2O, Na_2O, TiO_2
Binder:	Heat/1472 degrees Fahrenheit
Emphasis:	Information Laden/Typical Games

EUXITHEOS [the Potter] (signed) and EUPHRONIOS [the Painter], *Sleep and Death Lifting the Body of Sarpedon,* c. 515 b.c. The Sarpedon Vase, Calyx-krater. Archaic-Classical Style—Red Figure vase. Metropolitan Museum, New York.

Origins of Color Pigments:	Terra cotta clay with iron oxide and iron-rich ochre clay slips (paint).
Clay and decorative slips:	Alumina, iron, calcium, magnesium, manganese, nickel, kaolin, potassium, sodium, titanium, chromium, copper, vanadium, and barium
Binder:	Heat/1472 degrees Fahrenheit
Emphasis:	The artist and the craftsperson become mutually dependent on one another. Greek daily life seen through clay vessel decoration.

The clay body (vase) and the clay slip (paint) only require heat as a binder because the clay body and slips have identical elements. The vase clay body, black gloss, and red clay slip all contain the same elements (see *Origins of Color Pigments*), but different percentages. A natural bond exists between them because they are, each one, composed of all eight material elements. The heat from the kiln produces a permanent binding, or bond.

The term *black-figure* vases means that the image was painted with clay slip, which contained heavy concentrations of manganese and iron oxides. The black surface, additionally, was burnished to produce a glossy surface. The red areas are quite simply the bare clay body of the vase. The clay body also has amounts of iron, but not the same percentage as the black figures. Before the *first firing,* the colors of the pot surface were red-orange with dark red-orange figures. Once the first oxidized firing was finished, the entire surface was virtually the same color. The first initial firing creates a more permanent and damage-resistant vessel. The *second firing* was accomplished by the introduction of green wood into the hot kiln in order to produce a smoky reduction* firing, which transformed the figure into black, glossy, high-contrasting color against the red-orange background. Finally, in the *third firing,* the kiln once again is fired by allowing

Figure 1-11 Black-figure amphora depicting Ajax and Achilles, c.540 BC. Ceramic. Vatican Museums and Galleries, Vatican City, Italy.

---

* Reduction refers to the restriction in the intake of oxygen into the kiln, and/or the affect of burning only part of the oxygen in a kiln environment, altering the hues on a given ceramic surface. Heat, as well as oxidation or reduction atomsphere transform the surface into different colors and mood effects.

more air into the kiln (oxidation firing), which caused the unpainted background areas to return to the red-orange color of the clay; the glossy surface remained black.

The colors of black and red-orange were striking to say the least. The might, power, and influence of the Greek civilization are somehow felt by the high-contrasting colors of these elegant works. The colors of any ceramic venture are very different than a fresco or painting. Pigments of paint are fired to achieve optimal color to create the painting. With ceramic colors, they quite often transform into different colors and moods by the introduction of heat.

Red-figure vases are obviously the opposite. Instead of the figure appearing as black, it is the background, which is painted black, that reveals the bare clay red-orange figure. Such is the case with the Calyx-krater. Firing for *red-figure* pottery is the same then as *black-figure*.

Figure 1-12(A) Terracotta calyx-krater (bowl for mixing wine and water), c. 515 BC; Archaic. Signed by Euxitheos, as potter; Signed by Euphronios, as painter. Greek, Attic. Obverse View.

Figure 1-12(B) Terracotta calyx-krater. Reverse View.

The famous potter Euxitheos first made this beautiful form on the potter's wheel. After much consideration about the accuracy of the form, as well as determining its appropriateness for the painted subject matter, he went about producing this perfected clay piece, and then signed the finished vessel.

Euxitheos was then responsible for the three firings, which would follow the painting of the surface, executed by the artist Exekias. Thomas Hoving, former director of New York City's Metropolitan Museum of Art, claimed that it was the painter Exekias who eventually "gained the prize."

Who deserved recognition? Those in support of the potter say that without the vessel, there is no painting. The form had to be carefully thought out and designed in consideration of the drama that would take place on the piece. Additionally, the skill and experience of the potter was required to fire the piece without incident three separate times.

Those who argue in defense of the painter will say that without the painting, it is a mere pot, a utilitarian and unimportant piece. They say that the creativity and skill of the painter has transformed the clay pot into a magnificent 360-degree *clay theater.* Certainly, without the painting it would normally be thought of as *craft.* Now that it has the embellished surface, it becomes *art.* Additionally, the introduction of high color contrast to what would otherwise be a solid red-orange surface is significant. The seductive qualities of the red-orange ground, as opposed to the mysterious black background, excite the senses and stir the imagination. So, is it color that validates the vessel or the form of it?

ROMAN ART

753 B.C.–337 A.D.

Dionysiac Mystery Frieze, c. 60–50 b.c. Villa of the Mysteries, Pompeii, Italy.

Origins of Color Pigments: Cinnabar (red) [mercury II sulfide], hematite and Egyptian blue (violet/purple), various iron oxides and lead tetra oxide (red-oranges), crushed limestone, mollusk shell, bird eggs [calcium carbonate] (white), and burnt ivory and bone [carbon-based materials] (black)

Binder: Clay slip

Emphasis: The mighty Roman Empire was known as the most civilized, yet brutally barbaric society. The Roman Empire ruled the known world as a single government, attempted to create a world of one language, was highly evolved in the arts, and a mighty war machine. Roman arts were the height of classical perfection, including using color as a mood enhancer.

When we left the *Greek stage,* observed on the Sarpedon Vase, we experienced a type of *theater in the round,* with high contrasting but limited ceramic colors. The Roman style continued in that unspoken tradition of surface performances, but on a much grander scale and color palette. On this typical Pompeian fresco, the supreme architectural stage

Figure 1-13 Mural From the Villa of the Mysteries, Pompeii.

unfolds its drama. It is at Pompeii where we begin to see more lively and saturated color than at any other previous period. This is where we also see more varieties of hues, the mixing of two primary pigment colors (Egyptian blue [synthetic color] and yellow ochre) to create a secondary green. We are now seeing tinted light blues (background in *Narcissus*) a mixture of azurite and white.

The Pompeii artists also had become skilled at creating a certain amount of *atmospheric perspective* in the *Narcissus* fresco. The foreground with its opaque light oranges of the figure contrasted with the very translucent light background, which is quite an accomplishment for fresco pigments. The Romans discovered that they produced the most convincing results when they applied up to nine layers of lime plaster, the last being a combination of lime plaster and fine aggregate crushed marble. The layering, and especially the marble on the finished surface, helped to create greater surface strength and more translucency on the painted surface. In fact, it is this layering that was responsible for the development of more brilliant *reds of cinnabar*, as we see in the Dionysiac Mystery Frieze.

The mood and emotional response generated by the energy of this saturated red is intensely seductive, and creates an appropriate mood. The Dionysus Mysteries involve a semi-secret cult brought to Italy from the Greeks. Many of the poses in this fresco drama are very classical, and the entire stage is set with ritual and mysterious body language. The predominant warm tones of orange, red-orange, and saturated red not only speak volumes about the Dionysus cult, but about the Romans as a people. Warm reds were the prevailing colors throughout this city of leisure and wealth, and certainly the mood conveyance of red and red-orange hues is paramount in reflecting (as well as the symbolical reference) a culture critically involved with the sensual aspects of humanity.

Figure 1-14 Pompeii Bakery.

A Portal To The Ancient World Has Been Opened

In 62 a.d., the nearby Mount Vesuvius erupted, covering the entire city of Pompeii with volcanic ash and debris. For more than 1,600 years the city was lost, but in the year 1748, after the accidental discovery of the city, excavations began. What was to be found was astonishing beyond comprehension. The volcanic ash, which settled over the city in the coming days after the eruption, had created a protective seal over the city. According to some accounts, it had rained intermittently, which caused rapid cooling of the hot ash as it settled over the city. The hard shell had all but created a type of hermetic seal, which is why we have such beautifully preserved examples of Roman culture, as seen largely in the pigmented frescos.

In previous centuries, very little was known about ancient Rome. Thanks to the discovery, we now understand that the city was a playground for the wealthy, a resort for vacationing Romans. We know, in some cases, the names and occupations of the inhabitants in particular houses, as well as the general attitudes and culture of the people.

The elegant and sometimes provocative frescos with their colored pigments can be appreciated by their careful rendering of tints and shades indicating their understanding of value gradations. Additionally, there was a general knowledge of the mood connection to color, as observed in their careful handling of saturated color and hue variations.

Figure 1-15 *Narcissus at the Fountain.* Fresco Painting in the House of Marcus Lucretius Fronto at Pompeii.

EARLY CHRISTIAN AND BYZANTINE ART

29 A.D.–1453 A.D.

JUSTINIAN, *Bishop Maximianus and Attendants,* c. 547 a.d. Mosaic (north wall apse) San Vitale, Ravenna, Italy.
Theodora and Attendants, c. 547 a.d. Mosaic (south wall apse), San Vitale, Ravenna, Italy.

Origins of Color Pigments:	Gold leaf (gold), iron, copper (greens and blues), copper/cobalt (dark blues), reduced copper (dark reds), antimony oxide (opacifier), manganese.
Glass Tile Formula:	Soda-lime-silica with magnesium and soda carbonate
Binder:	Cement/lime plaster
Emphasis:	The early Christian world, free from Roman tyranny. Constantine issues the *Edict of Milan* (313 A.D.) proclaiming that Christianity is to be legal.

Tesserae or Byzantine mosaic tile adorns the interior of the first *Christian church* in Ravenna, Italy. One of the central components within any church is to create closeness to God; a heavenly ambiance is certainly second to none for the physical representation of being heaven bound. The Holy Bible mentions *gold* often, but particularly significant is when God declares that He will set up a new earth, a new kingdom where pain and suffering no longer exist, and war is no more. In the New Testament Book of Revelation, Chapter 21, verse 18 John records the following concerning the New Jerusalem: "And the building of the wall of it was of jasper: and the city was pure *gold,* like unto clear *glass.*" The apse of San Vitale (below) is adorned with small mosaic tiles, known as *tesserae* (small glass tiles). In fact a great deal of its interior consists of tesserae gold artwork. The interior is *luminous with a heavenly golden glow,* as if to be a threshold to heaven itself. The emotional appeal of specific colors is paramount here. One must feel the *mood of heaven* by the effects of light to create its color palette within the church.

The small square tesserae tiles create color by laying gold *leaf* between two pieces of glass. The remaining colored tiles are also glass, but with specific oxides that are made to be molten with the glass when fired, and then cooled to their respective colors (*see Origins of Color* for colors of tiles).

Another important color technique, which came into more prominence in early Christianity, was the *encaustic* painting technique (*Virgin [Theotokos] and Child between Saints Theodore and George,* page ___), which was basically colored pigments and beeswax on wood panel. Encaustic painting has its origins in Egypt and is one of the most enduring forms of painting, because wax seals and protects the colors of pigments.

SCALA / ART RESOURCE, NY.

Figure 1-16 San Vitale. Interior towards the east (altar). S. Vitale, Ravenna, Italy.

Color's role here is significant, in that it reinforces the focal point of the composition. There is more defined and opaque color, including the red cushion that she is seated upon. Mary's deep blue gown, purple shoes, and golden footrest all continue to pull the eye decisively toward the center icon. The light yellow-orange (gold) of the footrest, halo around the head of Jesus, and His mother are aligned vertically with the centered heavenly ray of light overhead. The expressions of their faces and the overwhelming blueness of the robe create a very somber and respectful mood, which is the emotional appeal that we would expect to feel. Finally, in the eleventh to twelfth centuries we see tempera on wood, which consisted of earth and synthetic pigments. There were two types; one was composed of egg yolk, powdered pigments, and water. The other was called casein, which was powdered mil protein, powdered pigments, and oil or water. Egg was preferred, especially because it was a superior binder. Tempera also produced great luminous/translucent colors, more so than other methods of the past, as evidenced in the Vladimir Virgin.

Emperor Constantine converted to Christianity and was declared as the first **Holy Roman Emperor** by the Pope. This was an amazing and unique event, because prior centuries demonstrated Rome to be the great persecutor and enemy of Christianity. Now, the function of both the Pope and Caesar had been combined; a type of quasi-divine position.

Constantine moved the capital from Rome to the Greek city of Byzantium or **Constantinople.**

Later in the fifth century, Emperor Justinian (Christian) receives credit for creating the first **golden age** of Byzantine art and architecture. He was responsible for the construction of over thirty churches in Constantinople (which does not include surrounding cities and churches).

Figure 1-17 *Byzantine Mosaic of Emperor Justinian and His Retinue,* c. 6th century. A mosaic from San Vitale Cathedral in Ravenna, Italy, shows the Byzantine Emperor Justinian the Great surrounded by his retinue.

SCALA / ART RESOURCE, NY.

Figure 1-18 *Madonna of Vladimir,* c. 11th-12th century. Russian Icon. Tretyakov Gallery, Moscow, Russia.Virgin).

ERICH LESSING / ART RESOURCE.

Figure 1-19 *Virgin and Child with Two Saints,* c.395-1453. Byzantine icon. St. Catherine Monastery, Mount Sinai, Sinai Desert, Egypt.

ARCHIVO ICONOGRAFICO, S.A./CORBIS.

Figure 1-20 *The Court of Theodora*, c. 6th century.

EARLY CHRISTIAN AND BYZANTINE ART   **19**

THE MIDDLE AGES

EARLY MEDIEVAL ART 500 A.D.–1000 A.D.

Chi-rho-iota Page, folio 34 recto of the Book of Kells , Illuminated Manuscript, Late eighth to early ninth century. Tempera on Vellum. Iona, Scotland.

Origins of Color Pigments: Oxgall (black), yellow ochre (yellow), red lead (red), woad/indigo (blue), kermes (red/violet), red and yellow ochre (orange).

Binder: Egg white/fish glue

Emphasis: Fusion of Christianity, Greco-Roman heritage, and non-Roman cultures in the north.

The Middle Ages were responsible for the building of huge churches, better known as cathedrals, as well as the creation of the illuminated manuscript. The emphasis here will be the manuscript itself. No other time in recorded history have we seen such elaborate artworks posing as books. The Book of Kells, which is where this page is located, was created to be displayed on the church altar. The Word of God through this particular age in Europe, was illuminated or clarified by the affective use of the Illuminated Manuscripts and Capital letters. The visual communication became important in a world where illiteracy was uncommon. The passage from the Bible here is the beginning account of Jesus Christ in the Gospel of Saint Matthew. The actual Greek letters are XPI: chi-rho-iota, along with the two words—autem (seen as h) and generatio. The entire passage reads, "Now this is how the birth of Christ came about."

The function of color for the manuscript is equally obvious, as is the role of a cathedral interior (Ravenna church, for example). *Illumination* is the key word. The church is illuminated by light and the colors of yellow-orange (gold) are manifested on the interior, creating a heavenly or respectful ambiance. Manuscripts are an illuminated form of the Bible, glorifying every letter of every word, and ultimately the Word of God is clarified—it is illuminated (both spiritually and physically) as though directly from heaven itself.

Within the gothic cathedrals of the same time period , we see large colored glass windows, which illuminate the interior of the building, just as the manuscripts illuminate the soul.

Figure 1-21 Cathedrale Saint Etienne, c. 12th century. Auxerre, France.

Figure 1-22 Chi-Rho page, *Book of Kells,* fol. 34. c. 800. Illuminated in Iona-Kells-Northumbria. Trinity College, Dublin, Ireland.

Kermes was used for brilliant red-purples, which was a very expensive and exotic pigment. Kermes is an insect (Coccus Ilicus) found only in the oak trees in the Mediterranean region. The pigment could only be obtained by grinding up the pregnant female insects.

ROMANESQUE ART

1050 A.D.–1200 A.D.

Scenes from the Life of Christ, c. 1150 a.d.–1170 a.d. Stained glass window—detail. Chartres Cathedral, France.

Origins of Color Pigments: Silica, lime, and ash (flux) [lead]. Copper reduction (red), copper oxidation (blue), copper oxidation/reduction/oxidation (green), beechwood ash and sand-silica, potash, manganese and iron with temperature variances [add manganese for purple] (yellow and purple).

Binder: Lead (tracery) flux/ash (lower melting point) otherwise not applicable

Emphasis: Romanesque, meaning "Roman-like." Architecture such as cathedrals had certain similarities of Roman building styles; barrel and groin vaults, etc.

The Romanesque period ushered in the age of the cathedral and colored glass windows.

When considering color's role in stained glass windows, it is important to remember that the illuminated manuscripts have a commensurate role. The cathedral illuminates one's physical surroundings, as well as the soul, and the manuscript brings light and truth to the heart.

The colors of stained glass windows serve to illuminate Biblical stories by converting the sun's light into brilliantly

Figure 1-24 Piazza dei Miracoli with Cathedral and Leaning Tower, Pisa. Duomo, Pisa, Italy.

SCALA / ART RESOURCE, NY.

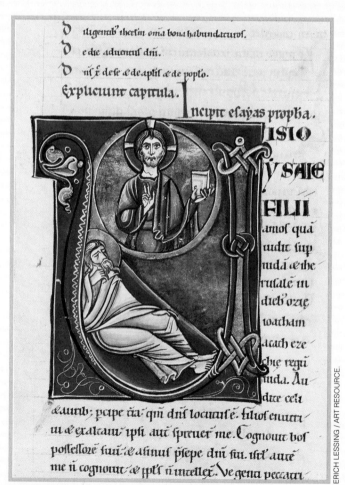

Figure 1-23 Bible of Saint Sulpice de Bourges, France, 1150-1200. MS 3. The vision of Isaiah; Initial V. Bibliotheque Municipale, Bourges, France.

ERICH LESSING / ART RESOURCE.

Colors of Precious Stones

Jasper: Deep reds, yellow.

Sapphire: Blue, light red (pink), yellow or green.

Chalcedony: Waxy white.

Emerald: Green.

Sardonyx: Various.

Chrysolite: Yellow, yellow-green.

Beryl: Blue-green.

Topaz: Light red, yellow.

Chrysoprasus: Light yellow-green.

Jacinth: Red, Reddish-blue, dark purple.

Amethyst: Violet.

Pearl: Translucent white.

lit facets of glass. Quite literally, the Biblical passages are *enlightened* (spiritual) by the *illuminated* colors (physical) from the light of heaven. In reality, the cathedral, stained glass windows, and illuminated manuscripts receive their inspiration from the Biblical passage from the book of Revelation, Chapter 21: 18–23. Referring to the New Jerusalem, God's new heavenly city, the description of it reads as such:

> (18) And the building of the wall of it was of Jasper: and the city was pure gold, like unto clear glass. (19) And the foundations of the wall of the city were garnished with all manner of precious stones. The first foundation was jasper; the second, sapphire; the third, a chalcedony; the forth, an emerald; (20) The fifth, sardonyx; the sixth, sardius; the seventh, chrysolite; the eighth, beryl; the ninth, a topaz; the tenth, a chrysoprasus; the eleventh, a jacinth; the twelfth, an amethyst. (21) And the twelve gates were twelve pearls; every several gate was of one pearl: and the street of the city was pure gold, and it was transparent glass. (22) And I saw no temple therein: for the Lord God Almighty and the Lamb are the temple of it. (23) And the city had no need of the sun, neither of the moon, to shine in it: for the glory of God did lighten it, and the Lamb is the light thereof. [King James Translation—1611 A.D.]

ART RESOURCE, NY.

Figure 1-26 *The Life of Christ.* New Testament cycle (lower half of window). Cathedral, Chartres, France.

It is more than apparent now from where the cathedral's inspiration is derived, with its colors of windows. Color is the main event for Romanesque cathedrals in order to create the perfect heavenly ambiance. We will see that concept come to fruition in the Gothic period next.

ALINARI / ART RESOURCE, NY.

Figure 1-25 View of the Chartres Cathedrall, Chartres, France.

Chartres Cathedral's windows were donated by various peoples of the time. Merchants, artists, nobles etc., all came together to fund these windows, most of which are intact today. The cathedral was not only a worship center, but a civic center as well. It was the focal point of the city and a symbol of the spiritual, as well as power.

GOTHIC ART

EARLY GOTHIC 1140 A.D.–1193 A.D.

High Gothic, 1194 a.d. – 1304 a.d.

Late Gothic, 1305 a.d. – 1400 a.d.

ROGIER VAN DER WEYDEN, ***Deposition, Center panel of a triptych from Notre Dame hors-les-murs,*** c. 1435 a.d. Oil on Wood. Louvain, Belgium.

Origins of Color Pigments:	Light ultramarine [sodium sulfide] (blue), cobalt [cobalt aluminate] (blue), Vermillion-cinnabar [mercury sulfide] (red), cobalt violet, [cobalt phosphate] (violet), azurite, Naples yellow [lead antimonide], zinc white.
Binder:	Linseed oil
Emphasis:	Much about the creation of the huge stone Gothic cathedrals built all over Europe with magnificent interiors and grandiose, colored windows. The countryside churches in small villages gave way to the rise of huge cities with giant cathedrals, which in turn became civic centers, as well as a place of worship.

Figure 1-27 *Deposition.*

The late Gothic period will be our focus on color. This period is known for its many and grand cathedrals, stained glass windows, and the transformation from egg tempera painting to oil-based pigments. The Gothic period saw different and immensely beautiful tempera paintings because the artist used the *whole egg*, which created a silky luster rarely seen before. Even so, artists wanted a more durable and better drying substance for color that would resist severe cracking, which was evident in egg tempera paintings.

The **Deposition** (below) illustrates the new *versatility of oil paints* over tempera. The highly competent use of tints and shades, gradations a chromatic value is unparalleled to this point. It is *color saturation extraordinaire*. Oils greatly extended the drying time, so that the artist could spend a greater amount of time creating the value gradations of colored pigments. This kind of clarity, saturation, and depth of space is largely attributed to the difference in pigment binders (egg as opposed to oil). Many times, the mood of a painting with a primary triad of saturated colors would subtract from the serious nature of a theme such as this. However, because of the *varied degrees of chromatic value* seen in the gold background, the *darker interspersed colors of fabric*, and the *grieving faces and body language of the figures*, the normally jubilant colors instead transition down to the somber hopelessness of the composition's story.

PHOTO BY THE AUTHOR.

Figure 1-28 *Notre-Dame.* Stained glass window. Notre-Dame, Paris, France.

Egg tempera has an odd quality about it. While wet, it is very temporal by nature and washes off easily; however, when it dries completely it is permanent and has great longevity. This is particularly true of the Gothic addition of the ***whole egg.*** For this reason we have an abundance of paintings that have survived through the centuries. Tempera paints have some of the most brilliant and saturated colors, with amazing luminosity and clarity.

RENAISSANCE ART

EARLY RENAISSANCE [LATE GOTHIC] c. 1400–1450 A.D.

High Renaissance, c. 1450–1570 a.d.

SANDRO BOTTICELLI, *Birth of Venus* (next page), c. 1482 a.d. Egg Tempera on Canvas. Galleria degli Uffizi, Florence, Italy.

Canvas: Linen/22 threads per cm.

Origins of Color Pigments: Saffron (orange-yellow), raw sienna (yellow), azurite (blue), atacamite [copper chloride] (light green), verdigris [copper acetate] (dark blue), rose madder [*Rubia Tinctorium* root] (light red), lead (white)

Binder: Sudan Black B and Amido Black AB2, animal glue, and gum

Emphasis: The great age of Humanism brought about the rebirth of classical art. Pursuit of Humanism and classical texts. Artists wanted to study the old Greek-Roman art forms, and give new life to those classical forms.

Even though many fifteenth-century artists continued to use tempera through the Renaissance, this was also a time of transition, moving away from tempera to the versatility of oils. The use of tempera had reached its prime. The critical difference here is that now we see *tempera on canvas (linen) ground*, rather than panels of wood. Another issue that makes this painting particularly relevant is that most Florentine painters were not particularly interested in color, because theirs was a more science-based approach to paintings. Botticelli, a Florentine painter, however, demonstrates a high degree of concern about color and its emotional draw. The mythological goddess of love (Venus) and surrounding figures are seen with elegantly detailed tints and shades of hues, against a somewhat flat and simplistic background. In fact, the figurative element of the composition seems to be completely isolated from what almost appears to be a fresco wall, while the four figures are liberated from it in full three-dimensional illusion. These forms are created by delicately maneuvered chromatic values, transforming the composition into a cool and sublime mood. Here, color performs its magic by alluring the spectator into its breezy surroundings, while the figures themselves separate forward into the viewer's space.

Figure 1-29 Krokos: Greek Red Saffron of Kozani Crocus flowers.

The compositional *color temperature* variation of the cool background hues, contrasted with the warm foreground, contributes to the separation of the two planes in this allegorical fantasy.

Saffron, one of the organic dyes in the *Birth of Venus,* is the world's most expensive spice. There have been times in history when saffron was more costly than gold. Seventy-five thousand Crocus flowers *(sativus Linnaeus)* are required to produce one pound of saffron filaments. There is a natural bond between the organic colorant and egg tempera.

Figure 1-30 JAN VAN EYCK, ***The Arnolfini Wedding.*** Wedding picture of Giovanni Arnolfini and Giovanna Cenami, Bruges, 1434. The couple conclude the marriage by joining hands. A small dog is a symbol of fidelity, the lone candle in the chandelier symbolizes Christ as witness. Oak, 82 x 60 cm. NG 186. National Gallery, London, Great Britain.

Figure 1-31 *Birth of Venus.*

FERNANDO YANEZ DE LA ALMEDINA, *Saint Catherine,* c. 1510 a.d. Oil on Canvas. Museo Del Prado, Madrid.

Origins of Color Pigments: Red lake [mixed with silica: glass particles] (red/crimson), yellow smalts* [glass colored by lead antimonite] (yellow), orpiment [arsenical sulfide yellow and orange realgar] (deep orange), green glass [cobalt blue and iron/yellow] (green)

Pigments reached new heights with the addition of ground colored glass to the paint, creating even more transparent and brilliant hues.

Binder: Unknown

Emphasis: The Renaissance was a period where painting reached new heights of accomplishment. Never before have we seen such extraordinary color prowess, not to mention the amazing ability of artists to represent life itself, so well. The overwhelming *warm* tones in the composition contrast with the *cool* green fabric of St. Catherine's robe. The senses are controlled and riveted as well by the extreme saturation seen in the red robe. The painting seduces the eyes with its richness of hues, and produces a tranquil, yet passionate mood. Her face projects a type of Mona Lisa calmness, but the colors are authoritative and energized. A remarkable composition in the history of color.

TITIAN, *Venus of Urbino,* c. 1538 a.d. Oil on Canvas. Galleria degli Uffizi, Florence.

Origins of Color Pigments: Verdigris [finely powdered] (green), madder [plant roots] (red), yellow orpiment and orange realgar (Light to dark red-orange), orange-yellow [glassy lead antimonite] (yellow-orange), glasslike ceramic frits, and zinc white

Binder: Linseed oil

Emphasis: This was an important period because not only did painters universally change to a ground of canvas, but color itself was changed to a great degree by the Venetian painters. Titian was one Venetian painter who was best known for his color compositions. The incorporation of sand (silica sand) or powdered glass into the colors of pigments created greater luminosity than ever before. Layering of pigmented color, one over the other with glass as an ingredient, pulled in more light to the composition than was ever before possible. *Tonal color* was Titian's forte, which involves the *cadence of the same color* and altering

Figure 1-32 *Saint Catherine.*

it by a range of tone and hue variations throughout the painting. The balance of color throughout the composition actually organizes the placement of forms. The composition is divided into extreme foreground and background existence. The dark curtain pushes Venus into our personal space and creates a *warm tonal* mood seduction, while the figures in the background are seen more candidly through a shift of color and tonal variations.

---

* Occasionally, Smalts would be yellow, as well as blue.

Figure 1-33 *Venus of Urbino*.

According to one of Titian's peers, Palma il Giovane:

> Titian [employed] a great mass of colors, which served...as a base for the compositions....I too have seen some of these, formed with bold strokes made with brushes laden with colors, sometimes of a pure red earth, which he used, so to speak, for a middle tone, and at other times of white lead; and with the same brush tinted with red, black and yellow he formed a highlight; and observing these principles he made the promise of an exceptional figure appear in four brush strokes....Having constructed these precious foundations he used to turn his pictures to the wall and leave them there without looking at them, sometimes for several months. When he wanted to apply his brush again he would examine them with the utmost rigor...to see if he could find any faults....In this way, working on the figures and revising them, he brought them to the most perfect symmetry that the beauty of art and nature can reveal.... [T]hus he gradually covered those quintessential forms with living flesh, bringing them by many stages to a state in which they lacked only the breath of life. He never painted a figure all at once and...in the last stages he painted more with his fingers than his brushes.*

Venetian artists such as Titian began the adaptation of finely ground glass into their color pigments. The Venetians were known for their professional *color-sellers* as well as their fine glass. Venetian glass is still the most highly prized glass throughout the world today.

---

* Quoted in Francesco Valcanover, "An Introduction to Titian," in *Titian: Prince of Painters* (Venice: Marsilio, 1990), 23-24.

BAROQUE ART

1585 A.D.–1700 A.D.

NICOLAS POUSSIN, *The Dance of Human Life,* c. 1638 a.d. – 1640 a.d. Oil on Canvas. The Wallace Collection, London, England.

Origins of Color Pigments: Umber and ochres (earth tones), azurite (deep blue), malachite [copper carbonate hydroxide] (dark green), realgar, (red-orange), smalt [cobalt-blue ground glass] (blue), orpiment [arsenic sulfur mineral] (bronze yellow), Naples yellow, vermillion (red), bone black and lead white

Binder: Est.: Poppy or walnut oil

Emphasis: Baroque cannot be all inclusively described because it encompasses a wide range of historical and artistic advancements. Basically, however, Baroque was very dramatic and complex. You might be able to summarize its serious themes or style as excessive *dynamism* with very serious themes.

The Baroque period in art was dynamic to say the least, and at the heart of this energy was mood. A popular French Baroque convention for painting (art) was an ordered system for conveyance of emotion to the viewer. The ancient Greek theories in music come into play at this point. The modern-day *keys* of music were derived from a variety of Greek *modes,* which in turn were representative of the different emotions. The *Ionian* mode corresponds to *The Dance of Human Life* because that particular mode was assigned to *cheerful and joyous* moods. The painting itself creates a type of lyrical connection to the visual response. It is the poetry of color. This hexadic color harmony employs the colors of the spectrum to further enhance the gaiety of the dance itself. In fact, color is the key component of the painting, from the rich hues of the foreground to the illuminated heavenly host blazing through the sky. Poussin's work is an excellent example of a Baroque method of painting that became popular. The *underpainting* technique, which we will discuss next in Jan Vermeer's work, is one of the foundations for the enhancement of color brilliance seen in this lively and stimulating composition.

Figure 1-34 NICOLAS POUSSIN, *The Dance to the Music of Time*, 1640.

THE WALLACE COLLECTION.

Figure 1-35 GIAN LORENZO BERNINI, *The Ecstasy of Saint Teresa.* Cornaro Chapel, S. Maria della Vittoria, Rome, Italy.

JAN VERMEER, *Girl With a Pearl Earring (Head of a Girl),* c. 1665 a.d. – 1667 a.d., The Mauritshuis, The Hague, Holland. Oil on Canvas.

Origins of Color Pigments: Yellow ochre, vermillion (heated cinnabar), red madder (madder plant root), red ochre, raw umber (natural earth), ultramarine blue (natural ground lapis lazuli) indigo (indigo plant) weld (from the weld flower), white lead, charcoal, and bone black

Binder: Est.: Poppy or walnut oil stimulating composition.

Girl With a Peal Earring has from time to time been referred to as the **Dutch Mona Lisa,** and in some ways possesses the same thought-provoking mystery about her as does the *Mona Lisa.* The differences, however, are quite clear. The extreme contrast of the dark green background in Vermeer's master painting projects the figure into the immediate space of the viewer, as well as enhances the three-dimensional effect. *Leonardo da Vinci* himself noted that there seemed to be a greater degree of lightness occurring in an object when the background was dark. Certainly, there is a great deal of luminescence, particularly seen in *the girl's* face and turban. Additionally, rather than a pose she seems to have just turned her head in time to notice the viewer.

There are other reasons why there is such a difference. A technique referred to as **underpainting** was created during this time, and Vermeer was at the forefront of its becoming popular. Underpainting began with the whole of the composition being mapped. Every figure and form is first painted with neutral colors or tones of white. In other words, the painting exists first as a monochromatic version of the final work. Other than lead white pigment, warm brown tones, blacks, and ochres were occasionally used to achieve the underpainting as well. For the *Girl With a Pearl Earring,* various thicknesses and amounts of *lead white* formed the underpainting. This method of painting created greater volume in forms, and better distributes the light and dark values for the best possible illumination. *Glazing* further increased luminosity in pigments. A good example of glazing is seen in the girl's turban. There is one layer of ultramarine blue with additions of white (tinted) for the first layer. The next layer consisted of a thin transparent layer of pure ultramarine. Additional layers can be added to create even greater degrees of radiance, or "shine-through." The eye optically mixes the layers to create the illusion of a "stained glass" effect, in a sense. The background is actually a super dark transparent green, created by transparent layers of *weld* (a yellow flower) [yellow] over indigo (plant) [blue].

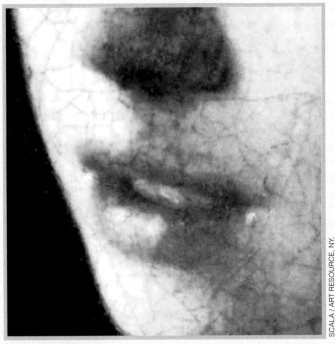

Figure 1-36(A) *Girl with the Pearl Earring.* Detail.

Figure 1-36(B) *Girl with the Pearl Earring.* Detail.

Figure 1-36(C) *Girl with the Pearl Earring*.

ROCOCO ART

1700 A.D.–1800 A.D.

Jean-Honoré Fragonard, *The Swing*, 1766. The Wallace Collection, London, England. Oil on Canvas.

Origins of Color Pigments: Viridian [hydrated chromium oxide] (green w/blue tones), Prussian blue [ferric ferro cyanide, iron] (blue), white zinc, cadmium reds [cadmium selenide] red, cinnabar [red mercury sulfide] red, and lead tin (yellow)

Binder: Poppy oil

Emphasis: Opulence, grace, carefree, and playful. Focuses on the aristocracy of society.

The Swing is without a doubt the quintessential Rococo painting, as the *Basilica of St. Alexander* is to architecture. The volume and space in this painting is created by the tints and shades of blue-greens. The Baron's mistress on the swing is illuminated by a blue haze within the surrounding darkness of thick foliage. Her complementary tints and shades of red further add to the focal point in the composition. Dark and light hues of blue-green are the key to this painting. The lightness and brilliance of the red dress is very much accentuated by the dullness of blues and blue-greens. The dress itself is exemplary of the Rococo aesthetic. The flamboyant,

carefree nature of the woman, kicking her shoe off in the direction of the suitor as he gazes under the girl's skirt, depends on these color complements to create the emotional appeal. The dull hues of color seen on the suitor, on the gentleman pulling the swing, and the garden statues, are all subservient to the highly intense light reds and whites of her garments. The painting is both sensuous and playful in this dyad harmony of two colors; it carries moods that convey a sensuous calm in the darker blue-green hues, as well as the playfulness of carefree lighter red hues.

Figure 1-37 Johann Michael Fischer, ***Benedictine Abbey Church Ottobeuren, Nave and Choir,*** 1737-1792. Abbey, Ottobeuren, Germany.

Figure 1-38 *The Swing*.

NEOCLASSICISM

1730 A.D.–1800 A.D.

Jean-Auguste-Dominique Ingres, *La Grande Odalisque,* 1814. Oil on Canvas. Louvre, Paris.

Origins of Color Pigments: Cobalt [oxide] (blue), indigo (blue-violet), iron oxide (yellow ochre), zinc oxide (white), azurite (blue), Naples yellow/lead tin yellow

Binder: Linseed or walnut oil

Emphasis: The Neoclassical style was embraced by the leaders of the French Revolution, and therefore most associated with the revolt. This art movement was not unlike the revival of Greek/Roman classical forms in the Renaissance, yet with more fervor about the ultimate in perfection, better known as *idealism,* which portrays the human form far better than reality. It was the combination of classical antiquity and Romanticism, seen here in like manner to the reclining Venus, which has been painted in various forms throughout history.

*L*a Grande Odalisque is the *grand* finale of illusionist textures, created by Ingres' color prowess. The artist is a lover of clarity. His extravagant silky curtain and sheets, in contrast with the fur covering on the bed as well as the peacock feathers, are just the beginning of the chromatic and tonal harmonies created. The ultimate synthesis of neoclassical clarity, the sophisticated richness of texture, and the exoticism of the Romantic movement (following section) is formulated in this composition. The tactile silkiness of the harem girl's skin has reached the zenith of chromatic tonal shifts. The luminous light red-orange hues of her body are heavily contrasted against the dark muted green wall and blue-green headboards in the background space. The shimmering blue curtain aids in the separation of the background from the foreground, and provides a type of transition between the dullness of the background and the luminous figure in the foreground. Additionally, it is a contest of compliments where warm and cool colors create contrast and dynamic color forms. The dark blue-greens of the background recede quickly, as well as pushes the figure into the spectator's space. This dark, dull color is critical in order to further accentuate the soft and subtle nature of her skin tones, as she turns her head confronting the viewer. This is the rebirth of classical figures in the nineteenth

Figure 1-39 *Grand Odalisque*.

century, but now with a full complement of chroma, in order to bring back the ultimate in color sensuality.

In the tradition of the reclining nude female, Marie-Guillemine Benoist, who was one of Napoleon's painters, renders the unexpected. Typical was the light skin of classical painters. Typical was the light skin of the classical painters, but now in the Portrait of a Negress, Marie-Guillemine Benoist paints an unconventional and beautiful dark skin lady. The exotic figure demonstrates a stark contrast againt the yellow wall and the classical white drapery. The turban and gold earring remind us of Romantic characterizations. It is elegance in color richness, as the dark skin is emphasized by the uncomplicated background and high contrasting white fabric. It is mood par excellence.

Figure 1-40 MARIE-GUILHELMINE BENOIST, *Portrait of a Negress*, 1800. Canvas.

ROMANTICISM

1790 A.D.–1850 A.D.

EUGENE DELACROIX, *Liberty Leading the People,* 1830. Oil on Canvas. Louvre, Paris.

Origins of Color Pigments: Iron oxide, ivory black, yellow ochre, cadmium yellow, cobalt blue, cerulean blue, sienna, vermillion, madder, and lead white

Binder: Linseed oil

Emphasis: Romanticism is one of the most difficult to define, because it is more about attitude or a particular state of mind, rather than a specific style. It may even depend on mood and emotional variances of a given artist. This is most certainly the departure from the conventions of specific styles and movements."

The comparison of color function between Overbeck and Delacroix is striking. *Italia* and *Germania* are crisp, clearly illustrated forms in a very definable space with a more saturated and opaque palette. The painting almost seems more Neoclassical than Romantic, especially with its general absence of brush strokes. *Liberty Leading the People* is more painterly; brushstrokes are evident, as is the luminescence of the composition. It is comprised of *tonal variations* rather than color differences, and exhibits a high degree of translucence in the paint, as opposed to the opaque, solid disposition of Overbeck's work. The two figures are obviously the focal point because they are centered forms—saturated drapery against the more highly tinted background. *Liberty*, on the other hand, is the focal point with the highly translucent and luminous direction of light. Ultimately, the French flag becomes the focus with its perfectly saturated red.

Figure 1-41 FRIEDRICH OVERBECK, *Germania and Italia,* after 1828. Oil on Canvas. Gemaeldegalerie, Staatliche Kunstsammlungen, Dresden, Germany.

Both paintings are clearly from the Romantic period, however, because they are both symbolical of a greater ideal. *Italia and Germania* symbolizes the north and the south, which were long-standing enemies. It depicts the personifications of two countries, reconciled in spite of their differences. *Liberty Leading the People* is much the same, in that liberty has been personified to lead her people to freedom and prosperity over a corrupt government.

The significance of Delacroix's work here is that his application of color was uniquely different.

Liberty Leading the People is uniquely luminous, and yet there are fewer colors, with almost no saturation, which was normally more associated with luminousness.

Delacroix's new technique was to employ glowing pastel colors as the underpainting on top of a white base (ground). Thick paint was then built up over these thin washes of tonal color. The luminous variations of tonal orange values create an indisputable somber, yet urgent emotional appeal. This composition recording the French Revolution in progress produces an emotional response to our senses that is both desperate and hopeful. The dark shadows feel dismal and reveal death and destruction, and yet the mood is hopeful as the luminous diffused light exposes Liberty and her ragtag band of citizens literally climbing over the bodies of their enemy.

Figure 1-42 *Liberty Leading the People*.

REALISM

1830 A.D.–1900 A.D.

JEAN-FRANCOIS MILLET, *The Gleaners,* 1857. Oil on Canvas. Musee d' Orsay, Paris.

Origins of Color Pigments: Yellow ochre, burnt sienna, cadmium yellow, iron oxide, raw umber, ivory black, cerulean blue, and lead white

Binder: Linseed oil

Emphasis: Realism took a very different turn in that social awareness or the *reality* of life became the focus. Rather than the embellishments typically seen in a composition, it became the *truth gauge* for social conditions and attitudes. Far from the *Classical* styles and concepts of *Idealism,* real conditions of society were rendered or translated by the painter into color mood visuals. Realism; therefore, in a common color composition, would exhibit common drapery without any of the embellishments, or melancholy moods.

The Gleaners brings to mind the former Romantic period in that there is a profound sense of *oneness* with nature. The departure from that, however, is the obvious class distinction portrayed. Three laborers toil at the backbreaking task of gathering wheat remnants. Only the poor glean a farm for the small bits of usable wheat, but the wealthy would never concern themselves with such trivial concerns. Additionally, there is no attempt to alter the hazy atmosphere into a pleasant sky with beautiful billowy clouds.

The color condition in this painting produces an austere mood. The tonal variations of orange hues throughout the composition tell us that it is late afternoon, and we have a sense of weariness from a day of hard labor picking up scraps of wheat. The mood here is created by both body language and the color.

The entire scene is illuminated with its ultra-light violet sky, illuminating the orange value throughout the field. Notice the wheat field's radiant hues contrasted against the darker opaque foreground figures, and how they are pushed forward into the immediate ground. Millet further creates deep space—the worker with the red scarf and white garment is contrasted against the darker indigo of the second figure. The tints and shades of orange throughout the composition also give us the sense of a large expanse, and the intensity of the violet sky exacerbates the distance even more so. This is a classic case whereby the *light recedes* into the background, creating an enormous expanse.

Thomas Eakins' painting, *William Rush Carving His Allegorical Figure of the Schuylkill River*, demonstrates variances of the Realism movement. When compared with *The Gleaners,* we immediately notice the quintessential difference between its backbreaking toil and the frivolous pursuits of the artist with his nude study in the comfort of his studio. This painting demonstrates the fundamental difference in tonal values in hues. Eakins' painting consists of variations in red-orange, and all but the figurative element (clothing) is very dark. The illuminated clothing next to her exaggerates her nudity, especially because the only saturated color in the painting is a portion of the *red chair pad* and the *blue*

garment. The fact that her attire is next to her rather than being worn is a contradiction to the artist's work, which actually sculpts her body *with* clothing. The *Allegorical Figure* and her clothing are indeed obvious as the overwhelming focus, as the artist struggles in the background to bring life to his sculpture. The artist is barely recognized because of the low-key hues of his environment, as if we are not supposed to see that the sculpture has clothing. Conversely, the model seems to be truly alone because of the extreme contrast of dark and light hues. There is a somewhat somber and lonely mood by her mere presence contrasted against the deep red-orange of her surroundings. She is, in fact, withdrawn within her own world and so the focus *for her,* as well as the *viewer,* is her own form.

Figure 1-43 Stage Actress Sarah Bernhardt, c. 1862. Portrait before her debut.

Figure 1-44 *The Gleaners*.

Figure 1-45 THOMAS EAKINS, ***William Rush Carving His Allegorical Figure of the Schuylkill River,*** 1876. Oil on Canvas on composition board.

IMPRESSIONISM

1850 A.D.–1920 A.D.

EDGAR DEGAS, *Dancers in the Classroom,* 1880. Oil on Canvas. Sterling and Francine Clark Art Institute, Williamstown, Massachusetts.

Origins of Color Pigments: Paris-Prussian blue, Naples yellow, red and yellow ochre, zinc white, alizarin [madder lake] (red), Indian yellow, and ivory black

Binder: Nut oil

Emphasis: The Impressionists were very concerned about the colors of light. Their paintings often reflected the nature of color's source, which is white light. Their studies concerned the nature of light as it changed colors during the time of the day, seasonally, or in weather conditions. Whether in Claude Monet's work, who often was considered the master of the *colors of light,* or Edgar Degas' light-filled dance studio, light and its affect on color was at the forefront. Certainty, Impressionist color was about optical *reality* rather than the social realities seen in Realism. Within that optical truth, their subject matter was a preference for genre settings rather than political motivations as seen in the past.

Yellow, blue, and red-orange hues set up a type of triadic color harmony, or more specifically, a chromatic unity. The radiant blue dresses carry the eye to the very back of the room. As light from outside floods into the room, it illuminates and seems to provide additional energy to the figures. The blue costumes are the key factor in this painting. The unity of the entire scene is carried out through the translucent light blue hues of the dancers' costumes. The composition is both energized and calm. The yellow hues bring energy and exuberance into the room, while the blue values equalize the mood and bring the energy level down somewhat. The dancers themselves reflect both energy and calm. Their movement, as well as the visual splashes of light (seen on background figures) create the energy, as opposed to the relaxed and tranquil foreground setting of the composition. The entire room consists of shaded or muted colors, which seems to expound on the blue costumes, exaggerating the playful yet serious mood of the study of ballet for these young girls.

Figure 1-46 EDGAR DEGAS, *Dancers in the Classroom* (formerly titled *The Dancing Lesson*), c. 1880, oil on canvas, 1955.562.

Figure 1-47 Claude Monet, ***Woman with a Parasol,*** c. 1875. Oil on Canvas.

The term ***Impressionism*** has its origins at the Paris exhibition ***Salon des Refuses,*** which were works rejected by the official ***Salon.*** One critic wrote, "What on earth is that?" referring to the exhibition of an artist's work. Further excerpts from his analysis were as such: "Perhaps . . . but the impression is there," and "Well, it's a funny impression!" The artists rather liked the term, and so began referring to themselves as the ***Impressionists.***

POST-IMPRESSIONISM

1880 A.D.–1910 A.D.

VINCENT VAN GOGH, *Four Cut Sunflowers,* August-September 1887, Otterlo, Rijksmuseum Kroller-Muller. Oil on Canvas.

VINCENT VAN GOGH, *Haystacks in Provence,* June 1888, Otterlo, Rijksmuseum Kroller-Muller. Oil on Canvas.

Origins of Color Pigments: Ultramarine blue, cobalt blue, citron yellow, carmine, emerald green, mars black, and zinc white

Binder: Nut oil

Emphasis: Post-Impressionism is best exemplified by two pairs of artists. The first pair, Seurat and Cezanne, will reaffirm prescribed and ordered values (albeit in more abstract terms), while it was van Gogh and Gauguin who expounded the virtues of the emotional/mood content of color. This period often emphasized saturated color and heavy impasto broken color to lure the viewer.

Vincent van Gogh, one of history's most profound artists, used color to construct *emotional responses* in his compositions. The four cut sunflowers seem to take on a personality of their own. The exuberant movement of brush strokes is commensurate with the *mood* created by the yellow/yellow-orange petals, as the flora seem to choreograph themselves across the composition. The high contrasting ground of deep blues and greens, as well as conflicting directional brush strokes, further exaggerate the visual appeal and movement of flowers.

This epic colorist used the medium to invite the viewer into the composition—after all, who wouldn't be tempted to investigate the *Haystacks in Provence*. The warmth of golden yellow-orange haystacks immediately pulls the eye into the field. The contrasting coolness of the violet, blue, and green sky invites us to walk down to the distant village, only after being enticed by a brief confrontation with the ladders.

Van Gogh knew better than anyone that color's primary objective was the expression of mood. He said regarding the importance of color: "…I don't mind so

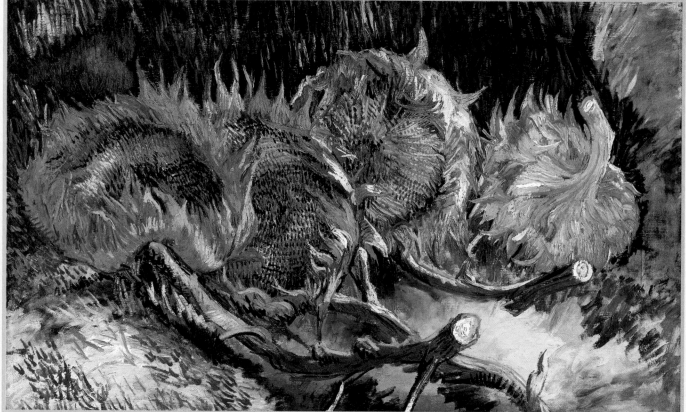

Figure 1-48 Four Cut *Sunflowers*.

Figure 1-49 *Haystacks in Provence.*

much whether my color corresponds exactly, as long as it looks beautiful on my canvas, as beautiful as it looks in nature." A paragraph later he said, "Here is another example: suppose I have to paint an autumn landscape, trees with yellow leaves. All right—when I conceive it as a symphony in yellow, what does it matter whether the fundamental color of yellow is the same as that of the (actual) leaves or not? It matters very little." Certainly, his desire is more about the creation of appropriate emotional content concerning the autumn leaves; the mood of that season, of that moment, can only be interpreted by subjectivity of the artist's perception. How can I best translate to the viewer exactly what I am feeling about the autumn landscape? We must conclude that it is not in the accuracy of seen optical color, but within the inner senses of the artist; therefore, van Gogh's color responses are more truthful to that end.

Figure 1-50 PAUL GAUGUIN, *Peasant Women in a Breton Landscape*, 1894. Canvas. Musee d'Orsay, Paris, France.

PAUL GAUGUIN, *Peasant Women from Brittany,* 1894, Oil on Canvas. Musee d'Orsay, Paris.

Large flat planes of color are typical in Gauguin's work. Like van Gogh, the realistic version of form in space is not a priority, but it was color that became the vital element in the composition. The *illusion* of space was not a concern for Gauguin; he merely created the *implication* of it by a series of large-to-small color planes. The subject matter and space that it occupies is simple for us to understand in many different styles, but it is the saturated to dark hues in the composition that gives us a critical look at the emotional and mood content in a given painting. In the *Peasant Women from Brittany,* the painting actually conveys the mood of the artist, and like van Gogh, perhaps Gauguin lives part of his life vicariously through his work. While creating the composition of lively and jubilant hues, the painter is at rest—he has entered that tranquil memory of past experiences. Post-impressionism takes us into a new world where *color* is not simply one of *elements of art,* but is paramount to the painter.

TWENTIETH-CENTURY PAINTING

1900 A.D.–1930 A.D.

Cubism and Associated Styles

MARIE LAURENCIN, *Guillaume Apollinaire and His Friends* [among them Marie Laurencin, Pablo Picasso, and Fernande Olivier], also called *Gathering in the Countryside,* 1909. Oil on Canvas. Musee National d'Art Moderne, Centre Georges Pompidou, Paris, France.

MARCEL DUCHAMP, *Nude Descending a Staircase, No. 2,* 1912. Oil on Canvas. Philadelphia Museum of Art. Louise and Walter Arensberg Collection.

Origins of Color Pigments: Vermillion, cadmium red, burnt sienna, raw umber, emerald green, lemon yellow (hansa), zinc white, and ivory black

Binder: Linseed oil

Emphasis: Cubists are *reorganizers* of shape and form in space. They organize recognizable objects into the basic truths of the form, without concern for the original or realistic representation of it. Picasso said regarding his artwork, "To paint is to first destroy," and "A painting is first of all a sum total of destructions." *Nude Descending a Staircase* by Duchamp is simply that. The figure's form has been reorganized into a monochromatic composition of fractured *planes of movement.* It is a summary of pure form and movement.

Marie Laurencin paints Guillaume Appolinaire (center) with his group of artist friends. Picasso (on his immediate left), Picasso's mistress Fernande Olivier (Picasso's left) and Marie Laurencin (lower corner), among others. The painting has been simplified into flat planes of color. In these early days when Picasso was forming his ideas about cubism, we can see the influence of early cubist concerns in Marie's abstracted figures, that are morphing towards fractured planes. The integration of color and form, with the formalized horizontal line of faces, creates a relaxed and peaceful composition.

This painting demonstrates that both color and form have been married into simple form, with minimized value gradations. The reds and greens mingle with the more neutral tones in the composition, which helps to produce a stable mass of forms.

Figure 1-51 *Guillaume Apollinaire and His Friends* [among them Marie Laurencin, Pablo Picasso, and Fernande Olivier], also called *Gathering in the Countryside.*

Figure 1-52 *Nude Descending a Staircase (No.2).*

EXPRESSIONISM

WASSILY KANDINSKY, *Improvisation VII (Composition VII), 1913.* Tretyakov Gallery, Moscow, Russia.

WASSILY KANDINSKY, *Market Place in Murnau,* 1908. Fundacion Coleccion Thyssen-Bornemisza, Madrid, Spain. Canvas.

Origins of Color Pigments: Vermillion, cerulean blue, cobalt blue, cadmium yellow, lemon yellow, red and yellow ochres, zinc white, and mars black

Binder: Linseed oil

Emphasis: Expressionism was at the forefront of working with color's primary attribute, which is the creation of *mood and emotion*. The major difference between the cubists (Fauvists) and the Expressionist painters, was the minimal concern about structural and formal composition, and more in favor of color. The *expressive* qualities of color were considered far more powerful and essential to convey the more important issues, which were spiritually based (i.e., the manifestation of *inner emotions*).

The Market Place in Murnau (Figure 1-54) demonstrates Kandinsky's struggle to express the pure spiritual essence of color mood. He begins to abstract his images, while increasing or exaggerating the saturations of the original hues in the *Market Place*. Like the expressionists, Kandinsky soon realized that representational forms of color possessed severe limitations, not to mention the limitations of the canvas' boundaries. It became a mood-quest in a manner of speaking, working toward expressing the limitless boundaries of the spirit of emotion, by the choreographing of non-objective form and color.

Finally, Kandinsky's work had managed to evolve from the restrictions still seen in the *Market Place* in 1908, to better representation of the "Spiritual of Art" seen in *Improvisation VII* (Figure 1-53) in 1913. Color and line had become the physical manifestation of a non-tangible musical composition. Said to be Kandinsky's most complex work, *Composition VII* would seem at first glance to be a pandemonium of color. On closer examination, it is a carefully orchestrated hexadic color harmony. It is rather the controlled chaos of colors in space, harmoniously traveling across the composition. As successful as he was, Kandinsky realized that he would never completely accomplish bringing the non-tangible into the physical world.

Figure 1-53 *Improvisation VII (Composition VII).*

Figure 1-56 *Les Demoiselles d' Avignon*.

In this painting, Picasso demonstrates the typical juxtapositions of fractured planes so often observed in his work. The fractured colors in this abstraction of human form, fills the composition, demonstrating a new and dynamic method of representing form in space. Color, as well as form, takes an unconventional departure, which was key in the changing of attitudes, in terms of how these elements had been traditionally viewed. The cool and calming blue abstracts interact with the warm red hues to create a tranquil display of the young ladies in Avignon.

SURREALISM

Salvador Dali, *The Persistence of Memory,* 1931. The Museum of Modern Art, New York, NY. Oil on Canvas.

Frida Kahlo, *Self-Portrait with Changuito,* 1945. Fundacion Dolores Olmedo, Mexico City, D.F., Mexico. Oil on Canvas.

Origins of Color Pigments: Magenta, vermillion, cerulean blue, iron oxides, zinc white, and ivory black

Binder: Linseed oil

Emphasis: Surrealism was originally intended to express a genuine thought process. Aesthetics, morality, and reasoning were liberated from art, which were considered to be the controlling forces. Rather, free association according to Freud's psychoanalytic technique explores the imagination in the world of myths, fantasy, and even dreams. It is, in fact, a surreal approach to art.

A painter of thoughts and emotions, Kahlo often used color to record the *real* Frida. Though she appeared happy (according to her friends), it was a façade for emotional torment. For this painter, color was the natural expression of mood. Even though *Autorretrato con Collar* appears to be a confident Frida, the color palette demonstrates her real situation or *mood*. There is a lack of translucent color; only heavy opaque hues exist, which seem to dominate the mood of the painting. The artwork is one of complementary contrasts. A cold and icy background lingers, while the figure itself seems almost hot with anger, as if the temperature of the composition is on fire with neganergy. The hues of her skin seem as strong, vibrant, and commanding as does her very presence.

Figure 1-57 *The Persistence of Memory*.

Figure 1-58 *Self-Portrait with Changuito.*

Point of Interest

Kahlo's paintings were a physical representation of her spiritual condition. It has been said by many who were close to her that her most impressive paintings were executed during those times when she was in deep depression. *"My painting carries with it the message of pain...Painting completed my life... I believe that work is the best thing..."*

Frida Kahlo

ABSTRACT EXPRESSIONISM

Hans Hofmann, *Autumn Gold,* 1957, Oil on Canvas. National Gallery of Art. Washington D.C. Robert and Jane Meyerhoff Collection, 1996.81.4

Origins of Color Pigments: Alizarin crimson, ultramarine blue, Indian yellow, cadmium yellow, cobalt green, viridian green, dioxazine purple, titanium white, and mars black

Binder: Linseed oil

Emphasis: Originally a term used to describe Kandinsky, *Abstract Expressionism* first referred to Kandinsky's nonfigurative and nonrepresentational paintings. By the time Abstract Expressionists had graduated from the Surrealist movement, the New York school of artists began to concentrate more on the expressive qualities of paint and color. As with the Impressionists, color in the composition generated the light as opposed to nature where light illuminates color.

*A*utumn Gold by Hofmann is the pure form expression of color, which imitates a type of architectural construction in thick imposto paint. This painting could be much about the color of red, even though there are many hues other than red in the compositional space. The shaded hues of green create a high contrasting barrier between the tinted light hues of yellow and green on the right side of the painting. It is this setup of color saturation contrasted with tinted and shaded hues that exaggerates the saturated and translucent red.

Mood Associations of Colors Within in the Painting

SATURATED COLORS	SHADED HUES	TINTED HUES
Angry	Depressed	Joyful
Energized	Quiet	Playful
Passionate	Mysterious	Revealing
Sensuous	Somber	Peaceful

Figure 1-59 *Autumn Gold*.

COLOR FIELD PAINTING

HELEN FRANKENTHALER, *Nature Abhors a Vacuum,* 1973, Acrylic on Canvas. National Gallery of Art, Washington D.C. Patron's Permanent Fund and Gift of Audrey and David Miruish, Toronto, Canada.

Origins of Color Pigments: Cadmium red, cadmium lemon yellow, iron oxides, zinc white, and mars black

Binder: Acrylic emulsion

Emphasis: Typically large planes of translucent washes, oils, and ultimately acrylic paint became the standard for expressing the spiritual condition of the artist. Color field paintings were pure chromatic abstractions that were most often calm and even meditative in character.

Frankenthaler's work consists of large planes of translucent washes, which forces the viewer to contemplate the unadulterated character of color. Void of any references to the real world, her paintings replicate the natural colors of the earth—some compositions with movement, some that are quiet and tranquil. The translucency of color in *Nature Abhors a Vacuum* allows the maximum amount of light into the composition, hence the vibrancy and glow of warmth felt in the hues. The mood pulls the viewer into its very dreamy, nonthreatening environment, and color has no pretense as it creates a simple presentation of itself.

Mark Rothko's 1968 painting *Untitled* is even less associated with real references, in that it is a veritable palette of light. The color field doubles as a panel of radiant energy, and yet at the same time projects a serenity that is not usually associated with orange and yellow.

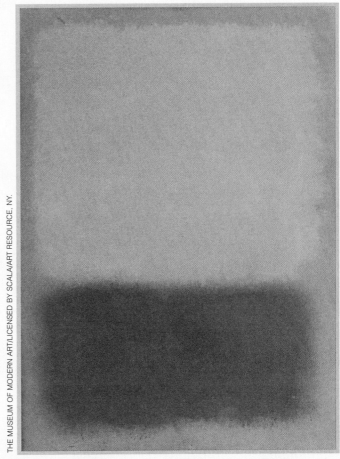

Figure 1-61 *Untitled*.

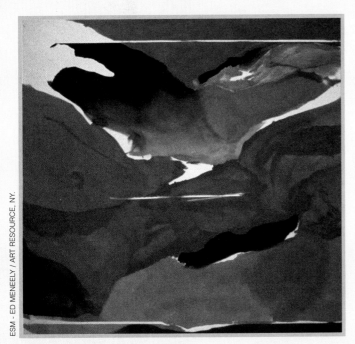

Figure 1-60 *Nature Abhors a Vacuum*.

Point of Interest

Mark Rothko's color field paintings became successively darker as he grew older and realized his own mortality. Suffering from depression, Rothko eventually renders his canvas into a field void of color. Just before his death from suicide, he had implemented an achromatic palette, producing canvasses in dark grays and black.

PHOTOREALISM

AUDREY FLACK, *Queen,* 1975–6, Oil and Acrylic on Canvas. Louis K. Meisel Gallery.

Origins of Color Pigments: Indian yellow, cadmium orange, cadmium yellow, crimson, cerulean blue, ultramarine blue, phalo green, chromium oxide green, dioxazine violet, titanium white, and mars black

Binder: Linseed oil and acrylic emulsion

Emphasis: Photorealism was first and foremost about the artist's romance with the camera. In the fifteenth century, Leonardo da Vinci used the camera (obscura) to aid in his perspective drawing; in the nineteenth century the camera was used to help painters *imitate the reality of nature.* In the twentieth century, Photorealism (Painting) turned it around by using *painting to imitate* the reality of camera images. For the photorealists, it is the photograph by which they build the composition.

Flack's fully saturated composition of hexadic color harmony is difficult to read in terms of mood components because there is an equal representation of color. The painting is actually more about representation, and of course, symbolism. Even though we want to clarify a mood from the vibrant red of the rose or the intensity of yellow in the apple, there are too many pure colors to derive a typical mood sequence. It is perhaps because of the obvious color palette that we want to make more of it than is there. Suffice it to say that we can make sufficient observances of color balance throughout the painting. Red objects move from left to right across the canvas, as does yellow across the bottom, and green peppered in diagonally. Light violet, blues, and gray accentuate the saturation of the orange, apple, and rose, not to mention additional smaller objects.

> I always wanted to draw realistically. For me art is a continuous discovery into reality, an exploration of visual data which has been going on for centuries, each artist contributing to the next generation's advancement. I also believe people have a deep need to understand their world and that art clarifies reality for them.
>
> Audrey Flack

Figure 1-62 *Queen*.

CONTEMPORARY

1990 A.D. – CURRENT

FRANK STELLA, *Cantahar,* 1998. Mixed Media on Canvas. Imaginary Series. Coll. of the Artist.

Origins of Color Pigments: Lithographic inks - 48-color lithograph, screen print, relief, etching, engraving, and aquatint

Binder: Oil with lithographic resins, rosin acid-based materials, hydrocarbon resins, and alkyd resins latex coating binders

Emphasis: Contemporary styles are varied and nonspecific. Normally, there are a myriad of styles at the turn of the twenty-first century.

A composition so rich with color movement, tints and shades, and intensity, Cantahar is a saturated extravaganza of color. The mood variables projected are both calm and energized. The energy of the saturated yellow and red captivates and moves the eye throughout the canvas with a certain authority or command, while the blues (particularly the center blue area) and greens give calm and control to this perceived color chaos. The perfect placement of hues throughout creates a perfectly color-balanced composition of the seven spectral colors. Dark or heavy colors are minimal (shades) and excessive tints are absent, while there is a bounty of brilliance that would make a strong case for celebration, dancing in the streets—a veritable compositional Mardi Gras of moods.

Color plays a complex role here as it scatters its playful and yet very serious elements throughout the masterpiece, as if a symphony is being played out. Though jubilant, there is a certain serenity of color that is choreographed across the paper surface. There is movement of color, some rapid, some slow, and to a particular degree, seems to have commensurable attributes with Kandinsky's compositions.

Figure 1-63 *Cantahar.*

SUMMARY

At the very heart of these textbook components is the development of the student's critical thinking and problem solving skills. Knowledge of color and its attributes is of course vital, but it is the development of critical thinking skills in color that separates the mediocre from the extraordinary color designers. Also, a significant beginning to understanding color attributes, lies within *Color Equations*. It provides an introduction to color in a historical sense and serves as an additional complement to understanding the complexities of color. There are no single components, however, which stand alone as more important than the other, but each of those parts and chapters is a map—roads that lead to the extraordinary understanding and use of color.

CHAPTER TWO

Figure 2-1 Sir John Everett Millais, *Mariana*, 1851. Oil on Panel. Based on Shakespeare's character Mariana in his play *Measure for Measure*. Tate Gallery, London, Great Britain.

2

THE SOVEREIGNTY OF LIGHT

COLOR PHYSICS, COLOR SATURATION, INTENSITY, AND VALUE

THE TWELVE–PART COLOR CIRCLE

There are many complexities and variations about the theory of color. The very reason for the designation *color theory* tells us something about the nature of the subject itself. During our discourse, we will discover aspects about color that are both factual and theoretical. Some attributes of color are *written* in *stone*, whereas others are interpretive in nature.

Let's begin with the very basics: the *twelve-part color circle*. We want to illustrate how the twelve-part color circle is developed from the triadic color harmony of red, yellow, and blue. These three equilateral colors on the color circle are known as *primary colors*. They exist in and of themselves and cannot be created by the mixing of other colors. Put another way, we can say that all other colors are produced by various mixtures of primaries. They are the foundational source of all other color amalgamations in the subtractive color world.

By separating a circle into twelve equal parts, we will first establish the *primaries* of yellow (top), red (lower right), and blue (lower left) into an equilateral triangle. Next, the *secondary* colors of orange, green, and violet are established. They are located equilaterally as well, arranged with a space between each primary and secondary.

A secondary color is achieved by the mixing of two *primaries,* for example:

Red + Yellow = Orange
Red + Blue   = Violet
Yellow + Blue = Green

Figure 2-2 Itten Color Circle.

RICHARD EWING.

Now that we have established the primary and secondary colors, we have one more set of colors to create: *intermediate* colors (see footnote regarding tertiary explanation).*

The intermediate (tertiary) colors are inserted between one primary and one secondary and are made by mixing one primary and one secondary as follows:

Red + Orange = Red-Orange
Red + Violet = Red-Violet
Blue + Violet = Blue-Violet
Blue + Green = Blue-Green
Yellow + Green = Yellow-Green
Yellow + Orange = Yellow-Orange

This establishment of color with its own distinctive location within the color circle is the same sequence of color seen in a natural rainbow, as well as the natural spectrum of colors seen through a clear prism.

Figure 2-3 Twelve Part Color Circle with Color Harmony Indicaters.

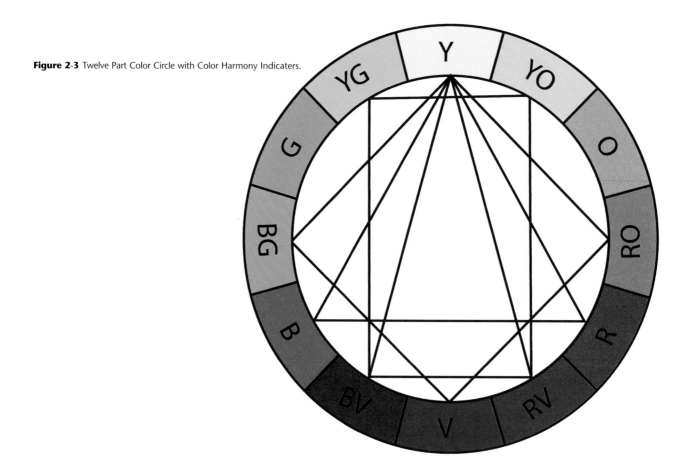

*Here is where theory interjects itself. Speculation as to whether or not the term tertiary holds the same meaning as intermediate color occasionally arises. Today most artists use the word tertiary and intermediate interchangeably.

THE VISIBLE COLOR SPECTRUM

In Sir Isaac Newton's *Opticks; Treatise of the Reflections, Refractions, Inflections and Colours of Light,* he investigates his theory that *the source of all color is light* by careful observation of the primary source of light, which was considered to be rays from the sun itself.

He began the analysis of light by focusing the sun's light into a clear triangular prism.

A narrow slit was first cut into a flat board in order to concentrate the light. The light was directed through the narrow opening and onto the prism. As the white light refracted through the prism, it in effect separated the colors of light into seven distinct bands of light. This process refers to the visible spectrum and tells us that **white light is the source (purest) of all color.** In order to confirm that color exists in white light, the process was then reversed, so that the colors of light were redirected back through another prism, condensing them back into white light.

The *rainbow* is another accurate source of the effects of sunlight directed through a prism. You will notice that when a rainbow occurs, there is always sunlight present, albeit a mere opening in the cloud formation. A rainbow occurs after rainfall, while there still is moisture in the air.

Tiny water droplets each act as very small prisms, which together act to create one of the many wonders of nature.

Figure 2-5 demonstrates how white light strikes a droplet of water [A]. At this point some of the light is reflected away, while some enters the droplet. That which enters is refracted to [B]. Once again, some leaves the droplet, while the remainder will reflect back [C]. The visible spectrum is separated into bands of identifiable color to produce a rainbow.

The close-up photograph of a rainbow at Jasper National Park (next page) gives us a better understanding about the colors of light. Red, which has the longest wavelength, is evident while violet with its shortest wavelength is more difficult to distinguish. Interestingly, some theorists disclaim indigo as a legitimate spectral color because it often is difficult to see. The difference between the spectrum's blue and violet is marginal, but one must learn to see that it is visible. Because so much of the color is reflected out of the water droplet, rainbows tend not to have such sharp distinctions from one color to the next. For that reason, it also is difficult to see indigo, especially because it is a narrower band of light. Most assuredly, it does exist.

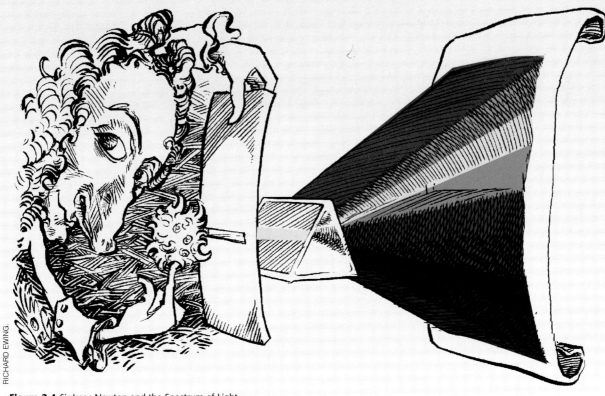

RICHARD EWING.

Figure 2-4 Sir Isaac Newton and the Spectrum of Light.

Figure 2-5 White light is the source of all color.

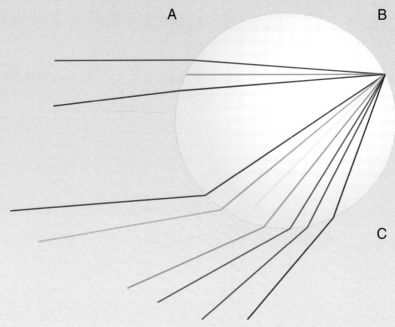

Figure 2-6 Rainbow at Jasper National Park.

LIGHT

In 1873 mathematician and theoretical physicist James Clerk Maxwell presented his formula known as "Maxwell's Equations," which brought forth the concept that electrical charges actually interacted via a force field. He demonstrated that there could be a marriage between electricity and magnetism. In fact, he soon realized that the electromagnetic wave had the exact same speed as light (300,000 km/s), and that the joining of these two forces resulted in the actual creation of light. It was this new finding that opened our eyes to the world of light.

Soon came a profound realization that there were new kinds of light, which all had various and specific wavelengths depending on the amount of energy emitted by a given wave. Basically, shorter wavelengths would equate to greater energy and longer waves generated a lower energy, yet all electromagnetic waves are actual energies that vibrate throughout the known universe.

As we can see from Figure 2-7 depicting light measured in terms of wavelengths, the gamma and X-rays are the *most energetic* and yet have very *short wavelengths*. Next, a very familiar form of radiation from the sun is ultraviolet, which is responsible for human maladies such as burns and skin cancer. All of the aforementioned lights emit the most harmful radiation to the human life form. The invisible ultraviolet is one step higher than the visible spectrum of violet, which can be seen.

Next, decreasing in energy, the *visible color spectrum* can be seen on the chart, and occupies a very small area of the total spectrum of light. This is the region of the most importance to us because artists and designers rely on visible color.

The visible spectrum is bordered on the low side by infrared, which has wavelengths too long to see—basically beyond the color *red*. Of course, we have previously mentioned the other side of the color spectrum bounded by ultraviolet, which also is out of visible range from violet. The lowest energy levels with the *longest wavelengths* are microwaves and radio waves. We now know that for the major part of the electromagnetic spectrum most lights cannot be seen, and in fact it is but a fraction of that light scale that is visible.

Each member of the visible spectrum of color also has a particular wavelength and energy level. Because red is closest to infra*red* light, it has the longest waves but the lowest energy level, whereas violet, which is closest to ultra*violet,* has the highest energy level and the shortest waves (see Table 2-1).

Additionally, colors with the longest wavelength not only have the lowest energy level, but are the least refracted colors as well. Violet, on the other hand, has the shortest wavelengths, highest energy level, and the greatest refraction of all visible colors.

The Electromagnetic Spectrum

On either side of the familiar (but tiny) visible rainbow of red, orange, yellow, green, blue, indigo, and violet lie vast bands of nonvisible radiation. The higher the energy of the radiation, the shorter its wavelength. The spectrum divisions between the different forms of radiation overlap because the names derive in part from how the radiation is generated and the technology used to detect it.

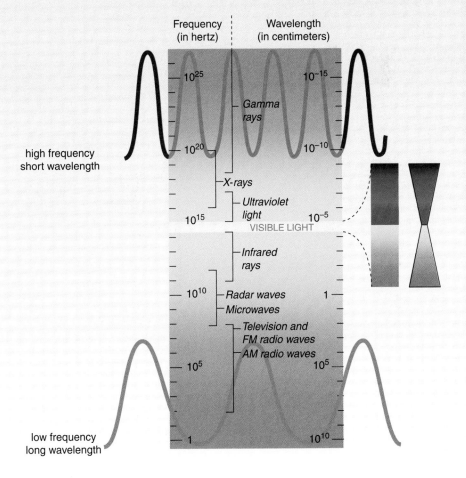

Frequency (in hertz) / Wavelength (in centimeters)

high frequency short wavelength

10^{25} — 10^{-15}

Gamma rays

10^{20} — 10^{-10}

X-rays

Ultraviolet light

10^{15} — 10^{-5}

VISIBLE LIGHT

Infrared rays

10^{10} — Radar waves — Microwaves — 1

Television and FM radio waves — AM radio waves

10^{5} — 10^{5}

low frequency long wavelength

1 — 10^{10}

Figure 2-7

The Visible Spectrum—Wavelength Standard

COLOR	WAVELENGTH IN MILL MICRONS	FREQUENCY IN CYCLES PER SECOND
Red	800-650 (longest wave)	400-470 (lowest energy)
Orange	640-590	470-520
Yellow	580-550	520-590
Green	530-490	590-650
Blue	480-460	650-700
Indigo	450-440	700-760
Violet	430-390 (shortest wave)	760-800 (highest energy)

Table 2-1.

It is still a mystery in terms of how exactly the *eye-to-brain* function works, because we do not know how we actually discriminate wavelengths. We do, however, know about actual colors of physical *objects* themselves. When superimposing a green filter over a red filter and then placing them in front of white light, the result will be black. These complements (red and green) cancel each other, because the green filter absorbs all other spectral colors except green. Commensurately, the red filter does the same. All of the color has been *stolen* and nothing is left but black.

The colors of physical objects, as well as pigments, are *subtractive* because their colors are the result of absorption. A red apple does not contain color in and of itself, but it is the light that is responsible for the production of red in the apple. It is the *molecular constitution* of the apple's surface that absorbs orange, yellow, green, blue, and violet, reflecting *only red* back to the viewer's eye. The purer the white light source (sun), the redder the apple will appear. If we were, for example, to illuminate the apple with a green light, which is the complement of red, then the apple will appear black, thus canceling each other. Complements will complement each other side by side, and defeat each other when combined. The results are commensurable for all other complements as well.

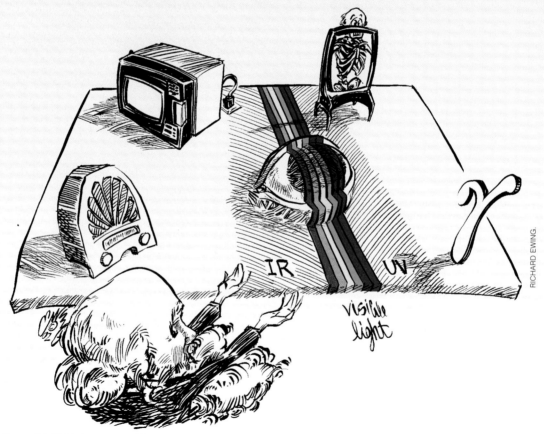

Figure 2-8 Visible Spectrum and Sir Isaac Newton.

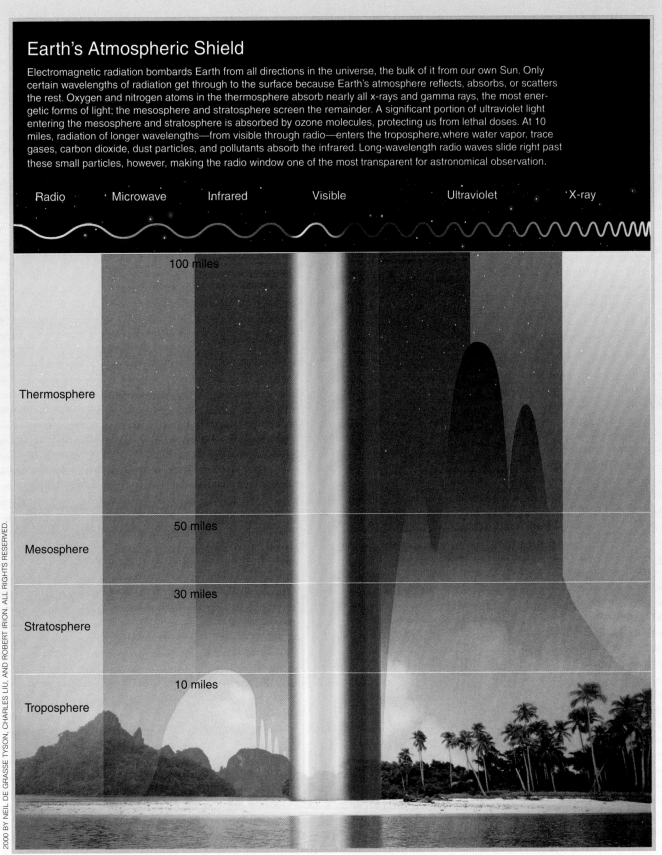

Earth's Atmospheric Shield

Electromagnetic radiation bombards Earth from all directions in the universe, the bulk of it from our own Sun. Only certain wavelengths of radiation get through to the surface because Earth's atmosphere reflects, absorbs, or scatters the rest. Oxygen and nitrogen atoms in the thermosphere absorb nearly all x-rays and gamma rays, the most energetic forms of light; the mesosphere and stratosphere screen the remainder. A significant portion of ultraviolet light entering the mesosphere and stratosphere is absorbed by ozone molecules, protecting us from lethal doses. At 10 miles, radiation of longer wavelengths—from visible through radio—enters the troposphere, where water vapor, trace gases, carbon dioxide, dust particles, and pollutants absorb the infrared. Long-wavelength radio waves slide right past these small particles, however, making the radio window one of the most transparent for astronomical observation.

Radio · Microwave · Infrared · Visible · Ultraviolet · X-ray

100 miles

Thermosphere

50 miles

Mesosphere

30 miles

Stratosphere

10 miles

Troposphere

Figure 2-9

Earth's Atmosphere

Another interesting side note about light (color) wavelengths is to observe why the colors of the earth's atmosphere change throughout the day. During a sunrise or sunset the light rays from the Sun hit the Earth's surface at an angle, and therefore travel through greater distances or larger volumes of atmosphere before reaching the Earth's surface. The reason a sunrise has a reddish tone and sunsets change from yellow to orange to red is that the blue wavelengths are fragmented and dispersed, which then allow more of the red, red-orange, and yellow wavelengths to reach the terrain.

Intermediate color (tertiary) is the result of mixing one primary and one secondary color. The term intermediate seems to be a better fit than tertiary, because it describes hue between or *intermediate* of one primary and one secondary color. Many still use *tertiary* to mean the same, but for this textbook we will use the word *intermediate*, which is the more accurate term. There was a time when tertiary actually meant the *mixing of two secondary colors*, which is vastly different than a primary and a secondary result.

Tertiary color is commonly referred to as the mixing of one primary and one secondary color. However, we also know the combination of those two colors are known as *intermediates* because the resultant color is located *intermediately*—or between—the primary and secondary colors. Officially the dictionary defines the word tertiary as being "of the third order, or rank," which would infer that two colors are mixed to produce the one. That being the case, intermediate and tertiary color could be one in the same because there is no specific designation. Interestingly

enough, the term tertiary has been known to refer to the *mixing of two secondary colors* as well.

What may better support the idea of the term *tertiary* is the dictionary definition. The definition here indicates a certain weakness on the part of the third color. For example, primary yellow is the purest yellow; it's created by no other combination of colors. A secondary orange is a blend of yellow and red, which results in yellow-orange. On the other hand, intermediates are just that—between, or in the middle of the primary and secondary color.

Normally, two secondary colors will create (depending on percentage of the mix) resultant brown hues (one example), which is more or less a range of shaded orange to red tones. This is very different than how we see the intermediate hue.

Additionally, this should not be confused with the mixture of two *complements*, which produce a neutralized, or grayed effect (these issue will be discussed in greater detail later in the text). For the sake of continuity, we will let the terms intermediate and tertiary remain as interchangeable at this point.

COLOR SYSTEMS

There are two categories of color primaries: *additive* and *subtractive* processes. Additive primary color deals with the *properties of light,* which are **R**ed, **G**reen, and **B**lue **(RGB).** These are typically seen in the design world dealing with computer screens and various digital applications. Subtractive color, on the other hand, refers to the three primary *physical pigments of* **R**ed, **Y**ellow, and **B**lue **(RYB),** classically thought of in terms of a painter's palette of colors. Additionally, subtractive color primaries are linked to computer processes in relation to the printing inks of **C**yan, **M**agenta, **Y**ellow, and black **[K],** better known as **(CMYK).**

RYB Subtractive Color - Primary Triad of Red, Yellow, and Blue

White light is the source of all color (seven spectrum colors). When a subtractive, or pigmented, color surface receives that light, it basically absorbs all of the colors in the ray of light, except for the specific colors represented on that surface. In Figure 2-11, for example, the sun's white light containing red, orange, yellow, green, blue, indigo, and violet is flooding the plant's surface.

It is the molecular constitution of green (chlorophyll) in the vegetation that is recognized by the *green ray* and is therefore revealed as green. The remaining colors are not recognized and are simply absorbed into the surface. The color of *green* is not absorbed, but reflected back to the viewer's eye.

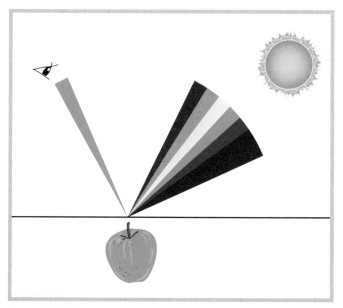

Figure 2-10 Subtractive Color RYB.

Figure 2-11 Subtractive Color.

Figure 2-12 Thailand's Flora and Fauna: Green Chlorophyll.

The photosynthetic green pigment is additionally responsible for the life of the plant, because photosynthesis helps plant life obtain energy from sunlight. It is therefore important to realize that light is not only comprised of specific colors, but also carries energy as well.

Certainly, when we think of the romanticized version of fine arts and the old master painted canvases, subtractive color seems most often associated with the processes of subtractive color. It wasn't until the twentieth century that subtractive color began to take on an additional application, which has become the CMYK printer inks associated with the computer RGB process.

The next page briefly introduces four of the many varied color circle systems. The color circle system began in the eighteenth century with Sir Isaac Newton, who gave birth to the color circle, and continued on with Johannes Itten's subtractive color circle created in the mid-twentieth century. The color circle is a derivative of the spectrum of light as it was seen by Newton's experiment reflected onto the wall.

1. **Newton's** (Figure 2-13) color circle, seen on the right-side page of his 1704 publication, shows the first color circle. Newton had only the seven spectral colors at unequal angles, just as it would have been seen on the spectrum of colors projected onto a given surface. No balance adjustments were made. He basically joined two ends of the spectrum.
2. **Goethe** (Figure 2-14) recognized the very essential function of symmetry and complementarity's role in color's characteristic. Goethe's 1810 publication *Theory of Colors* points to a very basic concept in color today. Goethe was first to realize the importance of the non-spectral color of *magenta*.
3. **Munsell** (Figures 2-23 and 2-24) carefully organized colors with a specific number system. While Goethe

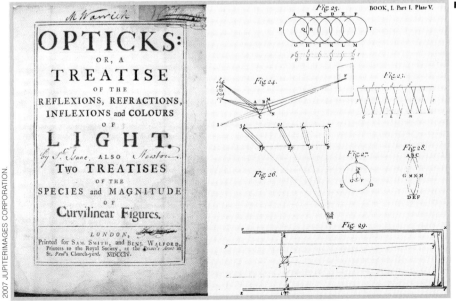

Figure 2-13 ISAAC NEWTON (1642–1727), *Opticks.* Second edition London 1794. Cover.

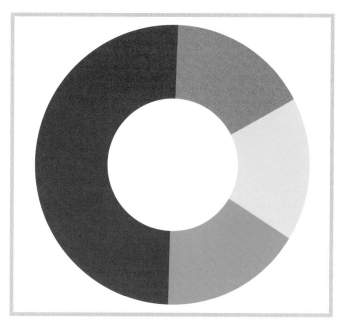

Figure 2-14 Goethe's Color Circle.

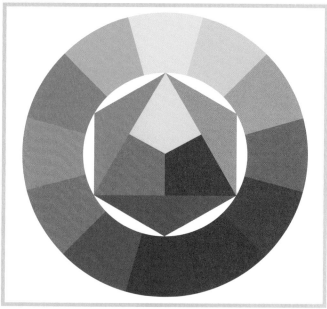

Figure 2-17 Johannes Itten's Subtractive Twelve-Part Color Circle, 1961.

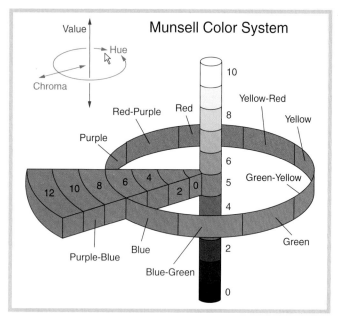

Figure 2-15 Munsell's Color Order System.

remained general and confined to the primary and secondary colors, Munsell dealt with all colors and hues. His number system located any color in the Munsell structure based on decimal increments on hue, value, and chroma ranges.

4. Itten's color circle (1961) was finally adopted by most color theorists until now. It is more concise than Goethe's, yet less extravagant than Munsell's. The primary, secondary, and intermediate range of colors are displayed equally. The center triangle and hexagon indicate the complementary colors, as well as triadic and hexadic harmonies.

RGB Additive Color - Primary Triad of Red, Green, and Blue

The *additive colors* are quite different than subtractive in that they are colors of light and not pigments. Additionally,

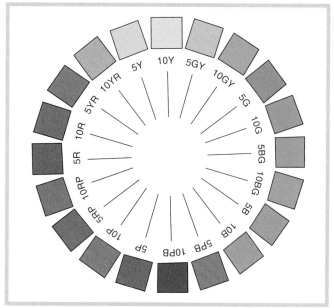

Figure 2-16 Munsell's Hue Circle.

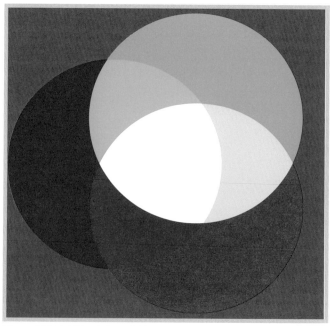

Figure 2-18 Additive Colors – RGB.

Figure 2-19 Basic electron orbital path around a proton and neutron.

their primaries are red, green, and blue, typically recognized in computer and digitally related applications as *RGB. The absence of yellow is conspicuous, and is produced by mixing red and green light.*

The actual origins of the primary colors of light should be of interest to the student of color. It is of particular interest because the twentieth century has been revolutionized by the creation of the computer, color printers, and other digital functions such as the camera. The core of the RGB function is found deep within the atom itself.

Because all matter is composed of atoms, we must conclude that the elemental foundation of color lays within these tiny particles. The atom contains a nucleus of protons (positively charged) and neutrons (neutral) (one proton and neutron are pictured here for simplification). An orbital path of one or more negatively charged electrons circumnavigate these bundles of protons and neutrons.

Electrons carry with them groups of elementary particles called photons, which move at the speed of light. Photons, when passing close to another electron, can be absorbed, transferring energy and momentum.

The smallest *provable* particles are known as *quarks.* Each proton and neutron carries bundles of three quarks each; one red, one green, and one blue quark for each

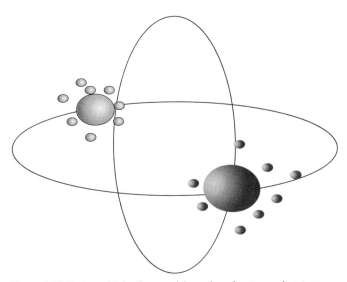

Figure 2-20 Electron orbital paths around the nucleus of protons and neutrons.

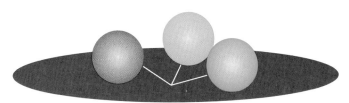

Figure 2-21 Inside the proton and neutron are bundles of quarks.

Figure 2-22 Subtractive Colors – CMYK.

bundle. Each RGB group of three quarks are bound together, so often there are many groups of RGB quarks inside a proton or neutron, and they are in constant movement. The RGB symbol you see on your computer screen ultimately makes reference to the color quark.

CMYK Additive Color - Cyan, Magenta, Yellow, and Black

CMYK brings us back to the subtractive model, but this time the specific hue of blue, red, and yellow. Cyan (blue) and magenta (red) must be very specific in hue in order to produce the most accurate representation of color possible. Typical to the subtractive model, the colors revealed are those that are not absorbed.

In order to illustrate the difference in specific CMYK inks, we need only to examine the previous *pigmented RYB subtractive process:* RYB: Red and yellow produce orange [CMYK: Magenta + Yellow = Red], RYB: red and blue produce violet [CMYK: Magenta + Cyan = Blue] and RYB: blue and yellow produces green [CMYK: Cyan + Yellow = Green]. Although the mixture of CMY produces black, it is not a pure black, so black is included with the triad colors as a pure source. Additionally, because we are referring to printing inks, combining CMY to produce black would soak the paper and use too much ink. The independent black will create a cleaner line than attempting to align (register) the three colors, not to mention the cost savings of using one color source over three.

Point of Interest

Color charts known as a digital color checker (Figures 2-23 and 2-24) are a grid of either 24 or 140 patches of perfect saturated color. These charts are typically used in: 1) graphic arts to check printing or proofing processes, 2) in photography applications to check paper, film, light, and filters, 3) in the television industry to check cameras, monitors, film, and light, 4) electronic publishing to check scanners, monitors, and various proofing procedures.

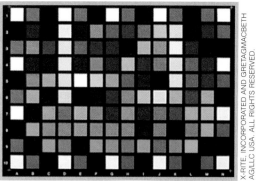

Figure 2-23 24 patch color checker in Adobe Photoshop.

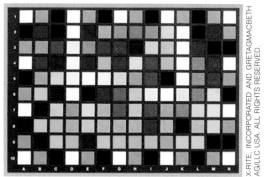

Figure 2-24 140 patch color checker.

These two Macbeth ColorCheckers© are used in the color industry to register color accuracy. The smaller chart, typically used for the profiling of digital cameras, consists of 24 color patches that basically imitate the general colors of life, such as skin tones, foliage, sky, terrain, and so on. The larger version (SG Color Checker), consisting of 140 color patches, is more specific and includes the original 24, plus a 17-step gray scale and 14 various skin tones. These checkers examine and compare the digital color reproduction to any given actual color scheme. In terms of the camera, a grid of *subtractive color inks* (checker) are being calibrated to an *additive color* digital device.

Summary: The *additive and* subtractive models are as follows:

Red, yellow, and blue (RYB) = subtractive primary triad of *pigments*

Red, green, and blue (RGB) = additive primary triad of *lights* [quark bundles of RGB]

Cyan, magenta, and yellow (CMY) + black (K) = subtractive primary triad of *inks* [CMYK]

COLOR ANONYMITY AND THE ATOM

A Word About Color Anonymity

Color theory itself possesses a certain ambiguity and mystery, as well as its particular fact-based representations. Occasionally, the student will observe what seems to be *ambiguity*, and yet what appears to be vague in reality is nothing more than subjectivity. From time to time, color does seem to be contradictory, and yet we learn to accept its two-sided character.

The fact-based characteristics of color are the observations that we can *visually see* as well as evaluate, and are not subject to interpretation. They are what they are.

Other attributes of color anonymity are hidden within the *mysteries unseen by the naked eye*. Concrete knowledge about the science of color is derived from this aspect and helps to develop a clearer understanding about its function. Here we will briefly focus on the mysteries of the unseen and smallest unit of color, the atom.

The Atom

Originally, the idea that natural occurrences can be explained in terms of elementary ingredients was first recorded in the Greek town of Miletus of Ionia in the sixth century B.C. (c. 625–547 B.C.). The initial concept of the atom, however, came about a century later by Democritus and Leucippus (c. 480-c. 420 B.C.). Their idea was that all matter was made up of indivisible and eternal particles. The Greek word *atomos*, which literally means "that which cannot be divided," seemed an appropriate name to describe the nature of their theory, thus the use of the name *atom* was first used.

Around the same time, **Aristotle** and **Plato** were spending hours arguing their philosophical differences. Plato's approaches were always on a more spiritual plane, but it was Aristotle who was more connected to the earth with his scientific views.

Soon enough, Leucippus' idea about the atom was put to rest in favor of Aristotle's more popular notion that there

Figure 2-25 SHIJO, *The Atom Revealed.*
Symbolic Color Abstraction #1.

RICHARD EWING.

Figure 2-26 Plato's approaches (philosophy) were always on a more spiritual plane, but it was Aristotle who was more connected to the earth with his scientific views.

were instead four fundamental substances: air, water, earth, and fire. At this point the atom was nothing more than a solid mass; the idea of a nucleus with even smaller particles was unknown. Of course, Aristotle was unable go much farther than to hypothesize about *matter*, because his methods for turning theory into fact were limited, to say the least. The whole issue about the existence of the atom slowly died out and remained dormant for the next two millennia.

More than thousand years later, in 1662, the atomic hypothesis awoke when Irish physicist **Robert Boyle**

admitted that the only way to make sense of gases being compressed was to acknowledge the atom itself. The slow discovery of this atomic premise continued in 1808 when **John Dalton** proposed that all matter comprises atoms. Toward the dawn of the *atomos* years in Greece, it was thought that the atom itself was the basic building block of matter, but in 1897 **Joseph Thomson** gave us experimental proof that the atom actually had an internal structure, beginning with the electron.

THE DISCOVERY OF THE ATOMIC STRUCTURE: COLOR QUARKS

The Electron and the Photon

It was **Joseph Thomson** who discovered the first particle, the *electron,* and its mass. The electron maintains an orbit inside of the atom around the nucleus at an enormous velocity of 186,000 mps (the speed of light). The energy variances between electron orbits determine the energy level of the light that is to be absorbed. When an electron changes the level of its orbit from higher to lower, it immediately emits a *photon,* which will carry borrowed energy (surplus) away from the original electron, only to be absorbed by another. The energy from the photon is actually the difference registered between the first and final orbit's state. It was **Albert Einstein** who realized in 1905 that light existed as small bundles of energy, swarming around the electron like bees on a hive. He referred to them as photons. It was Einstein who actually completed Max Planck's research on photoelectric effects and thus indentified the photon.

The Nucleus

Soon after, **Lord Ernest Rutherford** proposed and later proved that the atom had a heart, a very small area in the

PHOTO BY THE AUTHOR.

Figure 2-27 SHIJO, *The Nucleus of the Atom.* Symbolic Color Abstraction #2.

PHOTO BY THE AUTHOR.

Figure 2-28 SHIJO, *The Course of the Electron and Its Photons.* Symbolic Color Abstraction #3.

center of the atom, which he named the **nucleus.** In reality, the nucleus of the atom is so small that it has a ratio of a grain of rice to a football stadium—the stadium representing the atom and the rice being the nucleus. Now, we can begin to partially assemble the atomic structure. So far, we have electrons simultaneously orbiting a nucleus and exchanging photons, which all exist inside of the atom.

The Proton

It was the uncovering of the nucleus and its structure that also led **Rutherford** to the detection of the **proton** in 1919. Protons contain an electrical charge. In fact, they all have the same type of charge, which causes them to repel one another. The atomic nucleus is partially composed of these protons.

The Neutron

The proton is companion to the **neutron** within the nuclei. The neutron also resides inside of nucleus with the proton as revealed by **James Chadwick** twelve years later in 1932. Because neutrons are not identical to protons, and protons are all charged alike, it is the neutrons that help separate protons from each other. Stable nuclei will typically contain an equal amount of protons and neutrons.

Figure 2-29 The energy contained in a single atom causes one to stand in awe as to how it is all held together.

The Nucleons

When the proton and the neutron are referred to as a unit, they are called **nucleons.** A nucleus contains pairs of protons and neutrons held together by this nuclear glue.

The Quark

It seemed that the mysteries about the atom had all been uncovered. Then in 1963, the American physicist **Murry Gell-Mann** finally discovered the basic building block of all atomic nuclei throughout the universe, the **quark.** The quark has been a particularly important discovery about the atom, especially to color theorists. The *smallest* of all provable particles resides within the proton and neutron structure as bundles of quarks. Each bundle is referred to as a baryon (baryon wrapper), which contains one quark each of red, blue, and green. Just as it is with the additive color primaries, the three quarks when combined together create white light. At last, the source of color is found in the smallest particle of the atom. These RGB bundles of primary colors of light are represented on your computer monitor, such as in Photoshop and so on.

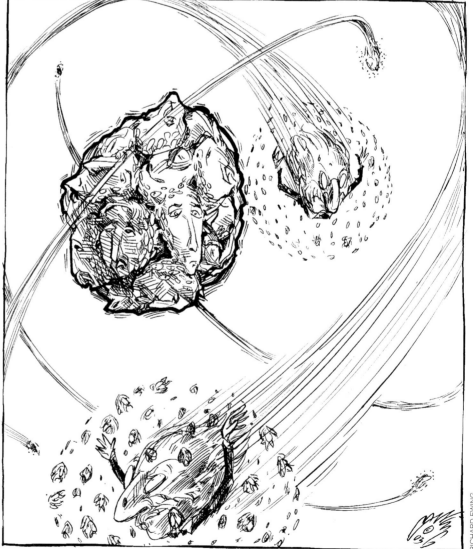

Figure 2-30 Harry N. Abrams, Inc. The Eagle Nebula from the Hubble Telescope.

UPI/DRR.NET.

SMASHING MARBLES

The Origins of Color and Color Sightings

I really can't remember how many times my friend and I spent the night on top of a mountain when we were younger. At the ripe age of fifteen we would lie under the warm summer stars, so many and so brilliant. The Milky Way, luminous and silent, spread before us across the heavens in a glorious array of sparkling jewels. We never ceased to be amazed about the boundaries of space and what mysteries lie beyond our ability to imagine.

Planets, stars, galaxies, and the universe were truly a *dynasty of light* within their own right. All of humankind had looked upon, wondered, and studied through the centuries what was now ours to contemplate. Seldom has humanity had such case to wonder and imagine as when looking upon heaven's lights. What was actually out there and how far did the universe extend? These were questions we would ask ourselves each time we lay on the mountain.

"So, how far does the universe reach, before the end?" I inquired passively.

The answer was not what I was expecting, and snapped me into an obsession of inquiries.

"What? I know you are smarter than that. What's the matter with you?" my friend exclaimed. "Surely you are joking?"

"What do you mean, what do I mean?" I replied indignantly. "It seems pretty obvious that there has to be an end to everything. After all, nothing can simply go on forever . . . especially nothing!" Void of any knowledge concerning Einstein's theories, I continued, "You have to be able to prove that. How can you just say something that ridiculous?"

"That's it! You have found the answer. There must indeed be a *gigantic wall* out there with a big sign that says *The End,*" he said, becoming more obnoxious by the second.

"Yeah, that's it," I replied.

"So, what's behind the wall?" was his final question.

We lay out under that wonderful and warm summer sky thinking about our problem, until at last, we fell asleep from mental exhaustion.

We awoke determined to find the answer. We found ourselves in my dad's garage that afternoon. You should see the great stuff this man had in his little kingdom. I always loved that workshop, with the essence of everything that was my father. His collection of tools and . . . . . hammers!

"That's it, the hammer!" my friend quipped. "You still have those great big boulder marbles?" .

PHOTO BY THE AUTHOR.

Figure 2-31 Marbles.

SMASHING MARBLES   **79**

"Sure, right here! But why?"

"Just give me the marble, will ya?" I had no idea what a hammer had to do with marbles, but I always knew he was a little weird.

We sat down in the center of the concrete floor. It was a cold slab, and I wasn't happy at all about it, but my interest was sparked and so I endured.

"Put the marble on the floor and cover your eyes," he said.

Szwaaaack! The fragments of glass seemed to crackle through the air at enormous velocity. Eyes uncovered, we wondered where the marble had gone. The fragments were so small that what remained was a tiny mound of powdered glass fragments.

"Pick out a single piece of glass, and set it over here on the floor," he suggested. "Here, use these tweezers. You'll need them to isolate the fragment."

I had a tough time of it, getting that tiny piece of glass, but I finally segregated the piece.

Kaathud! Down came the hammer on the fragment. Absent were sounds of crackling glass fragments this time, only the cold thud of the hammer's steel head on the floor. By this time, I was sure my friend had some odd obsession about destroying things.

"What are you doing?"

"Never mind, now get another piece of that marble," he demanded.

"There isn't another piece, look around!"

You guessed it . . . "wham" . . . the hammer came down on what was nothing more than a tiny powder fragment on the floor. He proceeded to elaborate on the continuous process of striking each smaller piece, until . . .

"Until there is nothing left, whatsoever," I burst out in self-righteous declaration. With a disappointed look on his face, he began to explain that I was as clueless about this demonstration as I was uninformed about the *infinite space* issue the night before. Soon enough, however, he began to reach me as he drew out illustrations on the back of sandpaper sheets, with my dad's favorite drafting pen. We got to the point where the molecule was smashed, and then the atom, the nuclei, and finally the smashing of the protons and neutrons within the nucleus. The only thing left to disintegrate was the smallest provable particle, the quark.

"Aha!" said I "There you have it, there is nothing left to smash," thinking back to my end of the universe theory.

"No, you see, they hypothesize that there are smaller particles yet, something called *strings,* you see!" He continued as if to convince himself with every word.

It was then that I realized that matter could not be forced into nonexistence, anymore than you could say that there was an end to outer space.

Later, as I was contemplating color as a student at the university, I was at a certain quandary as to where color came from. I thought back to my childhood dilemma with my more enlightened friend, and realized that it was the quark that held the secret.

As I studied I found that quarks were bundled together as inseparable groups of three: one red, one green, and one blue, which also are the primaries of additive color, or the RGB seen on my computer monitor. I learned that these *quarks* of red, green, and blue combined together to produce *white light,* and therefore energy. The exact opposite is true of the subtractive primaries, or pigments, which combined to create black.

Suddenly everything became clear. Even the Earth's solar system, with the planets in orbit around the Sun, seemed to strangely replicate the electrons and photons in orbit around the atom's nucleus. In fact, when nuclei actually collide and then connect together, the result is nuclear fusion. The same is true of our Sun. As these nuclear forces are liberated they create massive amounts of energy. From the smallest particle to the largest bodies in space, from the quark to the supernova, we understand more about the source of color, the *dynasty of light.*

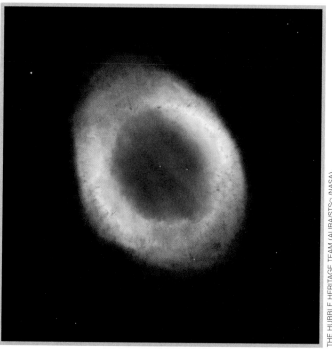

Figure 2-32 The NASA Hubble Space Telescope has captured the sharpest view yet of the most famous of all planetary nebulae: the Ring Nebula (M57). The colors are approximately true colors. The color image was assembled from three black-and-white photos taken through different color filters with the Hubble telescope's Wide Field Planetary Camera 2. Blue isolates emission from very hot helium, which is located primarily close to the hot central star. Green represents ionized oxygen, which is located farther from the star. Red shows ionized nitrogen, which is radiated from the coolest gas, located farthest from the star. The gradations of color illustrate how the gas glows because it is bathed in ultraviolet radiation from the remnant central star, whose surface temperature is a white-hot 216,000 degrees Fahrenheit (120,000 degrees Celsius).

THE HUBBLE HERITAGE TEAM (AURA/STScI/NASA).

THE CARBON ATOM—CRYSTALS AND CATHEDRALS

We have discussed both the purest (outer) source of color, which is produced by the sun's white light, and the *inner* resource of color, the atom's quark. Let us now shift our focus to one of the most dynamic examples of light and color, and to a subject that we are very familiar with—the diamond. We will see that the *white diamond** is really one of the best examples for illustrating the effects of *additive* color. Colored diamonds also will be used to create a better understanding of the nature of *subtractive* color. First, however, let us briefly discuss the nature of the diamond's *atomic structure*.

A diamond's molecular structure is comprised of five *carbon atoms* that form a *tetrahedron*. One atom is in the center with the other four surrounding it and equally spaced. Each tetrahedron arrangement is bonded at an equal distance from the other, creating the crystal structure of the stone. It takes four tetrahedrons to develop the interior, or core, of the diamond unit cell. The four corners of each unit cell are constructed of *carbon atom tetrahedrons* in their respective unit cells. Outer atoms of similar core tetrahedrons are in turn bonded to atoms, which are part of the other unit cells. This network of interconnected crystal structures creates the ultimate hardness for which the diamond is so well known.

The diamond actually is an excellent visual link between the unseen inner color quark and the very obvious spectrum often seen through a prism or in the form of a rainbow.

We know that the unseen color quarks are the smallest verifiable particle of the atom, and the outer evidence of color is produced by pure white light from the sun. When we direct a ray of white light at a clear prism the light is refracted through this triangular-shaped crystal, which separates the beam of visible light into the component wavelengths of the seven spectrum colors. So the energy of pure white light is interpreted into color escaping from the prism, and colored quarks of red, green, and blue are bound up within the atom, their energy also creating white light. The diamond, on the other hand, attracts the light. It is absorbed into the carbon crystal, and is then seen as color, trapped forever and eternally refracted within its many facets.

It wasn't until the nineteenth century that the crude uncut diamond was transformed into the ultimate source of color brilliance. A new cutting technique called *brillianteering* finally exploited the potential of radiant white light to reveal the uniqueness of a diamond's fire or its color dispersion. The *brillianteering* method gave way to the discovery of the *brilliant* cut. Basically, a brilliant cut diamond consists of 57 highly polished facets—28 facets at the bottom, 28 facets in the crown, and 1 at the point of the pavilion (culet). These facets act as tiny mirrors. The crown facets attract light into the diamond, which is then reflected by the 28 pavilion facets. In 1919, the ultimate brilliant cut was discovered by the 19-year-old math student Marcel Tolkowsky. He mathematically figured the appropriate ratio between facet angles opposite each other. This allowed the diamond to exhibit the *maximum refracted inner light without losing the essential reflected outer light.*

The round brilliant diamond has 56 exact symmetrical cuts (57 counting the culet), which is the ideal proportion for a round, brilliant-cut diamond. The diamond is uniquely beautiful because it is alive with ever-changing color (the fire) as one shifts from one viewing angle to another. This process of turning a crude, uncut diamond into the ultimate form then reveals the captive spectrum of color sparkle, or fire, within.

We are certainly familiar with many forms of spectral manifestations as seen through rainbows, bevel-cut glass, prisms, and celestial displays (auroras), to name a few. The diamond stands in a uniquely different category. A perfectly faceted diamond will put on the greatest show on earth. Captive within, the *fire's* color spectrum (dispersion) constantly changes, and seems convincingly alive. The white diamond is the ultimate in clarity and sparkle. It dazzles, and almost memorizes the eye as the spectrum of colors dance within the mirrored facets. Deep within the colorless diamond there is a world of fantasy, alive with its alluring sparkle, as if to commune with the spiritual nature of humankind itself.

There is another type of diamond, which assumes a completely different characteristic than the traditional *colorless*** or white stone. These are colored diamonds, or sometimes referred to as *fancies*. *Colored* diamonds have more of a mood association than do the colorless stones. Colored diamonds oftentimes, however, create more of a deep, dark, mysterious mood. Some are dazzling with clear radiant color, while others are permeated with deep saturated mood.

On the following page is a sample list of colored diamonds in terms of *saturation, hue, and lightness* from the Aurora Collection. In our lecture, we will discuss the similarities shared between the colored diamond and conventional color theories in subtractive and additive color applications. These similarities occur in hue, saturation, and intensity (brightness/lightness). For example, pigmented hues possess a certain brightness (intensity) factor, in a similar way that diamonds reflect light (lightness factor). Of course *saturation*, whether in color theory applications or within the *Aurora* collection, refers commensurately to color purity, as does *hue* in its naming of a color.

Once you have looked over the *saturation, hue, and lightness* list, look at the *Colored Diamonds* chart from the *Aurora Collection,* and study saturation and lightness as it relates to the particular diamond. Try to determine the level of saturation first (weak, moderate, or strong), without looking at the saturation information. You will notice that your judgment or recognition of saturated color may seem different than it is with pigmented methods of assessment.

---

*Note: A clear or transparent diamond is referred to as a white diamond in the industry.

**Note: The white diamond is also referred to as colorless, as opposed to the colored diamonds seen on the following color charts.

Saturation and Intensity in Pure White Light

Here is an actual photograph of intense pure white sunlight striking a five-carat-weight white diamond. The diamond itself is somewhat blurred as the intensity of light overwhelms the entire image. Notice the result of pure energy. We know that the atom and its component parts, such as the reaction found in photon (electron) exchanges and the RGB quark bundles, generates energy. Energy creates light, and light produces color. In this photo, we can see the results of that process in a very visual sense. Look at the discharge of color, as white light refracts through the ultimate prism of light. It is almost impossible to capture the true and complete colors within a diamond, photographically or otherwise. The colors are both saturated and intense, so much so that it cannot normally be recorded precisely. The diamond refracts the most saturated light possible, while it also exemplifies the greatest possible intensity in color.

Allowing the diamond to refract its colors directly onto a white surface (extending out from the crown), permits us to see *indirectly* just how pure "saturation" can be in light. Seeing the diamond's color on that surface is the absolute saturation or pureness possible in light. Looking *directly* then at the diamond allows one to see color in its ultimate "intensity."

Using Figures 2-33 through 2-36 and Table 2-2 study the relationship between conventional saturation and intensity in pigments, and that of the same found in colored diamonds. This will help you to clarify the difference between saturation and intensity, as well as the very nature of color itself.

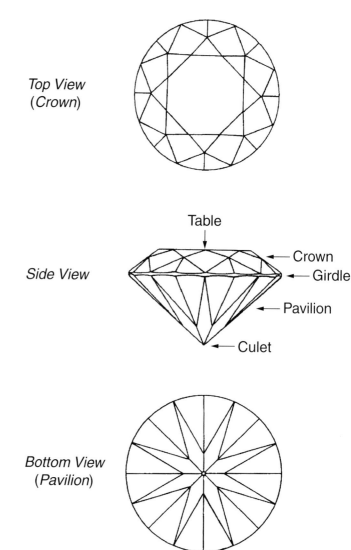

ASHLAND PRESS, INC. REPRINTED WITH PERMISSION OF ALAN BRONSTEIN/ASHLAND PRESS, INC.

Figure 2-33 Composite Part of a Facted Diamond. =The Round Brilliant.

Figure 2-34 Five-Carat, Round, Brilliant Diamond in White Sunlight.

PHOTO BY THE AUTHOR

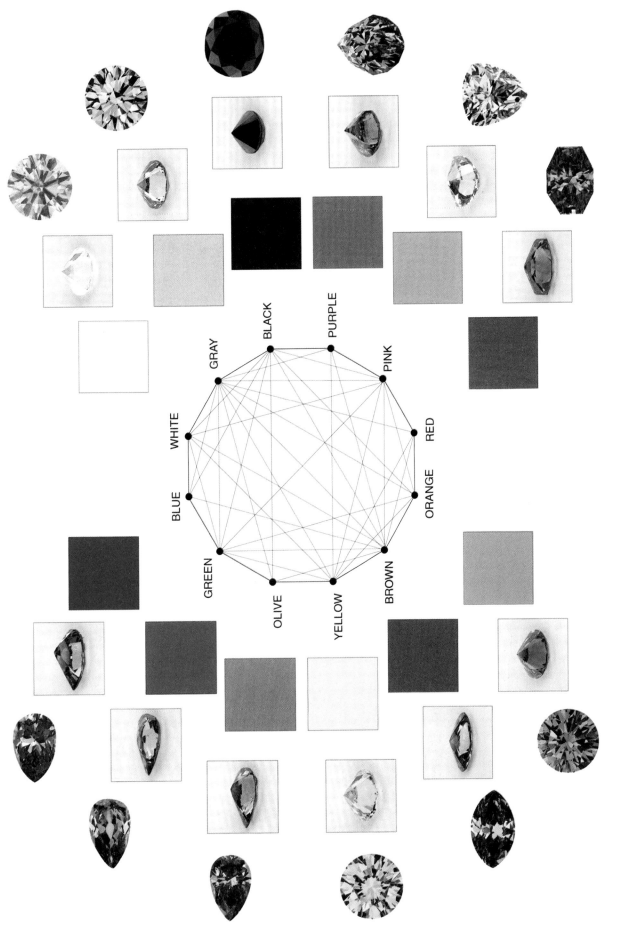

Figure 2-35 Diamond Color Chart (Color Cricle). Diamonds from the Aurora Collection.

SATURATION AND INTENSITY IN PURE WHITE LIGHT 83

Diamonds from the Aurora Collection

Number 45
Weight .... 0.49 ct
Measurements .... 5.08 - 5.17 x 3.07 mm
Shape .... round
Cutting .... modern brilliant
Common Name .... sapphire
Hue (HUE) .... blue (B)
Lightness (LIT) .... dark (Dk)
Saturation (SAT) .... weak (Wk)

"... Diamonds of a faint bluish tinge are not unfrequently found... the rich deep blue diamond is of extreme rarity... although writers describe these stones as possessing in an eminent degree the beauty of fine sapphires, no comparison can really be instituted, their blue color being peculiar to themselves — dark, verging on indigo, possessing a characteristic intensity which differs materially from the mild, soft hue of the sapphire..."

E.W. Streeter   1884

"... The Jagersfontein mine is... characterized by... exquisite fancy stones of deep sapphire-blue colour."

P.A. Wagner   1914

Number 46
Weight .... 0.49 ct
Measurements .... 5.11 - 5.14 x 3.07 mm
Shape .... round
Cutting .... modern brilliant
Common Name .... ochre
Hue (HUE) ....
.... brownish orangish yellow (br-o-Y)
Lightness (LIT) .... medium (Med)
Saturation (SAT) ... strong-very strong (St-VSt)

"... Coloured diamonds... fine deep golden yellow or canaries and pronounced fancy colours always find a ready market..."

M.D. Rothschild   1891

"... The deep yellow canary diamonds, the black, and brown, and many other shades are also unusual and desirable."

Marcus & Co.   1937

Number 47
Weight .... 0.50 ct
Measurements .... 5.10 - 5.14 x 3.07 mm
Shape .... round
Cutting .... modern brilliant
Common Name .... garnet
Hue (HUE) .... reddish brown (r-BR)
Lightness (LIT) .... very very dark (VVDk)
Saturation (SAT) .... weak (Wk)

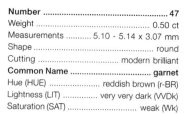

"... The princely collection of the late Mr. Hope possessed a diamond of a blood-red garnet shade..."

A.C. Hamlin   1884

"... diamonds of strong, rich, deep tints are extremely rare; so, too, are the garnet, hyacinth, rose, peach-blossom, and lilac colored specimens..."

G. Merrill   1922

Number 48
Weight .... 0.50 ct
Measurements .... 6.04 x 4.39 x 2.77 mm
Shape .... pear
Cutting .... modern brilliant
Common Name .... cinnamon
Hue (HUE) ....
.... pinkish orangish brown (pk-o-BR)
Lightness (LIT) .... medium (Med)
Saturation (SAT) ...... weak-moderate (Wk-Md)

"... Diamonds occur in all shades, from deep yellow to pure white and jet black, from deep brown to light cinnamon, also green, blue, pink, yellow, orange, and opaque..."

W. Crookes   1909

"... the Kimberley Mine... characterized by yielding brown stones... a considerable percentage of smoky and... Diamonds of a peculiar pinkish brown colour."

P.A. Wagner   1914

Figure 2-36 Diamonds from the Aurora Collection.

Saturation, Hue, and Lightness of Colored Diamonds

The following chart lists hue (color name), saturation, and lightness definitions according to appropriate institution.

HUE NAME AS PER STANDARD COLOR THEORY*	FORMAL HUE NAME AS PER AURORA**	COMMON HUE NAME AS PER AURORA	SATURATION STRENGTH AS PER AURORA	LIGHTNESS REFLECTED AS PER AURORA
Yellows:				
Saturated Yellow	Brownish-Yellow	Banana	St to VSt	Lt to Med
Light Yellow	Yellow	Maize	St	Lt to Med
Dark Yellow	Org/Brown-Yellow	Amber	Mod	Med
Blues:				
Blue-Violet	Blue	Blueberry	Wk to Mod	Med to Dk
Light Blue	Blue	Sapphire	Wk	Dk
Saturated Blue	Blue	Navy	Wk to Md	Med to Dk
Reds:				
Dark Red	Reddish Org-Brown	Chestnut	Wk	VDk
Light Red	Purplish Pink	Rose	Wk to Mod	Med
Dark Red-Orange	Orangish Brown	Mahogany	Wk to Mod	VDk
Greens:				
Light Yellow-Green	Greenish Yellow	Chartreuse	St	VLt
Yellow-Green	Yellow-Green	Grass	Mod	Lt to Med
Dark Green	Greenish Olive	Chameleon	Wk to Mod	Dk

SATURATION DEFINITIONS
Wk = Weak
Mod = Moderate
St = Strong
VSt = Very Strong

LIGHTNESS DEFINITIONS
VLt = Very Light
Lt = Light
Med = Medium
Dk = Dark
VDk = Very Dark

HUE DEFINITIONS
According to the respective conventions.

* Standard Color Theory = Taught in Traditional Additive/Subtractive Applications.
** Aurora = Aurora Collection by Alan Bronstein.

Table 2-2.

SATURATION AND INTENSITY IN PURE WHITE LIGHT

A THOUSAND NIGHTS FANTASY AND THE GOTHIC DIAMOND; A TRIBUTE TO LIGHT

In this short essay we will observe and discuss color in terms of its revealing source, which is white light. There are, of course, many important traditional aspects for the study of light and color, especially from a physics standpoint. In this discussion, however, we shall take a more comparative approach to the subject, using the *Gothic cathedral* and the *diamond* as the ultimate revealing source of light's substance, which is color. In this instance, we will take a closer look at the character or personality of color, its functional purposes, and its symbolic nature.

Recently, while in Paris we revisited Notre Dame, one of Europe's finest examples of Medieval Gothic cathedrals. So important is this cathedral that all signs in France that indicate the distance to Paris actually list the distance to Notre Dame. If you are 8 kilometers from Paris, you are, in reality, eight kilometers from the cathedral, rather than Paris' city limits.

Built in the twelfth and thirteenth centuries, this glorious structure, with its towering architectural vertical thrusts, immediately performs its task is to draw one's eyes toward the heavens, and ultimately to the source of light. Through the Middle Ages in the Christian world, light often has been synonymous with God, or the light emanating from God. Therefore, to look heavenward was to see the light of God Himself. This was an extremely important aspect of the Gothic cathedral, both seen on the massive exterior elements as well as the interior volume spaces. On the outside, Notre Dame's exterior reaches 300 feet above ground and dominates the entire area, as the Seine River flows around it.

Approaching the cathedral from the front, the second most noticeable aspect of the structure is the multiple figurative sculptures and reliefs, which form a strong horizontal band under the Rose Window. Many of these figurative reliefs and sculptures depict the last judgment, Christ and

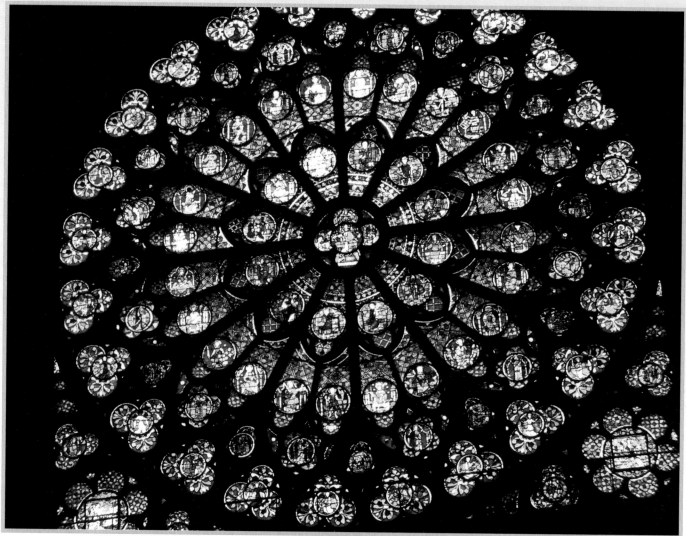

Figure 2-37 The Northern Rose Window of the Notre Dame Cathedral in Paris.

Figure 2-38 Rendering of Notre Dame – Front.

IAN WORREL.

the Church, apostles, prophets, and so on. Because many people of the Medieval period were mostly illiterate, these figurative elements would perform an extremely valuable function. The Biblical accounts came alive to greet the churchgoer, as this sculptural building reminded them of the familiar Gospel (meaning: *good news*) stories.

The value of the Paris cathedral became particularly evident by this point in history. Still in its youth, Notre Dame was to become a sanctuary of God's light and forgiveness; a retreat for the community in a world rapidly plummeting into chaos. Those were the years when the infamous *Black Death* struck down one-third of the entire population, from Iceland to India. Death and destruction were all around. Wars broke out in continuous waves of devastation, flooding the landscape with immeasurable carnage. Europe was at the forefront of it all, with France bearing one of the heaviest burdens. The cathedral became a temporal escape into a sanctuary of God's divine light; a small world of tranquility to experience a moment's safe haven.

Immediately upon entering Notre Dame, an overwhelming feeling of God's presence prevailed, as one's head would be immediately drawn upward 115 feet to the ceiling above.

A high ceiling was paramount in order for the Gothic cathedral to function properly with its stunning height pulling the eye upward to stand in awe of heaven's majesty searching for the mercy and grace of God.

One of the problems in the creation of these monumental ceilings was that of structural integrity. The ceiling itself, and more importantly the walls, which supported the entire roof structure, had to be properly reinforced. In the earlier Romanesque churches, massive walls were needed in order to support the barrel vault ceilings. The problem was in the massiveness of the walls. The actual wall mass restricted the number of windows, which in turn restricted the quality of light in the church. Basically, the fewer the openings, the stronger the wall. At some point, a conflict arose as to the function of a cathedral. Cathedral walls functioned primarily as buttressing to provide structural integrity. Larger windows would allow more light into the structure, but not adequately support the ceiling and roof, which were quite heavy. Large portal were needed to illuminate the overall interior. If one's eyes were meant to be lifted toward heaven, then the interior was too dark, the ceiling or height undetectable, thereby minimizing the effectual presence of a heavenly host. The obvious fix would then be to install larger windows to increase the amount of light needed to illuminate the cathedral properly.

The resultant outcome of this crisis for light was largely responsible for the concept of the Gothic cathedral itself. It was characterized by the advent of several new architectural changes: the *rib vaulted* ceiling, the *flying buttress* system, and lighter walls with large stained-glass windows. *Rib vaulted* ceilings consisted of four-part vaults, which were built on *pointed-arch ribs*. These rib vaults were more self-supporting than the old Romanesque barrel vaults, which was important because suddenly massive walls were no longer required. To further enrich the process, an exoskeletal buttressing system was created known as *flying buttresses*. This new buttressing system was comprised of an arm or arched wing that stretched out from the exterior walls to an independent vertical buttress, allowing the builders to open up large portals of light for *stained-glass windows*.

The Gothic cathedral became the ultimate expression of heaven on earth. As one enters the massive structure of the church, it is impossible to walk through without suddenly realizing the overwhelming presence of vertical space. Standing breathlessly, head lifted to the ceiling above, the windows suddenly burst into full view as if to declare the glory of heaven. As one enters the vast interior, the stained-glass windows of Notre Dame seem to explode into an array of transformed heavenly light. This illumination from heaven suddenly becomes a vast color field resultant from facets of saturated hues.

Perhaps the windows of Notre Dame become even more noticeable because it is one of the darkest of all Gothic cathedrals. The second-story gallery windows are fairly remote, and the massive honeycombed nature of the interior chambers restricts the free flow of light throughout the cathedral. In most cathedrals the light floods the interior spaces, turning them into luminous jewels of color, as opposed to Notre Dame, which suffers from its darkness. An amazing thing happens, however, because of the absence of light: the north and south transept rose windows actually become much more radiant and spectacular.

Certainly it is because of the dark and light contrast that causes us to see such an extreme sensation of brilliance. The fact is that Notre Dame's Rose Windows, especially the north window, are of the most highly regarded of all Gothic cathedrals. The radiating bars of tracery on the northern Rose Window extend out to an immense 31.5 feet in diameter from the center oculus. The Rose Windows tell a story, specifically Biblical truths about Jesus Christ and His church. Beginning with the northern transept window, we observe the Virgin Mary with Jesus at the center, surrounded by concentric rings of Old Testament prophets, judges, and clerics. The south transept Rose Window features Christ on the throne, which is surrounded by rings of apostles and church martyrs.

The use of light in Gothic windows was very important to the church because of its symbolic purposes. Light entering through the windows into the church was as though the divine light came from heaven, or God Himself, and was flooding the interior of the church. From the highest to the lowest, from God to humankind, the colors of heavenly light came down and bathed all within the House of the Lord.

> The church, by its beauty alone, acts as a Sacrament. . . . . . like the plain and forest, the cathedral has its atmosphere, its fragrance, its light and shadow, its chiaroscuro. The great rose with the setting sun behind it seems, in the hours of the evening, to be the sun itself, on the point of disappearing at the edge of a marvelous forest. But this is a transfigured world, where light is more dazzling than in ordinary life, and shadow more mysterious.
>
> —*Emile Male*, Religious Art, *1949*

The world of the Gothic cathedral is indeed transfigured by these enormous windows of light. An interesting note at this juncture would be to mention the existence of an authentic Gothic cathedral built in the twentieth century in our very own Washington, D.C. Begun in 1907, the Washington National Cathedral was completed 83 years later in 1990, and exemplifies of the Gothic cathedral in every aspect, including the interior light.

IAN WORREL

Figure 2-39 Rendering of Notre Dame – Inside.

These huge windows often seem like gigantic colored jewels, capturing not only the essence of perceived heavenly light, but of one's own imagination. As we compare light, we have looked briefly at the Gothic cathedral window but we would also like to call attention to its equal—the diamond.

The diamond is about romance. It is permanent, mysterious, and most definitely the stuff of which fantasies and dreams are made. What is it about fantasy that holds such intrigue? Certainly we occasionally nurture fantasies filled with never-ending possibilities and imaginations. One is often compelled to ponder the effects of illusion becoming reality. We know that fantasies often are developed from fragments of actual experience constructed by the many facets of our lives. The fantasy is assembled like many mirrors from the past. As the light of imagination reflects from each mirror, or memory, it reveals an exaggeration or fantasy, a total fabrication from our memories and desires. We may daydream or become so mesmerized that for a moment we live in that dream, only to be yanked back into reality moments later. They are *stolen moments* in time, revisited.

It seems as though our minds can create a thousand fantasies. Our imaginations take us far away—yet only for the *moment*. My most coveted fantasies many times reveal themselves in the form of daydreaming—visions filled with light and brilliant colors, as though those elements somehow helped to enhance the fantasy, or perhaps make it more credible. The colorful environment within my fantasies was always exciting and energetic, adding fuel to my imagination. Because of these *illuminations*, I have observed that light and color are essential elements in creating the emotion and mood of my dream world.

It is the absolute nature of light to expose its component of color. There are many demonstrations of color in the world: the tranquil blues within the ocean and in the skies, the passion felt in the color orange, the sensuousness of red, the celebration of yellow, or the peaceful rest of green meadows and forests. We can experience color through thunderous and explosive volcanoes, or the radiant translucency of a rainbow. All create an emotional response of one sort or another. How then would it be if we could experience the moods and emotions of all colors simultaneously? One of fantasy's greatest attributes is the ability to create intense emotional responses. Imagine then, all emotions experienced at one time.

Perhaps there is a symbolic reference for these combined moods. I am reminded of a particular warm and breezy late October night, as the fragrance of autumn flowed over the terrace, stirring the air in the room. The intensely moonlit evening conspired with the fall breezes to keep me awake. The warm temperatures that night did not correspond to the typical autumn colors in my mind. As I lay on my bed desperately trying to sleep, colors of summer—blues, greens and violets—dashed through my head, even though I knew the colors identified with that season should be variations of orange and red.

Unable to discern the season of my existence, I finally rose out of my sleep-deprived state to see for myself. Just then, an intense flash of blue and green light suddenly

It is also interesting to note here that the light of the interior spaces seem to replicate the hues of certain colored diamonds, found in the famous *Aurora Collection* of colored diamonds. Several diamonds have variations on the same color, but there is a diamond in that collection possessing a particular "burnt" orange color. The National Cathedral's larger inner spaces are a similar color of orange as seen in the diamond's interior, which in turn may be similar to how we would perceive the light from heaven itself. The windows and interior spaces are built to allow the maximum amount of light into the church interiors, similar to the diamond's construction. Of course, Gothic cathedrals vary in their effective light depending on the time of the year (sun's direction) and whether it is cloudy or sunny on any given day.

As we mentioned, the intensity of the north and south Rose Windows are significantly noticeable, as one notices the contrast of extreme saturated light seen in the window as opposed to the darkness of the interior spaces. Not because of any intention by the church builders, the darkness in the church became synonymous with the Biblical principle concerning the darkness in "man's heart." The windows then reveal their contrasting light, which then symbolize the divine light from heaven illuminating humankind's *dark heart*.

invaded my eyes, drawing me to my mother's heirloom diamond sitting just beneath the lamp. I soon became mesmerized as I began to contemplate the color of this rather large, five-carat diamond. As if to fall in and out of consciousness, I continued to stare closer into this all too familiar arrangement of carbon atoms, until I realized what was actually happening.

The diamond had in fact cast a spell over me with its bursts of radiating energy and ever-changing spectrum of hues. The ultimate performance of light and color had claimed its victim. The white light of the lamp was continuously being lured into the crystal, held captive and then dispersed into sparkling displays of color as the dream continued. My spirit remained captive as did the color in this crystal, and I danced within the facets until the spell was broken. There I stood in front of yet another Rose Window.

Nothing exhibits the attributes of light as does a perfect diamond, so brilliant and alive with clarity and fire. Close inspection into the physical and psychological dimension of the diamond allows to see dancing colors, moods of celebration, the feeling of warm summer nights, ...

Diamonds are not revered simply because they sparkle with color or because they are mere shiny baubles. They are spellbinding jewels, symbolic of fantasy fulfilled, of hopes and dreams that finally captivate and romance the viewer. A diamond can be a fantasy as well as a sophisticated charm of eternal elegance, or a symbol for good fortune and happiness. In a sense, we desire to enter the fantasy perhaps through the diamond's interior itself. To get inside is to live the fantasy and to experience the color and its power over us.

Because we cannot enter the diamond physically, or experience an affinity with it, we can only imagine how it could be instead by entering the Gothic cathedral itself. It is different in many ways and yet fundamentally the same.

The Gothic-style architecture with massive colored windows was crucial in bringing light into its space, and into the soul of humankind. The two important aspects about the construction of the cathedral were *space* and *light*. The first was to create an enormity of space by means of the cathedral's towering *vertical thrust*, with its high ceilings. The next step then would be to satisfy the light requirement by incorporating the use of external flying buttress systems. This in turn opened up wall space, allowing for the installation of larger colored windows to emit greater amounts of *light*. These new portals thereby were responsible for filling the space with radiant color of the heavenly *New Jerusalem*, referred to in the Book of Revelation. Diamonds and cathedrals both require accuracy and symmetry in their construction. They are both required to capture the optimum light, which in turn creates the color mood by which we derive inspiration and dare to dream.

It is one thing to imagine or create a *fantasy* through observing a diamond's color, but it is quite another to experience the *reality* and power of God himself through the interior spaces of the cathedral. When walking through the National Cathedral in Washington, D.C., an amazing

phenomenon seems to often happen. As you experience the mood of this building, you become aware of color immediately, as if walking through the *spectrum,* grandiose style. People who have not walked close to God or for that matter have not known Him at all often leave the cathedral in awe of God's presence. It is quite a spectacle to observe.

The 100-foot high, vaulted ceiling creates a startling and extreme space, one that leaves the observer without adequate words. Additionally, the presence of pure sunlight from heaven, which passes dramatically through the colored glass facets, can perhaps simulate the essence of a diamond for the participant. Is the cathedral a type of surrogate diamond? Certainly the original idea

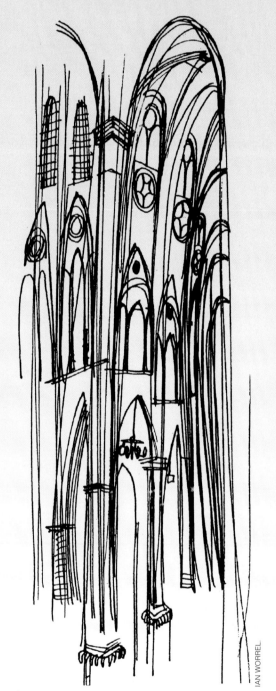

Figure 2-40 Rendering of Notre Dame – Upper Windows.

of the cathedral was that one could experience God's presence by His light, which is translated through the glass into pure saturated color. His light, therefore, was the source of color, which illuminated the chapel and further revealed the nature of God.

Through this brief study we have covered the components of light through both the diamond and the Gothic cathedral. The diamond can only be entered through a color fantasy world, one that stimulates our *imagination* and allows us to escape reality. The cathedral, on the other hand, can be experienced on a more physical and spiritual level, causing us to contemplate issues more *realistically*.

Diamond Characteristics

- Brilliance and Clarity: Quality of light (white light)
- Fire: The flashes of color refracted in the facets
- Light: Reveals color
- Saturation of colored diamonds

Cathedral Window Characteristics

- Purity or quality of light: Light from God Himself
- Intensity of warm and cool colors reflected from the windows
- Transforms light: specific radiant color
- Saturated stained glass

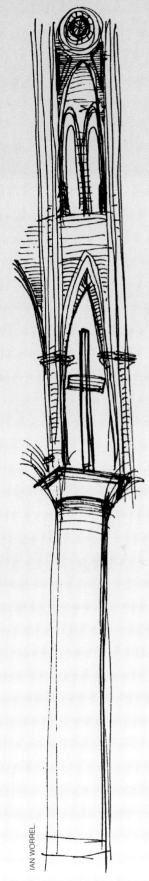

Figure 2-41 Rendering of Notre Dame – Column.

The Gothic Diamond

The Notre Dame Rose
Gothic petals transformed;
Facets for a portal of heaven's glory.
A rose window splashes
Translucent, illuminated color,
Over opposing vaulted walls.
Within a community's spiritual fortress,
The Rose endures, blossoming
And revealing
The "dynasty of light."

We understand, therefore
The diamond.
Not unlike Heaven's majesty,
It reveals
Faceted windows of
Sparkle and celebration.
Dazzling flashes of color
In a moment of time.
It is then a perfect choreography
Of color.
A fire that reveals
A "dynasty of light."

SHIJO,
Notre Dame de Paris
Paris, 2003

Figure 2-42 Interior of the Washington (D.C.) National Cathedral.

PHOTO BY THE AUTHOR.

SATURATION AND INTENSITY

For many years it has been said that saturation and intensity are one in the same. In one respect this is possible, depending on how the subject is approached. First, let's examine the true nature of saturation, and then intensity.

Our first task is to examine saturation in terms of its traditional definition. This is somewhat difficult in itself because definitions vary from text to text. Let's see if we can sort this out logically.

A general term for saturation:

Pigmented (subtractive color) saturation is the absolute purity of a hue. It is completely free from the influence of black, gray, or white; it is the pure intensity of a given hue. In colors of light (additive color), or prismatic hues, it is the color spectrum that possesses the maximum saturation or intensity of hue.

The problem that arises is with the term *intensity*, used twice within the paragraph. This is why we think that saturation and intensity are the same. In reality, there is a fairly distinct difference, even though there are some similarities.

Saturation

Saturation refers to the absolute purest state of a color and to primary or secondary colors in particular. In this example we will use yellow. In Figure 2-43, we see a saturated yellow patch on the left, after which various degrees

Figure 2-43 Intensity Scale with Additions of Violet.

of yellow's complement (violet) are added. The addition of violet changes the intensity of the yellow to a dull, lifeless hue. Just a small amount of violet has changed the character of yellow from celebration to an unhealthy pale hue. Its purity has been compromised, and eventually the yellow (weakest of all colors), is overcome by the violet (strongest of all colors).

The following is an exercise, which begins the process of critical thinking.

When you are in the process of learning a subject, it is often important to find out *why* it is so, or *if* it is the truth. Settling issues from your own research will help to build a solid base for your education in art. Please consider the argument about the similarities and dissimilarities between saturation and intensity.

Saturation (Figure 2-44) and intensity, it can be said, are *superficially* the same, but *fundamentally* different. Intensity is the degree of chromatic value changes that lead toward or away from saturation. It is, for example, the degree of brightness of yellow moving toward or away from its saturated state. Basic differences are that *saturation refers to purity of a color and intensity addresses brightness.* Yellow, in reality, becomes more intensified as white is added, and is therefore brighter than its saturated condition.

Traditionally we have said that the highest form of intensity is the saturated state of the color. That would be true if we say that *intensity* makes reference to *concentration,* yet we know that intensity also refers to *brightness,* which is not necessarily saturation.

Let's consider a different approach. If brightness equates to intensity, we could say that lightest yellow is the most intense (white additions) and the dullest yellow is the least (black additions), with *purity or saturation* residing between the two (see Figure 2-48). The problem with

Figure 2-44 Henri Matisse, ***The Red Studio,*** 1911. Saturated red dominates this composition to create a very specific mood response. This painting is not about intensity, but the *absolute purity* of *saturated color.* The overwhelming emotional appeal of this composition causes us to understand that this room has very special significance to the artist.

the two terms is that *brightness* itself can refer to either *intensity* (concentration) or *vividness* (saturation). The argument should best be resolved then at this point by stating that full intensity (concentration) would be the purest or saturated state, and *brightness* would then be better referred to as the *lightness* of a given color.

Intensity

As we begin to refer to intensity, it is important to note some of the differences between saturation and intensity. Although they may be similar in some respects, they are different by definition in other ways

Paul Gauguin's *Promenade at the Seashore,* (Figure 2-45) is not about saturation, but intensity. Unlike the purity of color in Matisse's *Red Studio* (Figure 2-44), Gauguin's seashore demonstrates his dispersion of tinted hues throughout the composition. Hues of light red, light yellow-orange and blue dominate the background and foreground scenery.

Both paintings demand serious mood responses; Mattise's *Red Studio* exudes the passion of an artist's studio, as it is saturated with red pure red color. Gauguin's *Promenade at the Seashore* demonstrates the calm and tranquil moods in the intensities of light hues throughout. One is about saturation, the other intensity, but each conveys its own specific emotional appeal by virtue of color saturation or intensity.

One of intensity's scenarios can also be seen in *Portrait of a Lady* (Figure 2-46). Notice that her face is illuminated with intensities from darker skin tones, to the more intense higher values of red-oranges. Her face

Figure 2-46 Roger Van Der Weyden, *Portrait of a Lady,* 1460.

is radiant with subtle value shifts. Intensity has a much wider range of possibilities than does saturation. Saturation is pure and exists in one state, but intensities are created by the addition of white and other translucent enhancers. Intensity or lack thereof, is more about tints and shades (chromatic values), mass, and believable illusion of space, all of which can be observed in this portrait. Here, the mellifluous nuances of the skin's tone is created by the harmonious surface of intensity changes. Intensity differences normally begin with the minor addition of another color or a complement, whereas values are accomplished by the addition of black or white to a color. As opposed to intensity, saturation has but one state or condition that it can exist in and instead creates powerful moods and symbols to manipulate the viewer's psyche. Saturation then becomes much more mood specific as a lone hue.

Bartolome Esteban Murillo's, *The Immaculate Conception of Soult* illustrates that intensity is the dominant force of the painting. There is no evidence of saturation in this composition, because the orange tones make a transition from lightest orange to darkest orange to red-orange. The range of intensities produced in this piece creates a very translucent, heavenly atmosphere.

Value

The word value in and of itself refers to achromatic (absence of color) conditions, such as black, gray, and white. It also refers to producing a lighter color by the addition of white, or making a color darker by adding black, and all gradations in between.

Figure 2-45 Paul Gauguin, *Promenade at the Seashore,* 1902.

Figure 2-47 BARTOLOME ESTEBAN MURILLO, ***The Immaculate Conception of Soult,*** after 1678.

ARCHIVO ICONOGRAFICO. S.A./CORBIS.

The center patch of Figure 2-48 is just as yellow as it can possibly get and is therefore saturated. The varying degrees of brightness of white (left side) involved with each yellow patch are all leading toward saturation. As soon as saturation has been reached (fourth yellow section from the left), black is then added and its results seen in the fifth section. The slight black addition has robbed the yellow of its liveliness, taking yellow away from its saturated state, into dullness.

Michelangelo's *Creation of Adam* also shows gradations of values. Both intensity and value changes are evident in the Sistine Chapel ceiling at Vatican City in Rome. This work is the artist's claim to fame, in part due to his exquisite use of value systems. A section of that ceiling is seen (Figure 2-50), in the form of the *Libyan Sibyl* (1508–12) illustrating quite well his prowess with values.

During the High Renaissance in Italy, it was the Pope who dictated an artist's destiny. Michelangelo desperately wanted to sculpt, and considered his focus to be in the realm of sculpture. A conflict arose when the Pope demanded that Michelangelo paint frescoes rather than follow his heart's desire, which was to sculpt. Really there was an enormous amount of blank wall space, and if you were ever desirous

of an art career in Italy, then one was beholden to work in the Church's medium of choice. So Michelangelo became painter by day and sculptor by night.

Van Dongen's *Portrait of Dolly* exemplifies the results of shading with small amounts of black added to yellow. Notice that (as with the yellow value bar example) yellow begins to exhibit a degree of greenness when there are additions of black. Also of interest are the effects of value, intensity, and saturation on the composition. The near saturation of the yellow background affects the *violet* in that it seems more intense, and the shaded green jacket seems much duller than it actually is. In the same manner, the yellow seems brighter because of the lack of saturation and intensity in the jacket, as well as certain violet hues seen in the hat.

Michelangelo's *Libyan Sibyl* is an excellent study in value gradations. This artwork is a small section of a larger whole seen on the Sistine Chapel ceiling at the Vatican in Rome. The artist's frescoes suddenly seem to "pop" away from the wall into three-dimensional space. His ability to create value systems had become highly accurate. The artist himself always revered sculpture more than painting a flat surface, but the Papal powers that be pressured him to paint frescoes because there was an abundance of empty wall space. That being the case, Michelangelo lived out much of his sculptural experiences vicariously through his painted frescoes. He was so inclined toward sculptural forms in space that he became one of the most renowned three-dimensional painters of all time.

We can see just after this short discussion that there are differences between saturation and intensity. Very simply, saturation exists in only one state, while intensity can exist, increasing or decreasing, in various stages, creating a range of three-dimensional possibilities.

A more subtle illustration of saturation, with intensity and value gradations, can be seen in the video still by

Figure 2-48 Yellow Value Intensity Scale.

ARTIST RIGHTS SOCIETY.

Figure 2-49 KEES VAN DONGEN, ***Portrait of Dolly,*** 1911.

Figure 2-50 MICHELANGELO BUANARROTI, *The Libyan Sibyl.* Detail of the Sistine ceiling. Sistine Chapel, Vatican Palace, Vatican State.

Shijo (Figure 2-51). The most evident illustration is on the surface of the arms and legs of Aiko's Warrior, particularly her left arm forward. Exactly in the center of her arm we see the most saturation, that is, the orangeness of her skin. As the shades move to the back of the arm, there is a quick change to a very dark value, after which we observe the fairly rapid change of the lightest intensity of orange on the top portion of the arm.

The entire photographic composition is comprised of darkest to lightest oranges, which are indicative of a monochromatic color harmony.

Finally, it is important to take a look at color from a different angle. The intensity of a color often relates to the intensity of the subject matter itself. We can take an ordinary subject, without the intensity of action, and turn it into a vibrant and brilliant display of color intensities, transforming the object into a theatrical performance.

SOVEREIGNTY OF LIGHT

The celebrated father of French Impressionism, Claude Monet, knew full well about the dynamic effects of light. He thought well beyond the scope of color visuals and lived for the imminent opportunity to catch light at its optimal time during any given day. Monet worshipped the omnipotence of light. He was the master of seeing color, for observing the hues that were actually seen by the human eye as opposed to preconceived notions of color. First and foremost this painter knew that the *authority of color* (Chapter 3), was first dependent on the *sovereignty of light.*

A brief study of Monet's paintings of the Rouen Cathedral will introduce the student of color to his prowess in light observation.

Monet was a student of light as well as color. To be able to see color clearly and understand it, one must first know something about the properties of light. The artist set aside several years of his life to make a thorough study of the Rouen Cathedral. In fact, he persuaded the landlord of an apartment building across the street from the cathedral to allow him to use a second floor apartment directly across the street. With a commanding view of the cathedral's façade, he began his acute studies of the play of light across its surface. He illustrated conspicuous distinctions between light in the morning and light at dawn.

In the early morning light, the top half of the cathedral is bathed in cool blues and violets. Monet layers the cool

Figure 2-51 Shijo, *Akiko's Warrior Sleeps: A Thousand-Nights Fantasy.*

composition with the blue's complement of orange, which further enhances the richness of light on the blue surface. The overall surface then is interpreted as light to dark violets. The portal itself is actually the emphasis, as the ever-lightening deep violet tones begin to expose the front doors and the entire portal itself. The viewer anticipates the approaching light, as it will soon immerse the entire structure. The intensity of the light on the top half of the building causes us to focus on the façade itself, because the bell tower seems to merge into the atmosphere and reach into heaven.

Now in the approaching night sky, we see the opposite as the cathedral is immersed in warm orange light with just the slightest amount of blue- and violet tones. Everything is the opposite; what was cool blue in the morning- is now its complement of orange at the reverse time of the day. The sun is going down rather than coming up, and the cathedral's light is being *consumed by the darkness*, as opposed to the morning *light overwhelming* the darkness. One might be tempted to think there was no difference, but Monet had become intensely aware that the early morning light is not the same as the late afternoon light. The mood content is radically different.

"I am worn out, I give up, and what's more, something that never happens to me, I couldn't sleep for nightmares. The cathedral was coming down on top of me, it was blue, or pink, or yellow," Monet records in a letter. His studies of the light's affect on the Rouen Cathedral had exhausted him to the point of despair. This was his commitment to the study of light and its component of color.

Light was so important to Monet that he once claimed that the only truly acceptable time to paint the façade of the cathedral was between 12:00 and 2:00 pm, when the light began to fall across the surface front from right to left. The strange thing about Monet's obsession with light is that he missed the most important aspect of light concerning a Gothic cathedral: the interior light.

I was interrupted today, and instead of working on twelve canvases, as I had hoped, I only worked on ten. There was a great celebration at the cathedral, the inauguration of the moment to the former Archbishop Bonnechose. A sung Mass performed by 300 who had come from Paris . . . bref, since this morning the portal was draped in black, which greatly hindered me; so I wanted to go to this Mass, but the seats at five francs had been sold out the day before; luckily, Madame Monier was able to obtain an invitation for me and I was wonderfully placed. It was marvelously beautiful and I saw some superb things that could be done inside, which I very much regret not having seen earlier.

Figure 2-53 CLAUDE MONET, *The Portal and the Tour d'Albane* (Morning Effect).

For a painter of light, this could only mean he was overwhelmed by the capture and transformation of heavenly light bursting through a multitude of stained-glass windows.

An artist who had spent his life focusing on the effects of light on painting in the *out-of-doors* now could see another entire world of possibilities for light effects. Indoors was a

Figure 2-54 CLAUDE MONET, *The Portal and the Tour d'Albane* (Dawn).

place that from outward appearances would seem void of any serious potential study of light. So massive, so visually heavy, and so intimidating, why would one think to study light on its interior? Yet as we can see in this chapter, the *interior* of the Gothic cathedral is most certainly a fortress for the majesty and *sovereignty of light.*

Thailand's temples are an interesting *highlight* in our discovery of color function. We continue to look at light and color and its significance of the ambiance, which it creates for a structure. Interestingly enough, the western world (Notre Dame de Paris) deals with color from within; light enters through the colored-glass window in order to create a deeply respectful ambiance. Thailand's use of color is similar in that the temple surfaces are constructed of *colored glass*, yet meant to be viewed from the exterior rather than the interior.

You will recall that the colored translucent facets of glass in the Notre Dame de Paris transformed pure white light (as it passed through the window) into a spectrum of saturated color. The function of color within the interior space of the cathedral is to transform its space. The interior function then, is twofold: 1) the colored-glass windows are transformed into saturated color, which are a spectacle in themselves, and 2) the interior spiritual ambiance is created by the collection of these hues.

Figure 2-55 Pagoda Rooftop within the Grand Palace.

PHOTO BY THE AUTHOR.

PHOTO BY THE AUTHOR.

Figure 2-56 The Dragon (Naka) Gate, Doi Suthep Temple, Chaing Mai, Thailand.

PHOTO BY THE AUTHOR.

Figure 2-57 The Dragon (Naka) Gate, Doi Suthep Temple, Chaing Mai, Thailand—Detail.

Let's view the colors of glass from a completely different culture. The Thai culture is unique in its use of colored glass. Throughout Thailand you will see colored-glass tiles, which make up the exterior surfaces of palaces and temples. The Grand Palace in Bangkok is one of the most amazingly beautiful sites in the world. The surface construction of the images and architecture consists of gold and colored-glass tiles. The overwhelming difference between the cultures is that Thailand's temples use light and color to produce an exterior ambiance.

The glass tiles of Thailand's temples and palaces are actually small colored-glass mirrors (see dragon and detail on the following page) of translucent reflecting colors. An atmosphere of stimulating color awaits the participant. The mood is one of both awe and respect as one becomes overwhelmed with color extravagance. This, of course, is quite opposite to the Rose Window of Notre Dame, which pulls in the light and transforms it into a quiet ambiance of worship. Colors of light in both applications create effective mood responses, though very different.

The function of color can be quite different from east to west. When asked why the temples, for example, are so ornate with color, a young Thai woman explained, "The glimmering colors and high intensity of the golden structures were quite a contrast to ordinary daily life. The Thai people traditionally have been hard-working people, many of whom were farmers; people who grow crops, rice, and so forth. Of course, the average person was exposed constantly to the earthen colors of fields, vegetation, and blue skies, which are indeed calming and tranquil. Coming to the temple,

PHOTO BY THE AUTHOR.

Figure 2-58 Little Thai Girl.

however, was stimulating and exciting, and the world became transformed into a color paradise, creating a celebratory mood for social interaction and worship. Actually, there is a beautiful correlation between the reflective color tiles and the *reflection* of one's own spiritual condition. Life is spiritual happiness and joy; the reflective translucent colors of the temple are perhaps symbolical, in terms of how we should live our lives transparently."

Figure 2-59 Grand Palace—Detail of the Grand Palace Temple Columns.

Figure 2-60 Thai Hill tribe family.

It is indeed an extraordinary event to visit the Grand Palace and witness the splendor of color. **The variances of colored-glass tiles can be seen between the gold leafed tiles (Figure 2-57) of the dragon, and the tight fitting Temple glass tiles – Figure 2-61.** A Typical Hill Tribe Family and . . . . . *the love of saturated colors, seen here in their typical community dress.*

Figure 2-61 Temple Glass Tiles—Detail.

THE COLOR STAR OF JOHANNES ITTEN

By William Jaynes

Objective:

This project will provide the student with an understanding of the three-dimensional relationship of color, which is more thoroughly expressed as a *sphere* than by a color circle. Johannes Itten's color star is nothing more than a three dimensional color sphere that has been interpreted onto a two-dimensional flat plane. The star contains the relationship of *hue, value, and saturation*. Additionally, the student will gain a clearer understanding of the inherent *light and dark* value aspects of hue.

Project:

Color Star: The student will create two well-crafted stars. The first will be a color star, which is the pure hue relationship derived from the traditional color wheel. This part will contain the subtractive primaries of yellow, red, and blue, with secondary colors of orange, violet, and green. Additionally, the intermediate colors of yellow-orange, red-orange, red-violet, blue-violet, blue-green, and yellow-green incorporated. Once the color wheel of the star is painted, the student will tint (pure color plus white) two steps toward the center, with the center resulting in pure white. Next, shade (pure color plus black) two steps outward, resulting with the star tips becoming black.

Value Star: After the color star is completed, the student will translate the star into a *value* star. The value star will be painted next to the color star. Think of the value component as color, which has been drained of its hue, or think in terms of the computer, which is able to translate a true color image into a gray scale mode. In successful translation, the value star will contain the same value weight as the color star.

Test the value translation by photocopying the color star on a color copy machine, but be sure that you set it to *gray scale mode*. The black and white photocopy of the color star should closely match the painted value star.

Figure 2-63 Johannes Itten's Color Star.

Figure 2-64 Johannes Itten's Color Star (achromatic).

Summary

In Chapter 2 we discussed:

1. Color physics. The 12-part color circle, as well as the *visible* spectrum, which is a small part of the total electromagnetic spectrum.
2. Primary, secondary, and intermediate colors of *subtractive* color.
3. *Additive* colors of RGB, which involve computer screens and various digital color applications.
4. CYMK, which involves the use of *subtractive* printing inks.
5. Color quarks and their origins in the atom, as well as their relationship to additive color models.
6. Various color wheels of Newton, Munsell, Goethe, and Itten.
7. Value, saturation, intensity.
8. Diamonds and their relationship to light, color, and Notre Dame de Paris.
9. The sovereignty of light and its relationship to Claude Monet's Toud' Albane.
10. Color grid and color star project to demonstrate the use of saturation, intensity, value, and hue.

Coming up in *Chapter* 3 we will further research light and color in the cathedral, in order to more fully grasp the power of color, or the *Authority of Color*.

CHAPTER THREE

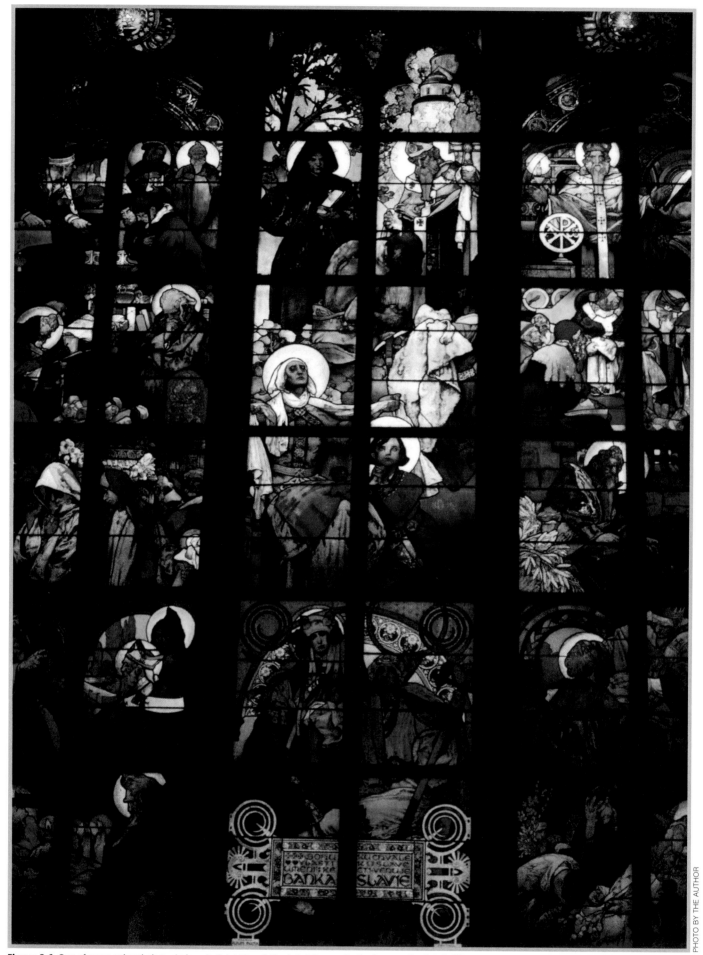

Figure 3-1 One of many colored glass windows in Saint Vitus Cathedral at Prague Castle, Prague, Czech Rebublic.

3

THE PROPERTIES
OF LIGHT
AND COLOR
AUTHORITY

In the previous chapter we discussed the Sovereignty of Light and its endowment of color over the world. Our emphasis was primarily on the interior of the cathedral's inner qualities of light, transformed into its seven component parts or colors. Often we focused on the atmospheric color conditions on the inside of the Gothic cathedral because of its overtness, yet at that point we had not discussed the more subtle exterior surface colors as they change over the period of a day.

It is vital to create the most careful observations in order to create a greater sensitivity to the more restrained color surfaces. Consider how Notre Dame de Paris changes in color (see Figures 3-2 through 3-5) as the day progresses. It is not merely an achromatic cathedral created by a darkening sky; it is the transformation of the surface color from an advancing sun.

Notre Dame de Paris (Figure 3-2) is observed late in the afternoon on the south side. Note that the surface is a *very light and radiant yellow*. The sun is at its highest here during the spring, and creates the brightest radiance of light in a 24-hour period. This is the peak of the cathedral's most intense color.

Notre Dame de Paris (Figure 3-3) is a bit later in the afternoon, and we can now see a substantial change in the exterior surface. The radiant light yellow surface has lost some of its intensity, and has been reduced. The *yellow has dulled* considerably, with the slightest indicator of a *violet tinge* on the lower shaded area.

Notre Dame de Paris (Figure 3-4) has now completely lost its yellowness, the intensity level has greatly reduced to the point where the lightest surface is now *lightest red-orange*, with more prominent *violet* tones appearing in the shaded regions.

Figure 3-2 Notre Dame de Paris: Image One.

Figure 3-3 Notre Dame de Paris: Image Two.

Figure 3-4 Notre Dame de Paris: Image Three.

Figure3-5 Notre Dame de Paris: Image Four.

Notre Dame de Paris (Figure 3-5) has now lost much of its *red-orangeness*, and reflects a *dull orange* with slightest *violet* hues. What began as a very *light yellow* intense surface has now become a very dull *red-orange* to *violet* cathedral. The architecture has taken on the *yellow's complement* at sunset. As the sun's white light diminishes from the surface, the sunset itself becomes more *orange to red-orange*.

These are some of the light and color issues that critical thinking colorists learn to discover. Gaining a greater visual sensitivity to the colors of light on a surface is paramount in the learning process. Claude Monet struggled with the subtle nuances of color in his paintings of the Reims Cathedral for several years. We realize after our eyes have become sensitized to color that our brain often tells us that the cathedral is nothing more than colorless, while our eyes actually see yellows, oranges, red-orange, violets, and indigos. What we think we see and what we actually see are often two different things. The secret, then, is to learn to question what we think we see through critical and often lengthy observation of a surface's color.

Also in the previous chapter, we discussed saturation, intensity, and value and produced a color chart exhibiting these three aspects of color. We also talked about the largest or most prevalent sources of color, which is light emanating from the sun, to the smallest provable particle, such as the quark. We studied the Gothic cathedral in general and its role with light and color, the diamond, the carbon atom, and the electromagnetic spectrum—all within their relationships to light.

In this chapter we want to pursue more specifics about light and color, especially as it pertains to what we refer to as the *Authority of Color*. Essentially, color has the influence and command of establishing focal points, depth of space, and so forth. Its chief function even more so is the psychological ramifications, that is, the establishment of the emotional appeal and the mood control of the viewer/patron.

Additionally, we will take a more critical look at color mixing by using a more sensitive collection of colors. As you have noticed by now, colors such as *cadmium red light* are more difficult to maneuver in the direction of orange. This red hue often is interpreted as orange itself, because it is so far from the conventionally used red of *quinacridone magenta*, for example. Cadmium red light is the lightest official red on the market and is often interpreted by the viewer as orange rather than red.

The color mixing project proposal for this chapter deals with yellow exclusively, because yellow is the most intense and yet weakest color. We have learned that yellow is the most easily influenced of all colors by the addition of the slightest amount of black, for example. Using these very sensitive colors for our next project will help to develop a greater sensitivity about the process of color mixing. As indicated before, we are eliminating the conventional primaries, and substituting them for a more minimal palette in order to *fine-tune* the colorist's sensitivity for optimal desired results and the recognition of subtle nuances.

CONVENTIONAL PRIMARY MIXING COLORS	PROJECT PROPOSAL CHOICES
Quinacridone Magenta Cadmium Red Light	Quinacridone Red
Hansa Yellow Cadmium Yellow Light	Hansa Yellow
Phthalo Blue Cerulean Blue	Ultramarine Blue

Even though the conventional primaries are more easily controlled and achieve the more "expected" result, the project proposal primaries are designed to create a more diverse experience in color mixing. Certainly it is appropriate to experience all of the primary triad possibilities, and it is encouraged as your color education continues.

Before moving into your next project proposal or an alternative project, please take the time to read the essay by Isaac Asimov (Page 134).

We most certainly know of Asimov's prowess as a *science fiction writer*, but many are not aware that he was also a *scholar of atomic science*.

It was his profound understanding of the science of atoms that gave his fiction additional credibility (not to mention the added creative potential). You will find his essay an effective tool in the further study of the nature of light, the source of all color.

This chapter begins with further observations of light and color at two Gothic cathedrals, one Gothic chapel, pigmented illustrations (paintings), and a *real-life* observation as to the influence and authority of color.

Not far from the coast of central Japan lies the mountainous resort area of Hakone. The *highlight* for this segment can be seen in the sculpture park of the Hakone open-air museum. The towering **Symphonic Sculpture** is a colored-glass, cylindrical structure whose summit can be accessed from the interior via a spiral stairway.

This cylindrical cathedral exudes a symphony of moods. Surrounded by the colors of light, one begins to climb the spiral staircase; some quickly in anticipation, others slowly to the top. There are warm zones of reds, oranges, and yellow hues, and cool areas with saturated blues, greens, and violets transitioning around and toward the top of the tower.

Figure 3-6 Symphonic Sculpture, Nobutusaka Shikanai, Hakone, Japan.

PHOTO BY THE AUTHOR.

Figure 3-7 Symphonic Sculpture: Spiral Stairway.

PHOTO BY THE AUTHOR.

Figure 3-8 Symphonic Sculpture: Detail.

Ascending the stairs, the participant is immediately surrounded by an orchestra of color as sectors of warm and vibrant hues suddenly invade calm neighborhoods of cool greens and blues. The viewer becomes the audience (partaker) in this theater in the round, with *energetic* bursts of choreographed color harmonizing with *tranquil* hues.

In a sense, it is very much like attending an opera with its many instruments, all in accord with one another as the conductor dictates. In the opera, the conductor determines any change of rhythm or cadence as the music creates the mood. In similar fashion, the participant controls the visual tempo of the Symphonic Sculpture by the pace of the climb. It is a visual hexadic color harmony, which reaches its intermission when arriving at the top, and played out in its entirety on the descent.

Because of the cylindrical nature of the structure, the saturation of colors are not all fully seen at the same time. As one rotates around the interior, the colors reveal their saturated nature little by little, as dictated by the direction of sunlight entering the sculpture chamber.

PHOTO BY THE AUTHOR.

Figure 3-9 Symphonic Sculpture: Interior Colored Glass.

THE AUTHORITY OF COLOR

Notre Dame de Paris

We return back to Notre Dame de Paris in order to begin our discussion about the *authority of color*. More specifically, we take our pilgrimage directly to the south Rose Window—the *Gothic Diamond*. One need only attend a Sunday service at the cathedral to fully understand the symbolic and spiritual ramifications of the cathedral's colored windows, as well as the interior ambiance of the church. The cathedral was built and used during the Middle Ages, a period from approximately 400 to 1400 A.D., which was marked by Christianity's central role. The cathedral was used as a spiritual and community center; it was in fact the focal point of the city, where people of the community went for encouragement and spiritual strength. It remains a spiritual and community center today. Parisians still gather together for worship at the cathedral, as well as on the common gathering grounds at Notre Dame. Eight hundred years later, people are still coming, if for nothing more than to enjoy an afternoon of "people watching," as the cathedral remains the focal point of Paris. As we discussed in Chapter 1, it is ground zero for all distances measured to Paris. Notre Dame is of the foremost examples of light and color, and a superb illustration of the authority of color, and indeed light itself.

There are some points of interest that should be discussed briefly before we discuss color authority itself. When we look at the floor plan of Notre Dame de Paris, we can see that the basic interior plan of the cathedral replicates a cross; the cross by which Jesus Christ was crucified as told by the Scriptures. Actually, the transept illustrates the horizontal of the cross, while the altar (see Figures 3-10 and 3-11), chancel, choir, crossing, and center aisle represents the vertical post of the crucifix. There are, of course, many cathedrals throughout France built in the crucifix form, some even more obvious as a cross than others. The transept of the cathedral is the horizontal representation of the cross, which has on its left end the South Rose Window, and on its right end the North Rose Window. The left hand of Christ, then, was nailed where the South Rose Window would be, and the right hand on the side of the North Rose Window. The north window is predominantly cool greens and blues while the south window, with its reds and blues, appears as a enormous warm violet jewel.

The narthex and West Rose Window would be at the impaled feet of Christ, while the chancel and altar indicate the head of Christ; above this are five radial chapels with thirteen colored-glass arched windows. The Rose Windows, then, represent the three initial major wounds.

A Rose Window does not exist at the head of Christ. Rather, there is the chancel and altar, and behind that radiating chapels joined in a half circle at the east end, all referred to as the ambulatory. These chapels are adorned with elegant stained-glass, arched windows throughout (Figure 3-11), and exist where the head of Christ would be on the cross. As we discussed in the Chapter 1 essay, *A Thousand Nights Fantasy and the Gothic Diamond; A Tribute to Light, light* becomes a symbol of God's eternal light. A light coming into a world of darkness, or the darkness in the human heart, exemplified especially in the Middle Ages.

Historians often refer to the Notre Dame de Paris as being the darkest of all major High Gothic cathedrals. This at first would seem to be a serious problem, because the cathedrals were redesigned with flying buttresses (chapter 1) or an exoskeletal system in order to allow more light into the inner space. Much of the light that enters the smaller chapels along the side aisles is absorbed or transformed by the time it reaches the actual side aisles of the church. Also, much of the light is absorbed by the areas in the cathedral with deep niches where few windows exist. However, it is precisely the fact that this is an extremely dark cathedral, that we are encouraged to use it as an example of light and color. Let's find out why.

As we indicated, the darkness of Notre Dame also symbolically represents the dark and light contrasts of the human struggle or condition. The dark side of humankind is represented by the dark interior of the cathedral as opposed to the light side of a loving and caring God. Good and evil, love and hate, celebration and agony, light and dark—these always provide contrast and emphasis when paired together. That being the case, we observe that the brilliance of saturated colored windows are surrounded by the darkness within each chapel.*

The contrast of dark space against an illuminated color panel is striking, and it is the dark areas that emphasize color all the more. We have a symbolic match then—the darkness of the human heart and the light of Heaven illuminating the soul. A building constructed in dark times with the hope of salvation, the light of the kingdom of Heaven enters every colored portal. Of course, the nave (sanctuary) is always lighter because it is at the heart of God.

We are first tempted to think that the darkness will be the all-powerful and consuming force, but soon enough we discover that the lighting of a single candle demands the darkness to flee. One single candle illuminates, if only slightly, that which is in the darkness.

As more candles are lit, greater amounts of energy are created and, therefore, more light is generated that reveals and creates color. Once this sovereignty of light has established the authority of color, the commanding role of color begins to manipulate the human senses.

As we look to the South Rose Window, it is in a very real sense what we would hope a diamond to be. This huge circular window reveals the ultimate in color authority—saturated color developed by pure white light. The window is faceted color brilliance, and its fire cannot be compared, written about, or photographed with any degree of adequacy. The only possible way to comprehend

---

*Windows on the south side tend to illuminate the chapels on that side much more adequately during the Sun's most advantageous time of day, as opposed to the north side windows that are quite dark by comparison. The optimal illumination period for the south side is in the late winter and early fall, whereas the north's best time is mid-summer. These would be the exceptions to an otherwise darker period of the year for chapels within the cathedral.

Figure 3-13 Cathedral Chapel Window.

Figure 3-14 Candles in Notre Dame's *Transept* Section of the Cathedral.

Figure 3-15 A Family Lights Candles on Easter Sunday in Notre Dame's *Nave* Section.

Figure 3-16 South Exterior View of St. Severin.

in the Figure 3-17 how much light floods the interior as opposed to Notre Dame. The ambiance is quite different from many Gothic cathedrals as the entire main sanctuary is radiant with white light as opposed to absolute color. Color is not overt by any stretch of the imagination. We see minimal color and the absence of serious color ambiance is quite unexpected. Of course, as one views the entire nave, every quiet and subdued hue of color can be observed on the walls and floor as well as on the chairs themselves. The interior nave of the church has an environment of subtle color and intense pure light.

It is intriguing to realize that the nave area gathers such an enormous quantity of light while surrounded by various extremely dark smaller chapels. Unlike the main sanctuary, the adjacent chapels are each enhanced by a colored window. It is the darkness of these lower chapels that enhances the colors of each chapel window.

Two aspects about light and color in this cathedral are important. First, the chapels are recessed far back from the actual sanctuary, where the main source of light prevails. This effect contrasts with the small chapels that are minimally illuminated, facilitating the creation of very dark chapels. Secondly, though the chapels are dark, they actually display exquisitely beautiful colored windows, thanks to the darkness in each chapel. It is the dark quality of the chapel that creates a full spectacle of

elegant and saturated color. This symbolically matches the spiritual teachings of the age, which identified "mankind" as lost in darkness, which was then contrasted to the holy light of God.

Sainte Severin chapels each create a mood of their own. One could say that symbolically, the center nave (sanctuary) exposed the worshipper to God's pure light and the

Figure 3-17 Interior Groin Vaults and Windows of Sainte Severin.

Figure 3-18 Interior View of Sainte Severin's Interior Chapels Viewed From the Nave Through the Side Aisle.

Two Dimensional Images of Color

The more complex issues about the colored windows, as opposed to clear windows, lies within the churches' two-dimensional images of color, and how they relate to the exterior three-dimensional images. Color makes historical references, symbolic gestures, and strong visual scenarios, all designed to instruct and manipulate the senses. The matter becomes so complex that it cannot be adequately discussed in its entirety, but will be addressed occasionally through the text. We will allow the subject to surface from time to time, in order that we may have a selection of various examples.

A more immediate and obvious contrast can be seen between the Notre Dame de Paris exterior and interior. The exterior statuary relates to the interior ambiance both in symbolism seen in the windows and the message preached from the pulpit. A slightly more complex relationship has to be seen symbolically, between the seemingly colorless or perhaps monochromatic nature of the statuary, and the color that is represented spiritually through the figurative sculptures.

Let's examine the nature of the color represented by the exterior figures (Figure 3-20), though unseen. We understand by now that color is expressive, just as

heart of God and therefore exposed the worshipper to the nature of their individual sins. After bathing in God's holy light, one could confess one's sin in the chapel, after which God would receive the rejuvenated worshipper back into the arms of salvation, fully forgiven.

Figure 3-20 Central Portal of Notre Dame's West Façade: Left Jamb Depicting St. Peter, St. John, St. Andrew, St. James, St. Simeon, and St. Bartholomew.

As a child, I attended a church with my parents (much smaller, of course), that was much that way, or at least in terms of the windows. I remember specifically thinking how "ugly" the windows were every Sunday as I approached from outside the church. They were dull and lifeless. How could they build something so completely unattractive? Once inside, I couldn't understand where the ugly windows had gone. All I could see were beautiful arrays of colors, in what oddly enough seemed to be in the same location as the unsightly windows. I would run out repeatedly, trying to believe that they were really the same windows.

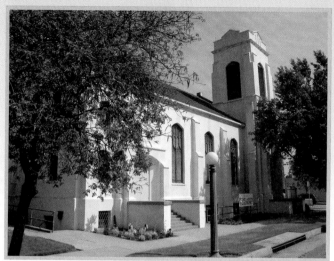

Figure 3-19 Author's Childhood Church.

the faces on the sculptures are communicative. Take a look at the figures from left to right and see whether or not you can identify the subtle differences of their facial expressions: The first figure seems stern and very somber, and if we were to assign color to it, perhaps we would say deep blue. The second figure is peaceful or content, perhaps a lighter blue or even yellow. The third figure seems somewhat sad; the weight of a true violet may indicate that mood. The fourth stands calmly, the fifth is perhaps inquisitive, and the last stands humbly before the Lord (unseen in this photo). There are many scenarios by which color can relate here. Bible verse, when compared with the cathedral, could indicate that the exterior, or outer shell of humankind, is a façade, yet the inner person is the genuine article, so to speak. It is the condition of the heart of the person that can be filled with the joys of a God-centered life, which then translates from a rather colorless* void into a life of light and vibrant colors.

Figure 3-21 Back side of the Notre Dame Choir: The Risen Christ with His Disciples.

The figurative sculptures on the cathedral's façade beckon the sinner to come in and hear the message of salvation. Once inside, the peace of God's love radiates from the windows of colorful glass figures, filling the chamber with the spiritual atmosphere of its color. This was the message of the church during the Middle Ages, and the principle motivation behind its construction.

Once inside, one can observe beautiful figurative wall reliefs in full color. These are actually scenes created in a full narrative of the life of Christ, just behind the choir walls. The interior of the cathedral begins to have a very galleried effect; it is a type of visual music, an orchestrated ambiance of color.

When we return to the outside of the structure, the windows are all but lifeless in terms of color. The exterior stained-glass windows vary from light blue-green, deep blue-gray, or deepest gray-violet, depending on the time of day. The exterior is so radically different that it is almost shocking to realize it is the same window. The interior window illuminates into a *translucent* portal of Heaven's glory, while the outside demonstrates a very *opaque* and forbidden or closed-off surface. The windows are so dependent on the transfusion of light that the difference between the outside surface and interior is striking.

Notre Dame de Paris

At Notre Dame de Paris, the exterior walls as well as the interior are much the same in terms of the building materials and surface quality. A very light orange and absorbent-textured surface, the material seems as ordinary as one could expect. However, in the absence of color stimulation, the statuary makes up for the difference. The exterior (Figure 3-22) is the elegant expression of High Gothic with its multitudes of figurative works. It seems more a case for mass than volume as the overwhelming

---

*Of course, to color theory students, the exterior is not colorless, but by the average definition and to the common person, it does seem to be colorless.

sculptural sense of the building dominates the area. The color stimulus, which is minimal on the exterior, is more than compensated for by the beauty of the stained-glass tracery and three-dimensional forms. Once inside the intensely lit exterior, saturated windows of color, sculptural reliefs, and sedately colored walls create a color spectacle hard to imagine.

The minimal representation of three-dimensional figures in the interior is subtlety transformed by color softly splashing over the wall surfaces, particularly notable in the south chapels.

The authority of color establishes its own interior mood through the saturated windows. It transforms the walls, often splashing elegant displays of color over the wall surface, which changes constantly as the day progresses.

Rainy days present a window of richly saturated colors and deep shades. The deep reds are luscious and full, and mysterious ultramarine blues immerse the mind in fantasy. It is a truly beautiful and quite different experience. Even while the brilliance of the windows are diminished from low light, the colors are still evident and inspirational. The interior of the church also has changed accordingly. The mood is very somber, so much so that the interior relies on sources other than the sun itself. Lamps and candles must be lit to recreate the atmosphere

once again. Whether the sun fully or partially illuminates the interior, color transforms the interior space in such a way that ultimately *our emotional state* is seriously affected. This is just one example of the power and *authority of color.*

So, it is now clear that the colors in the individual facets of glass found in the tracery on any given stained-glass window function to evoke an emotional response. To create the appropriate mood is always at the forefront of any color application. The windows, such as the Rose Window, were most assuredly no exception. The stories that are told in each window often correspond to the energy expressed by the colors, increasing the mood complement of the story and its emotional state. Second, and more importantly, it is the combined ambiance of colors created within the actual atmosphere or space of the cathedral that produces a very somber and respectful environment. There is no doubt concerning the suggestion of a heavenly environment existing for those who would enter these gates of Heaven. The cathedral is open to all of its citizens, a hope of protection and salvation in a troubled time. Still today, we can observe people wandering into Notre Dame and watch as the psychological effect of colors in light help deliver to them a moment's peace and quiet.

The reader may have noticed by this point that the windows' dominant colors are usually blues and reds.

Figure 3-22 West Rose Window, Notre Dame de Paris.

Figure 3-23 Interior Chapel Wall.

The typical basic four colors are red and green, blue and yellow, with red and blue dominating the window plane. In most cases, these hues are very saturated color. Because saturated color is the purest form of a color, it is therefore the most authoritative. In every case, saturated color is used almost exclusively throughout the High Gothic cathedrals in France. Red exhibits its warm, passionate, and energized moods, and the coolness of blue keeps it calm and reflects a certain quietness. They rule with great authority throughout the composition. *Saturation is authoritative.*

Sainte Chapelle

We have discussed Notre Dame de Paris as it pertains to color authority, focusing mostly on color saturation, and then Sainte Severin, which indicates high intensity color contrasted to saturated color. Now let us take a look at another very different example of a Gothic structure: Sainte Chapelle. It is situated just a few blocks away from Notre Dame.

Sainte Chapelle, a late Gothic architectural chapel, was consecrated in 1248 A.D., and originally was not simply a religious icon, but had political ramifications as well. It is reported that Louis IX purchased the *Crown of Thorns* and a fragment of the *True Cross* from the crucifixion of Christ, and had them enshrined at Sainte Chapelle. The cost of the relics were actually quite a bit more than was the initial cost of the building itself.

Even though the chapel windows depict more than 1,100 Biblical stories, it is very difficult to decipher them, because of the intensity of light and color that fills the room. This royal chapel was the example of what may perhaps be waiting in Paradise, or at least the simplistic version or earthly vision of it, especially for the king and his family. It was a type of connection or symbolic confirmation of the king's authority over the people, given by God himself.

The composite parts are simple. One enters through the west end narthex area directly into the nave. There is but one room featuring a gilded altar at the opposite end. There are no side aisles, only one huge space surrounded with stunning vertical colored-glass windows reaching to the very top of its groin vaulted ceiling.

The ribs of the vaults, as well as the colonnades, are primarily of gilded gold, creating an even stronger vertical thrust toward heaven. It is impossible not to look upward when one first enters the structure. Integrated with the gold surfaces are intricate designs of saturated blue and red, which also correspond to the blue and red hues in the stained-glass windows. All create a perfect harmony of illuminated color through the entire interior space.

Let us say that if the south Rose Window is the diamond of Notre Dame de Paris, then Sainte Chapelle is the diamond of Paris. Of course Sainte Chapelle differs greatly from Notre Dame in size as well as color effects. Notre Dame is, of course, an oversized church (cathedral), whereas Sainte Chapelle is really a huge chapel. Sainte Chapelle no doubt accomplishes what we would hope a cathedral would, in that it is the *ultimate depository* of light and color. It summarizes both Chapters 1 and 2 in that it epitomizes both the *sovereignty of light* and *the authority of color.*

To enter Sainte Chapelle is to walk through a fantasy created by color and light. It is neither about saturated color or intensity specifically, but it is each individual piece of colored glass combining together, mixing colors in the atmosphere itself to create an unparalleled heavenly ambiance. The brilliance of color is overwhelming as it seeks to illuminate the very soul of every person who enters. In reality, it seems almost impossible to absorb the

Figure 3-24 North Side Exterior View of Sainte Chapelle.

Figure 3-25 Interior of Sainte Chapelle.

composite aesthetic effect of Sainte Chapelle. It is as if to feel an array of multiple moods and emotions. It visually dazzles, it is color and light supreme. It is the authority of color to control all who enter.

THE AUTHORITY OF COLOR

Jean-Auguste Dominique Ingres

At this point, we turn our attention from mineral pigmented glass to oil pigmented paint on canvas. Let us observe the function of colors by examining a painting by Jean-Auguste Dominique Ingres, in a different approach to the authority of color.

In his preliminary drawing of *Odalisque with a Slave*, the work resolves the figurative decisions of placement, position, proportion, and gesture, as well as the determination of value and the like. Many times artists use drawing as a preview for what later becomes a painting, dealing with all of the other compositional elements first before resolving the most important element of color.

The drawing, effective as it may be, is severely limited in its emotional appeal. What we do see in terms of

emotion is realized by facial expression alone. Perhaps body positioning may enhance the mood to a degree, but the drawing remains minimally charged with emotion without color. Fundamentally, a certain degree of emotion is expressed, but it is somewhat deplete of mood. We cannot imagine the mood fully without its source, which is color.

Once color is added, the picture changes from a mere drawing to an elegant, sophisticated composition, complete with emotional richness. Suddenly the authority of color becomes evident. As color is developed, we see the painting emerge as a living document, complete with warm sensuous reds and passionate oranges, complemented by stable and calming green hues. The contrast of her light orange skin makes reference to the more saturated orange skirt of the musician, which in turn connects to the saturated red hues in the remaining composition. The painting then makes a transition from saturated reds in the background to orange in the immediate middle ground, and then to the lightest orange hues observed in the foreground figure. The saturation of red and orange, in unison with the intensity of lightest orange, dominate and direct the eye exactly where the painter wants the viewer to focus. The authority of color controls the viewer's emotions and dictates our mood. The color now enhances the expression of emotion on the figures' faces to complete the total emotional scenario.

In order to make a stronger point about saturation and the authority of color, we will make a comparison between Ingres' *Odalisque with a Slave* and Bernini's *The Ecstasy of St. Teresa*.

As it is with the artworks of Bernini, *The Ecstasy of St. Teresa* translates mood and emotion through recognizable images. The realistic and dramatic body positions and facial expressions create a body language that convinces us that there is a high degree of emotion. In this case, it is the familiarity of subject matter that helps the viewer to clearly understand the mood of the artwork. The mood and emotional content is obvious without any color representation and there is very little that color could do to greatly expound on that in this particular artwork. In Bernini's *The Ecstasy of St. Teresa,* the flowing drapery and the soft and sensuous expression of St. Teresa's face contrast against the background's stark vertical light rays.

Odalisque with a Slave (Figures 3-26 and 3-27) also demonstrates a sensuous position, as we observe the nude's soft curves contrasted against a harsh geometry of architecture. Ingres, however, presents us with a painting lush in saturated color, especially noticeable in the red columns and drapery that contrast against her tinted light red skin and suggesting a greater degree of sensuality. Here, saturation plays one of its finest roles through the *authority of color.*

Ask yourself if *"The Ecstasy of St. Teresa* (Figure 3-28) were to be a color composition or painting, what colors would I use?" Considering that color does create mood, what colors would we use to empower the figures to their maximum desired effect? Consider the theatrics of the piece, and then ask yourself if you would use reds and oranges. Perhaps, perhaps not! After all, the reds may be too extreme coupled with the drama of the figures.

In any case, in Bernini's work it is the *dramatic and theatrical* effects of the sculpture that convey the emotion. It is clearly *color authority* that dictates mood in Ingres' work. Both works are equally effective; it is simply a difference of figurative gestures.

Fairfield Porter

Finally, we want to examine the work of American painter Fairfield Porter. One thing we know about effective design or artwork is that it seeks to capture one's attention and then effectively plots a way by which the viewer will be held hostage long enough to create the

Figure 3-26 Jean-Auguste-Dominique Ingres, ***Odalisque with a Slave,*** c. 1858. Drawing.

Figure 3-27 Jean-Auguste-Dominique Ingres, *Odalisque with a Slave,* c. 1839–1840. Painting.

appropriate mood. It may be by means of subject matter, texture, figurative expression, proportional extremes, scale, spatial uniqueness, or variations thereof. It is, however, the controlling factors of color that are generally responsible for the impact of a work. The use of intensity, saturation, and value will always dominate color compositions or objects. The authority of color seems to have a certain majesty.

The painting *Katie and Anne* (Figure 3-29) has the initial impact that light is somehow flooding in from the outside. In fact, the room seems to be lighted with an impossible deluge of color and light. Yet the interior is much lighter than the outdoors itself. The painting attracts our attention first and foremost by the saturated hues of the carpet, the blouse on the woman, and the long stemmed flowers in the background vase, all a very saturated yellow. Though the yellow does not spatially dominate the composition, it does overwhelm the painting by virtue of its saturated condition. Of all the colors, yellow is most certainly the brightest.

SUMMARY

In Chapter 3, we presented:

1. The brief study of how atmospheric light colors change **exterior** hues of the cathedral, as in Monet's study in Chapter 2.
2. We explored the effects and Authority of color through the Gothic cathedral model.
3. The mood or ambiance of the **interior** space in cathedrals is a paramount function of colored windows.
4. The additional function of the saturated windows as to depict Biblical stories and principles transposed into saturated color as a result of light from the heavens.
5. The specific functions of light and light waves.
6. Color Grid project to demonstrate the use of saturation, intensity, value, and hue.

Figure 3-28 GIAN LORENZO BERNINI (1598–1680). ***The Ecstasy of Saint Teresa.*** Cornaro Chapel, S. Maria della Vittoria, Rome, Italy.

Figure 3-29 FAIRFIELD PORTER, *Katie and Anne*, 1995. Oil on canvas. Hirshhorn Museum and Sculpture Garden, Smithsonian Institution.

Two Androids and a Baby

I had a very interesting and rather humorous incident on a recent return trip from Paris.

It begins on the initial journey to that great city. On that plane, there was a young couple sitting on the other side of the aisle with an infant perhaps six months old. The situation remains vivid in my mind, because the child complained intermittently for half of the trip. At some point the entire passenger population seemed to be on edge, in various degrees; myself included. How absolutely lovely it was to arrive in Europe. As much as I love children, I couldn't wait to get off of that plane!

Finally, as the day arrived for my return back to the states, I was blissful to say the least. My research had gone very well. After all, it was springtime in Paris, and my work was productive and inspirational beyond my expectations. My mood was definitely as good as it gets.

As we began to board the aircraft, I was already looking forward to refining my notes on the return trip. As I was settling into my seat, I began to do my usual scan of who my neighbors would be for the next 12 hours. Amazing! Who should I see perched across the aisle from me . . . that's right, *the* baby!

What are the odds that I would be sitting in the exact same seat, and the same three people in their respective seats, on the return home? Hard to believe. My joy turned to somber trepidation as I glared at the sweet little bundle of innocence. Wondering when "baby" would fire himself up again, I leaned over to give him a smile. He was an adorable child, full of smiles, and of course loved the attention of other people.

As soon as the wheels left the ground, the baby began his proclamations.....he was bored to tears, as expected. The parents began their usual routine of bouncing, an occasional gentle shake (always made him smile) and then a quick feeding. Bounce, shake, and feed, that was it.

After an hour of repeated fussing from the baby, I finally gave up trying to do any creative writing. The parents themselves sat quietly hour after hour, smiling at

Figure 3-30 Teddy Bears and Pigment.

the fussy baby and completely unbothered by the whole adventure. It was as if they were almost without feeling. These two parents, even though loving and caring, were clueless as to the solution. At the exact moment I closed the lid to my computer, *the light went on!* Here I was doing research on color theory, when I suddenly realized that the environment around the baby was almost completely colorless in the dim light. As the baby was being bounced, he was facing a muted light-blue bulkhead, looking at absolutely nothing but a blank wall. The parents both wore light blue, and the seats were of comparable hues; it was a monochromatic, dull environment.

What parents would not bring one single colorful toy on a 12-hour flight? They were...*androids*, that's it! Two androids and a human baby.....completely without emotion. Everyone in the aircraft was irritated but the parents.

Bounce, shake, and feed, bounce, shake, and feed....shake that baby....somebody stop the madness!

Eureka! I suddenly realized the answer. I think sometimes that I am perhaps a bit slow myself, because it took me two trips across the Atlantic to figure it out. I reached up to my overhead compartment, where I had a large bag of specialized pigments purchased in Paris—red, orange, yellow, green, blue, and violet, fist-sized jars perfect for the baby.

My parents' generation had a saying: "Silence is golden." That term never made more sense than it did that day. For the duration of the remaining trip, the baby required no more than a little stimulus. He was completely under the domination of color. We live in a world of color. Color entices, lures, and captivates the subconscious, as one falls under the power of *color authority.*

LIGHT

by Isaac Asimov

Particles and Waves

If we are prepared to admit that all matter is composed of atoms, then it is reasonable to ask if there is anything in the world that isn't matter and, therefore, isn't composed of atoms. The first possibility that might spring to mind is light.

It has always seemed obvious that light is immaterial. Solids and liquids can be touched, have mass, and therefore weight, and take up space. Gases cannot be felt in the same way that solids and liquids can, but a moving gas can be felt. We have all experienced high winds and we well know what a tornado can do. Then, too, air will take up room so that if an "empty" beaker (actually full of air) is plunged, open end down, into a tank of water, the water does not fill the beaker unless, somehow, the air is allowed to escape. In 1643, the Italian physicist Evangelista Torricelli (1608–1647) showed that air had weight and that this weight could support a column of mercury 76 centimeters (30 inches) high.

Light, however, has none of these properties. It cannot be felt, even though the heat it might produce can. It has never been found to have perceptible mass or weight, and it does not appear to take up space.

This doesn't mean that light was dismissed as unimportant because it was insubstantial, however. The first words of God, as given in the Bible, are: "Let there be light." What's more, under the name of fire, it was the fourth of the ancient Earthly elements, on a par with the three material ones of air, water, and earth.

Sunlight was naturally considered to be light at its purest. It was white light, unchanging and eternal. If sunlight were made to pass through colored glass, it would pick up the color of the glass, but that would be an earthly impurity. Again, when objects burned on earth and gave off light,

Figure 3-31 Rainbow at Jasper National Park.

Figure 3-39 James Clerk Maxwell.

magnetic behavior. They have been known ever since as Maxwell's Equations.

Maxwell's Equations (whose validity is confirmed by all observations made since) show that electric fields and magnetic fields cannot exist separately. There is, indeed, only a combined electromagnetic field with an electric component and a magnetic component at right angles to each other.

If electric behavior and magnetic behavior were similar in all respects, the four equations would be symmetrical; they would exist in two mirror-image pairs. In one respect, however, the two phenomena do not match each other. An object can be either positively charged or negatively charged. In magnetic phenomena, on the other hand, the magnetic poles do not exist separately. Every object that shows magnetic properties has a North Magnetic Pole at one location and a South Magnetic Pole at another location. If a long magnetized needle, with a North Magnetic Pole at one end and a South Magnetic Pole at the other, is broken in the middle, the poles are *not* isolated. The end with the North Magnetic Pole instantly develops a South Magnetic Pole at the break, while the end with the South Magnetic Pole develops a North Magnetic Pole at the break.

Maxwell included this fact in his equations, which introduced a note of asymmetry. This has always bothered scientists, in whom there is a strong drive for simplicity and symmetry. This "flaw" in Maxwell's equations is something we'll return to later.

Maxwell showed that from his equations you can demonstrate that an oscillating electric field will produce, inevitably, an oscillating magnetic field, and so on indefinitely. This is the equivalent of an electromagnetic radiation moving outward, in wave form, at a constant speed. The speed of this radiation can be calculated by taking

the ratio of certain units expressing magnetic phenomena to other units expressing electrical phenomena. This ratio works out to nearly 300,000 kilometers (186,290 miles) per second, which is the speed of light.

This could not be a coincidence. Light, it appeared, was an electromagnetic radiation. Maxwell's equations thus served to unify three of the four phenomena known to pass through a vacuum: electricity, magnetism, and light.

Only gravitation remained outside this unification. It seemed to have nothing to do with the unified three. Albert Einstein, in 1916, worked out his general theory of relativity, which improved on Newton's concept of gravitation. In Einstein's interpretation of gravity, which is now widely accepted as essentially correct, there should be gravitational radiation in the form of waves, analogous to electromagnetic radiation. Such gravitational waves, however, are much more subtle and feeble, and much more difficult to detect, than are electromagnetic waves. Despite some false alarms, they have not yet been detected at this moment of writing, although virtually no scientist in the field doubts that they exist.

Extending the Spectrum

Maxwell's Equations set no limitations on the period of oscillations of the field. There could be one oscillation per second or less, so that each wave would be 300,000

Figure 3-40 Woman Demonstrating Static Electricity.

kilometers long, or more. There could also be a decillion oscillations per second or more, so that each wave would be a trillionth of a trillionth of a centimeter long. And there could be anything in between.

Light waves, however, represent only a tiny fraction of these possibilities. The longest wavelengths of visible light are 0.0007 millimeters long, and the shortest wavelengths of visible light are just about half this length. Does this mean there is electromagnetic radiation we don't see?

Through most of human history, the question as to whether light existed that could not be seen would have been considered a contradiction in terms. Light, by definition, was something that could be seen.

The German-British astronomer William Herschel (1738–1822) was, in 1800, the first to show this was not a contradiction after all. At that time, it was thought that the light and heat one obtained from the Sun might be two separate phenomena. Herschel wondered if heat might be spread out in a spectrum just as light was.

Instead of studying the spectrum by eye, which noted only the light, Herschel studied it by thermometer, which measured the heat. He placed the thermometer at various places in the spectrum and noted the temperature. He expected that the temperature would be highest in the middle of the spectrum and that it would fall off at either end.

That did not happen. The temperature rose steadily as one progressed away from the violet, and reached its highest point at the extreme red. Astonished, Herschel wondered what would happen if he placed the thermometer bulb *beyond* the red. He found, to his even greater astonishment, that the temperature rose to a higher figure there than anywhere in the visible spectrum. Herschel thought he had detected heat waves.

In a few years, however, the wave theory of light was established and a better interpretation became possible.

Figure 3-41 William Herschel.

IMAGE SELECT / ART RESOURCE.

Sunlight has a range of wavelengths that are spread out by a prism. Our retinas react to wavelengths of light within certain limits, but sunlight has some waves that are longer than that of the visible red, and is therefore to be found beyond the red end of the spectrum. Our retinas won't respond to such long waves, so we don't see them, but they are there anyway. They are called infrared rays, the prefix coming from a Latin word meaning "below," for you might view the spectrum as going from violet on the top to red on the bottom.

All light, when it strikes the skin, is either reflected or absorbed. When absorbed, its energy speeds up the motion of the molecules in our skin and this makes itself felt as heat. The longer the wavelength, the deeper it penetrates the skin and the more easily absorbed it is. Hence, although we can't see the infrared, we can feel it as heat, and the thermometer, for similar reasons, can record it as such.

It would help, of course, if it could be shown that infrared rays were actually made up of waves like those of light, but with longer wavelengths. One might allow two beams of infrared rays to overlap and produce interference fringes, but no one would be able to see them. Perhaps they could be detected by thermometer, with the temperature going up each time the instrument passed through a "brighter" area, and going down each time it passed through a "dimmer" one.

In 1830, the Italian physicist Leopoldo Nobili (1784–1835) invented a thermometer that would do the job. One of his coworkers was the Italian physicist Macedonio Melloni (1798–1854). Because glass would absorb a great deal of the infrared rays, Melloni made use of prisms formed of rock salt, which is transparent to infrared rays. As a result, interference fringes were set up and Nobili's thermometer showed that they existed. By 1850 Melloni had demonstrated that infrared rays showed all of the properties of light without exception—except that they could not be seen with the naked eye.

What about the other end of the spectrum, where violet light deepens into darkness? That story began in 1614, when the Italian chemist Angelo Sala (1576–1637) noticed that silver nitrate, a perfectly white compound, darkened on exposure to sunlight. We now know This happens, because light contains energy and can force apart the molecule of silver nitrate, producing finely divided silver, which appears black.

About 1770 the Swedish chemist Karl Wilhelm Scheele (1742–1768) went into the subject in more detail, making use of the solar spectrum, which wasn't known in Sala's time. He soaked thin strips of white paper in solutions of silver nitrate, let them dry, and placed them in various parts of the spectrum. He found that the strips of paper darkened least quickly in the red, more quickly as one went farther and farther from the red, and most quickly in the violet. This happens (as we now know for reasons that will be explained later) because light increases in energy as one goes from red to violet.

Once Herschel discovered infrared rays in 1810, however, it occurred to the German chemist Johann Wilhelm Ritter (1776–1810) to check the other end of the spectrum. In 1801, he soaked strips of paper in silver nitrate solution

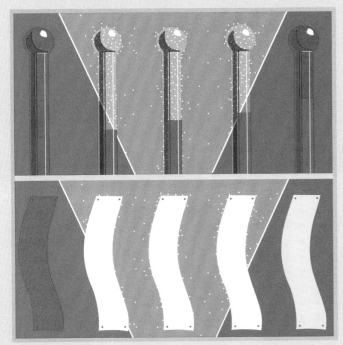

Figure 3-42 1. Infrared Light. In 1800, when William Herschel placed his thermometer in the dark area beyond the red end of the spectrum, he was surprised to record the highest temperature. **2.** Ultraviolet Light. In 1770, Karl Wilhelm Scheele found that paper soaked in silver nitrate solution darkened most quickly when exposed to violet light. In 1801, John Wilhelm Ritter exposed the paper in the dark area beyond the violet and the paper darkened even more rapidly.

and repeated Scheele's experiment except that he placed strips of paper *beyond* the violet, where no light was visible. As he suspected they might, the strips of paper darkened in this lightless region even more rapidly than they would in violet light. This represented the discovery of ultraviolet rays, where the prefix is from the Latin for "beyond."

Infrared and ultraviolet radiation existed just at the borders of the visible spectrum. Maxwell's Equations made it seem that there could be radiation far beyond the borders. If such radiation could be found, then Maxwell's Equations would be supported very strongly, for without them no one would have suspected such radiation might exist.

In 1888 the German physicist Heinrich Rudolf Hertz (1857–1894) made use of a rectangular wire, with a gap in it, as a detecting device. He set up an oscillating electric current in his laboratory. As the electric current oscillated, moving first this way, then that, it should emit electromagnetic radiation, with the radiation wave moving up while the current is going one way and then down when it is moving the other way. Such an electromagnetic wave should have a very long wavelength because, even if the oscillating electric current changes direction every small fraction of a second, light can move quite far between changes.

Hertz's rectangular wire would gain an electric current if the electromagnetic wave crossed it, and there would be a spark across the gap. Hertz got his spark. In addition, as he moved his rectangular wire here and there in the room, he got a spark where the wave was very high or very low, but no spark where it was in between. In this way, he could map the wave and determine its length.

Hertz had discovered what came to be called radio waves, which lay far beyond the infrared radiation and could have wavelengths of anywhere from centimeters to kilometers.

No one questioned Maxwell's equations after that. If there was a luminiferous ether, it carried electricity and magnetism also. If there was another ether, it existed only for gravitation.

In 1895, by the way, electromagnetic radiation was discovered far beyond the ultraviolet, with wavelengths exceedingly small. We will get to that later, after we consider a few other matters.

Dividing Energy

Electricity, magnetism, light, and gravitation are all forms of energy, where energy is anything that can be made to do work. These forms of energy certainly seem different from one another, but one can be turned into another. As we have already seen, electricity can be turned into magnetism, and vice versa, and a vibrating electromagnetic field can produce light. Gravitation can cause water to fall, with the falling water turning a turbine that can force a conductor through magnetic lines of force to produce electricity. Interconversions of energy and work represent the field of thermodynamics.

Such conversions are never completely efficient. Some energy is always lost in the process. The lost energy does not, however, disappear but makes an appearance as heat, which is still another form of energy. If heat is taken into account, then no energy is ever totally lost, nor does any energy ever appear out of nowhere. In other words, the total amount of energy in the universe seems to be constant.

This is the Law of Conservation of Energy, or the first law of thermodynamics, which was finally placed in compelling terms in 1847 by the German physicist Hermann Ludwig Ferdinand von Helmholtz (1821–1894).

In a way, heat is the most fundamental form of energy, for any other form of energy can be converted *completely* into heat, while heat cannot be converted completely into nonheat energy. For this reason, heat is the most convenient phenomenon through which to study thermodynamics; a word, by the way, which is from the Greek for "movement of heat."

Heat had been closely studied by scientists ever since the first truly practical steam engine was invented in 1769 by the British engineer James Watt (17__ _ _ _ 1919). Once the Law of Conservation of Energy was unde_____ _ _ _ study of heat became even more intense.

After the advent of the steam engine, there were two theories of the nature of heat. Some scientists thought of it as a type of subtle fluid that could travel from one piece of matter to another. Others thought of heat as a form of motion, of atoms and molecules moving or vibrating.

The latter suggestion, or the kinetic theory of heat (where kinetic is from a Greek word for "motion"), was finally established in the 1860s as the correct one when Maxwell and the Austrian physicist Ludwig Eduard Boltzmann

Figure 3-43 Waters of the Parana River rush down the spillway of the newly-opened Itaipu Dam, the world's largest hydroelectric dam. Foz Do Iguacu, Brazil, November 4, 1982.

(1844–1906) worked it out mathematically. They showed that everything that was known about heat could be interpreted satisfactorily by dealing with atoms and molecules that were moving or vibrating. As in the case of gases, the average speed ("velocity") of motion or vibration of the atoms and molecules making up *anything* is the measure of its temperature if the mass of the atoms and molecules is also taken into account. The total kinetic energy (which takes into account both mass and velocity) of all of those moving particles is the total heat of the substance.

Naturally then, the colder an object gets, the slower the motion of its atoms and molecules. If it gets cold enough, the kinetic energy of the particles reaches a minimum. It can then get no colder, and the temperature is at absolute zero. This notion was first proposed and made clear in 1848 by the British mathematician William Thomson (1824–1907), better known by his later title of Lord Kelvin. The number of Celsius degrees above absolute zero is the absolute temperature of a substance. If absolute zero is equal to –273.15° C, 0° C is equal to 273.15° K (for Kelvin) or 273.15° A (for absolute).

Any body at a temperature higher than that of its surroundings tends to lose heat as electromagnetic radiation. The higher the temperature, the more intense the radiation. In 1879, the Austrian physicist Joseph Stefan (1835–1893) worked this out exactly. He showed that the total radiation

increased as the fourth power of the absolute temperature. Thus, if the absolute temperature was increased two times, say from 300° K to 600° K (that is, from 27° C to 327° C), then the total radiation would be increased 2 × 2 × 2 × 2, or 16 times.

Formerly, about 1860, the German physicist Gustav Robert Kirchhoff (1824–1887) had established the fact that any substance at a temperature lower than that of its surroundings would absorb light of particular wavelengths, and would then emit those same wavelengths when its temperature rose above that of its surroundings. It follows that if a substance absorbs *all* wavelengths of light (a "black body," in that it reflects none of them), it will emit all wavelengths when heated.

No object actually absorbs all wavelengths of light in the usual sense of the word, but an object with a small hole in it does so after a fashion. Any radiation that finds its way into the hole is not likely to find its way out again and is finally absorbed in the interior. Therefore, when such an object is heated, black-body radiation—all of the wavelengths—should come pouring out of the hole.

This notion was first advanced by the German physicist Wilhelm Wien (1864–1928) in the 1890s. When he studied such black-body radiation, he found that a wide range of wavelengths was emitted, as was to be expected, and that the very long and very short wavelengths were low in quantity, with a peak somewhere in between. As the temperature rose, Wien found that the peak moved steadily in the direction of shorter wavelength. He announced this in 1895.

Stefan's Law and Wien's Law fit our experience. Suppose an object is at a temperature a little higher than that of our own body. If we put our hands near that object, we can feel a little warmth radiating from it. As the temperature of the object rises, the radiation becomes more noticeable and the peak radiation is at a shorter wavelength. A kettle of boiling water will deliver considerable warmth if our hand is placed near it. If the temperature is raised still higher, an object will eventually give off perceptible radiation at wavelengths short enough to be recognized by our retinas as light. We first see red light because that is the light with the longest wavelength, and is the first to be emitted. The object is then redhot. Naturally, most of the radiation is still in the infrared, but the tiny fraction that comes off in the visible portion of the spectrum is what we notice.

As the object continues to rise in temperature, it glows more and more bright. The color changes, too, as more and more of the shorter-wave light is emitted. As the object continues to grow still hotter, it becomes even brighter and the color undergoes another change as more, and shorter, wavelengths of light are emitted. The glow becomes more orange, and then yellow. Eventually, when something is as hot as the Sun's surface, it is white-hot, and the peak of the radiation is actually in the visible light region. If it grows still hotter, it becomes blue-white, and eventually, although it is brighter than ever (assuming we can look at it without destroying our eyes in the same instant), the peak is in the ultraviolet.

This heat/light progression created a problem for nineteenth-century scientists because it was difficult to make sense out of the pattern of black-body radiation. Toward the end of the 1890s, the British physicist John William Strutt, Lord Rayleigh (1842–1919), assumed that every wavelength had an equal chance of being radiated in black-body radiation. On that assumption, he worked out an equation that showed quite well how the radiation would increase in intensity as one went from very long wavelengths to shorter wavelengths. This equation, however, didn't provide for a peak wavelength, to be followed by a decline, as one approached still shorter wavelengths.

Instead the equation implied that the intensity would continue going up without limit as the wavelengths got shorter. This meant that any body should radiate chiefly in the short wavelengths, getting rid of all of its heat in a blast of violet, ultraviolet, and beyond. This is sometimes called the Violet Catastrophe. But the Violet Catastrophe does not take place, so there must be something wrong

with Rayleigh's reasoning. Wien himself worked out an equation that would fit the distribution of short wavelengths of black-body radiation, but it wouldn't fit the long wavelengths. It seemed as though physicists could explain either half of the radiation range, but not the whole.

The problem was taken up by the German physicist Max Karl Ernst Ludwig Planck (1858–1947). He thought there might be something wrong with Rayleigh's assumption that every wavelength had an equal chance of being radiated in black-body radiation. What if the shorter the wavelength, the less chance of it being radiated?

One way of making this seem plausible is to suppose that energy is not continuous and can't be broken up into smaller and smaller pieces forever. (Until Planck's time, the continuity of energy had been taken for granted by physicists. No one had wondered if energy, like matter, might consist of tiny particles that couldn't be divided further.)

Planck assumed that the fundamental bit of energy was larger and larger as the wavelength grew smaller and smaller. This meant that for a given temperature, the radiation would rise in intensity as wavelengths grew shorter, just as the Rayleigh equation indicated. Eventually though, for wavelengths shorter still, the mounting size of the energy unit would increase the difficulty of getting enough energy into one place in order to radiate it. There would be a peak, and as the wavelengths continued to decrease, the radiation would actually decline.

As the temperature went up and the heat grew more intense, it would be easier to radiate the larger energy units and the peak would move in the direction of shorter wavelengths, just as Wien's Law would require. In short, the use of the energy units that Planck postulated completely solved the problem of black-body radiation.

Planck called these energy units quanta (quantum in the singular), which is a Latin word meaning "how much?" What counted, after all, in the answer to the black-body radiation puzzle was how much energy there is in the quanta of different wavelengths of radiation.

Planck advanced his quantum theory, and the equation it made possible for black-body radiation (which agreed with the actual observations both for long wavelengths and short wavelengths), in 1900. This theory proved so important—far more important than Planck at the time could possibly imagine—that all of physics prior to 1900 are called classical physics, and all of physics after 1900 are called modern physics. For his work on black-body radiation, Wien received a Nobel prize in 1911, and Planck received one in 1918.

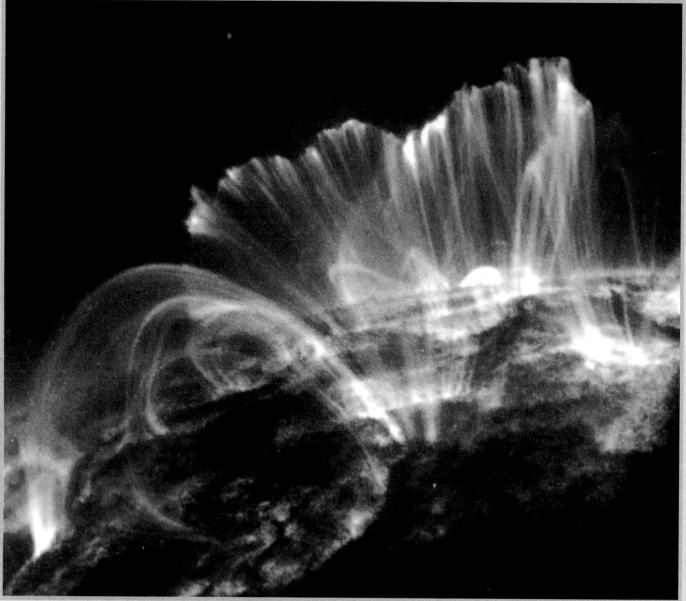

SOHO (ESA & NASA).

Figure 2-44 Solar Magnetic Arcs. This TRACE shows numerous spectacular coronal arcs.

PHOTO BY THE AUTHOR.

Figure 2-45 Mountains above the Dole Pineapple Plantation in Hawaii.

Objective:

Mixing the foundational *subtractive primary* pigments to demonstrate value, intensity, and saturation while establishing the resultant *secondary* colors of orange and green.

Four Groups of Color Mixing

There will be four rows of 9 patches each per grouping. Using one primary cool and one primary warm, you will be creating the optimal saturated secondary colors of orange and green. One of the four groups may produce an unexpected result. Try to determine which one and why?

The Project [*We will use group one as an example*]:

1. Begin with the second row of larger patches (group one). The left side patch (see yellow patch) is painted first, directly from the container (Hansa Yellow). Next, the right side blue patch also is applied with (see blue patch) paint directly from the container (Ultramarine Blue).

2. First, pour a small puddle of Hansa Yellow (HY) onto a nonabsorbent surface. Next, (a) separate a smaller amount of the color from the main HY puddle and add white to lighten the value of HY. (b) Apply that to the small square (indicated by dark gray) under the **HY** patch. Once more, (c) add even more white to the same puddle to intensify it (indicated by the light gray patch), and apply to the patch under the previous. Lastly, (d) separate another small amount of HY from the original puddle, and add a small bit of black, shading it to darker hue (note: black does not make *dark* yellow). (e) Apply it to the first square, first row (indicated by the black square) **(f)** Discard the two small patches of tinted and shaded HY. You are finished with the first line of color.

3. Next, add a very small amount of Ultramarine Blue to the original HY puddle, which will change the HY to a *slightly* greenish yellow. Apply that mixture to the second patch on the second row (indicated by the yellow patch with a slight green tinge) and repeat the entire process again, until the entire group is filled in. Remember, your ultimate goal is to incorporate the appropriate additions of Ultramarine Blue each time, in order that the fifth patch in the second row is an accurate saturated green (indicated by the green patch).

Group One
Hansa Yellow   **Ultramarine Blue**

Group Two
Cadmium Yellow Lt.   **Ultramarine**

Hansa Yellow   **Quinacridone Red**
Group Three

Cadmium Yellow   **Quinacridone Red**
Group Four

Dimensions of the color grid patches

- 1st row: ¾" × 1"   Shades: add black
- 2nd row: ¾" × 2"   Saturation
- 3rd and 4th row: ¾" × 1"   Tints: add white: Intensity/value
- 1" between   Horizontal space between top and bottom groups
- 1½" between   Vertical space between left and right groups
- 18" × 24"   Paper or overall composition size (Horizontal Landscape Format)

CHAPTER FOUR

Figure 4-1 Complementary Contrasting Composition of Orange and Blue, Waimea Bay, Oahu, Hawaii.

4

CONTRAST

INTRODUCTION TO CONTRAST

Understanding the functions of color contrast is vital as we learn about creating the illusion of compositional depth and distance (or the lack of it) as well as the forming of three-dimensional mass and focal points. Color contrast also is one of the chief components when we create emotional responses and mood contrasts.

Our primary focus, of course, will be on color contrast investigations. The very nature of contrast varies from high to low, depending on the degree of dissimilarity between values. Usually, when we refer to the maximum amount of difference in contrast, we are referring to *polar* or *diametrical* contrast. Color contrasts are very efficient at leading the viewer's eye to a desired location within a given composition or area.

As we study contrast through various projects and written assignments, it is important to remember the significance of contrast's character. We live in a world of contrast—good and evil, love and hate, happy and sad, winners and losers, rich and poor, peace and war—not to mention the various cultural contrasts in our communities and around the world. Some of these contrasts are about choice, while others are predetermined. Because the world itself is made up of these variables, it then becomes more logical and obvious why color contrasts are significant. We must remember as we continue through the text that *color's most valued asset is mood,* which is commensurate with the character of contrast, which also produces an abundance of mood variables but by different means. We know as artists and designers that emotional responses are at the heart of the matter, and it is contrast that provides one of the keys to such response. Let's take a look now at the diversity of contrasts available to us.

Figure 4-2 HARRY CALLAHAN, *Chicago*, 1950. The extreme light and dark contrast of the foreground trees and the background creates powerful imagery, as well as a very lonely composition on a cold, icy day. See if you can discern the true colors of this photograph.

PHOTO BY THE AUTHOR.

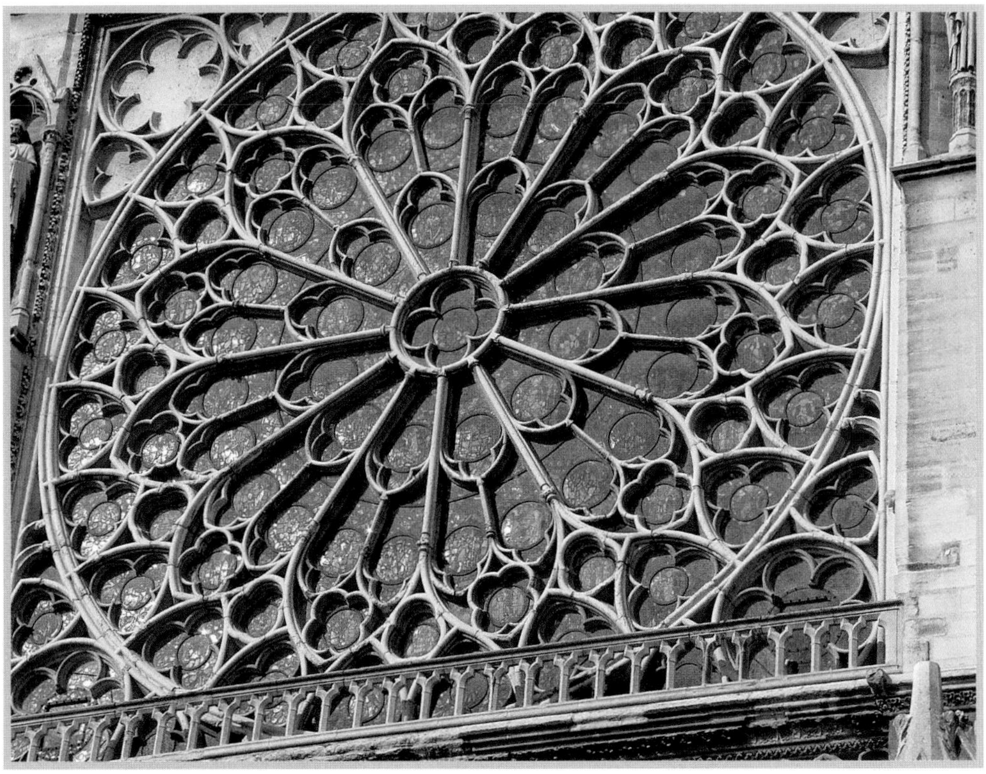

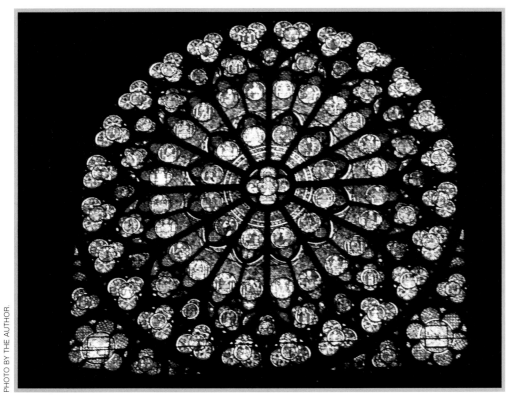

Figure 4-3 Exterior view of the South Rose Window, Notre Dame de Paris.

The exterior of the South Rose Window of the Notre Dame de Paris (above) is flooded with spring sunlight, constantly bombarding it with the full spectrum of colors. The window, with its enormous size and Gothic elegance, remains significant because of its beautiful tracery, structural integrity, and actual function to translate light into color.

The interior of the South Rose Window of Notre Dame de Paris is quite another view. The high contrast of the solid Gothic tracery against the translucent colored glass radiates the sun's light throughout the cathedral. It is the effect of *dark and light contrast* that truly transforms this colored diamond into heaven's gate, or the Eye of God.

We will now discuss the various types of contrasts and their importance.

PHOTO BY THE AUTHOR.

Figure 4-4 Interior view of the South Rose Window, Notre Dame de Paris.

Figure 4-5 Sunday Morning Mass, Notre Dame de Paris. Even though this scene is not officially dark and light contrast, some of the dynamics of dark and light contrast are evident here. The very dark violet foreground silhouettes against the bright yellow lights of candles, creating partially dark and light contrast of violet and yellow. The remainder of the composition is in contrast to the windows, creating the dynamics commensurate with the mood of this Catholic Mass.

Figure 4-6 PABLO PICASSO, *The Charnel House*, 1944–45. Achromatic Painting.

DARK AND LIGHT CONTRAST

The most extreme contrast is required for dark and light contrast. Therefore, it is optimally demonstrated in achromatic black and white and chromatically in violet and yellow. Extreme contrast always creates the most commanding statements. Certain essential functions are defined with the use of contrast, but before we look at the various examples of that, let's look at Picasso's *Charnel House* as an example of extreme contrast.

We notice that not only are there extremes of light and dark, but the weight of the painting is light to dark (or light to *heavy*), from top to bottom. The top one-third of *Charnel House* is contour line, which causes the viewer's eyes to immediately shift downward to where the heavier, more weighted area of the composition remains. This weightier area is created by the employment of extreme

black and white contrasts, juxtaposed with gray fragmented shapes. The dark areas dominate, pulling the figures of this disaster scene down to the floor. The contrast also creates a fragmented house of destruction, adding to the chaos illustrated by the linear elements.

The evidence of dark and light contrast in the skyscraper composition (following page) is clear, and easily understood. The dark foreground arch frames the buildings in the background, which creates a very specific focus as well as a greater depth of space. Additionally, it forms a certain mystery in the viewer's mind in terms of what is beyond what one can actually see, not to mention the curiosity of why this particular building may be important to the artist.

More so than the previous image, the embracing couple is the only possible focus (Figure 4-9). The expression on the woman's face, together with the surrounding darkness, creates a very somber mood indeed. The mysteries and moods that dark and light form together

Figure 4-7 Spacecraft launching from earth at night. In this image of an explosion, light and dark create a sudden moment of fear and anxiety; the foreground dark zone provides a barrier between the viewer and the possible danger in the background.

Figure 4-8 Las Vegas skyline framed by dark archway.

Figure 4-9 *Letters from Iwo Jima.*

will always be a paramount attribute of that particular contrast system. The film itself had many dark and light contrasting scenes, and is certainly consistent with the gloom of war and death that loomed over the island of

Iwo Jima during World War II. In this film clip, the full impact of impending war can be felt particularly because the most important features are emphasized; their faces and hands.

Let's take a closer look at the character of violet and yellow. We know that in the case of these complements, the maximum possibility of chromatic contrast can be achieved. Yellow has the most *intensity* of the spectral colors; it emits the highest degree of brightness possible in color. Yellow is also, however, the *weakest* of all colors. The addition of the slightest amount of its complement violet, for example, will severely change the character of yellow, so much so that it will create an almost sickly, dulled response to the viewer. It is very susceptible to any outside invader.

Violet is the extreme opposite of yellow because it is the *least intense* of all spectral colors. If yellow possesses the maximum brightness possible, then violet has the most *dullness,* and is therefore the strongest. If we are to add the commensurable amount of yellow to violet, as we did violet to yellow, the result would be of no consequence. In fact, if we were to triple the amount of yellow to violet, we would still be unable to discern the difference. Violet, because of its strength, simply "eats" the yellow. Because yellow is so weak, it will then take a considerable amount of yellow to allow our eye to see the change.

In Figure 4-10, yellow and violet are obviously the two dominant colors in this composition, which is defined as a dark and light contrast photo. Two pairs of complements can be seen in this dark and light image; violet and yellow, as well as yellow-orange and blue-violet.

Additionally, in the case of this natural environment, the play of colors of light (additive) illuminates the horizon, adding to the depth of space while creating the very dark violets. The two complements in this atmospheric "real-life" composition make clear the effects of extremes

Figure 4-10 Lone Tree and Sunset.

that can be seen in dark and light contrast; whether black and white, or violet and yellow.

The Nature and Function of Dark and Light

There are many opinions about light and dark receding and advancing in a composition, as well as warm and cool colors. Actually, all of them are true, depending on the contrast and value scenarios in a given composition. It is the arrangement of achromatic and chromatic dark and light (contrast) and dark to light (value) objects that cause the eye to *roam* a picture plane in space. Let's take a brief look at some examples to see specifically why these things are true.

Let's begin with the general notion that light, or light colors, advance into the viewer's space. If we were to look at a simple sphere, we would immediately understand that if light is illuminating its surface, then the light would first make contact with the closest point on that surface, which means that light does advance because it is closest to our eye. Anywhere there is an illuminated object, the light will advance and the darker areas will recede. We are identifying specific objects *(object light)* to lend credibility to this rule. Similarly, a portrait is the same in that the areas that receive light first are the closer points to the viewer's vision, and so obviously light advances again, and so on. The rule of *object light* is therefore steadfast in that light advances and dark recedes.

The light in the *Grande Gallery* recedes into what seems to be infinite space, as perspective and light lead the eye into the distance. It also is the contrast of the light against the dark that helps to emphasize and push the first gallery of columns and its arch forward into the viewer's

space. We see that the darkness from the long gallery hall diminishes rapidly, leaving an ominous and depressing dark foreground. Dark colors are clearly advancing while light recedes.

Edward Poynter's magnificent painting of *The Cave of the Storm Nymphs* (Figure 4-12) illustrates the nature of dark and light at its best. It is an issue of background, middle ground, and foreground contrasts that creates depth of space, as well as the dramatic effects of the composition. The background light contrasts against the middle ground rocks, or opening to the cave, which brings the dark portal forward. The foreground, then, becomes somewhat lighter as the figures come closer into our space.

The picture has an intensely lit scene of a sinking ship in a turbulent ocean. The middle ground dark contrast brings stability to the situation because it provides a solid defense against the storm. Those two factors of dark and light contrast are important, because the viewer needs to feel the contrasts between the chaos and peace and the turbulence and calm of the situation. Finally, the foreground is neither dark nor light, emphasizing the delicate nature of the predicament between the Nymphs themselves, and the brutal fury from where they came. Light and dark contrasts are seen especially emphasized on the immediate foreground figure. The three nymphs almost seem to be the same person, slowly progressing her way forward into a lighter and safer area of the cave. Each figure gets progressively lighter as she comes forward into space, and finally, light floods the foreground form, emphasizing that she is the first of the three to have solace from the storm.

It is *compositional light* that is creating spatial depth by the dark and light contrasts between the background, middle ground, and foreground. *Object light,* on the other hand, is creating extreme light and dark values, emphasizing the bodies of the nymphs, which enhances the drama

Figure 4-11 Hubert Robert (1733–1808), *Fantastical View of the Grand Gallery of the Louvre.*

SCALA/ART RESOURCE, NY.

Figure 4-12 Sir Edward John Poynter, *Cave of the Storm Nymphs*, 1903.

of the disaster. The fear created in this work relies heavily on the light and dark contrasts of the color palette.

The same effect, in a complete reversal of mood, can be seen in Frederick George Cotman's *One of the Family*. (Figure 4-13) Again, we have the light background, (especially noted is the intensity of light through the window), dark middle ground, and the fairly well-lit foreground.

This time, however, the dark wall of the background emphasizes the environment of the horse, as opposed to the atmosphere of the people inside.

We know by now that dark and light contrast also functions as an emphasis element. Focal points often are generated by the use of dark and light contrasts. In David Roberts, *The Israelites Leaving Egypt,* (Figure 4-14) we see

Figure 4-13 FREDERICK COTMAN (1850–1920), *One of the Family*, 1880.

a reversal of the previous examples. Rather than a dark middle ground, we instead see a well-lit middle ground.

Here, even though the dark advances into our space, the emphasis is clearly on the middle ground. The focus is on the thousands of Jews enslaved in Egypt who have finally been set free by Pharaoh because of God's persistent plagues on the land. They are seen both preparing and leaving Egypt. Notice the extreme contrast of dark in the foreground and the right side of the composition. One cannot help but focus one's attention on the center lighted area.

A number of examples can be seen throughout the text, in terms of dark foreground and light backgrounds. Please take the time to locate and study these effects in terms of how exactly dark and light function.

Third-Class Carriage (Figure 4-15) illustrates the importance of light to dark hues, because the figures of lighter values are in the viewer's space, with the help of the darker background. As these working-class people pack together in the cramped space of the train, the obvious focus is on the two foreground figures. It is important for the artist to portray the life and hardships of these working-class people. Not one single person in the train is wearing a smile, but it is especially true of the two ladies in the foreground. The people in the background seem to be less important to the artist, because they are obscured by the receding darkness in the back of the carriage. The two women illustrate one of the most revered paintings of the French Realist movement in the nineteenth century. Because of the contrasting advancing light, we are able to understand exactly what the artist

Figure 4-14 DAVID ROBERTS, *The Israelites Leaving Egypt*, 1828.

Figure 4-15 HONORÉ DAUMIER, *Third-Class Carriage*, 1856–1858.

BURSTEIN COLLECTION/CORBIS.

intends. We can easily read their faces as they demonstrate the realistic hardships of physical work.

Akihiko's Muse (Figure 4-16) is a classic light and dark scenario. In this case, it is neither black and white nor yellow and violet, yet it exemplifies the power of light and dark contrast. It is important to point out that even though black and white and yellow and violet are normally the best contrast opposites, other colors often demonstrate that quality as well. Here there is a sharp contrast of light and dark between the foreground and the background.

The almost luminous red-orange figure of the muse makes a serious contrast against the dark ground behind her. One of the keys to this division of space is the luminosity of the figure, which actually contrasts against the more opaque background.

Also, the depth of space is enhanced by the luminous reflection of the candle's light on the upper portion of her extended leg, reinforcing the depth of space. Our immediate logical reaction would be to think that the brightness of the candles are diminishing the illusion of

Figure 4-16 SHIJO, *Akihiko's Muse.*

PHOTO BY THE AUTHOR.

Figure 4-17 The flag of the United States of America is one of many perfect examples of *hue contrast*.

depth, but it is the diagonal line of the luminous leg against the dark background that helps to effectively split the composition.

HUE CONTRAST

In dark and light contrast, we discussed the two most extreme contrasts: black and white, and violet and yellow. Contrast of hue is actually the simplest form of contrast that we will be discussing. It is easy to understand, and there are no complex issues regarding hue contrast.

Hue contrast must incorporate no less than three colors in order to be effective. These hues, however, must be clearly distinct from one another such as the three primaries. Red, yellow, and blue are the most clearly defined hue contrasts, and far enough away from each other to provide the ultimate contrast. Although these colors can be changed in value and intensity, the further away they are from the saturated primaries, the less effective the contrast.

Some possibilities are:
Yellow, Red, and Blue
Yellow, Green, Blue, and Red
Green, Blue, Orange, and Black
Red, White, and Blue

The possibilities are seemingly endless as long as there is a reasonably distinguishable contrast between the hues. Proportions of the primaries can be altered by nominal value changes, such as the addition of white (tinting) for greater brightness (intensity), or adding black (shading) for less intensity, or dullness. A shaded red then will still

Figure 4-18 PAUL GAUGUIN, *Tahitian Landscape*, 1893.

Figure 4-19 Hue contrast can be many combinations of color, but they must have a considerable distance between them in terms of contrast value.

Figure 4-20 Little boy in prague takes time for a quick lunch.

In the photo above, the little boy in red, blue and white easily catches the eye in a crowded lunch hour street by a tram stop in Prague. Hue contrast is evidenced in a different respect here, with the saturated red and blue against the dull blues of the cobblestone walkway. Normally, hue contrast is regarded mostly in terms of saturated colors, which are in their boldest state, side-by-side contrasts with one another. In this situation, the hue contrast of red, blue and white are the more exaggerated by the dullness of color in the cobblestones. We are only observing the little boy as representing hue contrast, rather than the entire composition. If were to look at the composition as a whole, then we would be seeing saturation contrast, rather than hue contrast."

provide high contrast between itself and saturated yellow, or a tinted violet against blue will do the same. Of course, two shaded or two tinted hues will offer less contrast, and will eventually lose any significant contrast.

The effects of hue contrast offer many possibilities for the expressive nature of color. The contrast of these hues can be significant to forming emotional responses such as a burst of joy, celebration, or sudden grief and despair. This type of contrast is such that it is obligated to produce a response.

In early 1891, Paul Gauguin methodically packed his bags and said farewell to his wife and children forever. His desperation to escape the complications of city life, such as it was in Paris, filled him with the hope that he could find solace in Tahiti, where he could paint his abstract color fields undisturbed.

In Paul Gauguin's *Tahitian Landscape* (previous page), we see an exemplary composition based on hue contrast. Yellow, green, violet, and red (red-orange) control the mood of this warm composition. Gauguin's passionate response to the island world was his last stand. The landscape is one of his most emotional gestures yet. His love for the primitive, for the simple and uncomplicated world, and the sensuality discovered in his new Polynesian wife burst out onto this canvas. This painting is intensely rich with emotional responses, which hue contrast is famous for accomplishing.

Figure 4-21 ROY LICHTENSTEIN, *Forget It! Forget Me!*, 1962.

Roy Lichtenstein's *Forget It! Forget Me!* illustrates yet another aspect of hue contrast. We already know that the construction of hue contrast in a composition is capable of setting up a range of emotions or moods. The placement of one color next to another is critical in the creation of the appropriate mood. We understand that a moderately shaded red next to a yellow can change the character of one over the other. Color placement in hue contrast can either complement the other, or steal away the attention of the other. One may exert power over the other, while another will totally destroy its partner and thereby gain all of the attention.

Forget It! Forget Me! (Figure 4-21) serves to illustrate the effects of hue contrast and its varying moods. The dominant and controlling color in the picture is obvious, as this very saturated red separates the two people in their dispute. The placement of red in the center between the man and the woman acts as a barrier, symbolizing their dispute. Red is a dynamic color and has contrasting characters within itself. Red can be angry and hateful, or it can be sensuous and passionate. Yellow, on the other hand, can be quite jovial or celebratory by nature, as blue can be rather stable or calming. Also, it is permissible to introduce black or white to the composition of hue contrast. A white space in contrast to a blue or indigo patch will cause the blue/indigo area to appear to be darker and more mysterious. White next to yellow, however, can rob the color of some of its brilliance, and white next to red can take away a portion of the color's saturation. The addition of black next to red or yellow will cause the same hues to appear lighter and more intense. The defining element here is the

Figure 4-23 A Group of Impromptu Performers in Paris.

black outlining of the characters, which provides a greater definition and contrast between the contrast of hues.

Hue contrast is not unlike certain aspects of the atom that we studied in Chapter 1, which is a bit like harmony and chaos at the same time. The effects of hue contrast, because of their striking differences in color, often create a certain harmonious chaos of moods and emotional responses. If Picasso had been a colorist rather than a form artist, he most certainly would have often employed the use of hue contrast—for as he said, "A painting is first of all, a sum total of destructions."

Lastly, a familiar association of hue contrast would be found in the various tribal cultures of the world, such as the Native American Indian. With saturated hue contrasts, beautiful costumes of dyed fabrics, bracelets, and necklaces of colored stones, ceramic beads, and colorful feathers emulate the energy expressed in the tribal dance.

Even within a situation such as an impromtu performance on the streets of Paris (see Figure 4-23), the performers seem to understand the "attention-grabbing" necessity for color stimulus. In this case hue contrast dominates the scene. Saturated red, green, and yellow dominate the composition with contrasts of hue, and even though they are not consciously orchestrating intentional hue contrasts, there often is a subconscious understanding about saturation and contrast in the novice of color. The performance takes place in the square in front of Notre Dame de Paris, where thousands of people come out during a weekend day to enjoy the warm sun and listen to the bell tower chime on Sunday. With all of the diversions simultaneously occurring that day, these young people drew the attention of the majority of people in the square with their pure colors and equally intense music.

COMPLEMENTARY CONTRAST

Complementary color is just that—two colors that complement each other. They are colors that exist directly opposite of each other on the color circle. Complements harmonize and balance one another, causing the other to appear even better or sometimes more saturated than they actually are. Such is the case between Arnofini's bride's green dress and the red fabrics of the bed. The bed seems saturated, when,

Figure 4-22 Yellow-orange, blue, and red often provide outstanding hue contrast, even though there is a shaded red ground.

Figure 4-24 JAN VAN EYCK, *The Marriage of Giovanni Arnolfini and Giovanna Cenami*, 1434.

Figure 4-25 JAN VAN EYCK, *The Marriage of Giovanni Arnolfini and Giovanna Cenami*, 1434, Achromatic.

Make a comparison study between the chromatic painting and this achromatic version in order to determine how values function within a composition. Notice that the red and green values are balanced equally (50%). That is because red and green possess equal value. There is, however, a slight difference between them, only because the green dress is somewhat shaded and the bed fabric is tinted. If they were equally saturated, there would be no difference whatsoever. Conversely, the complements of blue-violet and yellow-orange on the left side of the composition creates a noticeable contrast between the two, because yellow and violet are not equal in value.

in fact, it is not fully saturated. When we look at the color circle, we understand that the primary colors are always present in complementary pairs consisting of one primary and one secondary color. These complements are red and green, orange and blue, and yellow and violet.

Complementary colors also possess a contradictory character. They not only complement one another, but they also can destroy or cancel each other. There is a very destructive nature about their relationship, and it is unusually similar to human behavior. If they get too close to one another, they automatically eradicate each other. Complementary colors are in fact mutual enemies as well as lovers. The mixing of two complements will always cancel chroma, and neutralize their ability to be effective. The mixing of two complements then create gray. So both complements possess strong chromatic powers; when linked side by side they complement and become more powerful, yet when they get too close they become enemies and are transformed into achromatic values.

An even more peculiar aspect of complements is that if you were to remove eleven of the twelve colors of light on the color circle, mixing the removed eleven colors would result in the complement of the color left behind. For every color on the circle, regardless of which color is segregated, the other eleven colors will mix to be its complement. This very peculiar phenomenon creates a visual after-image that a camera cannot record, even though the eye is able to see it: the eye requires a color to be balanced. When the color is absent, the eye will then compensate, or spontaneously manufacture the complement.

Jan van Eyck's painting is certainly one of the finest examples of complementary color and its effects. It uses both complements of yellow and violet (seen more subtly), and green and red (more obvious). The red and green complements are dominate because the violet is of course a stronger and duller hue, as is the yellow more intensified or less saturated.

The main event of complementary effects in Jan van Eyck's painting (Figure 4-24) is on the side of the bride. (Although she seems pregnant, her dress is merely gathered in front.) Many say the bed chamber itself is saturated red, but if we look at the very center of the composition, we will see true saturated red. The bed chamber appears at first to be saturated when it is actually tinted somewhat with white. The reason for this miscalculation is that the green dress *complements* the red and thereby causes it to look more red, or saturated, than it really is.

The bride is the focal point. Some say that their joined hands are the focal point, but that is a compositional focal point, not a color directive. Although the hands are indeed important, both compositionally and symbolically, it is rather the face of the bride that continues to pull

Figure 4-26 Hawaiian flower exemplifies a complementary contrast of red and green.

our attention away from the hands. There is an extreme contrast set up between the face and head piece, and the near saturation of the green and the red. Her head radiates, or is luminous far more than their hands or the face of the groom. Compare the achromatic version next to the chromatic version and you will see that this bears out to be true. The values are darker everywhere in the composition than is her face and head piece.

Meadow at Moritzburg is a classic in terms of what complementary color harmonies can produce emotionally. The vibrant and emotional quality of this expressionistic painting is evident in this composition. Even though red and green complements are equal in color balance, it is

sometimes the case where the two become too static, or predictable, and so it is sometimes necessary to introduce another color, or in this case a different complementary scheme. The complementary orange and violet structure in the foreground of structures removes the static from the otherwise obvious approach to complements.

Gerard's *Cupid and Psyche* presents a much subtler approach to complementary contrast. In fact, the contrast doesn't even seem to quite fit because we think of contrast as being more evident. Here is where the student must become more critical in his or her approach to the art of seeing. Split the composition diagonally from the lower right corner to the upper left corner. In the right upper diagonal side of the composition we see complements of light oranges and light blues. Cupid's body is a very light orange tone, his wings are darker orange, and the sky presents itself as a fairly light blue. The lower left diagonal, where Psyche sits, imparts complements of red and green. The red drapery on which she sits quietly helps the eye to see the slightest light red tones in her body. The green further enhances or creates a visual response with the viewer seeing more red in his skin than is perhaps there. The effects of complements here are the extreme opposite of *Arnolfini and His Bride,* where van Eyck paints an overt complementary harmony, as opposed to Gerard's very restrained or quiet set of complements.

This flower and its foliage are complementary, one to the other. The red seems redder than it is because of the green background. In fact, the red actually is not a saturated red, but the dark contrast directly behind the flower as well as the surrounding green, which gives us the notion that it is very saturated. Conversely, the yellow border of the flower's cup prevents the red and green from

Figure 4-27 MAX HERMANN PECHSTEIN, **Meadow at Moritzburg**, 1910.

Figure 4-28 FRANCOIS GÉRARD, **Amor and Psyche**, 18th century.

JAMES WORRELL/GETTY IMAGES.

Figure 4-29 Orange and blue create a powerful image. The orange prevails over the blue because the perfect balance of orange and blue is 33 1/3 to 66 2/3 percent. Clearly, the lack of balanced values are evident here as 50/50. The fruit jumps out at the viewer, almost as if they are floating over the blue surface.

forming the best possible contrast, as it becomes a type of buffer zone.

WARM AND COOL CONTRAST

Warm colors are identified as red, orange, and yellow, while cool colors are green, blue, and violet. Warm and cool colors can be identified as having an actual warmth or coolness to them, respectively. Red, orange, and yellow visually warm and cool colors are equally cold or cool. To be more specific, the totality of warm colors are identified

as yellow, yellow-orange, orange, red-orange, red, and red-violet. Specific cool colors are yellow-green, green, blue-green, blue, blue-violet, and violet. In terms of opposites or complements, the *strongest* (not highest contrast) would be red-orange and blue-green.

When referring to *color temperature*, we can imagine warm colors generated from an orange fire, or imagine the warmth of the sun's yellow heat, in contrast to a blue sky with its cooling breezes, or the chilling deep waters of blue-greens in the ocean. Temperature opposites also are responsible for the viewer's mood response. Consider for a moment some of the differing scenarios that warm and cool are similar to:

Warm and Cool *Properties* Could Express:

Warm and Cool	Rare and Common
Transparent and Opaque	Light and Heavy
Wet and Dry	Deep and Shallow
Sun and Shade	

Warm and Cool *Personalities* Could Express:

Excitement and Calm	Peace and Chaos
Contentment and Depression	Hope and Despair
Brilliance and Gloom	

Saturated color contrasts normally demand a more powerful emotional response. Picasso's *Girl Before a Mirror* (Figure 4-31) sets up strong alliances of warm and cool saturated and high intensity contrasts. The emotions of the artist seem be linked to the *Girl Before a Mirror* by his response to warm and cool contrasts. The color associations are commanding as this painting makes a case for the warm and cool nature of color, as well as serving as an example of hue contrast from our previous discussion.

Picasso's color schemes reflect the energy associated with the artist's life, as we will discuss later in Chapter 6.

Warm and cool contrast creates dynamic compositions of majesty and glory as we see in Murillo's *Immaculate Conception of Soult* (Figure 4-34) seen on the following

JUPITERIMAGES.

Figure 4-30 Cool colors are literally cool in terms of physical temperature. If one were able to touch a single cool blue ray of light, there would be a cool/cold sensation. The mood of blue here creates a very cool and tranquil composition.

KATHLEEN CAMPBELL/STONE/GETTY IMAGES.

Figure 4-31 Warm colors are literally warm in terms of physical temperature. If one were able to touch a single warm red ray of light, there would be a warm-hot sensation. Warm colors often create a variety of moods as well. The colors here are energized and passionate.

Figure 4-32 The Trevi Fountain in Rome is, in a sense, symbolic of Roman summer time. It is very hot by day and it is not until evening that Romans come out to play. This is a very popular place to hang out, recuperating from the day's heat. Because it is often too hot by day, it is the *warm glow* of the architecture representing hot days, and the coolness of the water seen in the night activities. The feel of color temperature in this image is in the opacity of the red-orange architecture and the green translucence of water.

Figure 4-33 PABLO PICASSO, *Girl Before a Mirror,* 1932.

page. This composition lies in serious contrast to Picasso's saturated colors, hard edges, and flat space. Murillo creates a subtle gradation of warm and cool contrasts. Especially noted is the absence of harsh contrast; rather we observe the careful variations of orange values that assist to create depth of space. The figure's blue robe contrasts against the misty red-orange background, which helps push the figure into the foreground. Even without the saturated color as seen in Picasso's work, the painting of Murillo surges with majesty and authority.

One of the periods of art in which light and warm and cool contrasts were important can be seen in the work of the Impressionists. Previously, we briefly studied the work of Claude Monet, particularly the Rouen Cathedral and the changes of color on its surface during the day or during the year, respectively.

Amedeo Modigliani's *"Seated Nude"* (Figure 4-35) illustrates the force of warm and cool contrasts in a more sensuous color scheme. Cool blues caress the right side of her body, while a warm shaded red supports her left side. The composition is diagonally split by the figure's light red-orange body, which ultimately creates a very relaxed and yet sensually energized painting. The blue is calm, the red is passionate, and the light red-orange unifies the two emotions of warm and cool colors.

Warm and cool contrast, in the case of Modigliani's *Seated Nude* (Figure 4-35), has a commonality with

Figure 4-34 BARTOLOME ESTEBAN MURILLO, *The Immaculate Conception of Soult,* after ca. 1678.

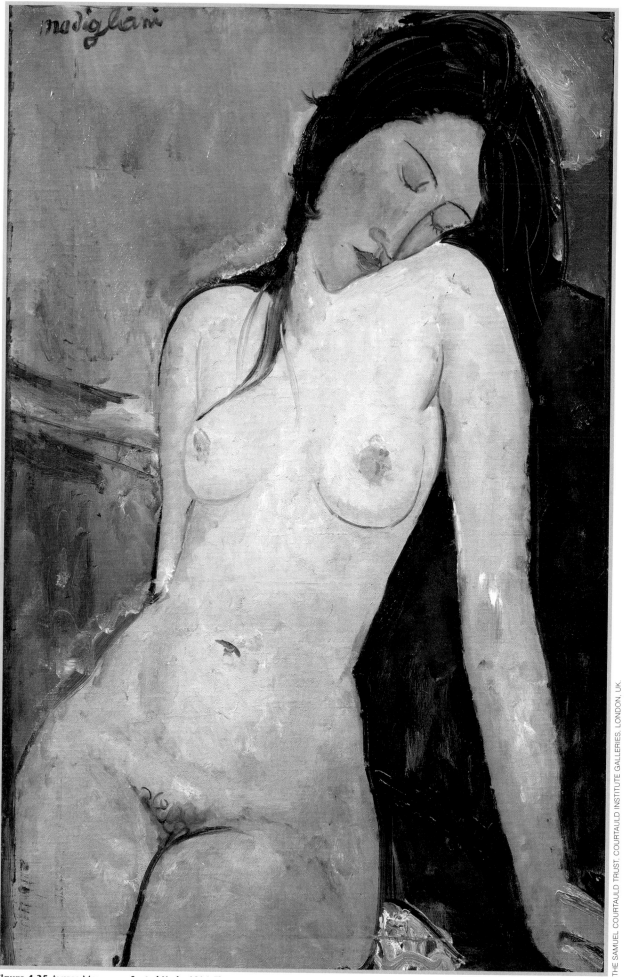

Figure 4-35 AMEDEO MODIGLIANI, *Seated Nude*, 1916. The contrasting cool blues and violets with warm reds and oranges in the seated nude composition commensurately creates a mood of both tranquility and sensuality.

Figure 4-36 Paul Gauguin, *Vision after the Sermon, Jacob Wrestling with the Angel,* 1888.

complementary contrast. The blue-green and red-orange of the composition also qualifies it as complementary contrast. What then, is the critical difference between complementary (which always has one warm and one cool) and warm and cool? The typical complementary composition is about one color complementing another. In *Giovanni Arnolfini and His Bride,* we can see that the green dress enhances the red bedspread, causing it to appear more saturated than it actually is, and commensurably the red bedspread causes the illusion of a more saturated green. They *complement* one another. *Seated Nude,* on the other hand, is not so much about complementing as it concerns itself with *temperature.* The *opaque* icy blue-green background *contrasts* with the *translucent* red-orange, which seems very warm. In fact, the figure almost seems to glow with heat. They are, in fact, extreme contrasts of color temperature in the same composition.

Warm and cool colors can apply to a single color as well. For example, Warm violets and cool violets may be produced by the addition of red or blue, respectively. The warm violet will actually have a slight red tinge and the cool violet will possess a bluish tone. The student may not immediately recognize a warm violet to be such when

confronted with the color, because it does take a little practice seeing the red in the violet. The same holds true when recognizing blue in a cool violet. Other variations exist, such as warm and cool black.

Paul Gauguin's painting of Jacob wrestling with the angel is important to note here. The *warm red* seems at first to be out of place in terms of what we would normally expect of an outdoor earth surface. Green or earth hues are obviously what we imagine, however; warm saturated red creates the extreme emotion or mood in the painting as Jacob wrestles with the angel. Certainly green tones would be inappropriate, because green is a calm color, so Gauguin proclaims that he wants to exude emotion rather than representational color accuracy. The robes of the nuns are a contrasting cooler violet, with higher contrasting caps, which diagonally divide the foreground from the background.

The greater the intensity, the harder it is to change warm and cool components. Yellow for example, turns yellow-green or yellow-orange rather than becoming a warm or a cool yellow. Violet is able to become either warm or cool because violet is the strongest (least intense) color, and therefore is not easily changed by the addition of blue or red. Yellow, conversely, is the weakest (most intense) color, and so it is too easily influenced by additions of another color, and therefore changes to another color.

Vision After the Sermon is an interesting study because of its high contrast between saturation and intensity. Rather than creating spatial differences, such as depth, it is actually responsible, in part, for generating flat space. The saturation of the red background is no competition for the white–capped[1] nuns in the foreground. We know that the *implication* of deep space is evident because of the perspective—large to smaller images, from foreground to background. We especially understand the implication of space because of the foreground. The nuns are not simply in the foreground, they are *in* the viewer's space.

In terms of illusion, however, the space is flat and so we do not feel a sense of depth whatsoever. The saturated red background is actually racing forward, while the white of the caps is receding into the composition, or the background. The more extreme the contrast between

these two entities, the flatter the composition becomes. Contrast directs attention toward the two wrestling figures in the background. Gauguin wasn't really interested in portraying realistic space or figures as much as he was concerned with registering the emotions of the conflict. In this Biblical account of Jacob wrestling the angel, the color and contrast affiliation is the key component in achieving the appropriate intensity of mood.

Saturation Contrast

The Character of Saturation

Before we discuss saturation contrast, let us take a brief look at what the term saturation actually means. Previously we discussed the properties of saturation in Chapter 1, but it bears repeating at this juncture. We know that the general

Figure 4-37 *Lara Croft: Tomb Raider* **PlayStation.** The saturated red background sets the stage for the characteristics of saturated contrast. Subtle nuances of saturated contrast in this composition occur when the values change from red to dark red seen in the background, as well as contrast between the saturated red and skin tones of Lara Croft.

[1]Actual colors vary, depending on printing. Caps are actually light indigo to blue.

description of saturation is the absolute purity of a hue, which is to say, its freedom from black, white, or gray. First, we'll explore the *general* definition in the purely *technical* terms. Second, we will look at the term saturation in a more *specific* sense as it relates to color "purity."

To do this we must explore the term *intensity* as well. Many have espoused that saturation and intensity are one in the same. In fact, this has been the popular language of this past century. We want to see why that is, and then propose a different approach to the two words. The general agreed-upon definition among the majority of theorists is that *saturation is the degree of the purity of a color (and its freedom from black or white) or hue as it is measured by intensity or brightness factors.* The well-known color theorist of the twentieth century, Johannes Itten, said saturation "indicates the intensity or purity of a color."

This formal or *general* definition of saturation refers to any given hue in its most saturated state. Whether a primary, secondary, or intermediate hue, it would then be whatever the most *pure state* of that hue could possibly be. We already understand that to intensify yellow, we add white. White is the vehicle that causes yellow to become brighter, or more intense. This is where the problem arises. Does a color become more intense (or brighter) as it moves away from the saturated state, or toward it? If intensity relates to brightness, then we would have to say that greater intensity is moving away from the saturated condition. So, how do we then interpret intensity? Intensity is identified in most circles as *the degree or amount of saturation, strength, or purity of any particular hue. A vivid or brilliant color is high intensity, whereas a dull color is low intensity.* This supports the notion that intensity moves *away from* the saturated state, as does dullness. But if intensity were the same as saturation, then would it not make more sense that greater intensity is working its way *toward* saturation, rather than away from it?

Intensity is certainly saturation's companion, if not the exact same family. To say that they are the same then requires some explanation. As we examine the evolving debate over this complicated definition, these are the types of questions we need to ask ourselves. We must be willing to give a deductive answer when the question arises, and then it is up to the individual to discern the differences between intensity and saturation.

To further explore what saturation is then, would be to offer the specific argument about the word *purity*, which is *commensurate to saturation*. Let's take *purity* to the extreme and be precise. Purity relates to color in the following ways:

- Primary colors exist in and of themselves. We cannot mix any other combination of colors to come up with yellow, blue, and red. They are the foundation colors for all others.
- Secondary colors are produced by mixing two primary colors.
- Intermediate colors (some say tertiary) are made by combining one primary and one secondary color.
- All of these colors have a saturated or pure state.

Figure 4-40 Saturation contrast is evident in other ways, in that the apple would be considered to be saturated, as opposed to the very light red of the background and remaining objects.

...... we have basically done so by changing the word from *purity* to *clarity*. Now we know why the primaries are not solely relegated to purity. So then purity is not in the sense that color be *untouched*, or virgin color, so to speak. Rather it is a state of *visual clarity*, which then quenches the argument that it would be any color that compromises the purity or saturation of a color.[2]

1. A color may be changed or diluted by the addition of black. Black actually dispossesses a color of its light characteristics, as to construct a type of filter in order to screen out a portion of the light itself.

As we consider *The Penitent Magdalene* (Figure 4-42), the primary color red seen on the figure's dress is an almost saturated red, or so it seems with the

Figure 4-41 Saturation contrast is easy to measure; it is either saturated or not. There is no guessing when it comes to understanding what is truly saturated. The true saturation point in this composition is the foreground banner. Even though we could say in a general sense, that the little girl's costume or perhaps the banner behind her is saturated, they are in fact not so saturated. The background is the obvious contrast to saturation, and does make the fore mentioned seem saturated, but we will hold fast to the true point of saturation in the foreground banner.

MEG TAKAMURA/IZA STOCK/GETTY IMAGES.

[2]Note: An emphasis of this text is to use and develop a student's critical thinking skills to indicate why such theory is true. Rather than always assuming everything you hear is gospel, why not investigate to see why it is true, or in some cases, questionable?

Figure 4-42 GEORGES DE LA TOUR, *The Penitent Magdalene,* 1638-1643.

Figure 4-43 JAMES ROSENQUIST, *Study for Marilyn,* 1962.

surrounding darkness (Figure 4-42). The background wall of violets and greens has been shaded with black, as well as the dark violet table drapery behind her leg. The red-orange objects on the table surface, as well as her skin tones and blouse seem all the more illuminated from the shaded, or dulled foreground, middle ground and background hues. La Tour was one of the great masters of saturation contrast.

2. A color may be changed or diluted by the addition of white. The effect of white additions are rather varied. Generally, white will cause the character of a pure color to become somewhat cooler, even if it is a warm color.

   Rosenquist's painting for the *Study of Marilyn* demonstrates how saturation contrast functions when white is added, intensifying the composition. The saturated red of the lipstick and fingernails has been extended into a very light tinted red throughout the rest of the composition. There is a wide variety of lightest red, to darker red, to the saturated red.

3. A saturated color may be changed or diluted with black and white (gray). The addition of gray will always cause a given color to have a certain neutrality or dullness.

   In O'Keeffe's *Black Iris,* what was originally blue and violet has the appearance of having been shaded, or neutralized by black and white additions. What we normally expect to see is more intense color in an iris,

Figure 4-44 GEORGIA O'KEEFE, *Black Iris,* 1926.

but instead we see an iris that demonstrates a very mysterious, almost depressed mood. The color of the flower has been drastically dulled so as to completely change the character of its original color.

4. A saturated color may be changed or diluted with its complement. The addition of green to red, for example, dulls the red progressively until the red seems almost black (depending on the hue of red).

Notice the green tints and shades on the sides of the mountains and in the clouds themselves in the painting *The Great Day of His Wrath* by John Martin. As the slopes of the cliffside progress downward and blend with the red, the area becomes darker and darker, creating an enormous contrast with the saturated red areas. Adding white to this dull red/green complementary mix will lighten the mixture to produce some very unusual tints and shades (see middle ground clouds, with lighter dull reds and greens).

John Martin's painting illustrates the power of saturated contrast. The center of the composition is a very saturated red-orange, in what appears to be an approaching smoky sunset. Below, the earth opens to reveal a lighter red-orange glow, which contrasts heavily against the darkest red-orange foreground. Fully half of the composition consists of a deep shaded red, which appears to have been dulled down by its complement of green.

Saturated contrast also can produce provocative emotional effects. Black added to violet seems to change the color to sudden dreariness. Such may be the case with

Simultaneous contrast basically refers to the manipulation of one color by placing it next to another. When placing a specified color next to another, one color will visually influence the character of the other hue in terms of value and intensity. Simultaneous contrast has an odd sort of similarity to that of complementary contrast in terms of psychological effects. Just as complements need each other, so do simultaneous contrasts when they pair with opposites.

One way simultaneous contrast functions is the pairing of two complements, especially red and green because they are of equal value. One should be able to see a thin gray line where the red and green meet in the center. This phenomenon has to do with mixing two complements. We mentioned earlier in the text that the mixing of two pigmented complements would result in the cancellation of the two colors. Basically, they physically cancel each other out. In simultaneous contrast, the eye mixes those two colors psychologically. Between the red and the green our eye produces gray.

Figure 4-45 JOHN MARTIN, *The Great Day of His Wrath*, 1851–53.

Simultaneous contrast can be created by contrasting achromatic values, chromatic and achromatic pairs, or by contrasting *near complements* of chroma. For reasons that we do not entirely understand, the human eye simultaneously requires the complement of any given color, and as we discussed in the previous chapter, the eye instinctively produces the complement in its physical absence. Needless to say, this effect enters into the psychological realm, because the actual complement does not have a physical existence, and cannot be recorded effectively. This experiment works best on a two-dimensional plane. Place two flat objects or pieces of paper in complementary colors together. Three-dimensional surfaces will create a gray shadow, which becomes a false substitute for the gray line that should be there instead.

Another way to achieve simultaneous contrast results can be observed in the above two examples. The gray squares are of the same value, but it is the influence of the saturated color that causes the gray squares to appear darker and lighter than the other, respectively. The gray square seems much more intense because the intensity of the yellow is causing the gray to lighten. The gray square also has a slight yellow tinge to it. The violet square influences its gray square, but in opposite fashion. The gray square is much darker because it is taking on the attributes of violet, which is the least intense, or darkest color. The gray square here clearly has violet tones. Needless to say, the remaining colors of red, orange, green, and blue will produce their own separate and commensurable influence over the same gray square.

The gray line effect can be measured in paintings as well as bar samples. The gray line effect diminishes when the hard-edged complements become less distinct.

The reproduction of Robert Indian's *Love* composition exhibits a reasonable example of *simultaneous contrast.* Both the saturation levels of the green and the red trick the eye into seeing that gray zone. In lesser effect, the *near complements* of red and blue will often produce a weaker version of that gray line.

Figure 4-48 ROBERT INDIANA, *LOVE,* 1967. This painting exhibits one version of simultaneous contrast. In the actual painting, the complements create a gray or neutral zone (line) between the green and the red letters.

as with yellow and blue, orange and violet, and red and blue. These all produce a variable gray zone, enhancing its neighboring color. In the case of orange and violet, for example, violet should cause the complement of orange, which is blue, to reflect back to itself. Orange in turn,

Figure 4-49 The influence of orange on the gray robe, as well as the additional walls and fixtures is obvious. The one saturated orange wall dominates the entire room in its ability to authority.

Figure 4-60 LA Gridlock.

Figure 4-62 The apple with the keyboard does not really function well as extension contrast. Although the apple is saturated red and the keyboard texture helps to draw attention to other areas (in a limited way), the remainder of the composition does not have the effective tints and shades of relevant contrasting colors to pull the eye through the composition. The apple remains the primary object.

of color balance. There are color contrast compositions, which incorporate percentage extreme ratios of as little as 3 to 5 percent, depending on the color, saturation, and intensity levels, plus imagery and emotional or mood concerns.

Of course, we know that mood content is polar as well, because saturated yellow has more upbeat qualities as opposed to the heavy and oppressing character of violet. Orange, while being fairly intense, does not have the equal brilliance to yellow. Because orange is much less intense, it is allowed more freedom within the percentage space. Blue also is less oppressive than violet, and commensurately, does not require as great of a percentage of space. This means that red and green are the perfect couple, because neither one requires more or less percentage space than the other. These ratios are only valid when the colors stated remain in their saturated form. Should any of these be tainted in any way, the stability or balance of contrast changes as well.

These are the basics of harmonious proportions. The term extension contrast then is allowing one color in the composition to dominate.

The warning flag at Waimea State Beach is a common site on the North Shore. It is a warning sign for those to think twice about going into the very dangerous surf. The red flag, in the lower center of the composition, is the first thing that the viewer notices. The saturated red flag controls the composition by virtue of its contrast extension. The vast expanse of blue is needed to balance the small amount of saturated red in the center. It actually takes that much blue in order to balance the small red flag in the picture. This is quite different from our standard color balance model, yet it does relate in an extreme sense. The smallest amount of red is balanced by the surrounding blues and orange sand, yet the flag

Figure 4-61 Warning flag at Waimea State Beach, North Shore, Oahu, Hawaii.

Figure 4-63 Pieter the Elder Brueghel, *Landscape with the Fall of Icarus*, 1558.

SCALA/ART RESOURCE, NY.

clearly dominates for attention. It takes a full extension of other colors out into the picture plane in order to balance the minor amount of red.

Another example of extension contrast can be seen in Pieter Brueghel's painting *Landscape with Fall of Icarus.*

The red shirt of the plowman in the center of the composition seems to perform brilliantly, as if to fight for attention in a vast expanse of light blue and light violet hues, against tints and shades of orange. Because the character of red is so aggressive, it holds credibility within the composition. The saturated red shirt of the plowman is not lost in the picture plane, as the tints and shades of dark oranges and light greens are not authoritative enough to keep the viewer's eye from the red shirt for any length of time. In one sense, the green and orange tints and shades are struggling to overcome the saturated red, while the red itself seems to be putting on a type of performance, trying to draw attention away from the other colors to itself.

In essence, extension contrast performs as an extreme version of color balance. Color balance is about specific percentages of complementary colors in harmony with one another, while extension is the competition of complements in a given space, or composition.

Extension contrast is captured in the photograph below which is a result of a two-hour traffic "snarl" in Southern California. At first glance, one is tempted to see the balance of complementary colors, yet the overall picture makes a better demonstration of *extension contrast.* The saturated orange shirt remains steadfastly in the center of the composition, while saturated blue pulls the eye out in every direction to see the entire picture. The greater part of the composition is neutral colors of gray values,

except the very background colors. Of course, this is not a perfect example, as is Brueghel's work, but it does serve to illustrate the *concept* of extension.

In the following essay, we will continue our studies of light and color. This time, we will begin to focus more closely on the functional components of light, the colors that are produced, and why. We will again look at the atomic structure, more specifically in relationship to colors produced by the particular elements in the outside natural environment.

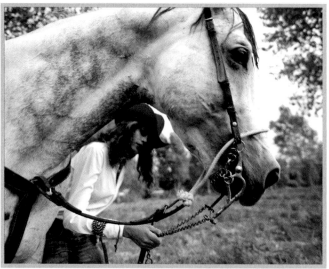

Figure 4-64 The equilibrium of color is dependent on the level of saturation of each complementary pair or color scheme. The only saturation in this photo is red. The remaining colors pale by comparison. In some cases, it is often necessary to create that imbalance in order to effect emotional appeal, mood, and dynamics in a given composition. Most certainly balance is a relative issue to the individual artist/designer, and knowing where and when to cross that line of balance.

HOLLY WILMETH/AURORA/GETTY IMAGES.

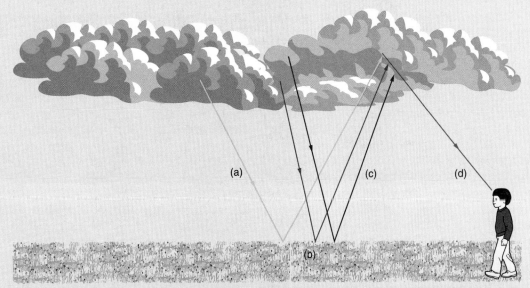

Figure 4-70 Reflected color in clouds. White sunlight (a) is scattered from cloud to hilltop. Flowering heather (b) absorbs green light preferentially, so blue and red are scattered preferentially (c) from the earth to water droplet and (d) back again. The cloud looks tinged with purple from the heather.

joins his image in the lake' and "the peasant drowns reaching for the moon." But the sea is not a faithful mirror. It is always darker than the sky because it does not reflect 100 percent of the light that reaches it, and it also is greener. The light that falls on the sea will be a mixture of white light radiating from the sun, white light scattered from clouds, blue light from the sky, and maybe a little light from the land. The light that travels from the sea to the observer comes by two routes. Some of it is reflected from the surface of the sea, and the color of this is the same as the color of the light shining on it. Other light may be reflected off the bottom of the sea; the color of this light obviously depends on the color of the sea bed. If this were covered with red coral, which absorbs all colors except red, the light reflected

from the sea bed would be red. The sea would be magenta, as the observer would receive a mixture of blue and red light. But even if the sea bed were silver sand, the light reflected from the bottom would differ from the surface reflection because the water itself is very weakly colored. It absorbs red light and so looks bluish green. The depth of the color naturally increases with the water's depth; the red component of sunlight is almost totally absorbed by a hundred feet of water. Looking down from a cliff or from an airplane on to the coastline of a calm sea, we find the shallows charted in pale aquamarine, which darkens with depth, through clear blue-greens to sapphire.

The absorption of red light by water is dramatically illustrated by the Blue Grotto in Capri. This cave is connected

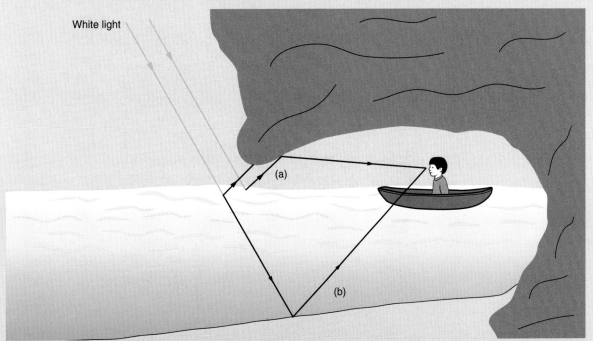

Figure 4-71 The Blue Grotto. Of the little white light which enters the grotto by path (a), much is absorbed by the rock. Most of the light reaching the boatman has traveled along route (b), passing twice through a 7-meter layer of seawater, which absorbs most of the red light.

to the open sea through a semi-circular hole only about 2.5 meters in diameter. Almost all the light which enters the eye of an observer inside the grotto has been reflected off the very pale sea bed about 7 meters below the surface. As the sunlight therefore passes through at least 14 meters of water, an appreciable proportion of its red component is absorbed. So the water looks gleaming azure.

As waves break, the water is flung into the air in a myriad of drops, and at each surface between air and water, sunlight is scattered, irrespective of wavelength, as from a cloud. So flying surf looks white, as does the foam at the sea's edge where air is momentarily encapsulated in bubbles of sea.

We return some twelve hours later to see the sun sinking behind black headlands in a blaze of red. The sunlight which reaches us has traveled through a much greater thickness of atmosphere at this late hour than it did around noon. Most of the blue light has been scattered away, as has much of the green and yellow; but the red and orange reaches us. As the sky to the east is dark blue, shading to emerald, a little blue light must have gotten through, and is being scattered back, together with light of the next highest energy, green. In an hour or so the only sunlight reaching us will be that reflected off the moon; and in moonlight we see no color.

Sunsets are much influenced by the number and size of water droplets and solid particles in the air and are particularly spectacular after volcanic explosions, which throw large quantities of very fine dust into the atmosphere. The scattering of light can also give rise to a range

Figure 4-73 Inside the Blue Grotto, Capri, Italy.

of less garish colors which can be seen when snorkeling on a sunny day in a calm sea. A swimmer who looks horizontally toward the sun, just under the surface of the water, sees the sea almost as golden green. Much of the blue and violet has been scattered away, and some of the red has been absorbed. An about-turn sometimes produces a transformation scene in which the color of the sea passes from green-grape and turquoise to a rich, though soft, blue-violet. When we are looking away from the sun,

Figure 4-72

promoted to regions even further from the center of the atom. The color of the light emitted when the atoms revert to the state of lowest energy is characteristic of that particular type of atom. The yellow flame to table salt is exactly the same as that produced by washing soda, caustic soda, or sodium bicarbonate and is caused by the presence of sodium.

Flame colors have long been used to identify chemical elements: a deep green flame is characteristic of copper, and pale mauve which is often seen over a wood fire, is caused by potassium, which is absorbed by plants from the soil. Nowadays, the intensity of flame color can be used to measure both the amount of the element which is present and the temperature of the flame. Atomic flame colors are exploited more frivolously by manufacturers of fireworks, who have access also to less familiar substances. The heads of "Bengal matches," for example, contain either lithium, which produces a rich crimson flame, or barium, which gives a lime green one. Relatively few elements, however, produce colored flames, which accounts for the rather restricted palette available to the pyrotechnist.

VEGETABLE COLORS

Since only a small fraction of dry land is covered with bare rock, sand, or snow, or with buildings, minerals make a limited contribution to the color of the earth's surface. Seen from the air, most of the land, as any air traveller can testify, is covered with vegetation: forest, grassland, crops, or scrub. During the growing season, leaves account for almost all the surface area of most types of plant. The landscape looks mainly green while the leaves are young, though the colors may change through yellow and red to brown as the year proceeds. But it is not solely the leaves which impart their colors to the landscape. A bare forest shows a range of subtle browns and the heather-clad hills of Scotland are smoky purple. Cultivation has brought us orchards of fruit blossoms and fields of spring bulbs. European farmland is studded with patches of dusky-blue lucerne and acid-yellow rape. Few British wildflowers, other than heather, monopolize enough expanse to determine the color of a distant landscape, but several provide

around ... cobalt nucleus in ... with chlo-
ride ...) when dry, and (b) after absorption of a little
water, .

which will emit light of other wavelengths. Coke, for example, burns with a clear blue flame, produced by excited oxides of carbon. The flames of domestic cookers and heaters differ from those of candles or fires because air does not just seep into the hot gaseous fuel but is premixed into the unignited gas. In coal gas, the color of the flame varies markedly with proportion of air in the mixture. A low ratio of air to fuel produces a yellow flame similar to that of a candle, while a high proportion of air to gas gives a hotter, clearer blue flame with a turquoise central cone, containing oxygen-plus-hydrogen groups. Natural gas is chemically more akin to candle wax, and—when mixed generously with air, burns with a blue flame composed of an inner cone similar to that at the base of a candle flame a paler, greener middle cone and a more purple outer cone.

Flames, like solids, can be strongly colored by the presence of very small amounts of impurities. A crystal of table salt will color the flame of a gas stove bright yellow. Pale mauve flames sometimes flicker over a particularly hot bonfire, and if any fine copper wire finds its way into a fire, it colors the flames emerald green. These colors are owed to individual atoms which have gained so much energy from the fire that one or more of their outer electrons has been

Figure 4-84 The Hills of Glen Quoich, Glen Garry, West Inverness-shire, Scottish Highlands.

Figure 4-82 Brilliant cut diamond on blue background.

or the observer, moves slightly the light which enters the eye is first of one almost pure color, then of another. Modern imitations may disperse and reflect light equally impressively. Their sparkle rivals that of a real diamond, though they lack its extreme hardness.

Some of the most beautiful colors of the mineral world are caused by optical interference. Precious opal, like soap solution, absorbs little visible light. It is made up almost entirely of silica and water. But part of the structure consists of regularly stacked spheres, and reflections from neighboring groups of these may interfere. Depending on the angle of viewing, light of one or more wavelengths is cancelled out. The opal acts as a diffraction grating. Legend maintains that the exact color of an opal is sensitive to the well-being of the wearer, and it is indeed possible that the spacing between spheres varies with changes in temperature and in the humidity of the skin. The mineral labradorite shows similar iridescence, usually in the color range from royal blue to kingfisher, green, and gold. These peacock colors are superimposed on a background of dull gray, which is caused by thin sheets of oxides of iron or titanium embedded in a colorless feldspar mineral. The iridescence arises through the interference of light reflected from different layers of oxide, the exact color depending on the spacing and orientation of the layers and on the viewing angle. The less exotic iridescence observed by Goethe on "the surface of stagnant water, especially if impregnated with iron," interference also arises from layers of iron oxide.

We have seen that many solids change color when they are heated. The change may be permanent. Clays and earth pigments, such as raw sienna, lose water on heating and acquire a much redder hue. Their structure is permanently

combine with oxygen and change color bright copper coin merely acquires a black coating of copper oxide, but for many substances, 'oxidation' is accompanied by burning. The light emitted by the flames often shows beautiful colors that depend on the substance being burned and on the rate of supply of both fuel and air to the different regions of the flame. We are so familiar with domestic flames from matches, candles, cooking gas, and fires that it may seem surprising that many of the changes which take place within them are extremely complicated and by no means fully understood.

If we look at a steady candle flame, we can see three main regions: a transparent blue base, a grayish semi-transparent central cone, and an opaque, bright-yellow outer cone. When the candle is lit, the wax liquefies, rises up the wick and vaporizes. Oxygen diffuses into the gaseous wax and combines with it, eventually producing carbon dioxide and steam while giving out considerable heat. At the high temperature produced, the wax breaks down into very small, highly excited groups of atoms (such as "dicarbon" and "carbon-plus-hydrogen") which, at the base of the flame, rid themselves of some of their energy by emitting blue light. Higher up the carbon atoms may join together and form relatively large conglomerates, or soot particles, which become "yellow-hot" and glow, forming the bright, opaque outer cone of the flame.

Flames produced when other substances burn may naturally contain other small, excited groups of atoms

The land of Japan is an interesting summary of contrast. Japan traditionally, is all about red and green. Through- out Japan the theme of humankind and nature is part of the past, and continues today. The red of humanity's *desire* as opposed to the *tranquil* green of the natural world are often opposites in character, yet they come together peacefully to complement one another. This entrance has an odd serenity about it. Even though the small shrine area is bathed in saturated red, it merely accents the remaining area, and tells those attending that this is a very important place. It's a great example of saturation contrast.

No matter where you are in Japan, complementary contrast dominates the landscape. At some point, one becomes so aware of this, that one begins to notice color harmonies, even in the less obvious—a young girl walks

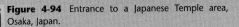
Figure 4-94 Entrance to a Japanese Temple area, Osaka, Japan.

PHOTO BY THE AUTHOR.

Figure 4-95 Girl with a red umbrella.

PHOTO BY THE AUTHOR.

Figure 4-96 Heian Shrine, Kyoto Japan.

PHOTO BY THE AUTHOR.

past creating a dyad harmony of red and green. The colorist will immediately notice that instant of color in time.

In Chapter 5, we will discuss the different color harmonies, one of which is a dyadic color harmony, in greater detail. Dyads are complements, one of which is red and green. Color harmony in Japan is paramount to truly understand Japan's past as a culture.

The dark, as opposed to light, provides stimulating contrast for the evenings. Notice the various functions of contrast:

Contrasts are seen in *serene* ancient castle settings and as *energized* modern cityscapes. Contrast also is obvious here as *the old and the new*.

Contrast comes in many forms color of lights in darkness, colors of contrast by day, serene and tranquil, as well as the old and the new. Life itself is full of contrasts, which ultimately can be translated into color functions such as symbolism, mood, and emotion appeal.

PHOTO BY THE AUTHOR.

Figure 4-97 Japanese Lanterns in Kyoto.

PHOTO BY THE AUTHOR.

Figure 4-98 Street Sign in Kyoto at Night.

PHOTO BY THE AUTHOR.

Figure 4-99 Osaka Castle, Osaka.

PHOTO BY THE AUTHOR.

Figure 4-100 Tokyo Shopping District—Sunshine City.

Summary

In Chapter 4, Contrast, we discussed;

1. The nature and importance of color contrast and its function to provide focal points, create depth of space, as well as to help color mood and emotional responses.
2. Once again, the Rose Window of the Notre Dame de Paris was briefly seen as an example of how contrast affects the interior space.
3. The seven various forms of contrast are dark and light, hue, complementary, warm and cool, saturation, simultaneous, and lastly, extension (balance).
4. The formation and function of color in air and water.

In the next chapter, *Tints-Shades and Value Systems,* we will study value and find out how our studies in contrast relate directly to this process. Contrast is the overt and obvious change of hues, values, and saturations, but tints and shades deal with the more subtle nuances related to contrast.

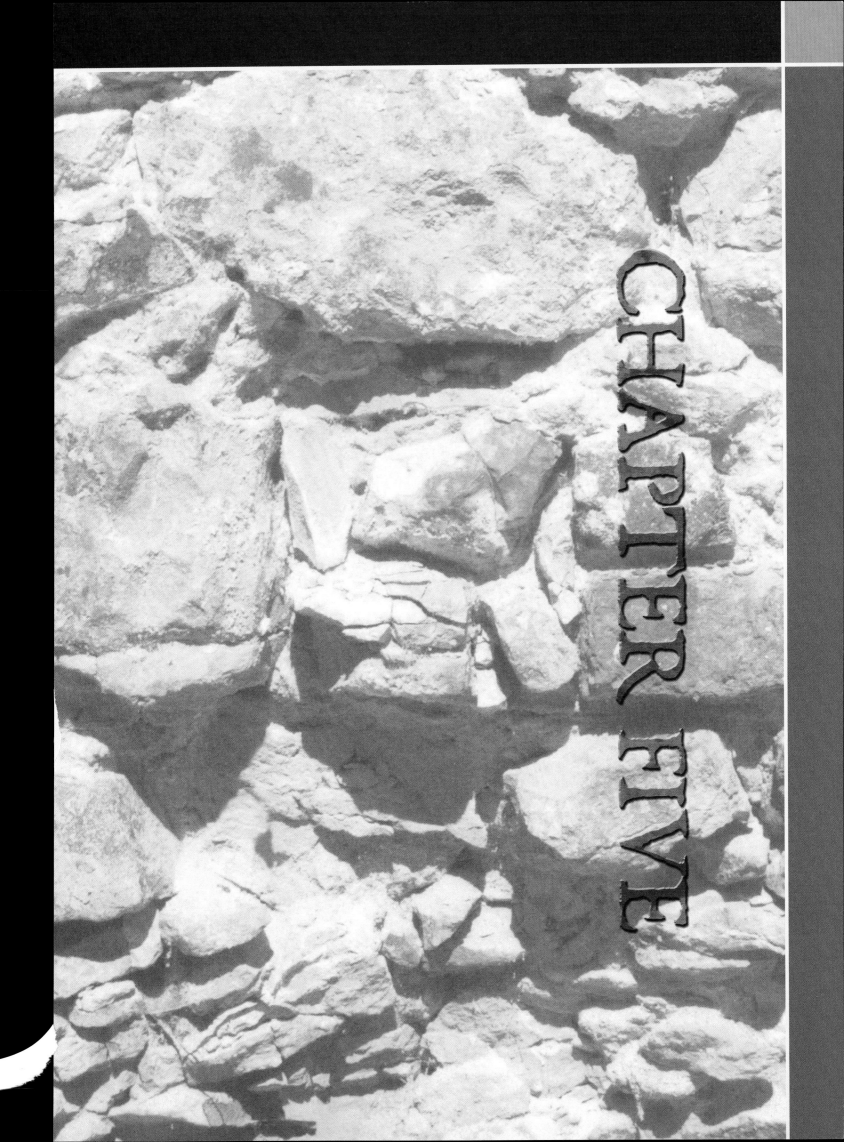

CHAPTER FIVE

Figure 5-1 Wat Rongkun, Chiang Rai, Northern Thailand. This extraordinary temple is unique in all of Thailand in that it is completely white. It is a very mysterious and intriguing site to behold. The temple pictured against the white clouds and translucent sky seems to be of another world, or a connection from this world to the next. This photo selection was made because of its excellent portrayal of the function of tints and shades. The value gradations in this temple distinguish the complex nature of shapes and forms that create the visual textures.

PHOTO BY THE AUTHOR.

5

TINTS AND SHADES—VALUE SYSTEMS

MASS, VOLUME, ILLUSION OF FORM IN DIMENSIONAL SPACE, AND FOCAL POINTS

Earlier in the text, we discussed values within chromatic and achromatic applications. In reality, *tints and shades* are another way of talking about value gradations—dark to light, chromatic values, and black to white gradations. *Tints* refer to the addition of white and *shades* refer to the addition of black to a given hue.

Attributes of the Value System:

- Manipulation of tints and shades consistently throughout a given composition controls the overall tonal quality of the artwork.
- Tints and shades create atmospheric perspective, controlling the degree of the illusion of depth of space.
- Tints and shades produce the illusion of form, or three dimensions in space, as well as limits dimensional capabilities. Tints and shades represent mass and volume.
- Tints and shades create extreme value gradations, which produce high contrasting areas or forms of high contrast. These results produce greater dimension and more obvious focal points.
- Illusion of surface texture.

In this chapter, we want to make investigations into tints and shades through specific examples in order to fully understand their exact functions. Without value gradations, all would be flat and without the illusion of reality. We will observe styles and time periods to see how tints and shades function as well as their overall importance in art.

Let's take a look at tints and shades (values) through a historical context.

THE CLASSICAL WORLD

Even the Romans understood the impact of tints and shades. As we take a look at some of the frescoes in the luxurious capitol of Italy within the lavish homes in the city of Pompeii, we can see evidence of the artist's struggle to understand how gradations of values functioned to indicate space and form.

In the house of Marcus Lucretius Fronto (Figure 5-2), this frescoed wall is rendered with the figures of Mars and Venus on the left. In the central area of the panel, Eros can be seen with groups of servant girls observing a scene nearby. We can almost detect the struggle of Roman artists who were striving to develop the idea of creating three-dimensional figures in space. Even though there is still a reasonable degree of flat space felt in the wall fresco, there are obvious attempts to create mass (form) by value variations seen in the drapery and fabrics worn by the participants in the picture. Even though artists had not at this point refined the process of value gradations, it is evident that they were well into understanding the subject. Furthermore, this elegant pigmented wall exhibits competent hue contrasts, creating a marginal depth of space in the composition.

Figure 5-2 Fresco Painting in the House of Marcus Lucretius Fronto at Pompeii.

THE MIDDLE AGES

In eleventh-century Gothic cathedral windows, we also see evidence of value variations within the individual glass constructions. The introduction of value gradations into stained glass was a major accomplishment early in the development of colors in glass. However, it wasn't until after the French Revolution that tints and shades were developed to their full potential. The variation of actual hues was not easily accomplished, but craftspeople did figure out how to introduce dark pigments into the colors of glass. The chapel window image found in St. Severin Cathedral (Figure 5-3) is an example of the important effect of tints and shades. The tints and shades of the drapery are skillfully controlled, creating a dimensional quality in the window. The values seen in the faces of Jesus and his disciples are essential to establish the expression necessary to convey the emotion of the situation.

An even more definitive use of values is demonstrated in this archival chapel (Figure 5-4) in *Notre Dame de Paris*. Here, we can see that tints and shades are very important in creating greater detail in the faces of the six figures. The delicate handling of tints and shades lends a believable texture to the skin and enhances the three-dimensional form itself.

Figure 5-4 Chapel Window of the St. Severin Cathedral, Paris.

Figure 5-3 Partial Window in Archival Room at Notre Dame de Paris.

The Renaissance Age

Early in Michelangelo's career, he knew he was to be a sculptor. The problem was the Pope needed walls embellished with Biblical references. This was a much higher priority for the church because its message would be available in a full grandiose visual format to both believers and nonbelievers. Basically, Michelangelo was told that he would need to conform to the wishes of the Pope if he were to survive as an artist in Italy. This was disconcerting to him, because he adored the medium of sculpting. In due course, Michelangelo painted for the Vatican by day, and sculpted for himself by night.

This bears mentioning because of his love for three-dimensional form. So much was his desire toward sculpting that we see it conveyed or converted into painted frescoes. Many believe that he actually sculpted vicariously through his frescoes and thus his incredibly accomplished results are seen on the Sistine Chapel ceiling (Figure 5-5). Never before had figures leaped off a flat surface in this manner. His ability to control *tints and shades* is astonishing to say the least. Michelangelo's control over value gradations was ever so tightly controlled, as if he were methodically chipping away at a sculpture. He meticulously developed his tints and shades.

Figure 5-5 Michelangelo Buonarroti, ***The Creation of Adam***, 1510.

Early American Realism

Turn-of-the-century American Realism artist Paul Cadmus records the famous event of Pocahontas saving Captain John Smith (Figure 5-6). Just as he is about to be slain for his illegitimate relationship with the young and seductive Pocahontas, she rushes in to protect him from death. He is spared because of her love for him, and as the story continues, all turns out well for them in this dynamic love story.

The dynamics of the Pocahontas love story also are visually reproduced in large part by the effect of tints and shades, or value gradations. This drawing is exemplary of the *chiaroscuro* value system, with borderline *tenebristic* effects (see the *three types of value variations* following this discussion), which illustrates the illusion of three-dimensional figures in space. The *chiaroscuro* system builds up a gradient of dark to light achromatic values across the composition that develops physically powerful figures. It is the strong gradations of values in the borderline *tenebristic* effects that help to create the severity of the situation, as the drama grows and the theatrical positions of the figures act out their roles. The value gradations actually produce a rather harsh transition, which again accentuates the extreme spectacle with its dramatic diagonal figures in the composition. Pocahontas is the key figure, because the powerful diagonal line created by her form interrupts the vertical stance of the two warriors and the horizontal band of kneeling figures. The diagonal line of her body is continued by the standing warrior's shoulder and left raised arm.

Figure 5-6 PAUL CADMUS, *Pocahontas Saving the Life of Captain John Smith*, 1939.

MODERN AND CONTEMPORARY

Shijo's imagery representing *Aiko's Dream* (Figure 5-7) is predominately about chromatic tints and shades. These strange abstracts seem to set up a certain flatness in the composition, while the tints and shades seen in the figures indicate a nominal degree of three-dimensional mass. This manipulation of tints and shades creates the *implication* of 3-D form, but not the *illusion*. Implication only infers a certain degree of form in space, but illusion produces the deception of being tangible. The intense yellow ground could be interpreted as the middle ground or background, and the same, respectively, for the violet triangular-shaped area. The use of tints and shades tends to confuse the eye, and therefore create flat, fractured planes of color that seem to overwhelm the potential for constructing the illusion of mass. Basically, tints and shades produce a certain mass, as well as the deception that there is measurable depth of space in the foreground, middle ground, and background. The flat planes, however, minimize those effects by their complexity of placement. The composition effectively creates the *dream state,* in that it is somewhat unclear and confusing—nothing is absolute or makes complete sense. The tints and shades help to invent the mysterious nature of these abstract figures as they transform from abstract simplistic forms to a more representational version.

Rousseau's dream imagery (Figure 5-8) is abstract and simple. Like Shijo's work, the images do demonstrate a certain degree of three-dimensional mass, yet in a limited way. The tints and shades are extremely consistent in their dark to light gradations across the flora and fauna in the composition. The background is constructed of uniform dark value variations, while the foreground illustrates a commensurable uniformity of lighter value gradations. The uniformity of gradient values in the foreground, background, and plant life tend to greatly flatten the composition. We know there is the perception of spatial depth, but the painting lacks the actual feeling or illusion of that space. However, the contrast of a horizontal band of very light tints and shades in the extreme foreground assists in creating limited illusional space.

Figure 5-7 SHIJO, ***Dream of Aiko.***

Figure 5-8 HENRI ROUSSEAU, *The Dream*,1910.

THE ANIMATED WORLD

Within the arena of *animation,* value gradations of tints and shades are imperative for creating certain types of contrast, which in turn creates focal points, dimensional mass, volume, and depth of space. The importance of tints and shades in animation, for example, can be illustrated by making a comparison between earlier animation and current applications in respect to their chromatic values.

Betty Boop, one of the early animated figures especially popular in the 1950s, was basically shapes defined by contour line, and then filled in with color, which is void of any value variation (see Figure 5-9, left image). In the earliest years of animation, value gradations in the figure (because they were all black and white) were mostly nonexistent. It was totally up to the viewer to imagine that they were seeing a three-dimensional form. Later on, a flat cartoon personality was typically rendered onto a clear sheet of acetate material. Next, that sheet was then inserted over a background scene, which had a full complement of value gradations.

With the help of shaded backgrounds, it became easier for the viewer to imagine this flat figure to be a three-dimensional form. During the early years, when television was a fairly new commodity, the viewer's imagination was the key component for animated forms, in a generation of so many new inventions.

In the twenty-first century, we find that hand-painted cels are rapidly becoming a thing of the past, as we have advanced to the point where we now employ more advanced technology. Digital processes have enhanced animation capabilities, and of course made the process much quicker and more effective.

Betty Boop's image (see Figure 5-9, right image) now has been created with the advantage of added chromatic values. The tints and shades have created an extraordinarily more believable image dimensionally. In much of animation today, with some exceptions such as the Pokemon series, the heavy line is no longer necessary, because tints and shades have produced a more believable three-dimensional form. The

Figure 5-9 Betty Boop. Classic Betty on Left. Right figure depicts Betty with added tints and shades.

Figure 5-10 The animated Laura Croft illustrates the magic of tints and shades to create the illusion of three-dimensional form in deep space.

contour line form today may only exist as a stylistic emphasis, but not necessary otherwise.

The *fully reclined figure* of Lara Croft (Figure 5-10) demonstrates tints and shades in the *chiaroscuro* value system, that is to say, the average gradation of dark to light, and back again. These value transitions here show us the importance of contrasts set up by tints and shades. The light to dark areas create the three-dimensional effects of the body. Her upright legs illustrate the most extreme value changes, and also create the maximum three-dimensional illusion. Compare the difference between her face, which is somewhat less dimensional than her legs, and the rest of her body. Dark and more subtle transitions of values occur in her face, while lighter and more severe gradations can be seen in her vertically extended legs. Her shoulders and arms reflect a moderate value range. Darker transitions in one area and lighter transitions in another help to create a greater sense of foreshortened space, moving the figure into its appropriate positions from the foreground to the background. Notice the slow transitions of shaded violets behind her right shoulder and arm. The contrast setup is significant between the right arm—with its rapid gradations of orange tints—and the background. The light tints of violet behind her elevated legs provide high contrast with the very intense light orange values of the legs.

Also apparent is the illusion of three-dimensional mass in space, as well as a certain perception of her skin texture. The slow and gradual yet wide range of warm orange

contrasted against violet tints and shades create the quiet and relaxed mood of the character.

KEY COLOR

We often use the terminology *Key* color, such as in a high key or low key composition. *Key* makes reference to the overall *tonal value*, whether in a painting, computer screen, or motion pictures. *Tone,* of course, can refer to shade, tint, color, hue, or value. In most applications, we

Figure 5-11 Li Man, Curse of the Golden Dragon.

use the word tone to refer more to the values and hues in a given composition, such as the film still of *Li Man* from the *Curse of the Golden Dragon* (Figure 5-11). This scene illustrates a dynamic contrast of *warm red tones.* It is basically tonally red, from tinted to shaded red tones throughout.

High key exhibits a very light or even white ground, and the images are illuminated to some degree as well. High key is more about *intensity* or tints, for that matter. Figure 5-12 is from one of the all-time classic films, *Gone with the Wind.* This image is an excellent example of *high key.* The background as well as Clark Gable and Vivien Leigh, is highly lit, and it is only the dark garments that provide any noticeable degree of contrast of value.

Low key, as demonstrated in Figure 5-13, is the opposite of high key in that we see a dark background and figures that are almost silhouetted. Low key is much less visible (low light) and is not about intensity, but rather very dark shades. Low key often addresses issues such as creating a mysterious or romantic mood.

audience had to rely solely on the actor's ability to convey emotion in order to create the appropriate mood response. By comparing the achromatic version of *Gone with the Wind* with the low-key color image, we can understand why color was such an extraordinary change for the television and movie industry. The low-key colors of the picture assist the actors in conveying the maximum emotion possible.

Figure 5-13

Figure 5-12 Vivien Leigh and Clark Gable in *Gone with the Wind.*

Figure 5-14 demonstrates what we call medium or intermediate key. Here we see a very *saturated* composition of pure colors with high contrast. Medium key is the *norm* of keys, or right in the middle of high-key low-key color. This key is what we see most often. Medium key is normally used in advertising, especially in terms of movie posters, billboards, and book jackets.

The original black and white version (achromatic values) of *Gone with the Wind* (Figure 5-15). At the 1939 début, the

Figure 5-14

Figure 5-15

The following image is another example of medium key effects. Several images are offered concerning this issue, in order to make clear the three key zones.

Figure 5-16 Medium Key—Chiaroscuro Relationship.

Medium key in Figure 5-16 also closely relates one of the value systems known as chiaroscuro, discussed on the following pages. The Italian word chiaroscuro gives reference to light and dark, and is used in the art world to discuss the effects of illusionary depth of space and the creation of volume and mass on a two-dimensional surface. Additionally, this should not be confused with ten-

nibrism, which is extreme and sudden value shifts of light and dark, particularly on figurative elements. Chiaroscuro is more about the compositional whole set-up by bold light and dark contrasts. The portrait above illustrates a moderate, yet bold transition of dark to light values on the skin, and creates an audacious light and dark transition in the figure/ground relationship.

Yet another illustration of the keys, particularly in skin tones can be seen in Figure 5-17, which demonstrative of chiaroscuro, but with a lighter figure and darker background. Notice that the value gradations create a bold

Figure 5-17 Medium Key.

Figure 5-18 High Key.

Figure 5-19 Low Key.

figure/ground relationship. The value transitions on the surface of her skin, is bold and creates a degree of mass not seen in the other two examples.

The high key photograph (Figure 5-18) is obviously quite different in that it is very intense and the gradations of value are very subtle. There is a figure/ground relationship here that is more intimate, since there is a relative closeness in values and less depth of space.

The low key example (Figure 5-19) has the least amount of light on the surface, and once again demonstrates a more delicate value shifts across the skin surface.

THE THREE VALUE SYSTEMS

Sfumato, Chiaroscuro, and Tenebrism

The value systems, whether chromatic or achromatic, have a certain relationship with contrast. Contrast, as we previously studied, is to draw a distinction between various color elements such as light and dark, complements, warm and cool, and the like. A composition normally possesses both contrast and value, but the difference between the two is dissimilarity of properties (contrast), and the range between light and dark, or *gradations* of light to dark (value). These gradations of value create the illusion of form in space.

Because the Mona Lisa is such a monumental western icon, we shall use that image as the emphasis for value. The painting owes its greatness to Leonardo da Vinci's

sensitive application of chromatic values. His delicate methodology of rendering tints and shades is second to none in the art world. Lets see why that is so.

Sfumato

The first of the value systems is the word sfumato, which can be defined *as the subtle gradation of values from light to dark and back again. It is as subtle as the variances in smoke itself.* Sfumato means vanished in smoke (*Italian*). da Vinci first created the effect of sfumato in painting. Attributes of sfumato are those that create the most subtle and delicate gradations of value. The Mona Lisa's face is comprised of subtle nuances of value gradations as a result of tints and shades. In fact, the entire composition is subtle and quiet with sfumato effects. Some say it was not finished because of the lack of detail in the background, and compared to the face of the Mona Lisa, it certainly does lack the detail we are accustomed to seeing. Yet the background has that smoky sfumato effect and the lack of detail helps us focus on the portrait of the lady herself.

The following page shows approximately how the Mona Lisa appears today (Figure 5-20), after her last restoration. The face of Mona Lisa is without question the most significant area of the painting, particularly because of its luminosity of tints. The Mona Lisa's face is, in fact, a series of thin layers of vermillion and burnt umber used in variations with lead white. Additionally, lead-tin yellow, iron,

Figure 5-20 LEONARDO DA VINCI, *Mona Lisa*, 1503-6, after the restoration.

Material Analysis of the Mona Lisa

SURFACE: Poplar Wood Panel.
BINDER: Walnut Oil.
TECHNIQUES: Thin layers of washes and glazes, particularly in translucent pigments.
SPECIAL SIGNIFICANCE: Stands alone in technical prowess and in the power of illusion.

ALABASTER: White - calcium sulfate [ground preparation coat-base].
AZURITE: Blue-copper - carbonate hydroxide [sky and landscape].
BITUMEN: Black to dark brown - bituminous coal [unconfirmed in the painting].
BURNT UMBER: Darkest yellow, appears as darkest reddish-orange - earth pigment [background].
CARBON BLACK: Black - charred animal bones or grape vines, soot (chemisorbed oxygen complexes) [face].
IRON OXIDE: Deep red to red-orange - iron and manganese oxide mixture gives burnt umber its specific hue, which is a key component in the creation of Leonardo's sfumato technique on Lisa [face and small amounts on flesh tones].
LAPIS LAZULI: Blues and blue-greens - feldspathiod silicates, calcite, sodalite and pyrite [distant ground and sky].
LEAD WHITE: White - basic lead (II) carbonate [flesh tints and sky].

LEAD-TIN YELLOW: Yellow - enhances luminosity in various colors [flesh tints, landscape, and small amounts in the dress].
MALACHITE: Green - basic copper (II) carbonate [landscape].
MANGANESE: Brown pigment - manganese oxide [flesh].
NAPLES YELLOW: Deep yellow-orange - lead (II) antimonite [flesh tints].
RED OCHRE: Dark red - earth pigment of anhydrous iron (III) oxide / silica and clay with iron [landscape and used to darken dress].
RED LAKE: Translucent red - from the Kermes Oak insect [flesh tones, mostly thin layers on the hands].
SAFFRON: Luminous warm saturated red-orange - red-orange stigmas create warm rich tones of red-orange, and the yellow stamens enhance translucency in pigmented color [unconfirmed, but likely used in the Mona Lisa].
UMBER: Dark yellow-brown - earth pigment of manganese and iron [landscape and flesh].
VERDIGRIS: Green - copper acetates [dress-often turned brown with oil].
VERONA GREEN: Blue-green to dull yellow-green - celadonite and glauconitic [landscape].
VERMILLION: Red - eerived from cinnabar, mercuric sulfide [flesh tints].
YELLOW OCHRE: Dull golden yellow or dark yellow - earth pigment of silica and clay; coloring agent is iron oxide [traces on the dress].

Figure 5-21 *Mona Lisa*—Achromatic Value.

Figure 5-22 The *Mona Lisa* Before Its Final Cleaning and Initial Restoration. The full effect of the *luminous* quality in her skin had been somewhat disguised for a number of years before the cleaning. The extraordinary sfumato technique, which is so eloquently demonstrated in *Lisa's* skin tones, could not be completely comprehended until the final unveiling in 2005. Layers of yellowing varnish had subdued *Mona Lisa's* smoky values, but now her greatest attributes as they create soft, supple skin and gives grace and sophistication the world's most famous lady.

Figure 5-23 Chiaroscuro in Real Life.

The Mona Lisa stands out clearly from his earlier work as well because he began using less lead white, which hindered or blocked the light generated by the surface. The use of less opaque white allowed the reflecting capabilities of the poplar ground to produce depth through the thin transparent colored layers.

Compare the almost miraculous gradations of value with those that are created in *computer programming,* and you will be all the more astounded at Leonardo's technique with pigmented value.

Chiaroscuro

Chiaroscuro is the *average gradation of value from light to dark, or from dark to light.* It is a step up from sfumato in that the gradation of values are less "smoky." In Picasso's *Renaissance Maternity* (Figure 5-24), chiaroscuro is demonstrated by the "moderate" succession of value gradients or steps toward dark, or conversely, to light. By "average gradation" we are talking about the standard term used to describe value successions in a general sense.

Chiaroscuro is the primary system used to create believable three-dimensional objects in space, whether by chroma or achromatically. It is neither smoky or extreme in its gradient. In Figure 5-23 average lighting seen on the woman's face, is another example of this effect. The value gradient is

and manganese have been detected in the flesh tones. According to Leonardo, the incorporation of *red lake* (from the insect of the kermes oak) was used as well. Pigments were actually ground into the binding agent, therefore creating various levels of refractive capabilities for the portrayal of volume and mass. This formula is applied in thin *translucent* layers of glazes, which produce an infinite possibility for tinting subtleties. Shading shadows are so precisely and gracefully blended, as the variations in smoke; hence, the word sfumato.

Figure 5-24 PABLO PICASSO, *Renaissance Maternity,* Dinard, Summer, 1922.

Figure 5-25 MICHELANGELO MERISI DA CARAVAGGIO, *The Conversion of Saint Paul*, 1660/1601.

moderate in its association with the surface skin. While the shaded side of her face seems "smoky" in gradient transitions, it is the overall facial surface, particularly the lighted side, which creates the unmistakable chiaroscuro.

Tenebrism

Tenebrism is the extreme and often sudden value gradation from light to dark and back again. Often tenebrism is so extreme in its gradation that it seems to shift suddenly from dark to light with little or seemingly no transitional area of gray values between. Tenebrism produces the most harsh tints and shades of the three value systems and is decidedly the most theatrical.

In *The Conversion of Saint Paul* (Figure 5-25), as is often the case in Caravaggio's work, we see the effects of tenebrism in full force. The actual account of this event is found in the New Testament book of Acts. To eliminate

any confusion, it is necessary to point out that Paul's name before his conversion was Saul of Tarsus. Saul was a Roman officer who regularly persecuted Christians, not long after the crucifixion of Jesus Christ. Christians were brought to Jerusalem on a frequent basis, as sanctioned by the emperor, and were persecuted and/or put to death for their faith.

One early morning, Saul sets off on a regular mission to search for Christians. Suddenly, a burst of intense light illuminates everyone in the search party, and Saul himself falls off of his horse from the resultant intensity of the light. As Saul lies on the ground blinded by the light, the Lord begins to speak to him by saying, "Saul, Saul, why are you persecuting Me?" Saul inquires as to whom he is speaking, and after a short conversation, he is led back into the city, where he stays with a certain disciple for a period of three days. After three days have passed, Saul's blind eyes unexpectedly are opened again. Saul's physical sight is not the only thing that was restored. His *spiritual eyes* also are opened. Saul converts to Christianity, and now *Saul of Tarsus* has become *Paul the Apostle,* who grew to be one of the foundation saints of the church.

Caravaggio builds extreme light and dark transitional areas of tenebristic values, focusing on the fallen figure of Saul. Even though light is flooding the surface of the horse's left side, Saul is still the focus. All through the composition, tenebrism reigns with the extreme dark to light conversions, with a minimum of transitional gray tones. The mass or three-dimensional form of Saul's arms are very tenebristic values. We are looking at an undetermined amount of deep space, mass, and focal emphasis, all a result of values in tenebrism.

Finally, a beautiful execution of tinted and shaded pigments can be observed in the ceiling of one of many rooms within the Palace of Versailles (Figure 5-26). The immediate observation is the high contrast between light and dark. The figure in the corner of the ceiling is in high contrast with the dark, low-key background. When standing in the room itself, it is almost impossible to discern whether it is the illusion of a three-dimensional figure or an actual sculpture. The execution of value gradations in this painted ceiling is astounding, as the extreme high contrast of dark and light causes the form to "pop" away from the rest of the painted surface.

The Versailles ceiling demonstrates two of the three value systems. The smoky background of the ceiling seems very reminiscent of the *sfumato* effects of Leonardo da Vinci's *Mona Lisa*. Also, the effects of *chiaroscuro* are responsible for the development of the illusion of three-dimensional mass in the foreground figure.

The maximum effect of contrasts of value are well planned by the architect and the artist. The highly recessed or vaulted ceiling omits much of the glare, which enters the room via the large palace windows (lower left corner). The optimal function of sfumato and high contrast is therefore allowed to accomplish its major function, which is to accentuate the figure and its mass.

Figure 5-26 Palace of Versailles, France—Interior Room; Corner Ceiling. Value systems can create a startling 3-D illusion. At the Palace of Versailles, a figurative form is revealed in the corner ceiling, which makes us feel an illusional separation from the wall. High contrast between the background colors and the foreground figure aid in the effects manifested by the figure's value system. This also is referred to as a *figure/ground relationship.*

SENSATIONS OF COLOR

by Hazel Rossotti

The homogeneal Light and Rays which appear red, or rather make Objects appear so, I call Rubrifick or Red-making; those which make Objects appear yellow, green, blue, and violet, I call Yellow-making, Green-making, Blue-making, and Violet-making, and so of the rest. And if at any time I speak of Light and Rays as colored or endued with Colors, I would be understood to speak not philosophically and properly, but grossly, and accordingly to such Conceptions as vulgar People in seeing all these Experiments would be apt to frame. For the Rays to speak properly are not colored. In them there is nothing else than a certain Power and Disposition to stir up a Sensation of this or that Color. For as Sound in a Bell or musical String, or other sounding Body, is nothing but a trembling Motion, and in the Air nothing but that Motion propagated from the Object, and in Sensorium 'tis a Sense of that Motion under the Form of Sound; so Colors in the Object are nothing but a Disposition to reflect this or that sort of Rays more copiously than the rest; in the Rays they are nothing but their Dispositions to propagate this or that Motion into the Sensorium, and in the Sensorium they are Sensations of those Motions under the Forms of Colors.

—NEWTON, *Opticks*

Since all Perception in the Brain is made
(Tho' where and how was never yet display'd)
And since so great a distance lies between
The Eye-ball, and the Seat of Sense within,
While in the Eye th'arrested Object stays
Tell, what th'Idea to the Brain Conveys?

—BLACKMORE, *Creation*

Do not the Rays of Light falling upon the bottom of the Eye excite Vibrations in the *Tunica Retina?* Which Vibrations, being propagated along the solid Fibres of the optick Nerves into the Brain, cause the Sense of seeing.

—NEWTON, Opticks

Two optic nerves, they say, she ties,
Like spectacles, across the eyes;
By which the spirits bring her word,
Whene'er the balls are fix'd or stirred.

—MATTHEW PRICE, Alma

Someone is given a certain yellow-green (or blue-green) and told to mix a less yellowish (or bluish) one—or to pick it out from a number of color samples. A less yellowish green, however, is not a bluish one (and vice versa), and there is also such a task as choosing, or mixing a green that is neither yellowish nor bluish. I say 'or mixing'

because a green does not become both bluish[1] and yellowish because it is produced by a kind of mixture of yellow and blue.

—WITTGENSTEIN, *Remarks on Color*, trans. By McAlister and Schattle

During the day, owing to the yellowish hue of the snow, shadows tending to violet had already been observable; these might now be pronounced to be decidedly blue, as the illumined parts exhibited a yellow deepening to orange.

But as the sun at last was about to set, and its rays, greatly mitigated by the thicker vapors, began to diffuse a most beautiful red color over the whole scene around me, the shadow color changed to a green, in lightness to be compared to a sea-green, in beauty to the green of the emerald. The appearance became more and more vivid: one might have imagined oneself in a fairy world, for every object had clothed itself in the two vivid and so beautifully harmonizing colors, till at last, as the sun went down, the magnificent spectacle was lost in a gray twilight, and by degrees in a clear moon-and-starlight night.

—GOETHE, *Theory of Colors*

Colors appear what they are not, according to the ground which surrounds them.

—LEONARDO DA VINCI, *Trattato della pi*

In the silent painted park where I walked her and aired her a little, she sobbed and said I would soon, soon leave her as everybody had, and I sang her a wistful French ballad, and strung together some fugitive rhymes to amuse her:

The place was called *Enchanted Hunters.* Query:
What Indian dyes, Diana, did they dell
endorse to make Picture Lake a very
blood bath of trees before the blue hotel?

She said: "Why blue when it is white, why blue for heaven's sake?" and started to cry again...

—NABOKOV, *Lolita*

Why blue: when I asked Nabokov "why blue?" and whether it had anything to do with the butterflies commonly known as the "Blues," he replied: "What Rita does not understand is that a white surface, the chalk of that hotel, does look blue in a wash of light and shade on a vivid fall day, amid red foliage. H.H. is merely paying a tribute to French impressionist painters. He notes an optical miracle as E.B. White does somewhere when referring

---

[1]Translator's Note: Wittgenstein wrote "greenish" here but presumably meant "bluish."

to the divine combination of 'red barn and blue snow.' It is the shock of color, not an intellectual blueprint or the shadow of a hobby ... I was really born a landscape painter."

—A. Appel, *The Annotated Lolita*

Every hue throughout your work is altered by every touch that you add in other places.

—Ruskin

When Anaxagoras says: Even the snow is black!
He is taken by the scientists very seriously
because he is enunciating a "principle," a "law"
that all things are mixed, and therefore the purest white
  snow
has in it an element of blackness.

That they call science, and reality.
I call it mental conceit and mystification
and nonsense, for pure snow is white to us
white and white and only white
with a lovely bloom of whiteness upon white
in which the soul delights and the senses
have an experience of bliss.

And life is for delight, and for bliss
and dread, and the dark, rolling ominousness of doom
then the bright dawning of delight again
from off the sheer white snow, or the poised moon.

And in the shadow of the sun the snow is blue, so blue-
  aloof
with a hint of the frozen bells of the scylla flower
but never the ghost of a glimpse of Anaxagoras' funeral
  black.

—D.H. Lawrence, 'Anaxagoras'

I had entered an inn towards evening, and, as well-favored girl, with a brilliantly fair complexion, black hair, and a scarlet bodice, came into the room, I looked attentively at her as she stood before me at some distance in half shadow. As she presently afterwards turned away, I saw on the white wall, which was now before me, a black face surrounded with a bright light, while the dress of the perfectly distinct figure appeared of a beautiful sea-green.

* * * *

As the opposite color is produced by a constant law in experiments with colored objects on portions of the retina, so the same effect takes place when the whole retina is impressed with a single color. We may convince ourselves of this by means of colored glass. If we look long through a blue pane of glass, everything will afterwards appear in sunshine to the naked eye, even if the sky is gray and the scene colorless. In like manner, in taking off green spectacles, we see all objects in a red light. Every decided color does a certain violence to the eye, and forces the organ to opposition.

—Goethe, *Theory of Colors*

A given visual phenomenon may not be perceived at all unless it is actively looked for.

—Burnham, Hanes and Bartleson, *Color*

The difference is as great between
the optics seeing, as the objects seen.
All Manners take a tincture from our won;
Or come discolor'd through our Passions shown.
Or Fancy's beam enlarges, multiplies
Contracts, inverts and gives ten thousand dyes.

—Pope, *Moral Essays*

For they sometimes appear by other Causes, as when by the power of Phantasy we see Colors in a Dream, or a Mad-man sees things before him which are not there; or when we see Fire by striking the Eye, or see Colors like the Eye of a peacock's Feather (Figure 5-27), by pressing our Eyes in either corner whilst we look the other way. Where these and such like Causes interpose not, the Color always answers to the sort or sorts of the Rays whereof the Light consists, as I have constantly found in whatever Phenomena of Colors I have hitherto been able to examine. I shall in the following Propositions give instances of this in the Phenomena of chiefest note.

—Newton, *Opticks*

Figure 5-27

Light and the Eye

The colors we see depend, we say, on the composition of the light which enters the eye. And this, in turn, depends on the composition of the original light and on the way in which the light is modified by encounters *en route* from source to eye, encounters with other light waves, with the media through which it passes, and with objects off which some or all of it may bounce. Since we were less than two weeks old, we could experience variations in the composition of the light as different sensations of color. But how?

In this section, we shall discuss the changes which occur when the light encounters the back of the eye. We shall discuss mainly human color vision, both normal and anomalous, but also will mention color vision in other vertebrates and in insects. We shall see that there is still much unraveling to be done before we can understand what happens *after* the light is absorbed by the eye—the optic nerve and the brain combine to play some odd tricks. Some of the sensations we experience seem but tenuously related to the encounter between light and eye. So while it is quite easy to give the specifications (of wavelength and intensity) for a ray of light, it is vastly more difficult to specify a sensation of color. Nonetheless, as we shall see, there have been numerous brave attempts to do so.

The eye is commonly likened to a camera. The light enters a dark chamber through an aperture which can be varied in diameter according to the intensity of the light, and it is focused by the lens to a light-sensitive backing. In both camera and eye, the light produces only small changes in the photosensitive material, but these are the starting points for a long series of changes which take place during the "processing" and which eventually produce either a photograph or a sensation.

In a young, normal, human eye (see Figure 5-28), the outer layer (the "cornea"), the lens, and the eye fluids are almost transparent. When the light reaches the retina, on the inner surface of the eye, it passes through layers of transparent nerve fibers, between capillary blood vessels and on to the photosensitive cells at the ends of the nerve fibers. These are backed with a layer of cells which contain black pigment and absorb stray light. The whole eye is enclosed in a tough outer skin which is an opaque continuation of the cornea.

The photosensitive cells are colored—they contain pigments which absorb visible light, and it is this absorption which forms the basis of our sense of sight. In the human retina, there are two classes of photosensitive cells called *rods* and *cones* on account of their (very approximate) shape. The rods are effective only in dim light and enable us to sense differences in brightness, while the cones respond to light of normal intensity and allow us to distinguish between different colors. So the eye behaves as a camera which contains two films, one for color and one for black and white only, as well as a photochemical device which selects the film appropriate to the lighting conditions.

The rods and cones are not distributed evenly over the retina. Opposite the center of the lens is a small yellow-brown pit, the center of which (the "fovea") contains only cones, 100,000 of them. There are no capillaries or nerve fibers between the lens and these foveal cells, but the pigmented edge of the pit absorbs some of the ultraviolet and blue light which might otherwise damage them. The rest of the retina is equipped with 4 million cones and 120 million rods. The concentration of the rods is greatest about 20 degrees from the yellow spot, while that of the cones decreases with increasing distance from it. But there is one point on the retina, at the junction with the optic nerve, where there are no photosensitive cells of either sort. This is the "blind spot."

When light strikes a photosensitive cell, a photon may be absorbed, and if it is, it will trigger off a series of changes which contribute to the sensation of vision. The probability of the photon being absorbed depends on whether the eye is adapted for bright or dark conditions, on the wavelength and intensity of the light and on the type of retinal cell on which it falls. We shall first see the way in which the rod cells respond, since these operate more simply than the cones.

It seems that all rods contain a single reddish-purple pigment called "visual purple" or *rhodopsin*, which consists of a protein combined with a substance called retinal, which, like carotene, has a long backbone of carbon atoms with small side arms (see Figure 5-29). When we have been in the dark for a while, the carbon chain is bent and slightly twisted near one end, and able to fit into an indentation in the surface of the protein (see Figure 5-30). If dim light enters the eye, a photon may be absorbed by the carbon chain, which then straightens out, untwists, and detaches itself from one of its moorings on the protein. This causes the shape of the protein indentation to change, and the other end of the chain to break loose. The pigment is bleached, and a signal may pass along the nerve fiber. This signal is identical for every proton absorbed, regardless of the wavelength of the light. The rod response is like that of a spring mousetrap which behaves exactly the same whether the trigger is released by a mouse or a rat (although the probability that it will be set off by one or the other depends on the relative numbers of each around and their relative liking for the bait). The rod cells are not, in fact, equally sensitive to light of all wavelengths. Photons in the middle of the visual region are absorbed most efficiently (see Figure 5-32). When viewed by weak moonlight, the dark green leaves of a holly tree (Figure 5-31) might seem a lighter gray than the bright red berries, because rods show their greatest sensitivity to green light.

If the illumination is increased, the rhodopsin remains bleached and the rod cell is inactive. But in dim light, the pigment, having lost its energy to the nerve, gradually reverts to its original, photosensitive state. The mousetrap resets itself spontaneously. Rods which have been inactivated by bright light readapt only slowly to the dark. The efficiency of our night vision increases markedly over twenty or thirty minutes and is not fully developed for about one hour.

Illumination which is bright enough to inactivate the rods also is bright enough to stimulate the cone cells and

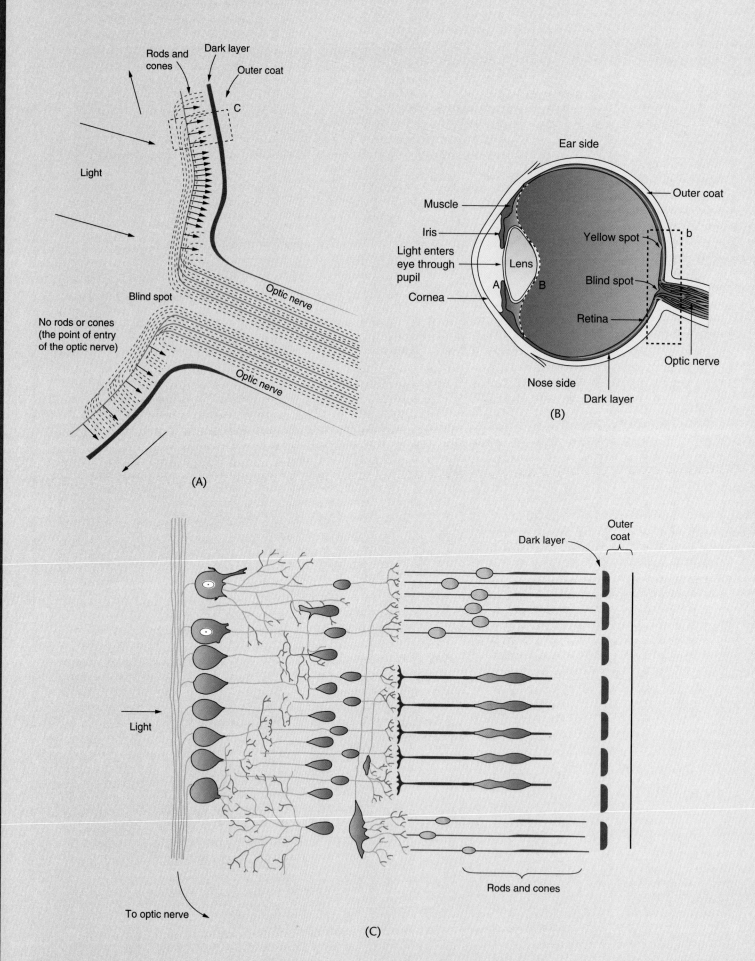

Figure 5-28 The Human Eye. (a) Horizontal section through center. The cavities A and B contain fluid. (b) Enlargements of region shown in box in (a) above. (c) Enlargements of region shown in (b) above, showing section through retina. (Adapted, with permission, from Figures 2.17, 2.18, and 2.19 in R.W. Burnham, R.M. Hanes and C.J. Bartleson, Color, John Wiley, New York, 1963.)

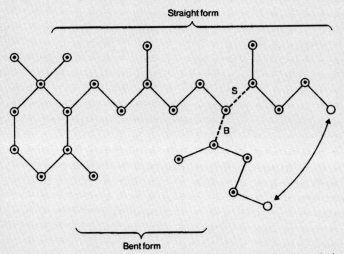

Figure 5-29 A Light Twist. The skeleton of the light-sensitive substance retinal. The end of the tail can twist, to give a bent form joined to the backbone by the dotted line B, or a straight form, attached by line S.

RICHARD WEISGRAU/MIRA.COM/DRR.NET.

Figure 5-31

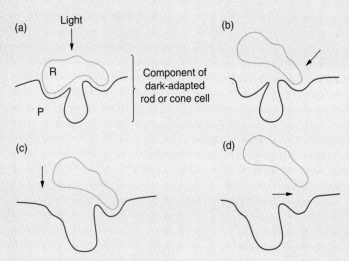

Figure 5-30 Changes in the Retina. Sketches to illustrate the mechanism of light sensitivity in the eye.

(a) A dark-adapted retinal group R adopts the bent form and fits snugly on to the puckered surface of a protein, P.

(b) When the retinal absorbs a photon, its "tail" straightens and forces the "head" away from the protein base.

(c) The protein surface, no longer held in position by the retinal, relaxes, and changes shape.

(d) The "tail" of the retinal breaks away from the protein, initiating an electrical charge which is conveyed to the nerve.

(Adapted, with permission, from R. Hubbard and A. Kroft, *Scientific American,* vol. 216, June 1967, p. 65.)

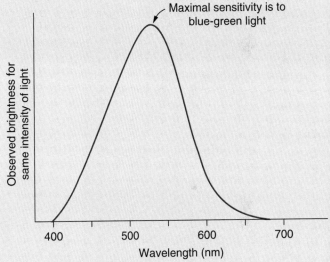

Figure 5-32 Brightness by Night. How the rod cells respond to light of the same intensity but of different wavelength.

so to allow us to perceive color. Cones respond to changes in the overall intensity of the light much more quickly than do rods and are fully adapted within seven minutes.

Each cone, like each rod, contains visual pigment, a molecule of which consists of a carotene-like carbon "backbone" partially folded into a cavity in a protein molecule. Although the retinal backbone seems to be exactly the same as that in a rod pigment, the particular protein which forms part of rhodopsin has not been found in cones. In fact, there are three different types of cones,

each containing a different sort of protein. So a cone will have one of three possible visual pigments. Each pigment absorbs light over much of the visual spectrum (see Figure 5-33a). The effect of the absorption of a photon is similar to that in rhodopsin, and does not vary with the wavelength of the light. For each photon absorbed, one carbon backbone straightens and one impulse passes to the nerve.

Each cone pigment, like rhodopsin, absorbs photons with varying efficiency according to their energy. Color vision is possible because the three cone pigments differ *from each other* in their sensitivity to wavelength.

We can see from Figure 5-33b that one of the cone pigments (A) absorbs most efficiently in the orange part of the spectrum, while another (B) absorbs maximally in the green region. The third pigment (C), which absorbs less efficiently than the others, has its absorption peak in

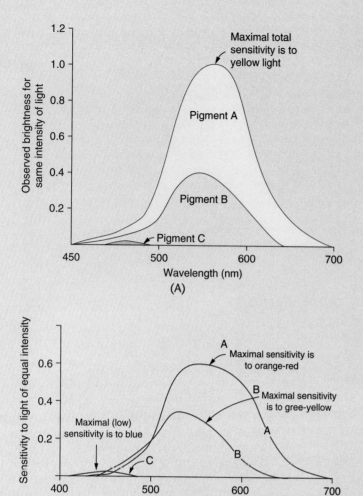

(A)

(B)

Figure 5-33 Brightness by Day. (a) The full line shows the combined response of the cone cells to light of the same intensity but of different wavelengths. The approximate contributions of the three systems of cone pigments are indicated by the differently shaded areas. (b) The approximate sensitivities of each of the separate systems. The valves are those estimated at the cornea by Smith and Pakorny.

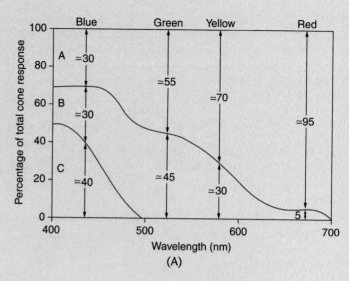

(A)

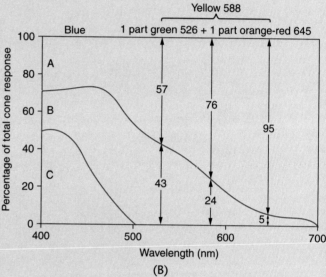

(B)

the blue, high-energy end of the spectrum. When we add together the separate contributions of the three pigments, we find (Figure 5-33a) that the total absorption also varies with wavelength, being most efficient in the yellow region. The percentage contribution of each pigment to the total absorption is shown in Figure 5-34, which perhaps provides us with the best key to the understanding of color vision because it shows us how the ratio of contributions varies with wavelength. Any light of "normal" intensity triggers off the three cone pigments in some ratio A:B:C, which depends on the wavelength composition of the light: and it is this *ratio* which produces a particular sensation of color. For example, a cone response in a ratio 33:42:25 gives a sensation of blue, while with one of 70:30:0 we perceive yellow (see Table 5-1).

Some response ratios can be produced both by the light of a single wavelength, and by a mixture of two lights, both of different wavelengths. We cannot distinguish by eye alone between a "pure" yellow light of one narrow

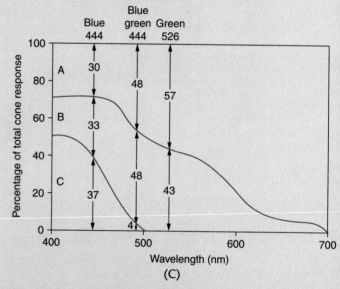

(C)

Figure 5-34 Cones and Color: Approximate percentage of total cone response attributable to each of the three pigments.

(a) The probable cone response rations A:B:C, which provide the sensations of blue, green, yellow, and red.

(b) The sensation of yellow can also be obtained by combining the responses of cone pigments A and B to green light and to orange-red light.

(c) The blue-green sensation obtained from light of 488 nm can never be exactly matched by mixing blue and green light as the percentage of B-cone response is maximal in this region.

Table 5-1 *Probable response of cone pigments to various wavelengths.*

Wavelengths (nm)	Approximate % of total absorption contributed by pigment			Color
	A	B	C	
420	29	21·5	49·5	violet
460	33	42	25	blue
490	48	48·5	3·5	blue-green
530	57	43	0	green
580	70·5	29·5	0	yellow
600	80	20	0	orange
620	88·5	11·5	0	orange-red
660	95·5	4·5	0	red

Table 5-2 *Probable cone response ratios for some pure and mixed lights.*

Color	A:B:C ratio	Wavelength of pure light of same ratio (nm)	Mixed light of same color			
			%	nm	ratio	color
Yellow	70:30:0	588	50	526	57:43:0	green
			50	645	95:5:0	orange-red
Blue	33:42:25	460			None	
Blue-green	48:48:4	488			None	
Green	63·5:36·5:0	560			None	
Red	95·5:4·5:0	660			None	
Magenta	64·5:23:12·5	None	50	460	33:42:25	blue
			50	660	95·5:4·5:0	red
White	63·5:34:2·5	None	34	480	43:49:8	blue
			33	540	59:41:0	green
			33	620	88·5:11·5:0	orange-red

wavelength range in the region of 580 nm and the mixture of green and orange-red lights, which gives the same response ratio (see Table 5-2 and Figure 5-34b). Green light of 560 nm cannot, however, be matched by a mixture. Since this wavelength is the lowest at which pigment C makes no appreciable response, any mixture containing light of lower wavelength would stimulate some contribution from pigment C. Nor can blue-green light of 488 nm, where the response of B-cones is maximal (see Figure 5-34c).

There also are some "non spectral" colors which can be made only by mixing. Mixtures of red and blue light give response ratios which do not correspond to that of any single wavelength light and which we perceive as shades of magenta. And if we mix blue, green, and orange-red light of roughly equal intensities, we obtain white light of ratio about 63·5:34:2·5, which is almost indistinguishable from the white light obtained by mixing all visible wavelengths at equal intensity.

Figure 5-35

So the cones allow us to distinguish colors by day and the rods enable us to see shapes at night. But the rods sometimes also contribute to vision by day. An object at the very edge of our visual field (behind the lines joining one eye to opposite ear) seems monochrome because the light which reaches us from it falls on the periphery of the retina where there are mainly rods and only few cones. Slightly nearer the center of the retina, there are rather few cone cells, and the perceived color is not quite the same as that produced when the same light falls on the cone-rich central region. It has been suggested that the sensation is attributable to the combined response of rhodopsin and of the three cone pigments.

The responses of rods and cones certainly both contribute to vision at the intermediate, twilight intensities of illumination. When the light is bright enough for us to see some color, but not bright enough to bleach the rods totally, the sensation is probably a result of the response of all four pigments. We have seen that rods absorb most

efficiently in the green region of the spectrum (~500 nm), whereas the total cone response is most sensitive to yellow light (550 nm). As dusk falls (Figure 5-35), our eyes therefore become increasingly sensitive to light of shorter wavelengths. At twilight, our most sensitive response is to blue-green light (510 nm) and so, before all colors turn to grays, they become gradually more blue, an effect first reported in 1823 by the Czech physiologist Purkinje.

Night is not always devoid of color. But although the full moon looks golden,[2] the moonlit world is colorless, as Walter de la Mare expresses it:

Slowly, silently, now the moon
Walks the night in her silver shoon
This way and that, she peers and sees
Silver fruit upon silver trees.

The intensity of sunlight reflected from the moon is just high enough to stimulate cone vision, at least in that part of the spectrum to which cones are most sensitive.

---

[2]But the moon is not always golden. Occasionally an unusually high proportion of the blue component of the reflected light is scattered, or bent, away from the observer. A "harvest moon" or "hunter's moon" (or a rising sun) low in the sky looks redder than usual. During a lunar eclipse the color of the moon may change, through orange to deep crimson. And, "once in a blue moon," atmospheric particles from a volcanic eruption or forest fire may be of exactly the right size to scatter all light of low and medium energy, with the result that only the blue component reaches the observer.

WOODFALL/PHOTOSHOT/DRR.NET.

Figure 5-37 Mature Male Satin Bowerbird (Ptilonorhynchus violaceus) displaying in it's bower to female.

MARIE READ/WOODFALL/PHOTOSHOT/DRR.NET.

Figure 5-38 Satin Bowerbird (Ptilonorhynchus violaceus), male, close-up showing violet eye.

blue objects such as scraps of paper and china, juice from blue berries, and feathers from smaller birds it has killed for the purpose. A male robin will defend its territory against a shapeless bunch of red feathers, although not against a bunch of brown feathers or even against a stuffed juvenile (brown) robin. Owls, however, have only rod cells, and so are totally color-blind. Three types of retinal cone cells have been found in hens and pigeons, whose color vision is similar to our own. The eyes of many birds, including these two, contain colored "filters" of oil droplets in the yellow-to-red range, but the effect of these on the color vision of birds is not known. In the frog, color vision appears to come with maturity—tadpoles seem to be color-blind. Lizards, which are active only in daylight and have pure cone vision, seem able to distinguish between meal worms dyed different colors, while the nocturnal gecko, with pure rod vision, is color-blind. Turtles, like birds, have colored, oil-drop filters, but their color vision seems to differ greatly from one species to another. Fish seem well able to distinguish colors. Sticklebacks and Siamese fighting fish react vigorously to red and blue in both courtship and defense of territory.

Though the compound eyes of insects have a totally different structure from the simple eyes of vertebrates, they contain visual pigments similar to our own. Many insects, such as bees, wasps, ants, dragonflies, butterflies, moths, beetles, cockroaches, and houseflies, can distinguish colors, but usually in a range different from our own. And some have color vision only in certain directions but are color-blind in others. Some parts of their color-sensitive insects respond to radiation of wavelength 390–300 nm in the ultraviolet range, which is invisible to humans. But most insects are insensitive to red light. Exceptions are a few butterflies and the firefly, which can detect light of a wavelength as long as 690 nm; as indeed it would need to if, as believed, it uses the orange-red flashes of its species to find a mate. Ants, however, are blind to red. When a colony is illuminated by a spectrum from sunlight, they carry their larvae into the red region but avoid the near ultraviolet. In addition to color vision, many insects, unlike humans, can distinguish between light that is of the same wavelength but polarized in different planes.

Much work has been done on the color vision of bees, who can distinguish between lights in the three color ranges: yellow (590–500 nm), blue-green (500–480 nm), ultraviolet (400–300 nm) (see Figure 5-40). For bees, the mixture of 440 and 360 nm and 650 nm, known as "bees' purple" by analogy with the mixture of the two extreme colors, red and violet, visible to humans. For bees, as for humans, there are pairs of complementary "colors" which together make up the whole range of the visible part of sunlight: ultra violet and blue-green, yellow and violet, blue and "bees' purple." Since bees cannot see light of a wavelength longer than about 590 nm, they are blind to

Figure 5-39 A flower with yellow petals would actually look more like this flower to the bee.

PHOTO BY THE AUTHOR

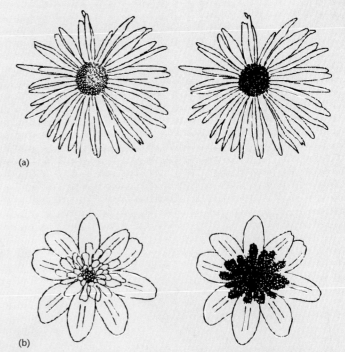

(a)

(b)

Figure 5-40 A Bee's-Eye View. The illustrated flowers on the left would be the result of photographs taken with normal film that responds mainly to visible light; those on the right would be the results of photos taken with film that records predominantly ultra violet radiation. The outer petals of the flowers, which seem yellow to us, reflect "bee's purple" to the bee (Figure 5-39). The centers, which absorb ultra violet and reflect only the yellow, would seem much darker, and could guide the bee to the nectar.
(a) Leopard's BANE.
(b) Lesser CELANDINE.
(Reproduced with permission, from R. L. Gregory and E. H. Gombrich, Illusion in Nature and Art, Duckworth, London, 1973.)

PHOTO BY THE AUTHOR.

Figure 5-41 Leopard's Bane.

WERNER BOLLMANN/GETTY IMAGES.

Figure 5-42 Lesser Celandine.

Although we have been able to establish that some animals can distinguish colors, only a few species have been studied in detail, and the part which color plays in their lives is largely a matter of speculation.

The Eye and the Brain

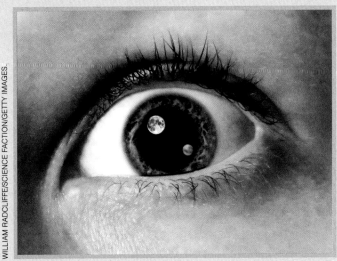

WILLIAM RADCLIFFE/SCIENCE FACTION/GETTY IMAGES.

Figure 5-43

red and orange, and so it might seem surprising that they visit such red flowers as poppies. However, poppies reflect not only red light but also ultra violet, and it is this which attracts the bees.

Photographs on film which is sensitive to ultraviolet light reveal complex patterns of guidelines on petals of some flowers which to us look plain white or a single color, but which are "variegated" in their power to reflect ultra violet radiation. Similar "latent" patterns on butterfly wings are thought to play a part in recognition and in courtship. If bees are shown two blackboards bearing the directions "Bees may feed here" and "No bees allowed," the bees always will collect on the correct notice, provided that the permissive text is painted with a material which reflects ultra violet light while the restrictive one is painted with Chinese white, which does not.

Are the writers of the excerpts on pages 174–175 merely being fanciful? If not, how can we reconcile the phenomena they describe with our earlier interpretation of color vision in terms of the absorption of photons by the three cone pigments? Our own experience confirms that there is more to color than the composition of the light which meets the eye. Colors provoke emotional responses. They appear to vary when physics suggests they should not and, contrariwise, seem constant when it seems they should vary. We sometimes see colors in the absence of what we might think would be the appropriate light, and indeed, in the absence of any light at all. A great number of types of change can take place both in the retina and in the brain after a photon is absorbed.

Some of our psychological responses to color may have a simple, geometrical origin. A red splodge often seems to advance from the page and to concentrate the viewer's attention toward its center, whereas a blue splodge seems to recede and to lead the eye outward. The apparent movement of colors toward, and away from, the viewer probably occurs because the lens of the eye (unlike that of a camera) is made of a single material and so is subject to "chromatic aberration." Light of different wavelength is bent, as by a prism or a raindrop, to a different extent. When the muscles which control the shape of the lens focus green light on the retina, the red light is focused a little behind it and the blue a little in front. To see a red object clearly, the lens must be the same shape as we need to see a green object which is slightly nearer, and to see a blue object, it must be adjusted in the opposite way. So reds seem to advance and blues to recede.

The impressions that blues (and yellows) spread while reds contract may well be because of the way in which the

Figure 5-44 Colors which recede or advance. (a) The eye receives light from a multi-colored object, M, when the lens is adjusted to focus green light on the retina. Blue is focused slightly in front of it and red slightly behind it. (b) When the lens changes to focus the blue light from M on to the retina, the eye is adjusted for the clear viewing of green (or white) objects, D, which are slightly more distant than M. Blue therefore seems to recede. (c) Adjustment of the lens to focus red on the retina also allows clear vision of a green or white object, N, which is slightly nearer than the source of the red light. So red seems to advance toward the viewer.

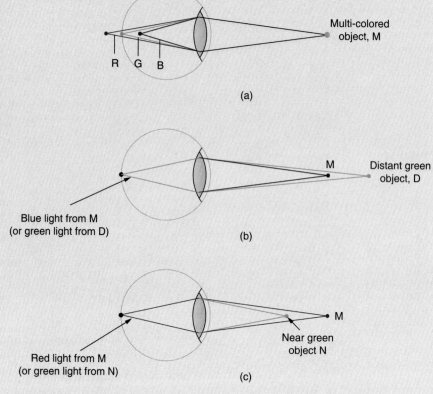

(a)

Multi-colored object, M

R G B

Blue light from M
(or green light from D)

M

Distant green object, D

(b)

Red light from M
(or green light from N)

Near green object N

M

(c)

cone pigments are distributed on the retina. We cannot see colors at the edge of our field of vision because only rods are present at the periphery of the retina, but as we bring an object nearer to the center of the visual field, we first recognize blue and yellow. Slightly nearer the center, we sense green, and still more centrally, we can see red. It is not surprising that blue, which we can see at the widest angle of color vision, tends to spread, and that red, which is visible only fairly centrally, tends to contract.

Color sensations may depend on intensity as well as on wavelength, even when the cones alone are responding. As the light gets more intense, both orange and yellow-green approach yellow, while violet and blue-green both become bluer. Only in three cases, yellow, green, and blue, does the color seem to be independent of the intensity. These colors are termed "psychological primaries" because each can be said, whatever its intensity, to contain no element of any of the others.

We do not fully understand why, out of all the colors, red, yellow, green, and blue behave in this way, though the cause probably lies in the absorption curves of the cone pigments. Indeed, there are many large gaps in our knowledge of visual perception, and particularly of color. But many of the effects mentioned in the chapter arise either from the highly complex set of nerve connections between the retina and the brain, or from the time lag in the recovery of a cone cell after it has absorbed a photo, or from a combination of both factors.

The rods and the cones are incorporated into very different "circuit diagrams" Impulses from individual rod cells do not travel directly to the brain, but first pass from a group of cells to a nerve center which transmits a signal to other centers, from which an impulse eventually reaches

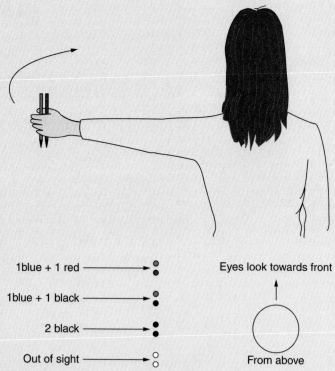

1blue + 1 red

1blue + 1 black

2 black

Out of sight

Eyes look towards front

From above

Figure 5-45 The Corner of the Eye. The girl, facing forward, holds a blue pencil and a red pencil out beyond her ear, and gradually moves her arm so that they come into her field of vision. She first sees both pencils as black, then perceives the color of the blue one, and finally recognizes the red.

the brain. Since the signal may have come from any one of a hundred or so cells, rod vision is very sensitive, although its definition is not of the very highest. It is likely that impulses from adjacent nerve centers are combined to give information about the *differences* between their

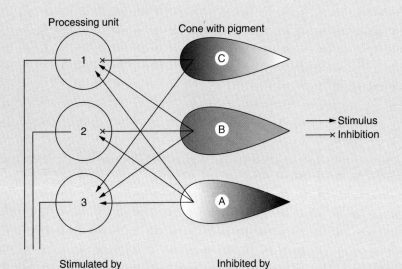

Processing unit | Cone with pigment

Stimulus →
Inhibition →×

Figure 5-46 Connections for Contrast. A possible scheme of nerve connections which would allow cone cells to monitor contrast.

Unit	Stimulated by response from pigment	Inhibited by response from pigment	Contrast monitored
1	A, B	C	Yellow/blue
2	A	B	Red/green
3	A, B, C	—	White/black

signals, which enables them to monitor contrast, and us to recognize shapes (see Figure 5-44).

Signals from the cones travel to the brain by various routes. Some cone cells near the center of the retina send combined responses straight to the brain, and this allows us to see extremely clearly, in color, in light of normal intensity. Other cones seem to combine their signals so that the activity in one cell inhibits the response of neighboring ones. The cones seem to be able to monitor both brightness and color (red/green and blue/yellow), and this could be achieved if the nerve connections were similar to those of the simplified scheme shown in Figure 5-44. A strong response from the cones also must be conveyed to the rod cells, in order to inhibit them when the light is bright.

It is thought that the first steps in the collation of cone responses occur in the retina itself, but that the brain performs most of the processing required to produce the sensation of color. It is certainly the brain which combines the signals from each eye. Colored stereoscopic pictures provide impressive application of binocular vision. A scene is photographed twice; once as viewed by the right eye of a stationary observer, and once as viewed by his left eye (see Figure 5-45). The right-hand one, printed in red, is superimposed on the left-hand one, printed in blue-green. This composite print is viewed through goggles with a blue-green filter over the right eye and a red filter over the left one. So the right eye sees black on blue-green, while the left eye sees black on red. After a second or so, the two signals fuse in the brain to provide a gleamingly three-dimensional impression in black on white.

Some people find that impressions from their two eyes do not fuse easily, if at all. The response of one eye sometimes entirely dominates that of the other, so that when viewing a stereoscopic picture through colored goggles, they would see a flat picture on a colored background. Very few people, who have defective color vision in one eye only, are in the unusual position of being able to

compare the sensations produced by normal, and defective, color vision, and to tell the normally sighted how the world looks to the "color-blind." And if the defective eye is strongly dominant, their supposedly binocular color vision also will be defective.

Some of the color phenomena which have most captured the attention of writers and experimentalists alike are those in which the effect of light on one cone cell is modified either by the simultaneous response of neighboring cells, or by some previous response, in eye or brain. One such effect is the way in which the inhibition of one cell by another enhances color contrast. If we stare at a bright red patch on a white card, it seems to develop a green line around the edge, whereas a yellow border appears around a violet patch. Sunlight on snow or whitewash looks yellowish, and the shadows bluish. But the light from the lit and shaded areas differs only in intensity. Its composition is the same. Even more impressive colored shadows can be obtained in theater lighting. In the same way, two patches of, say, blue and yellow, often look brighter and more contrasting when adjacent than when apart.

We know from studies of the electrical activity of individual brain cells that a cell which is receiving no stimulus is dormant, but it is not totally inactive. In the absence of any message from the optic nerve, it discharges steadily. When the retina is stimulated by a flash of light of a particular color, the electrical activity of the cell may be greatly increased or reduced to almost nothing or totally unaffected (see Figure 5-46). Different cells respond differently to different wavelengths.

Some brain cells appear to respond to color only if it occurs at the edge of an area. Such cells must play a crucial part in our perception of contrast, and hence, of shape.

The boundary between two colors produces interesting effects. A patch of bright color on a dark background appears, by contrast, brighter at the edges. A band of orange on deep green or brown appears almost to glow at the edges, like a strip light, in much the same way as

Figure 5-47 Stereo. An illusion of depth is produced by the fusion of two images within the brain.

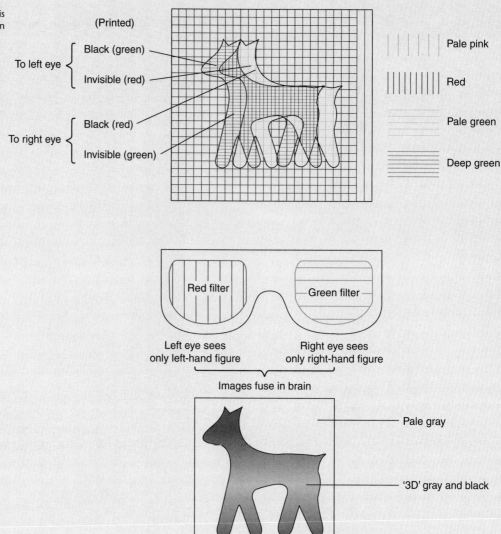

a series of wide stripes of increasingly paler gray seem, by contrast, to darken each of the boundaries. But, at the precise junction between two colors of similar brightness, the colors may become slightly paler, and so the contrast decreases. The effect is most marked when the two colors are complementary. For example, when yellow and blue stimulate adjacent cones, the response is much the same as if both cones had been triggered off by white light. The yellow and blue mix, not outside the eye but on the retina, so each of the patches look paler at the junction between them than it does further into the main area of color. This effect obviously becomes more important the smaller the patches of color. As early as 1824, Chevreul warned tapestry makers to avoid placing complementary colors next to each other if they wanted to produce brightly colored pictures. For the same reason, painters and stained-glass artists often outline areas of color in black, or separate them by a white line. But optical mixing need not yield only white. A mosaic of red and green gives a vibrant yellow. Such effects have been much exploited in textile design and painting and are the basis of color television.

Colors also become mixed on the retina if they follow each other more rapidly than about fifty stimuli per second. If the segments of a top are painted, the colors fuse when the top is spun (see Figure 5-48). Alternating slices of red and green become yellow, while blue and yellow become whitish, just as if lights were superimposed on a screen. A quite different effect, probably caused by different rates of recovery from fatigue to different wavelengths, is the stroboscopic color we see when we spin certain patterned black and white discs (see Figure 5-49). The actual colors experienced depend on the observer, and vary with the speed and the direction of rotation, the particular pattern and the light source. The top shown here, designed by Sydney Harry, is at its most impressive when viewed by the light of a color television set. Under fluorescent lighting it shows weaker colors, and under tungsten, or in daylight, none at all.

Color sensations may change with time if one or more sets of cone cells become tired, as when an observer is shown a series of flashes of very intense red light (620 nm). The color first seems red, then passes through orange and yellow to a green sensation, which holds for about thirty seconds before reverting gradually through yellow to orangeish-yellow, where it then stays. It seems that the barrage of high-wavelength photons is too great to be monitored for long by cones containing pigment A. Once the response is triggered, the recovery time is too slow

PHOTORECEPTOR CELLS AND ASSOCIATED INTERNEURONES AND SENSORY NEURONES

Originally, we studied the various forms of color (RYB, RGB and CMYK) and the various forms of those pigments and lights. You will notice in this illustration, that there are red, green, and blue cones. Each cone is sensitive to different colors in Newton's visible spectrum, which stimulates the three cells differently:

Red Light will stimulate the red cones
Cyan Light will stimulate the blue and green cones equally

Yellow Light will stimulate the red and green cones equally
White Light will stimulate all three cones equally.

RGB photoreceptors are found in the eye, just as we see RGB at work within computer and digital processes. See how many RGB examples you can think of, that are relevant to this study.

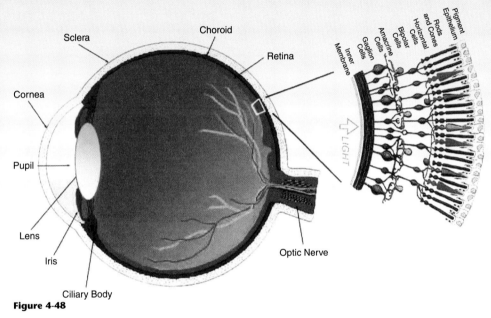

Figure 4-48

to maintain the appropriate response ratio A:B:C for 620 nm. So a higher proportion of photons become fatigued, but because they absorb a lower fraction of the photons than do the A cones, they become slightly less tired. So after about two and a half minutes, the response settles down to give an orange-yellow sensation derived from a lower ratio of A to B responses than would be expected for 620 nm.

Fatigue also seems to account for the engaging apparitions known as "negative after-images." If we stare hard at a colored pencil held against a white background for one or two minutes, and then remove the pencil, we can see a pencil-shaped patch of complementary color which moves across the background as we move our eyes. A red pencil gives a turquoise patch and a green pencil a magenta patch. It seems that when we look at a red pencil, the cones respond and become temporarily out of action in the A:B:C ratio appropriate to the wavelength. When white light falls on the retina, these fatigued cones do not respond, and the light from the

background produces a "white" response in the unfatigued cones, but a "white-minus-red" (i.e., turquoise) response in the pencil-shaped region of the fatigued cones. After a minute or so, the cones become reactivated and the after-image fades. Doctors and nurses wear bluish-green clothes when they do surgical operations so that they are not distracted by the bluish-green after-images of blood.

But not all negative after-images are as simple as these, or as Goethe's "well-favored" tavern wench. In 1965, it was found that if the eyes are "primed" by looking alternately at green and black stripes in one direction (say vertical) and red and black stripes in another (say horizontal), then the negative after-images which are obtained when we look at black stripes on a white background are linked to the direction of the stripes. If we look at vertical stripes, we now see magenta, and if we turn the pattern through a right angle, so that the bars become horizontal, the color changes to green. The connection between direction and color can persist for hours or even days without impairing every day vision in any way.

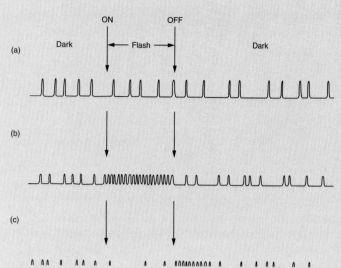

Figure 5-49 Brain waves. Some types of electrical activity of individual brain cells subjected to a bright flash of light.
(a) No response: the cell continues to 'tick over,' as in the dark.
(b) Activity increases during flash.
(c) Activity decreases during flash, but increases above normal level immediately afterwards.
Each cell may react differently to light of different wavelengths, and differently from its neighbors for light of the same wavelength.

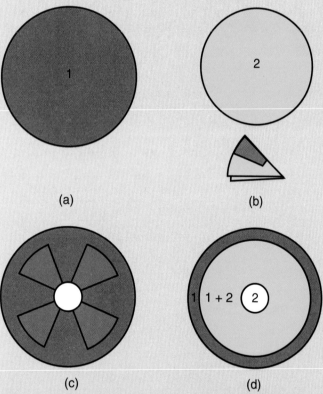

Figure 5-50 Colored Tops. Do-it-yourself color mixing. Circle of colored paper (1) mounted on circle of stout cardboard. Smaller circle of paper of different color (2), folded as shown, with shaded region cut way. Cut out glued concentrically on colored circle. When the cardboard circle is mounted (securely) on a child's top, or on the circular sanding base of an electrical drill, colors 1 and 2 are mixed in equal proportions when the disc spins. Best results are obtained with the brightest colors: a combination of fluorescent red and fluorescent green is particularly impressive.

Figure 5-51 Sydney Harry's Top. The original is 14.3 centimeters in diameter, and mounted on heavy cardboard with a sharpened matchstick as axle. It is spun by hand.

The exact explanation of this effect has not yet been fully worked out, but it is believed to hold the key to a greatly increased understanding of our perception of color, and of the nature of simple learning and memory. One thing is certain much more is involved than the mere time in which it takes a cone to recover from absorbing a photon.

Negative after-images of color complementary to the object are normally obtained when the illumination is fairly even. Incandescent sources may produce a positive after-image, a fleeting company of the object. In a darkened room, we may continue to see a candle flame for a moment or two after it has been blown out. And if you have a short enough name, you may write your whole signature across the night sky with a lighted sparkler, for the color lingers for an instant after the sparkler has moved on.

Perhaps the most impressive of all after-images is the "flight of colors" which we see after a very bright light has been shone into the eye, as when we have been examined by an oculist. Against a white ceiling floats a brilliant yellow patch with a magenta border, edged with turquoise around its changing amoeboid shape. The colors gradually change too, so that it becomes a negative after-image—blue, edged with yellow and red. The effect lasts for several minutes, changing shape and color like a spreading oil patch.

Visual information also can be stored for much longer periods. We can remember some colors for years, and our memory can modify the colors we now see. If two shapes, representing a leaf and a donkey, are cut from the same piece of gray paper and placed on the same background, most observers claim that the leaf is a greener gray than the donkey.

A similar expectation may be one reason why we say that a donkey, lit by the setting sun, is brownish gray, although the light which reaches us from it is akin to that scattered by rust or copper in daylight. But the state of adaptation of the eye also is important. It is thought that the retina can adapt to wavelength composition of the illumination, if this differs appreciably from white light, in much the same way as it adapts to changes in intensity. Those who use cars with slightly tinted green glass will know that, seen through the windscreen or a closed window, the surroundings look "normal" and the glass untinted. The eye is adapted to a faintly green background. But if we then partly wind down a window, that part of the scene we see through the open window now looks distinctly pink, while the adjacent part, viewed through the glass, is tinged with green. After a minute or so, however, the contrast fades, and both parts of the scene look untinted.

More dramatic illustrations of the interplay of adaptation and contrast can often be seen in theater lighting. The stage is lit from two widely separated spotlights, one white and one red, so that their spots exactly coincide on the white background, which our eyes, once they have adapted to the pink light, see as white. A dancer appears, and blocks the beam from the white spot, and where her shadow falls on the background, the only light which reaches us is from the red spotlight. So we see a red shadow on a white background. Her partner then emerges from the opposite wings, and blocks the beam from the red light. So where he casts a shadow, only white light reaches the background. But we do not see his shadow as white on a pink background, because we already see the background as white. So, instead of perceiving it as pink-minus-red, we see it as white-minus-red—as turquoise. The shadows of the *pas de deux* appear, not as red and white on pink, but more impressively, as red and turquoise on white.

A similar effect has been exploited by Land, who showed that red and white light could be mixed in such a way as to give sensations over a wide range of colors. He made black and white positive transparencies, photographing each scene twice, once through a red filter, and once through a green one. He projected them both on to a screen, the first with a red light, and the second with a white one, and when the images were superimposed, obtained, in addition to red and black, a range of colors from turquoise, through green and yellow, to orange.

We do not yet know if the mechanism by which we adapt to the color of the illumination takes place in the eye or in the brain. But there seems to be a series of brain cells, each of which picks up processed signals from a very narrow band of wavelengths. Between them, they span the visible spectrum; and it seems that each discernible color (including the non spectral purple) is associated with its own set of brain cells. Of these cells, a number will respond only in the presence of the background illumination. Thus some of the cells which respond to changes in the intensity of red light (but are insensitive to changes in the intensity of other colors) will respond to red *only* if it is mixed with light of other colors. Pure red light produces no activity in such cells. It may well be that observations of this type will eventually help us to understand why the perceived colors of objects depend so little on the light which falls on them.

But the extent to which the color of an object seems to remain constant also depends on who is looking at what. The color of a real donkey seems to change less with the illumination than does the color of a donkey in a picture. The colors of a naturalistic painting vary less than do those of a bold pattern, which are themselves more constant than an abstract picture with ill-defined regions of color. To a large extent, what we see depends on what we expect to see. Even to an artist, a donkey may, at a brief, casual glance, look donkey-colored. But if the artist is thinking about incorporating the donkey into a painting, he will be more sensitive to the light reaching him from the donkey at that particular moment than to the average color which the donkey would have if viewed by a lay-person in diffuse light.

Color sensations often may be even more dramatically altered by, or even produced by, factors other than light. Some forms of hysteria and hallucinogenic drugs enhance appreciation of color. Hallucinogens often provide experience of brightly colored patterns which bear little relation to the real world, and those about to suffer attacks of epilepsy or migraine may see ocolored rays and geometrical shapes before an attack. The blind, particularly if they are old, may have similar sensations, akin to seeing "golden rain" and colored patterns. In childhood, a pressure on a closed eye was enough to produce patterns as exotic as Catherine wheels or peacock tails. In adult life, a firmer touch, preferably on the upper part of the eye, is needed to produce an inferior but nonetheless impressive result. Electrical and mechanical stimulation of the optic nerve and the visual areas of the brain can make us see colors, as can some acute illnesses, and even a strong magnetic field. And so, of course, can memory and dreams. But although we can experience an immense variety of color sensations produced in these different, nonvisual, ways, we have as yet only a negligible understanding of any of the mechanisms involved.

Figure 5-52 Thai elephants at a soccer match, and [inset] author with Thai painter "Popeye" at a lunch break.

PHOTO BY THE AUTHOR.

We have taken a look at color sensations related to bees, ants, butterflies, and other creatures. We went a step further to discover the Bower bird, who collects only blue objects for his mate after completing her nest. We can even top that . . . how about elephants who paint?

During our research on color in these past several years, we have made additional jouneys to Thailand in order to research more thoroughly the *elephant artists*. Intrigued by this, we wanted to see if the elephants could paint representational objects in saturated colors. After putting together a team of people, we went in search of a very special young elephant (5 years old) to help us understand how these beautiful and gifted animals see color.

We met Popeye having his lunch in a bamboo thicket. He is one of Thailand's talented elephants. They have demonstrated a certain prowess in developing a sensitivity to color. For the past twenty years or so, certain elephants have been painting with color in the jungles of northern Thailand. A number of elephant camps entertain visitors with these artists, and offer the pachyderm paintings for sale to support the ever-growing population of elephants. Because elephants are respected and not made to work in difficult situations, sports and painting have been the substitute *job security*.

Our last expedition ended by introducing full saturated color to the elephants' existing knowledge about painting.

Popeye responds particularly well to red and green. Green we perhaps understand because his jungle habitation is made up of green fauna, but red is quite a different story. As we continue to research these kinds of questions, we are trying to determine if, for example, the elephant may indeed have a greater number of red cones in the eye than do other animals. These are yet to be determined.

Figure 5-54 Elephant team finds Popeye in a bamboo thicket.

It is always surprising in terms of how carefully the elephant's trunk manipulates the brush. He manipulates the brush with slow and calculated movements, and his responses to saturated backgrounds are quite different from that of a white ground or canvas, because his approach to the canvas is more cautious, as well as the actual application of paint to the surface. The sensation of color for Popeye is a study in progress, and to date is still being studied.

Figure 5-53 Popeye rejuvenated after lunch.

Figure 5-55 Popeye Paints the Tree Trunks First.

Figure 4-56 Popeye Adds Leaves to His Tree Composition.

Figure 5-58 Popeye's Snack: 50 lbs. of Bananas and Sugar Cane.

Figure 5-57 The Finished Painting: *Trees in the Jungle.*

Figure 5-59 Popeye's Paint Box.

Summary

The following concepts are particularly important to our summary of Chapter 5:

1. Tints and shades are foremost in their ability to create the illusion of mass and volume, as well as the implication of deep space. The surface gradients are able to portray illusion objects in space and surface texture. Tints are about intensity, whereas shades are about less intensity.

2. In our study of the *keys,* we demonstrated the three systems of high- medium-, and low-key color through movie clips.

3. The three-value systems were studied, beginning with Leonardo da Vinci's sfumato technique of gradients in the *Mona Lisa*, followed by the average gradation of value in Picasso's *Renaissance Maternity,* and then Caravaggio's tenebristic or extreme value gradations in his painting *The Conversion of St. Paul.*

4. The essay about the *Sensations of Color* covered the function of the eye in color vision, including certain animals' visual stimulus of color.

5. A project proposal to demonstrate the student's comprehension of chromatic values/tints and shades.

TINTS AND SHADES; MASS AND DEEP SPACE

The Project:

On a sheet of watercolor paper of specified size, render twelve spheres or eggs of varying sizes. You should form *three yellow, three orange, three green,* and *three white* spheres. Anytime that you paint or create a sphere on a surface, be sure that you make a cast shadow so, that the ball will appear to sit appropriately on the plane. Additionally, linear perspective should not be the main vehicle for creating the illusion of space—nor should overlapping—but rather chromatic value gradations. The spheres should have the illusion of three-dimensional mass by the manipulation of tints and shades. You must not only create round spheres, but also produce the illusion of deep space, whether by dark contrasts or *chromatic value gradations.* There will be four groups of three spheres that will illustrate either warm tints and cool shades or cool tints with warm shades.

The spheres need to have a light source, and should therefore be illuminated from one side or the other (Figure 5-60). The sphere then will demonstrate *highlights* to *base*

tones (see example on following pages), creating effective transitions of light to dark chromatic values across the surface of the ball:

- A *warm illumination* creates a *warm tint and shade,* but a *cool cast shadow.*
- A *cool illumination* creates a *cool tint and shade,* but a *warm cast shadow.*
- Use the blending, stippled, or broken color technique, or as demonstrated. Below are suggested formulas that will aid in your decisions. They are not "written in stone," only possible methods of color choices for the painting of spheres. You are allowed to make appropriate changes as long as you achieve a convincing composition of spheres in deep space.

Three Yellow Spheres (Figure 5-62):

- *Highlight* (warm tint) is white to very light tinted yellow.
- *Light tone* is light to medium yellow.

Figure 5-60

- *Half tone* is saturated yellow.
- *Base tone* or shade is yellow-orange. Shade with black.
- *Reflected light* is light orange-yellow.
- *Cast shadow* is cool-dark blue or violet tints and shades.

Three Orange Spheres

- *Highlight* (warm tint) is white to lightest tinted yellow-orange.
- *Light tone* is yellow-orange to saturated orange.
- *Half tone* is red-orange.
- *Base tone* is deep red-orange shaded with black.
- *Reflected light* is light red–orange.
- *Cast shadow* is cool-dark blue or dark violet.

Three Green Spheres

- *Highlight* (cool tint) is lightest tinted yellow-green.
- *Light tone* is light green to saturated green.
- *Half tone* is saturated green to shaded blue-green.
- *Base tone* is blue-green shaded with black.
- *Reflected light* is light blue-green.
- *Cast shadow* is deep shaded warm-red to red-orange.

Three White Spheres

- *Highlight* (warm tint) is white to lightest possible tinted yellow.
- *Light tone* is lightest yellow to lightest violet.
- *Half tone* is lightest yellow with violet shades. Mix them when partially *stiff*, so that you will not cancel the yellow.
- *Base tone* is violet.
- *Reflected light* is lightest violet tints.
- *Cast shadow* is cool deep violet.

Reference:

Tints and Shades

When referring to *tints* we are moving from gray to *white*:

When referring to *shades* we are moving from *gray* to *black*:

Figure 5-61

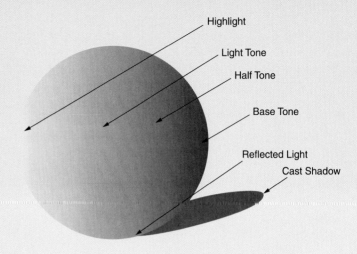

Figure 5-62

Project Objectives Summary:

- To formulate a proper understanding of how *tints* and *shades* function, particularly in terms of creating the illusion of three-dimensional *mass* and *depth of space*.
- To further clarify the effects of warm and cool temperatures and their effect of creating *believable shapes in space*, as well as facilitating mood variations.
- To form a clearer understanding of how value gradations function in all chromatic functions.

Please see the following image for an example of student resolution to the project proposal.

Student Examples:

Figure 5-63 Student Artwork #1.

SARAH CHEA.

Figure 5-64 Student Artwork #2, Sarah Chea.

PHOTO BY THE AUTHOR.

Figure 5-66 Sarah Chea.

Figure 5-65 Student Artwork #3.

CHAPTER SIX

Figure 6-1 FERNANDO YANEZ DE LA ALMEDINA, **Saint Catherine.** Color harmony through the ages were both intuitively and intellectually understood. The colors and their combinations were specified by royalty, from generation to generation. The general or overall harmony here is a tetrad (four basic colors) of reds, violets, yellows and greens (yellow-greens).

6

COLOR
HARMONY

INTRODUCTION TO COLOR HARMONY

Color harmony, in a very general sense, is a communications device that is necessary for all artists and designers to thoroughly understand. The development of working knowledge in harmony basics is the foundation for color theory itself. In a musical composition, we intuitively understand that music harmony is imperative for inspirational enjoyment. Indiscriminate spontaneous color applications are often somewhat like listening to music played from sheet music, with random selection of notes; it just does not make sense. In like manner, the harmonious whole of a given color composition is either visually lyrical, or not. (A complete explanation of this will be presented in Chapter 7.)

The harmony of color refers to the effect of color combinations on the human psyche and human spirit. Specifically, color harmony results when two or more colors are brought together to create particular moods and emotional responses by the viewer. In the first part of this chapter, we will study the conventional Western approach to color harmony. Next, we'll focus on the Orient for our summary of color's composite parts. Although color harmony serves similar functions from culture to culture, its composite hues vary considerably, as do the symbolic representation of those combinations. The second part of this chapter will entail the study of color as seen by the Japanese aristocracy in the Heian period 1,000 years ago.

In all situations and professions that require color resolutions, there are general hue formulas or color marriages that function optimally. The term *harmonious* can be used to define colors that are different from each other, as the same color with various values, or for colors that are only minimally different from one another.

Figure 6-2 Tranquility of a Dyadic Color Harmony of Yellow-Green Foliage and Red-Violet Bark.

Johannes Itten, a well-known color theorist in the earlier part of the twentieth century, said color harmony should not be considered "subjective," but rather should be moved into the "objective" arena. His comments were based mostly on the physiology of *afterimage* effects. An example of afterimage is gazing at a saturated *red square* for a few minutes and then closing the eyes, only to see a *complementary green square*. The same is true of an orange square, which produces a blue square and a yellow square to violet. The eye will always *demand the complement* of what also is known as *successive* contrast. In order to support objectivity in color harmony we need only to refer to the color circle. Our standard model illustrates that red is opposite of green, yellow to violet, and orange to blue. When we mix those complements, they have the effect of canceling each other to produce the achromatic value of gray. Imagine Wilhelm Ostwald's theory, for example, whose hypothesis of the color circle would actually put yellow opposite of blue, rather than violet. The result would not be gray, or the cancellation of color, but the two would instead create *green*.

Itten said that color harmony must be objective, whereas Ostwald believed that it should be subjective. We know that Ostwald felt his theory about harmonies was justified because certain groups of colors were "pleasing." These days we understand, however, that aesthetics are not the only criteria, but there is more to it—that is to say does not formulate well, in its all too simplistic approach (please see Ostwald's theory for greater clarity). On the other hand, color harmony cannot be entirely and unequivocally objective in all aspects. There has to be some room designated for subjectivity, even though it is certainly more objective by conventional standards. There are certain rules about color that cannot be denied, such as the *physiological* effects of successive contrast and simultaneous contrast, which has its place in the objective quadrant of color harmony. However, there are exceptions to the rules in some cases, because there are those who will always see color quite differently. We can say to any one person that their personal choice of color arrangements do not fit the conventional model of harmonic chroma, yet their choices will not always allow us to be overly dogmatic as long as people are individuals.

This brings us to *subjective* color. Certainly we can decide on any number of color harmonies or arrangements of our own choosing. That is not in and of itself the problem. There are certain formulas (harmonies), which presented in proper arrangement, produce specific and desired emotional results. Staying away from those factual conventions is sometimes risky when attempting to produce a very definite mood.

Subjective color is this: adherence to the rules or boundaries of color harmony conventions to a degree, with the freedom to chose those color harmonies that suit your needs. It is subjective in that you are free to make certain decisions about saturations, intensities, values, tints, shades, contrasts, color proportions, and so on. There are many color harmony variations—too many for us to cover in this text. Instead, we'll cover six traditional examples referred to as dyad, triad, tetrad, hexad, analogous, and monochromatic color harmonies.

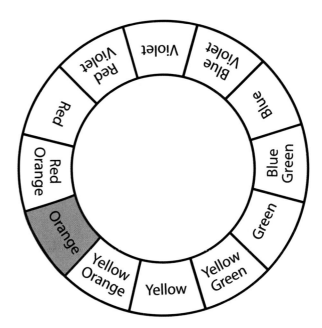

Figure 6-3 Monochromatic Harmony.

PHOTO BY THE AUTHOR.

Figure 6-4 Monochromatic Color Harmony of Orange: Three Persimmons.

SUNSET BOULEVARD/CORBIS.

Figure 6-5 Achromatic Composition of William Holden, Audrey Hepburn, and Humphrey Bogart. Remember not to confuse monochromatic (mono: one and chromatic: color) with achromatic (absence of color).

Monochromatic Color Harmony

Monochromatic harmony (Figures 6-3, 6-4, 6-6, and 6-8) refers to a composition of one color only, with gradations of light and dark value of that color. We have selected Picasso's painting *Two Nudes* to demonstrate how a monochromatic composition of red-orange works. There

Figure 6-6 Monochromatic.

Figure 6-8 PABLO PICASSO, *Two Nudes,* late 1906.

Figure 6-7 Monochromatic Figure.

are gradations of value from light red-orange to darkest red-orange. In this case it is about the tinting and shading of red-orange. The temperature of the painting remains warm throughout. The red-orange value gradations here also cause the figures to take on a very sculptural and stone-like appearance.

Two Nudes is an excellent example of one color with varying values. The entire composition is comprised of light, medium, and dark values of orange. The monochromatic use of color creates a very sculptural and stone like appearance to the figures themselves. The lack of color variation focuses the eye on the sculptural quality of these two figures.

Dyad Color Harmony

Dyad color harmonies (Figures 6-9, 6-10, and 6-11) consist of a pair of colors, which are opposite on the color circle. We know these pairs as complements, which always consist of one primary and one secondary color, as well as one warm and one cool. The power of complements often influences one another, depending on the specific hue combination. They are the *polite* pair, that is to say they exist to complement one another in order to create balance and harmony. Typically, strawberries are sold in green plastic containers,

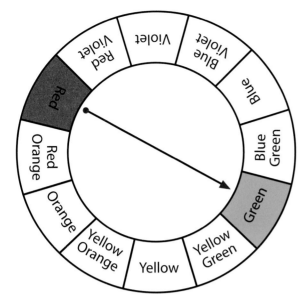

Figure 6-9

Figure 6-10 Dyadic Color Harmony.

Figure 6-11 Dyadic Color Harmony of Red and Green.

Figure 6-12

which enhance the redness of the berry itself. Test the theory, and put strawberries on a yellow surface instead, and you will understand the appeal of complements.

Triadic Color Harmony

Yellow, red, and blue are the strongest of the color harmonies, and are known as the *primary triads*. Some are triads of intensified color, or tinted triads, while others are significantly shaded reds, yellows, and blues.

Triadic color harmonies also can be seen in Richard Diebenkorn's *Berkeley No. 52,* (Figure 6-13) as a secondary triadic color harmony. Also, we can see clearly the secondary colors in the vineyard image of violet and orange grapes, contrasted against the green foliage. Notice how the intensity of light on the lower grapes actually seems to change to the hue of the grapes. At this point, it is prudent to review the difference between opaque and translucent color. Compare the difference in the opacity of the pigments of color in the painting and the translucence clearly observed in the grapes.

You remember, of course, our studies about compositional color analysis, and as a novice theorist, you may have discovered some difficulty in knowing exactly what to write about. If we were to do a complete color analysis of the grapes, we would have to discuss color elements such as *triadic color harmony, secondary colors, contrast, chromatic value gradations of tints and shades, intensity, saturation, translucence, and even emotional appeal.*

Remember, there are intermediate triads also, such as *yellow-orange, red-violet,* and *blue-green,* or *yellow-green, red-orange, and blue-violet.*

Figure 6-13 RICHARD DIEBENKORN, *Berkeley No. 52*, 1955.

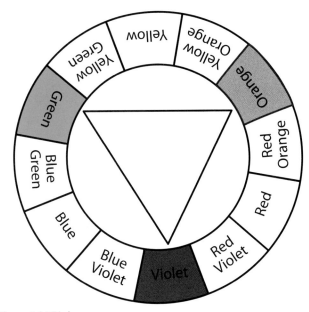

Figure 6-14 Triad.

JUPITERIMAGES.

Figure 6-15 Secondary Triadic Color Harmony.

PHOTO BY THE AUTHOR.

Figure 6-16 Triad (Primary).

RICHARD EWING.

Figure 6-17

Split Complementary *Triadic Color Harmony*

Split Complements also create a triadic color harmony, but the triangle is not equilateral.

Instead, the configuration of a split complementary from yellow, for example, would be yellow, blue-violet, and red-violet. The violet itself is no longer part of the harmony because one-half of it is moved to the left, and one-half to the right. The remaining colors are as follows:

- Violet: Yellow-orange and yellow-green
- Orange: Blue-green and blue-violet
- Green: Red-violet and red-orange
- Blue: Yellow-orange and red-orange
- Red: Blue-green and yellow-green

Jan Gossart, a sixteenth-century Renaissance painter (Figure 6-20), illustrates a skillful use of split complements, seen by the yellow-orange background buildings, the red-orange columns, and the blue sky, as well as the blue cloak on the figure.

Although the red-orange in the pumpkin patch seems to dominate the composition, the green and red-violet foliage not only serves to provide contrast and focus on the pumpkins, but also helps to lead the eye into the background space.

There is no concrete rule that the *principal* complement (green) necessarily has to dominate the composition. There can be variances of tints, shades, intensities, and saturations as long as there are two split complements involved. In this case, it is the saturation of red-orange that almost overwhelms the composition.

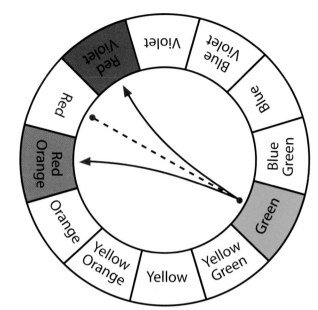

Figure 6-18 Split-Complement.

Figure 6-19 Split Complementary Triadic Color Harmony of Green, Red-Orange, and Red-Violet.

Figure 6-20 Jan Gossaert (called Mabuse), **_Danae._**

Tetradic Color Harmony

The *tetrad* harmony incorporates the use of two pairs of complementary harmonies in a single composition. Those complements are derived by a perfect square inscribed within the color circle. Each of the connecting points of the square indicates the colors that are to be used.

Three harmonies of the tetrad square are: (Figure 6-22)

- Yellow, violet, red-orange, and blue-green
- Yellow-orange, blue-violet, red, and green
- Orange, blue, red-violet, and yellow-green

Another tetrad can be formed by the use of a rectangle (Figure 6-24) inside of the color circle, instead of a square. These pairs are:

- Yellow-green, red-violet, yellow-orange, and blue-violet
- Yellow, violet, orange, and blue

The composition of Raphael's *Sistine Madonna* (Figure 6-25) has deep green curtains in the upper right and left corners, and on the outer robe of the right side figure. On the central figure of Mary, she wears a blue-violet outer robe with red. The left side figure is adorned mostly with yellow-orange with a bit of red. The surrounding ground of blue-violet also is apparent.

Raphael's entire composition consists of variations in blue-violet, red, yellow-orange, and green. You must look more carefully because there are few areas of saturated color throughout the composition.

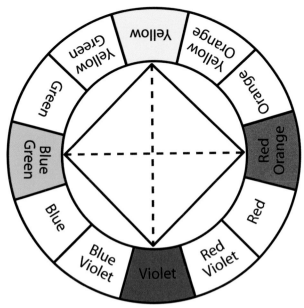

Figure 6-22 Tetrad.

Figure 6-23 Tetradic Color Harmony of Violet, Yellow, Blue-Green, and Red-Orange. The striking contrast can be seen between the light red-orange grapefruit and the dark red-orange wall. Additionally, the violet onions and yellow lemons set up a complementary contrast as well as the red-orange with the blue-green. Tetradic harmonies are easy to remember, because they are nothing more than two pairs of complements.

Figure 6-21

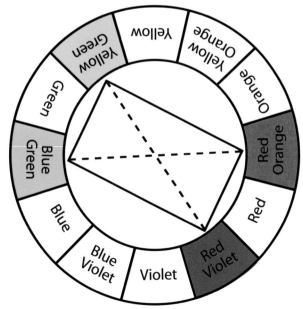

Figure 6-24 Tetrad.

Figure 6-25 RAPHAEL, *Sistine Madonna,* 1512–1513. Painted for Pope Julius II as his present to the city of Piacenza, Italy. The church at Piacenza was dedicated to Pope Sixtus II (left), on the right Saint Barbara.

PHOTO BY THE AUTHOR.

Figure 6-26 Tetrad.

Hexad Color Harmony

Hexadic color harmonies are derived from a hexagon (Figure 6-27) inscribed within the color circle. A hexadic harmony is the most colorful, as well as more complex because it consists of three warm and cool complementary pairs. It is easy to remember because there are twelve colors represented in the color circle. Every other color, or six colors, constitute a hexadic harmony. The two possibilities of hexads are:

- Yellow-orange, blue violet, red-orange, blue-green, red-violet, and yellow-green
- Yellow, violet, orange, blue, red, and green.

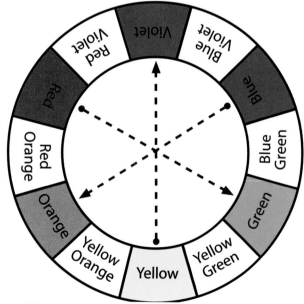

Figure 6-27

PHOTO BY THE AUTHOR.

Figure 6-28 Hexadic Color Harmony of Yellow, Violet, Green, Red, Orange, and Blue.

PHOTO BY THE AUTHOR.

Figure 6-29 Hexad.

USED BY PERMISSION OF THE LOUIS K. MEISEL GALLERY, NEW YORK.

Figure 6-30 CHARLES BELL, *Sixteen Candles,* 1992.

Analogous Color Harmony

Analogous color harmonies (Figure 6-33) are a family of hues that exist side by side on the color circle. As few as three and as many as *six* colors are normally used to qualify as analogous. They must all be joining colors on the circle, side by side. Both warm or cool harmonies may create an effective temperature mood. Warm analogous harmonies can be created (for example) by:

- Yellow, yellow-orange, orange, red-orange, red; or
- Red-orange, red, red-violet, and violet.
  Cool harmonies can be created (for example) by:
- Yellow-green, green, blue-green, blue, and blue-violet
- Green, blue-green, blue, blue-violet, and violet.

The dividing line between the warm and cool side of the color circle is: Yellow to red-violet (warm), and yellow-green to blue-violet (cool). Violet itself is normally considered on the cooler side, but is very susceptible to being either warm or cool with a small addition of red or blue, respectively.

There are no concrete rules that an analogous harmony must be either warm or cool. Analogous can be both, such as green, yellow-green, yellow, and yellow-orange. The only stipulation is that their connectedness cannot be broken, and no more than six.

The abstract painting of Nicolas de Staël (Figure 6-35) is constructed of rigid yellow-orange verticals and calm horizontals of yellow, red-orange and red. De Staël builds his landscape by incorporating a warm analogous color palette into the composition.

If we were to use temperature of color as a reference to this painting, we would have to say that it perhaps

Figure 6-32 Analogous Color Harmony—Yellow Lemons, Yellow-Orange Apricots, Orange Tangerines, Red-Orange Grapefruits, Red Tomatoes, and Red-Violet Onions.

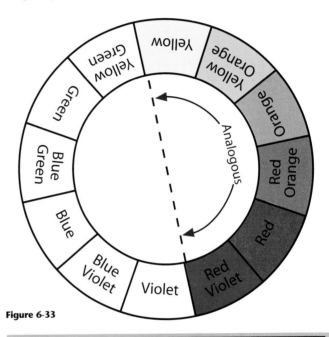

Figure 6-33

Figure 6-31

Figure 6-34 Analogous.

reflects a warm summer day. On the other hand, if we were to use the color symbolically, we may be tempted to call it a cool autumn day.

André Lhote's painting (Figure 6-37) creates an analogous warm and cool harmony of blue-green, blue, blue-violet, violet, red-violet, and red. Although there are both warm and cool hues, the overall effect is that of a somewhat warm composition. The redness of the figure, with the warm red-violet, seems to slightly dominate the temperature of the painting. The combination of warm and cool reflects a moderate temperature zone, to say the least.

In order to further explore color harmony, we want to go to another country—this time Japan. The following pages will first open up a general monologue about some general attributes about color in both the old (traditional) and new (modern) Japan. After that, we want to look at how the Japanese became the ultimate purveyors of color harmony in the tenth and eleventh centuries.

Figure 6-36

Figure 6-35 Nicolas De Staël, *Countryside.*

Figure 6-37 ANDRÉ LHOTE, *Bacchante*, 1910.

JAPAN: A LAND OF COLOR HARMONY

by Alan Burner

Since the earliest recorded history of the Japanese, color harmony has been an important aspect of the culture. In fact, color is at the core of its aesthetic sentiments, as we will see in the early Heian period and then in the newer and more contemporary Japan.

Color is especially at the center of concern for architecture, ceremony, dress (fabric design), and the Japanese garden. We will take a brief look at the specific color harmonies that represent Japan and the sentiment of its people.

Two Color Harmonies for Two Different Japans

Red and green dyadic harmony is part of Japan's history from early times. A typical scene that exemplifies the recognition of Japanese landscape is the saturated red architecture contrasted with the green foliage of nature. There already exists the symbolical harmony, or at least commonness of materials, between architecture and nature in that the structures of wood have been constructed from the very source of its contrast—the product of the green leaf. The artificial structure of wood has been painted red, which is in complementary color to the natural green foliage.

In the frame below we see a 50/50 balance of red and green, where neither color overpowers the other. It is this *dyadic color harmony* that prevails all over traditional Japan, and represents traditional Japanese color harmony. In a broader range of green landscape, it is the green that complements the red, and the red that complements the green.

The red Tori gate in the distance is most definitely a focal point, and yet it does not dominate the entire town because of the enormous amount of green landscape. The green of the surrounding area gives greater saturation to the gate, and the red of the gate certainly produces a more saturated green. It is the saturated red, which denotes *importance* in architecture, and it is the contrast of these two colors that signifies that which is constructed, as opposed to that which is natural.

Turning our attention to the photograph of the *Heian Shrine Pond on a Rainy Day*, (Figure 6-41) we observe both color harmony and the mood created by it. The pond image is a *monochromatic* green harmony. Notice the gradations and variances of green values in the garden. All of the plants have been carefully planned in their arrangements for optimal effect.

The monochromatic greens in the garden's foliage had a very quieting effect on students and faculty members. The tranquility in such a calm color harmony is quite amazing. Add a soft, steady rain to the mix and you will find it difficult to leave. The careful planning and placement of green hues are instrumental to the success of this color harmony.

Figure 6-38 July 1, 2004, Sports Page Announces Tigers Victory: The Color Harmony of Commercial Contemporary Japan.

PHOTO BY THE AUTHOR.

PHOTO BY THE AUTHOR.

Figure 6-39 Heian Shrine, Kyoto, Japan.

Elegant moments of harmony
Perhaps Murasaki's pond.
A work of art in beauty's rest
Rain splashed surface
Dances on lily pads of green.
Washed tranquil from the world
My heart is at peace
I can love again.

Shijo, Kyoto, June 2004

It is often the case, whereby one finds it impossible to express adequately, the experience of a given moment in time. As artists and designers, we struggle to express thos words, music, and color visuals, often to no avail. The more that we understand the issues with color attributes, in this case *harmony*, the more proficient we become in conveying our message. Let us not forget that it is the message or content of the color visuals that is responsible for translating the information to the viewer or customer.

Figure 6-40 Tori Gate at Hakone, Japan.

PHOTO BY THE AUTHOR.

Figure 6-41 Heian Shrine Pond on a Rainy Day, Kyoto.

Figure 6-42 Remembering a Sacred Moment of Tranquility with Kristi. Heian Shrine Pond, Kyoto, Japan.

PHOTO BY THE AUTHOR.

Figure 6-43 One of Many Tokyo Shopping Districts.

We have briefly discussed the typical colors that represent the older order of Japan as well as the traditional colors of Japan. Now let's take a look at the colors of *contemporary,* or present-day society in Japan, specifically within its larger cities. There is, of course, the old and the new, which exist side by side within most larger cities, but we want to focus on Japan's largest city in order to make a solid point.

Flashes of primary colors of yellow, blue, and red are everywhere in the city of Tokyo. These triadic color

PHOTO BY THE AUTHOR.

Figure 6-44 Small Udon Shop: Signage Must Also Compete. Tokyo.

harmonies have become symbolic of the new modern age for Japan's largest cities, especially Tokyo. This is not really surprising, because the primary triadic color harmony is the most powerful of all harmony combinations, and the idea is to capture the buyer's attention. At first sight, it would seem as though one sign would distract from the others, but it is the overall effect that draws crowds into the street. The Japanese are great team workers. By day, the streets are fairly calm and business is as usual. At night, signage had better be able to produce at least the same level of energy as the next, or one's business is liable to be engulfed in the night storm of primary harmonies.

Even the small stores must struggle to keep up with the energy and excitement of colors generated. By day all businesses are at equal standing, but by night when the crowds come out, the competition of color signage is intense.

A typical Tokyo shopping district (see surrounding images) is not simply amplified with visual primary harmonies, but color is audible as well. As one strolls the street, loud and commensurably energetic music seems to replicate the city's *visual clamor.* It is the symbolic stimulus blender, where all of the senses seem to overload into the proverbial buying frenzy. The trap has been set and is sprung. Basically, the energy of the city's yellow, red, and blue harmony creates the energy, which requires further support in the form of music. The city is the new

Figure 6-45 Primary Colors Prevail on Sega Poster, Tokyo.

PHOTO BY THE AUTHOR.

Figure 6-46 Primary Harmonies of a Game Palace Lure the Customer, Tokyo.

PHOTO BY THE AUTHOR.

Japanese society, which is in direct contrast with the old, traditional, quiet, complementary harmonies of red and green. This is but one example to illustrate the emotional and mood appeal of color harmony—one is tranquil, and one is energized.

Now that we have taken a brief look at Japan, both traditional and contemporary, let's begin to focus on the early beginnings of color harmony one thousand years in the past.

AN INTRODUCTION TO JAPANESE COLOR HARMONY: HEIAN PERIOD ARISTOCRACY

Because color harmony is no doubt the premier attribute of color, other than mood, our study of color harmony now shifts to a very different perspective. The primary birthplace of japanese color aesthetics and harmony, is recorded through a novel written slightly more than 1,000

years ago. Through this novel, we see the development of the arts in all forms, but more than any aspect it is its prowess of color harmonies that created such enormous aethetic ramifications for the next millennium in Japan.

The Tale of Genji is a very long love story. The novel was written 1,000 years ago in the ancient capital of Kyoto, by the Heian court aristocrat, Murasaki Shikibu.

The story revolves around the hero of the story, Prince Genji, the emperor's son. Through the earlier years, the exceptionally handsome prince often is involved in numerous romantic exploits, and continues to make the most of his position and good looks at the palace confines. At one point, Genji, who serves under the minister of the left, once again succumbs to his desires and spends the night with the daughter of minister of the right. He is confronted with the scandal and is unable to escape. Because of his indiscretion, he is forced to exile himself to the storm ravaged coast of Suma. Not surprising, Genji connects with a lady referred to as the "Akashi Lady" there, and they have a daughter.

Several years later, he is summoned back to the palace and restored with ever increasing influence. He begins to focus on his children at court, that the family may be able to marry into the appropriate political factions. Also, at this point, Kaoru (thought to be Genji's son, but in reality belongs to Kashiwagi) and Niou (Son of the emperor pregnant) pursue their own romantic quest, and both become rivals in love, which ultimately centers mainly around the impulsive and reckless Ukifune.

> Murasaki Shikibu's *The Tale of Genji* is *the* leading document in Japanese literature. Every citizen of Japan is aware of the Genji Monogatari and the story of the Prince. In every sense, it is the commensurable companion [notoriety and literary value], to the comedies, histories, tragedies and poems of William Shakespeare in England.

Another important feature and focus of this chapter is traditional Japanese color harmony, which takes us back 1,000 years ago to the Heian period in Japan; in particular, the aristocratic population of nobility up to the Emperor himself. This was a very important time for Japanese history and the development of Japanese aesthetic sentiment. Our basis for this period will center around Japan's most important literary achievement, the novel known as *Genji Monogatari,* or *The Tale of Genji*.

The author of this novel, the Lady Murasaki Shikibu, wrote this almost exactly 1,000 years ago, the closest estimation being between 1004–1006 C.E. This novel is one of the world's longest fictional texts, and is clearly Japan's most acclaimed novel throughout its history. The *Genji Monogatari* in Japan would be commensurate to Shakespeare in England, in terms of literary achievement and fame. All school children study *The Tale of Genji* in Japan. The novel is a fifty-four chapter love story that takes place in eleventh-century court life in Japan. It is Japanese aristocracy at its best—the emperor, empress, princesses, princes, ministers of the left and right, and ladies-in-waiting—all contribute to

Figure 6-47 Heian Shrine with Author's Students, Kyoto, Japan, 2004.

court life as aristocrats. They are concerned with a host of political factions, which helps to install them or their sons and daughters in a higher position within court life. The tale centers around Prince Genji, who experiences victory and defeat at court, the joys of life as an aristocrat, and the grief of exile, all from his own doings.

At this juncture, it will be important to see how the novel, Japanese aristocratic dress, court gardens and *color harmony* link together. The author's name Murasaki means *purple,* and part of her family name means *wisteria,* which is a lavender cascade of clustered blossoms, typically seen around Japanese gardens in the spring. The word lavender

Figure 6-48 Gravesite of Murasaki Shikibu in Southern Kyoto Area.

AN INTRODUCTION TO JAPANESE COLOR HARMONY: HEIAN PERIOD ARISTOCRACY   **281**

PHOTO BY THE AUTHOR.

Figure 6-49 Close-up of Murasaki Shikibu's Gravesite in Southern Kyoto Area.

PHOTO BY THE AUTHOR.

Figure 6-50 Court Carriage with Typical Layered Robes for Women, Genji Museum, Southern Kyoto Area.

(light purple or violet) refers to *affinity*. You will see in the following essay that affinity is a very important word. The fact that Murasaki Shikibu's name makes reference to these things gives important clues to look for within the essay itself.

Within the Japanese Heian garden itself, color was (and it still is) an important issue: the proximity of lighter greens to darker greens for contrasts; the positioning of

moderate greens as opposed to intermediate areas of color, and so on. The appropriate colors of bark, such as the red bark of a pine tree, the light-red flower of a cherry tree, or the white of a lotus blossom, are equally important in their placement.

Within court life, there also is the all-important aesthetic of appropriate dress. Fabric colors and motifs of the season must be appropriately layered to match the colors

PHOTO BY THE AUTHOR.

Figure 6-51 Typical Layering of Court Lady's Robes, Genji Museum, Southern Kyoto Area.

of a spring garden, for example, or autumn colors. For a lady to display poor taste in assembling the wrong color harmonies would mean a certain loss of status at court. The knowledge of proper color harmony uses at court was imperative for a lady.

Color was at the center of aesthetics, but there was much more involved. It was the court ladies who had command of artistic sensibilities. Painting, poetry, music, and writing were mostly the prowess of the aristocratic women. A woman's worth had much to do with her accomplishments in the arts. In fact, it is believed that in reality, it was *The Tale of Genji* that was largely responsible for the installation of Murasaki Shikibu at court.

Murasaki, both in the *Genji Monogatari* and the author, were gifted in the arts—painting, poetry, writing, and music. They had a special affinity for harmony, with many art forms, as well as color. Here, a mock up of Prince Genji is seen "peeking" to catch a rare glimpse of Murasaki playing the koto.

Below, a very early morning at Atami, Japan, is caught with a calm, quieting monochromatic blue color harmony. Note that the tranquility factor differs from the Heian pond (page 216), with its green monochromatic color harmony, and Atami Bay's (below) blue harmonies create very

PHOTO BY THE AUTHOR.

Figure 6-53 Genji Steals a Look at Murasaki's Musical Prowess, Genji Museum, Southern Kyoto Area.

sedate or tranquil environments. Both the Heian Shrine's pond green monochromatic color harmony and the Atami Bay blue harmonies are the result of a very sedate environment. It is easy to see why blues and greens are felt as calm colors.

PHOTO BY THE AUTHOR.

Figure 6-52 Atami Bay, Atami-shi, Shizuoka.

AN INTRODUCTION TO JAPANESE COLOR HARMONY: HEIAN PERIOD ARISTOCRACY   **283**

A CASE FOR COLOR HARMONY: JAPAN 785 A.D. TO 1186 A.D.

Color harmony is based on methodical color associations. Harmony continues to be the convention by which particular themes are established, as well as mood development and the creation of specific emotional content. These color accords are not exclusive to one culture, but are the vital link to expression for most social orders in the world today.

We find that by traveling through times past there have been standard color harmonies established, yet they have varied greatly from culture to culture through the stretch of time. Certainly we cannot expect all families of colors to have the same meaning for every group of peoples, yet no matter what group of people we belong to, we all understand the value of color harmonies. Whether by the creation of mood through color or the ability to focus attention to one or more areas in a composition, or the symbolical overtones, we intuitively understand harmonic legitimacy. Familiar color associations can be seen around the world. As we look at certain ethnic groups, we consider the costume form of dress of peoples in Africa, Polynesia, China, and Japan, or the Native American Indians across the United States, to name a few.

The organization of harmonious color schemes requires a certain sensibility. One culture in the distant past particularly sensitive to this was from the continent of Asia. As we travel back a thousand years in time, we visit the mother of aesthetic awareness—the Heian period in Japan. Here, emperors and empresses ruled over an aristocratic court of superior aestheticians, as princes and princesses procured the ultimate of all art forms. Whether dealing with aesthetics or politics, the Japanese in some way or another made important color decisions on a day-to-day basis.

Japan, 785 to 1186 A.D.

Color played one of its most important historical roles within the ranks of Japanese aristocracy during the turn of the first millennium. Nobility wove color harmony into the warp and woof of court life, from dress habits to garden aesthetics. One of the single most important aesthetic aspects or art forms of the day was the particular attention paid to how one was to dress each day. The obsession with court dress was practiced by all aristocrats, and was an important aesthetic statement about one's taste and sensibility, as well as one's position at court. This was particularly true of women in high court positions.

Interestingly enough, women had far fewer steps in their rank structure than did men. Yet what they lacked

Figure 6-54 Kashiwagi III—Genji Holds his Presumed Son Kaoru.

in color rank steps was more than compensated for in the number of layers of clothing required for females. In fact, as we will see, the splendor of color in women's dress created a dazzling spectacle, which could only have been described by *comparing the scene to a painting*.[1]

Let's begin our harmony studies, by making critical observations about this unique culture, specifically its dress habits, as well as the total aristocratic court scene.

Dress Code and Rank System in Heian Court

In the Heian court ranking system there were thirty grades of subject rank. With only a few exceptions, all of the highest three ranks, and most of the fourth and fifth ranked subjects, were actually permitted to attend the emperor at what was referred to as the Courtier's Hall. People from the fifth rank and up were considered the high ranking nobility, therefore, the sixth rank and down were considered low ranking, or minor positions.

The importance of dress in rank for the aristocrats was essential. The restrictions of color that were imposed at court allowed others to interpret the rank of another, even from a distance. This signaled what form the approaching relationship would take before actual human contact, and the color itself would make it possible to discern the difference between a courtier of the fifth rank and that of a sixth ranking courtier.

Because it was those of the fifth rank and above who received most of the attention at court, it is appropriate to focus on these higher ranks, particularly on the top three ranks. The lower ranks were not as elaborately dressed as the higher aristocrats. It was the visual structure of color harmonies combined that would indicate rank, which was more profound and well defined in the higher orders. In order to concentrate and focus on the vast complexities of all the ranks of dress, both men and women would typically allow themselves the occasional distraction of *okashi*.[2] This is a particularly relevant and important expression in aristocratic court dress as it relates to its affinity with nature. It is the quality and sensibility of *okashi* that draws our attention to the beauty and awe of court dress. It is that sudden awareness of beauty in court ceremony, with its various displays of color and motion, that forms the concept of the court's affinity with nature.

Dress Code and Types of Gowns for Women

Dress codes varied depending on the type of function that was being performed. Everyday dress was different than ceremonial dress, just as clothing worn in the spring time was in contrast to autumn, winter, or summer wear. Dress was traditionally changed before each of the four seasons began. This meant that specific colors represented each of the four seasons, and the robes of the aristocrats were changed accordingly. Consider the following example as Kenshi prepares her ladies-in-waiting for the Hojogi retreat:

> That evening, the ladies-in-waiting assembled before her in all their finery. Princess Teishi wore a coat in fallen-leaf colors over aster robes. Kenshi was a white figure, her two or three robes matched by her complexion.[3]

The particular colors, textile types, and layers involved could become quite complex depending on the occasion and office held by the person in question. Also, court

PUBLIC DOMAIN.

Figure 6-55 Typical Court Dress. From the Genji Monogatari Emakimono.

(Also see Ladies in Waiting of Lady Tamakazura's Court (detail), last page of this chapter.)

---

[1]*Murasaki Shikibu, Her Diary and Poetic Memoirs*, Bowring, Richard. Princeton University Press, 1982 p. 49, sc. 7. Murasaki Shikibu refers to Lady Saisho as she sleeps: "She lay with her head pillowed on a writing box, her face all but hidden by a series of robes, dark red lined with green, purple lined with dark red, over which she had thrown a deep crimson gown of unusually glossy silk; she made an enticing scene. Almost convinced that she had stepped right out of a painting, I pulled back the sleeve that covered her face."

[2]Okashi is the term used to express the beauty of the moment. Okashi is based on surface beauty such as court ceremony, color, action, and fabrics. Okashi can be expressed seasonally as spring. Spring illustrates the suddenness of being awe struck over beauty, as the new blossoms discovered on a tree, or an immense rainbow after a rainstorm. Spring, for example, is very Okashi!

[3]*A Tale of Flowering Fortunes*, William H. and Helen Craig McCullough. Stanford University Press 1980, Stanford, CA p. 744, Vol II.

dress, governmental dress, and attire of those residing at home varied as well. It is because of the infinite complex nature of aristocratic dress codes that I have decided to concentrate on court dress of the higher ranks for women. It was not unusual for a court lady to wear as many as fifteen layers of fabric types. Some of these variables will be covered later in the text.

Fabric in Rank

Listed here are the fabrics that were restricted for wear according to rank and office. It is important to remember that certain types of fabric and color harmonies were to be worn according to rank. There were even restrictions about the appropriateness of color to fabric combinations. Certain color and textile harmonies often were considered either appropriate or inappropriate, depending on the event and time of year. These conventions applied to both women and men.

Lower Rank: Plain and unfigured fabric, and bombycine.

High Rank: Damasks, gossamers, brocades, and certain types of embroidery.

Highest Rank: Deep *red* damask, embroidered *green* silk, and complex embroidered scenes on silk.

Many of the textiles seemed to indicate a certain kind of affinity with the body, clothing, and nature itself. The human form, natural textiles, and the physical aspects of nature will also be discussed in this text. We will analyze this particular form of affinity by illustrating that court fashion was the harmonious link between the human body and nature.

Dress Definitions for Women

The following are a few examples and descriptions of formal court dress, as well as the types of fabrics (for men's dress see the supplementary notes).

Jacket (Karaginu):   This was the outermost piece, and was usually the most elaborate. It was made from a variety of different silks, and depending on rank, it could be very elaborate. Sophisticated embroidery was common on this piece in the higher ranks. It was waist length.

Mantle (Uwagi):   Refers to full length, but falls short of being the same length as the trousers. The mantle could be either printed fabric or plain. Mantles were made of different types of silk; bombycine or brocade.[4]

Robes (Itsutsuginu):   Refers to sets of unlined robes that are combined together to create a specific color. Usually made of various silk gauze materials, gossamers, and damasks.[5] The first few layers are normally gauze, with the remaining layers being less sheer, made of either gossamer or damask. Layers can be as few as three and as many as fifteen.

Gown (Uchiginu):   Refers to trousers worn under the layers of lined robes. Most often, this piece was a crimson color, and made from beaten silk.

Train (Mo):   The train was the longest piece. Usually made from silk and/or brocade.

Rank Offices of Women

Before listing rank as it relates to women, it is important to point out that official rank was not awarded to women. Rank existed more in the form of "offices held" by a woman, which gave her commensurate privileges with a man's rank but without the same authority. These were *palace* ladies-in-waiting as opposed to ladies-in-waiting in *private* households.

Joro Class (upper grade):   Small group of ladies who were authorized to wear the forbidden colors and fabrics. This group consisted of the *Mistress of the Wardrobe*, two *Principal Handmaids, assistant Handmaids* of the third or fourth rank;—*daughters* and *granddaughters of the Ministers of State*.

Churo Class: (middle grade):   This was the largest group, and consisted mostly of *Handmaids* and *Palace ladies* (Myobu).

Gero Class (lower grade):   These ladies helped to sew costumes and related work. Usually belonging to *daughters of Stewards* and *Shinto priests* of leading shrines. These ladies-in-waiting were selected for office according to their skills in calligraphy, poetry, artwork, music, taste in dress, and manners. Usually, the lady who would demonstrate the highest degree of skill was the one who received the highest office at court.

Color Codes in Court Dress

One of the most complex problems in understanding court dress is that of the proper use of color. The applications

---

[4]BOMBYCINE. Also a silk fabric. Bombycine is a rich fabric between damask and brocade.

BROCADE. Any silk that has been woven into patterned colors, other than the sheer silks.

DAMASK. Another one of the silks. Because of its weave, produces a very satiny effect. Used as lining with gossamer.

[5]GAUZE. A very sheer fabric made from silk, usually worn closest to the body in layering techniques.

GOSSAMER. Sheer silks, but less sheer than gauze.

PHOTO BY THE AUTHOR.

Figure 6-56 Paper Tear Illustration of a Typical Heian Aristocratic Lady.

can only be *generalized* here because they varied considerably depending on rank and occasion, not to mention the exceptions granted for wearing certain colors. Below are the general color codes as they existed at Heian court:

Low Rank (sixth rank and below): Pale reds, most blues, browns, and certain yellows.

High Rank (fifth and above): Yellow-green, white, silver crimson, pale green, green over white lined with red, and yellow-green over red.[6]

Highest Rank: *Forbidden Colors*[7]; red and purple combinations, purple, yellow-green figured material, and deep purple (strictly forbidden color).

Monks and Mourning Attire: Gray.

THE STORY OF AFFINITY WITHIN THE JAPANESE ARISTOCRACY

The primary objective of this survey is to determine if there was an effort on behalf of the Heian court aristocracy to create the perfect affinity between themselves and actual nature. The main or direct link in creating that affinity most certainly would have to exist within the realm of court dress. The establishment of three types of affinity links at court will be discussed as follows:

1. **Indirect link to indicate affinity** or intermediate links refer to implicating affinity through an alternate

---

[6]Yellow-green over red could only be worn by the ladies-in-waiting of the Joro office (rank), and only pertains to jackets of figured silk and to printed trains.
[7]Forbidden colors could only be worn by those of the Imperial family, or the highest of court nobles. Forbidden colors varied somewhat with each new emperor.

source rather than a direct reference link. Indirect links include artwork, architecture, and interior furnishings. They are affinity indicators that are not as closely related to the person(s) in question.

2. **Surrogate link to indicate affinity** can be either a "stand-in" for the conventional link or method, or a substitute for the subject. Specifically, the exterior structured garden or a person such as Ukifune can act as a surrogate link or form.

3. **Direct link to indicate affinity** can be seen in court dress (fabric/clothing). Direct links are specific references to affinity. Directness must be involved with animate subject matter such as silk (silkworm), wisteria fiber (wisteria plant), and mulberry cloth (mulberry tree), and are used as direct links with the human form to create affinity with nature.

The *direct link* is the most important of the three links, and is the chief connecting factor in aristocracy's affinity with nature. The various links will be discussed within the framework of four basic Japanese text sources:

1. **From *Genji Monogatari:*** the chapter "The Picture Contest." This chapter involved an art competition between the Lady Akikonomu and the daughter of To no Chujo. The contest was important politically, because the results would be the installation of Akikonomu (winner of contest) as consort to the Emperor.

2. **From *Genji Monogatari:*** the chapter "Butterflies." This chapter records another contest involving Akikonomu. The Lady Akikonomu's fall garden was challenged by the Lady Murasaki and her spring garden.

3. **From *The Pillow Book of Sei Shonagon:*** the chapter "The Lady of the Shigei Sha." Lady Shigei Sha sent a letter off to her sister, the Empress, informing her that she intended to visit her in the near future. The apartments of the Empress were decorated and cleaned to a greater degree than ever before, as well as preparation of the ladies-in-waiting who also were dressed more elaborately than normal.

4. **From *Genji Monogatari:*** the chapter "Ukifune." Ukifune is the illegitimate daughter of the eighth Prince, and half sister to Oigimi and Nakanokimi. She becomes the victim of two male courtier's desires, whose names are Kaoru and Niou, and is whisked away to a small mountain cottage. Politically she is weak, as she does not have strong court backing, and ends up living out the rest of her life secluded in the mountains. Ukifune was known for her beautiful hair and petite size.

Beginning with "The Picture Contest," we are told about an elaborate gathering of Heian court aristocrats in order to determine who was the most accomplished artist. This contest was very important, because it would determine the

Figure 6-57 Takehawa II—Two Daughters of Lady Tamakazura Play "Go" Staking a Cherry Tree in the Garden and Sir Kurodo Peeps.

outcome of a *significant court appointment*—the selection of consort to the Emperor.

Lady Fujitsubo, Emperor Suzaku's consort, decides that because of recent endless debates on aesthetics in court and the large number of people involved, she would split the art contest into two sides. On the left side would be the *Akikonomu faction*, favored by Prince Genji, and the *Kokiden faction* would be on the right, which was favored by To no Chujo. Each side had a number of ladies-in-waiting as participants, and each side was in serious competition for their respective Ladies, Akikonomu and To no Chujo's daughter. The ceremony begins with the following scene:

> The day was appointed. The careful casualness of all the details would have done justice to far more leisurely preparations. The royal seat was put out in the ladies' withdrawing rooms, and the ladies were ranged to the north and south, and the courtier's seats faced them on the west. The paintings of the left were in boxes of *red sandalwood* on sappanwood stands with flaring legs. *Purple Chinese brocades* were spread under the stands, which were covered with delicate *lavender Chinese embroidery*. Six little girls sat behind them, their robes of *red* and their jackets of *white* lined with *red*, from under which peeped *red* and *lavender*. As for the right of Kokiden side, the boxes were of heavy *aloes* and the stands of lighter aloes. *Green Korean brocades* covered the stands, and the streamers and flaring legs were all in the latest style. The little page girls wore *green robes* and over them *white jackets* with *green linings*, and their singlets were of a *grayish green* lined with *yellow*. Most solemnly they lined up their treasures. The emperor's own women were in uniforms of the two sides.[8]

It is significant to note that it was the ladies who sat near the paintings, not the men. In this description, the dress (fabric) of the ladies-in-waiting and the page girls begin to resemble a oneness with the art work itself, not the men (it was the women who were the connoisseurs of art). If we examine the descriptions of the scene carefully, it becomes more difficult to separate the *inanimate art form from the animate*. It also is important to consider the following comparisons, seen in the previous paragraph, in order to see this concept more clearly:

Paintings on the Left

1. Paintings in boxes of red sandalwood on sapponwood stands.

8 *The Tale of Genji*, Murasaki Shikibu, p. 314.

2. Purple Chinese brocades under stands.
3. Little girls wore red robes.
4. Jackets were white lined with red.
5. Red and lavender peeped from under the jackets.
6. Oborozukiyo dressed the same as the little girls.

Paintings on the Right

1. Paintings in heavy aloes and boxes on lighter aloes stands.
2. Green Korean brocades covered the stands.
3. Little girls wore green robes.
4. Jackets were white with green lining.
5. Singlets were grayish green lined with yellow.
6. Kokiden dressed the same as the little girls.

The art of dress not only served as an aesthetic element as well as a messenger to signal that a competition was in progress, but also illustrated that the paintings had created a type of affinity with the fabrics worn by the ladies-in-waiting. The imagery and colors of the costumes, as well as the paintings, would illustrate a considerable affinity when considering the similarities of garden images and colors:

- The *red sandalwood* in contrast to the softer *tones of aloeswood*, yet the very fragrant quality of the aloeswood exits.
- Not only are the colors in contrasting complements, but the country from which the brocades originate are different. Also, the brocade is *under* the stands on the left, and *over* the stands on the right. As we continue down the list, *red robes* contrast and complement *green robes, red lining* to *green lining*, and so on. Because the time of the year happens to be spring, it is significant to note the play of *color* symbolism in dress. An example of this is the *purple brocades* and the *green jackets*, symbolic of the *plum tree* with its *green leaves* contrasted with the *purple plums*. The *white blossoms* seen in the jacket are contrasted with the *green leaves* in the lining, and so on. This preview of comparisons serves to illustrate how an *indirect* link is involved with linking people to nature through art.

It is important to note here just exactly what types of paintings were presented. These paintings were known as *emakimono*, which essentially means "narrative paintings." The *emakimono* assumes the form of a hand scroll (presented in a wood box—see last page illustration). When rolled out from right to left a story appeared. First the narrative section preceded by painted scene, usually consisting of a minimum of six but usually more illustrations.

The Suma emakimono decided the fate of the contest in the end, and was brought out by Prince Genji. These paintings contained scenes of Genji's exile on the Suma coast, where he had experienced extreme hardships in his struggle with the forces of *raw nature.* Gradually, Genji became part of these natural surroundings, as the effects of raw nature continued to physically batter him down. His robes illustrated the same subdued colors as his natural surroundings as he was tormented by constant storms, and his robes were wet from the rain as his body yielded to the winds of the Suma coast. With those images of the Suma coast in mind, the emotion of Genji's experience gripped those at court. They fought back the tears brought on by the visually powerful scrolls, as they felt the pain of their fellow aristocrat. Genji Monogatari records this:

> . . . .but there was no describing the sure delicacy with which Genji had quietly set down the moods of those years. The assembly, Prince Hotaru, and the rest fell silent, trying to hold back the tears. They had pitied him and thought of themselves as suffering with him; and now they saw how it had really been. They had before their eyes the bleakness of those nameless strands and inlets. Here and there, not so much open description as poetic impressions, were captions in cursive Chinese and Japanese. There was no point now in turning to the painting offered by the right. The Suma scroll had blocked everything else from view. The triumph of the left was completed.[9]

As the others looked on with To no Chujo, they were tremendously moved by the emotional content of the paintings. In fact, the *colors* and content of the artwork was so effective that most of those present had to struggle just to keep back their tears, as their hearts and minds were at one with Genji. The question that remains is how is it possible for a group of paintings to move people to such emotion?

In order to understand the emotional qualities of those paintings, it is necessary to establish the importance of the Emakimono, and its linking ability. There were three basic functions of this art form:

1. **Entertainment:** The most beneficial aspect of these scrolls pertained to the ladies-in-waiting, who were basically women of leisure. What better way to pass the time than to produce a *color document* or to enjoy a good story. With this abundance of time they also were able to perfect other art forms, such as writing, poetry, costume design (dress), music, and creation of the structured gardens.
2. **Competition:** Most importantly, and the particular purpose behind the picture contest, was the competition for court appointments. That very important political function was the reason for Akikonomu's installation as consort to the new Emperor; Genji had won the contest for her with his Suma scroll.
3. **Historical Documentation:** In Japan, these scrolls have provided valuable information from one generation to the other. The "Emakimono" is the visual source of information for what we know about Japanese Heian/Kamakura court life.

Figure 6-58 Suzumushi I—Genji visits the third princess of Suzaku-in when she is listening to the chirping of singing insects.

[9]*The Tale of Genji,* Murasaki Shikibu, pp. 314–315.

Because of the entertainment, competition, and documentational factors, we can see some very good reasons why the court developed this unparalleled sensibility. The paintings, which had accompanying poems, most likely had the same effect on the court observers (Suma Scroll), as an emotionally moving film does in the twentieth century.

It is important to reemphasize the startling effect that the Suma scrolls may have had on the others. Their hearts and minds were at one with a man who had experienced a form of affinity with raw nature, as he began to blend with nature. Accustomed to living around the structured and protected environment of the court life, Genji had felt the untamed wrath of raw nature, suffering the repeated effects of the storm. The paintings reflected the colors of his agony.

Up to this point we have been dealing with the idea of an *indirect link, such as art*. However, before examining the concept of a *direct* link, it seems more in order to examine the notion of a type of *surrogate* link. Art, architecture, poetry, and interior furnishings can all be considered a "surrogate" link, depending on the subject. However, in this text the *strongest* link is more committed to the *structured garden* and *court dress*.

Certainly it can be said that in particular places and certain times of the year, the natural forces of nature can be very harsh in Japan. These forces are very frightening and destructive at times, as was the account of Genji's exile on the Suma coast. It seems as though the aristocrats at court experienced the Suma coast through an intercessor or *surrogate link*, the painted colors of the emakimono compositions.

There were some possible reasons for the need of *surrogate* elements. Perhaps, because of the awesomeness of raw nature, they preferred to create their own environment as they wanted to see it rather than the way it actually appeared. Conceivably, being surrounded by such wealth and security for such a long period, they became too vulnerable to the insecurity offered by the real forces of nature. If that were true, a definite need for a substitute would have been created.

The *Lady Sei Shonagon's* aesthetic concepts define very well why the surrogate system existed. Many times, the Lady Shonagon is the *direct* link. To see that clearly, we turn to the *Genji Monogatari* chapter "Butterflies."[10] In "Butterflies," the issue of the *garden as an affinity link* surfaces again. The subject of court dress becomes successor and superior over the structured garden, as the garden acts as a mediator between the aristocrats and real nature.

The Butterfly Conspiracy

In order to discuss this thoroughly, it is first necessary to go back to the earlier chapter "Maiden" in *Gengi Monogatari*. Akikonomu wrote to Murasaki in a poem about the beauty of her autumn garden, inferring that *autumn* was the superior month to display a garden. Months later, in the chapter "Butterflies," as Murasaki's *spring* garden began to flourish she decided that it was time to respond to Akikonomu about the superiority of spring. She not only responded to Akikonomu with a poem, but dressed up some of her little girls to represent butterflies and birds. Once they were fully costumed, they proceeded to Akikonomu's residence to deliver floral offerings from Murasaki, while Yogiri delivered the poem: "She chose eight of her prettiest little girls to deliver them, dressing four of them as birds and four as butterflies. The birds brought cherry blossoms in silver vases, the butterflies "yamabuki" in gold vases. In wonderfully rich and full bloom, they completed a perfect picture."[11]

There was a type of indirect reference in that scene, because the butterflies and birds were presented as a *perfect picture painting*. Yet at the same time, the *direct link* of affinity became more obvious in the *costumes of the children as they fluttered around the garden*.

Affinity with nature was not only created within the confines of the garden, as we discussed about the *surrogate* link, but also in the *direct* link of dress. We not only observe the garden as an altered form of nature, but it also can be observed as a *motif* in the dress fabrics, art, and architecture. Imagine that we can see courtiers, ladies-in-waiting, and the children dressed with similar motifs all in the garden together. The furnishings as well as the apartment walls are finished in fine animal and floral motifs, which also correspond to those on the robes. As they move out into the garden, these motifs begin to merge with the actual forms of nature themselves. The *colors* match the *season* as well as the infusion of *color* harmonies seen throughout the structures, gardens, paintings, and fabrics. The picture becomes one of total affinity as the aristocrats—including the mock butterflies and birds (little girls)—move about within the natural elements that they represent.

All of the aristocrats were dressed with floral patterns and various motifs of nature. As they move among masses of blossoming plants and trees, they move in and out of similarly decorated interiors. Suddenly, the scene merges visually into a beautiful oneness—an infusion of affinity has been created. Consider the following account:

> The music for the dance of the
> Kalavinka bird rang forth to the singing
> of warblers, to which the waterfowl on
> the lake added their clucks and chirps,
> and it was with very great regret that the
> audience saw the dance come to an end.
> The butterflies seemed to fly higher than
> the birds as they disappeared behind a
> low fence over which poured a cascade
> of yamabuki.[12]

---

[10] *The Tale of Genji,* Murasaki Shikibu, pp. 418–429.

[11] *The Tale of Genji,* Murasaki Shikibu, p. 422.

[12] *The Tale of Genji,* Murasaki Shikibu, p. 423.

Figure 6 59 Hashihime Under the Moonlight—Daughters of Uji are playing music and Kaoru looks at them.

Even the ending was perfect as the butterflies and birds flew at different levels, both higher than the yamabuki fence. Suddenly they seemed to merge all together with the yamabuki, then in a moment they disappeared.

Akikonomu was greatly moved as she answered Murasaki's presentation:

> I weep in my longing to follow your butterflies. You put up fences of yamabuki between us.[13]

It was as if the Lady Akikonomu had felt a longing to experience this affinity with nature for a moment, as if to enter a dream state of oneness with those around her and nature. She had observed a visual blending of that scene; if only she could have been a part of it to experience the *union of the elements*.

The affinity element is illustrated once more when Prince Hotaru appeared suddenly at the competition, only to have learned that Tamakazura (Genji's adopted daughter) was already receiving letters from many of the courtiers. Because he also was interested in her, he proceeded to attach a spray of wisteria in his cap, swaying around like a willowing plant. He then said, "If there were not something rather special to keep me here, I think I would be trying to escape. It is too much, oh, really too

much." He then refused to drink any more, as he had consumed too much already. He continued by saying, "Lavender holds me and puts me in the mind of things. I mean, let them say what they will, to throw myself in."[14]

He divided the spray of wisteria at that point, and gave one of them to Prince Genji.

In Heian Japan, the meaning of the color *lavender* was *affinity*, and so the wisteria sprays were indicative of the Prince's interest in Tamakazura. Having given her father half of the wisteria flowers, he said:

> Please hold yourself in abeyance beneath these flowers, to judge if the plunge would have the proper effect.[15]

As we can see, affinity links were not always as dramatic and overwhelming as was the garden contest. Instead, it was subtle—the wisteria flower became a symbol of union between two people. Similarly, the color of lavender had reminded them of the union of two.

Seasonal dress was a powerful unifying element. When certain quests on Akikonomu's side arrived, they were issued formal attire with the *appropriate spring colors and motifs*. In order for people in court to successfully merge with nature a strict code was necessary. The codes for proper *colors*, fabrics, and prints were adhered to as

---

[13] *The Tale of Genji*, Murasaki Shikibu, p. 423.

[14] *The Tale of Genji*, Murasaki Shikibu, p. 421.

[15] *The Tale of Genji*, Murasaki Shikibu, p. 421.

Figure 6-60 The Hills of Southern Kyoto, the Area Where Murasaki Shikibu Wrote the Tale of Genji.

PHOTO BY THE AUTHOR.

Figure 6-61 Model of the Heian Court Residences and Palace Area.

PHOTO BY THE AUTHOR.

each season changed from one to the other. The attempt to become part of nature in the fine art of dress sensibility was constantly sought after by court aristocracy.

The following record from the *Tale of Flowing Fortunes* illustrates that spectacle of seasonal changes of color. At the *Golden Hall* (see following page) dedication in the year 1022, a description of Kenshi's ladies by Michinaga went like this:

Viewed from a distance as a brilliant sun rose in the sky, the very blinds screening the ladies in attendance on the various personages seemed extraordinary,

Figure 6-62 The Golden Hall, [previous original hall that was set on fire, was dedicated in 1022 A.D.] Kyoto, Japan.

to say nothing of the scene as a whole—the bombycines in *fallen leaf (yellowish-brown lined with yellow), maidenflower (yellow lined with green), bellflower (blue lined with green), and lespedeza colors (reddish purple lined with green),* and the *violet* curtains, shading to *purple* at the bottom, with their ornamental cords, cluster-dyed streamers, and elegant paintings appliquéd in *gold* and *silver* dust. Indescribably splendid sleeve openings and skirt edges spilled out from behind the blinds, so dazzling to the spectators that they could scarcely distinguish one from the other. *Red plum* and *wild-pink* peeled silk *(shiny material)* inner robes shone with brilliant luster, and there were bombycines and gossamers in *bellflower, maidenflower, lespedeza, fallen leaf,* and *rue* colors *(white with green lining)*, ornamental cords, formal jackets, trains—but I could not possibly describe everything. All the triple-layered *red* trousers were made of damask.[16]

These ladies were described much like one would talk about a beautiful sunrise. In fact, the beginning of the record began with a certain hint of affinity, as the "brilliant sun" was brought into the picture. The morning sun began filtering down through the delicate screens, into the room and onto the robes of the various ladies-in-waiting. Continuing with that aesthetic awareness, the *colors of the robes* were described in terms of their relationship to nature. (Bombycines in *colors of fallen leaf, maidenflower, bellflower,* and *lespedeza*.) Finally, a certain oneness was completed as "they could scarcely distinguish one from the other." The ladies in full court costume with their *colors of floral designs,* against the *colors of the natural setting,* had become visually unified.

Looking further into the concept of a direct link to affinity in court dress, the focus will remain mostly on women's dress for the following reasons:

- Women were the primary object of art—often more so than the artwork itself—as we see in the "Picture Contest."
- Women's clothing was more complex and elaborate than men's dress, and more layers were worn at one time.
- The affinity connection with women was much stronger, especially because skin tone was important for them. It should be noted here that women were more akin to the arts than were men. Women were totally involved with all of the arts and were well noted for their prowess in the arts.
- "The Picture Contest" and "Butterflies" chapters were primarily about women.

- Usually, it was the women who were in control of putting those functions together, and therefore they were responsible for the aesthetic success of the particular event.

In order to further understand the development of affinity and to cultivate its connections, it is logical to continue by discussing *court dress* as it relates to the *interior of a structure*. After which we will move to an outdoor scene in the highly organized garden. The first worthy example is an interior scene recorded by Sei Shonagon titled, *When the Lady of the Shigei Sha Entered the Crown Prince's Palace*.[17]

One day, the Lady Shigei Sha entered the Palace where ceremonies were being carried out with great splendor. She suddenly began thinking about the fact that she had never seen her sister the Empress. The following month, she wrote the Empress a letter advising of her intensions to visit. When the time had come, the Empress began decorating the Palace apartments more elegantly than she had ever before attempted. All of her ladies took great care in order to prepare themselves in the same manner. It is interesting to note here that "court procedure" dictates that the life of a court lady was mostly lived out within the interior world only. It was a rare occasion for her to exist to the outside world other than for travel. For this reason, it was even more important for the ladies and their interiors to function as one.

Our concept of these interior spaces is based on old woodblock prints, narrative scrolls, and various written documentations. Based on these sources, we will briefly discuss those interiors as they may have looked in the apartments of the Empress.

The interior spaces were very sparsely furnished, and for good reason. Moveable screens, sliding screen doors, curtains, and certain other walls were decorated with scenes of nature's landscapes and floral motifs. As often mentioned, the costumes were elaborately designed with motifs similar to their outside gardens. It would not be uncommon to see their robes of springtime consisting of embroidered garden motifs similar to their gardenscapes. Colors of their robes and jackets were in complementary color arrangements, and often commensurable to the existing colors in the garden itself. Therefore, when the ladies either entered an interior space or exited into the garden, the beginning connection with nature was born. The cycle of movement in and out of gardens and structures completed the picture of affinity.

The typical costume for a lady-in-waiting consisted of the following:

- One formal **Jacket** worn as the outermost covering. Usually designed with embroidery in a nature landscape motif. (Higher ranks)
- One **Mantle** underneath the jacket. Usually an animal, (cranes, etc.) or floral type of motif on a fairly dense

---

[16] *A Tale of Flowering Fortunes*, McCullough, p. 548.

[17] *The Pillow Book of Sei Shonagon*, Ivan Morris. Trans ed. (New York; Penguin Books), p. 128, #20.

PUBLIC DOMAIN.

Figure 6-63 Azumaya I—The second daughter of Uji shows a picture book. Lady Ukifune and Ukon reads a text.

silk, normally printed motifs as opposed to embroidered work. (Also depends on rank)

- One ***Train*** made of silk, 5 to 6 feet in length. Normally brocaded, depending on rank. Worn from the waist down about 12 inches past the end of the hair. (Depending if hair is full dress code length.)
- ***Robes*** were the layers worn underneath, and range from three to fifteen layers, combined to create *seasonal colors*. Sheer silks only were used.
- ***Trousers*** were worn underneath robes. Partially exposed, made from beaten silk. Always crimson in color.

Note: For complete details on dress, see introduction and supplementary notes.

In the transition toward affinity, Sei Shonagon records more concerning preparations for the Lady Shigei Sha:

> In the morning, I attended the Empress while her hair was being dressed. A four-foot curtain of state had been placed across the main hall, facing the back of the room. Her Majesty was seated in the front part of the room, while a group of ladies-in-waiting were gathered behind the curtain of state. Hardly any furniture had been put out, only a straw mat with a cushion for her majesty and a round brazier.[18]

It seems somewhat curious that there were so few pieces of furniture in the rooms, but then the reason for the sparse apartment interior becomes obvious. When we visualize the scene, imagine all of the ladies-in-waiting behind the curtain of state. Within the interiors, to one degree or another, there would be *harmonized colors* in patterns, nature landscapes, floral motifs on the costumes, and the like. Also, objects in the room reflected similar decorations such as curtains, screens, and other prominent areas, as well as in the traditional *tokonoma* (recessed wall area). Certainly, when we consider the possibilities of all aesthetic elements in the various rooms, there would have been no need for much else, without creating clutter and confusion.

Another noteworthy point about the furniture within the interiors was the feeling of impermanence that also prevails in nature. Seasonal change was not only involved with dress, but almost equally important was the seasonal change of interior space. Obviously, anything of permanence would have made it much more difficult to change the seasonal motif.

If the interiors did not coordinate with dress and with the season represented by the gardens, the ability to achieve true visual oneness would have been impossible.

---

[18] *The Pillow Book of Sei Shonagon.* Ivan Morris, p. 129.

Seasons change, as do interior spaces and fabric types at court commensurately. The ladies of the interior had become living art forms, and were responsible for the aesthetic furnishings. The visuals must have been astounding as suddenly the apartment interiors were transformed into a type of protected indoor garden.

Continuing in the development of affinity with nature, Sei Shonagon elaborates on the virtues of the Empress's complexion:

> Unusual though the combination was, Her Majesty looked beautiful. The color of her clothes went perfectly with her complexion and, as I gazed at her, I was impatient to have a proper look at the Shigei Sha to see whether she was equally pretty.[19]

It is precisely in that statement that the final link is formed. Favored among all women in court were the ladies with the lightest skin. Skin *coloration* and *tone* had to be perfect, or at least what they determined to be the most revered for standards of beauty.

In establishing a link to their natural surroundings, whether indirect, surrogate, or direct, the affinity source had to begin from the inside out, from the human form to the exterior jacket. The visual transition of affinity from human animate form to inanimate motifs had to be accomplished slowly, and more importantly, with subtlety.

Beginning with the inner most form (the human body) and then slowly making a visual transition from the inside robe to the outside jacket, the perfect complexion was first accompanied by the most sheer of inner robes. In many cases, the lightest color was worn closest to the skin, and usually white was the choice when dealing with seasonal dress. The visual transition from the surface of the skin to the first fabric was to be subtly varied in tone, and it was the most crucial step in creating affinity with outward surroundings as well as creating the perfect art form, the court lady. After the first of the sheer layers were put on, another type of sheer robe was applied, but with somewhat darker and more colorful layers. Many of the first layers were a very sheer silk known as gauze, and several layers were worn in the beginning transition. After the first layers, a sheer but less transparent silk robe of gossamer was put on. A somewhat thicker and even less transparent damask (silk) was finally added to complete the inner robe layering.

As suggested before, the most significant event in the creation of affinity with nature occurred in the layering process. It is safe to conclude that the proper selection of robes required the utmost skill in dress sensibility in order to complete the perfect dress scenario. The plan was to create gradations of silks one over the other, building expressive layers of fabrics until the final jacket crowned the assembly. These surface relationships created the framework to indicate the affinity experienced by the aristocrats.

COLOR BLENDING

Hue combinations in these surface relationships created specific *seasonal colors* appropriate for the particular season represented. This particular method of robe layering was commonly referred to as *color blending,* which produced court favorites such as *yellow-green* (A *green gauze* robe over a *yellow gauze*). The fabrics had to be sheer enough for the layering to be accomplished. One *color* is shown through the other, yet part of each robe had to demonstrate its *saturated color* as well as its translucent nature. So, part of the robe was to be seen as a *saturated green,* and the other that was a combination of the two colors, would appear with its intensity changed to *yellow-green.*

Gossamer and damask were used over the gauze in the layering process, but the combination of the two colors in these fabric did not create the suggestion of affinity in the same way as gauze. These two fabrics were considerably less sheer, or more opaque, and for that reason could not be blended in the same sensitive manner as gauze material. Normally, robes made with gossamer and damask were lined, gossamer lined with damask, or in some cases, damask lined with gossamer. The skill of overlapping materials was referred to by a specific name: *"Sweet Flag"* and *'"China Tree,"* and both were considered *summer colors.*[20]

Sweet flag robes consisted of a green robe with red lining. These were a court favorite to wear against the yellow-green gauze. *China Tree* robes were *pale purple* with a *green lining.* Again, the *blending of colors* was a very skilled art. Too much subtlety between layers, joined with *colorful outer garments,* would have downplayed the effect of the inner robes. Conversely, robes of too much *intensity* could downplay the mantle, train, and especially the jacket, all of which would have prevented any unifying of fabric with the person wearing the costume. The perfect progression of color layers was necessary in order to achieve perfect *color blending* with the exterior garments.

That brings us to the *mantle, train,* and the *jacket.* These garments were the *connectors* between the animate form (aristocrat) and the inanimate exterior layers, thus the creation of affinity. Exterior costume articles were made from heavier fabrics, embroidered heavy silk jackets, printed mantles, and heavy brocades or printed trains. An example of specific subject matter represented on the fabric was recorded by Murasaki Shikibu when writing about Governor Michinokuni's wife:

> When they finished serving, the women went out and sat down by the blinds. Everything sparkled in the light of the candles, and some women in particular stood out. Lady Oshikibu—wife of the Governor of Michinokuni and His

---

[19]*The Pillow Book of Sei Shonagon.* Ivan Morris, pp. 129–130.

[20]*A Tale of Flowering Fortunes,* McCullough, p. 226.

Figure 6-64 Yadorigi II—Nioi-no-Miya and the sixth daughter of Yugiri talk together for the first time.

Excellency's envoy, you know—had a beautiful train and jacket, both embroidered with the Komatsubara scene at Mt. Oshio. Tayu no Myobu had left her jacket as it was, but her train had a striking wave pattern printed on it in silver, not overly conspicuous but most pleasing to the eye. Ben no Naishi had a train printed with a very unusual design, as a crane standing in a silver seascape; as a symbol of longevity it was a suitable complement to the pine branches on the embroidery, a real touch of genius. Lady Shosho's embroidery, decorated with silver foil, was not quite up to the same standard as the others and everyone found fault with it.[21]

The types of fabrics and their organization, subject matter (motifs), and use of color all perform the task of creating a single unity or *harmony* with the sparkling lights of the candles. We can well imagine the effect of the candlelight reflected on the textured silver jackets and trains. Most of the specific hues remain unspecified, yet we have an idea as to what they were simply by remembering conventional summer color harmonies.

The scene was well planned. Instead of utilizing a floral motif or the *color blending* techniques to create the harmony, it was more about the unifying element of light. *Color* was still associated strongly in the event, because we understand that light is the source of color. Imagine for a moment the captured light during the evening, as it mingled within the colored fabrics with silver landscapes, then suddenly reflected off into the interior of the room, visually illuminating the jackets and everything around them. The robes, mantles, trains, and jackets have all been *harmoniously connected* now, and within the costume a certain statement about the transitional processes of affinity has been made. We can well imagine the delicate inner working of light transferring from one element to the other.

THE COMPLETED SCENARIO OF AFFINITY

Now that we have completed the costume, the stage can be set in order to complete the scenario of affinity. To accomplish this, an imaginary situation has to be created by combining the accounts of the "Lady of the Shigei Sha," "The Picture Contest," and "Butterflies" into a single event. We can easily visualize the interior apartments where the Empress, Shigei Sha, Sei Shonagon, and various ladies-in-waiting are installed. Imagine that they are all wearing formal court dress with their favorite embroidered jackets. The interior structure has been lavishly and carefully decorated, as the screens, doors, and curtains are all in the same motifs as those who are in attendance. The blending of visual aesthetics between the animate forms of the ladies in costume and the inanimate forms of the interior apartments is complete.

Arriving now at The Picture Contest, we see they are all present as contestants. All of the most talented ladies-in-waiting are arriving to take their places for the competition, and once more we see that the stage is set as the *indirect*

---

[21]*Murasaki Shikib; Her Diary and Poetic Memoirs.* Richard Bowring; Trans, ed. Princeton University Press. (Princeton, New Jersey 1982), p. 67.

link to the paintings. The paintings actually become somewhat obscured by the intensity of the costumes, and if it were not for the emotional intensity of the Suma scroll, certainly they would be. However, the *brilliance of color* in court dress has caused a certain blending or oneness between the artwork and the fabric. Court dress performs a certain amount of its own blending along with the emotional qualities of the Suma scrolls, in that they are both intense. One visual indication is by the *dress*, the other is emotionally indicated by the painted *scrolls*. Even with all of this evidence, one more link is still necessary to make this affinity complete.

The strongest link appears to take place in the *Genji Monogatari* chapter "Butterflies." Children are dressed as *butterflies* and *birds* and are scattered among the yamabuki flower. Ladies-in-waiting, courtiers, various attendants, and of course, the Emperor and Empress, are also involved within the garden environment. All are in formal court dress, and all are dressed with related garden and nature motifs, as the organization of court dress blends with and complements the highly structured garden. Not only are the people *linked* to raw nature, but now the costume fabric produced by the silk of the silkworm has moved back into its place of origin, the garden. This *surrogate* link also is used as a connector between the direct link and the raw aspects of nature outside of the court confines. With the visual linking process completed, we see the perfect affinity: a picture of nature with court aristocracy.

One final brief observation about this surrogate connection is best illustrated by the *Lady Ukifune*. Murasaki Shikibu writes about her in the last five chapters in the *The Tale of Genji*. One of the outstanding features Ukifune was so well known for was her hair. When discussing the *surrogate* form of the garden, it was presented in terms of linking the *motifs* of court dress to raw nature. Commensurate with that, Ukifune's hair would have been a *surrogate* form, linking her body to the costume and its *motifs*.

This takes us back to the transitional stage of linking the "white skin" of the lady to the exterior jacket. There could have been, at times, difficulty in blending the skin tones with the first robe, depending on the colors that were chosen. However, the dark hair—which is a product of the body—could have been used to link the body to the fabric by virtue of its high contrasting nature. It would serve as an alternate source as mentioned earlier but also as an *additional* linking device. Whether used as an *alternative* source in connecting the body to the costume, or as an additional supplement to help the robes connect. The hair was very important as part of the actual costume. The ideal hair length at court was approximately three inches longer than the height of the lady. Looking at the narrative scrolls, especially those of the Genji Monogatari, the hair flows down through and *mingles with the jacket, mantle, and train,* dispersing in and out of the *color folds,* creating a strong bond between the elaborate fabric and the lady herself.

Whereas the robes are successful in marking that subtle but all-important transition, the hair adds the perfect touch. The raven black hair contrasts sharply yet at the same time blends with the beauty of the court costume. The hair is not only a visual connection, but also creates a physical oneness with court dress.

There is a certain difficulty about presenting a completely clear picture of court dress. We are not able to appreciate, or fully comprehend it, in that we are limited by the amount of visual documentation, and of course, the inability to go back in time to observe the actual spectacle. More importantly we realize that even if we were able to be in attendance, it would have been impossible to adequately describe such an exquisite event with words alone.

Figure 6-65 Kaoru Visits Lady Ukifune who Lives in Sanjyo.

One of the masters of court aesthetics, Sei Shonagon, said this when she wrote several times about the frustrated attempts to provide an adequate description:

> It would be foolish to attempt a description of the courtiers' costumes, which were so splendid that they made everyone think of a grove of cherry trees in full bloom.[22]

If you have ever been to Japan in the spring, you know exactly what a powerful statement that is. Cherry trees in full bloom are a short-lived spectacle, rivaled only by summer fireworks. As summer approaches, the blossoms fall from the trees, creating a blizzard of color movement.

Summary of Affinity with Nature Linking Process

- Light skin.
- First inner *robes* of the most sheer of gauze.
- Additional *robes* of gossamer and damask: sheer silks.
- A *mantle* of heavier silk. Printed/unprinted.
- A *train*, usually printed or brocade: natural motif.
- The *jacket*, usually embroidered with natural motifs. (Higher Ranks)
- *Interior* apartments with related motifs and colors.
- The *paintings* of an art contest. Link of aristocracy to nature.
- The structured *garden*. Murasaki's garden: nature motifs, human form in perfect visual harmony with garden/fabrics. Ultimately links to *raw nature*.

Dress Definitions for Men

- *Over-Robe (Ue no kinu):* This was the outermost robe. Similar applications apply with men as with women concerning type of fabrics and designs.
- *Over-Trousers, Over-Shirt (Ue no hakama):* These are worn together with over-robes as formal court costume.
- *Under-Robe (Shitagasane):* This was a formal under-shirt.
- *Trouser-Skirt (Oguchi):* This was a wide, red trouser-skirt. Large openings in the legs.
- *Trouser-Skirt/Divided Skirt (Hakama):* Worn by both men and women.
- *Silk Trousers (Sashinuki):* These were worn loosely, and were laced.
- *Head-Dress:* This was given by the Emperor to nobility. The head-dress signified the fifth rank and above.
- *Baton:* The baton was ceremonial, and was given only to the highest ranking gentlemen at court.

FABRIC IN RANK

Listed next are the fabrics that were restricted for wear according to rank and office. It is important to remember that certain types of fabric and color combinations could be worn according to rank—even the colors used on particular fabrics had restrictions. These rules applied to men and women:

Figure 6-66 Heian Court Dress for Men, Genji Museum, Southern Kyoto.

PHOTO BY THE AUTHOR.

[22]*A Tale of Flowering Fortunes,* McCullough, p. 466.

Lower Rank: Plain and unfigured fabric, and bombycine.

High Rank: Damasks, gossamers, brocades, and certain types of embroidery.

Highest Rank: Deep red damask, embroidered green silk, complex embroidered scenes on silk.

Many of the textiles of that time period indicated a certain affinity with the body, clothing, and nature. The human form, natural textiles, and the physical aspects of nature have been discussed. We have analyzed this affinity by illustrating that dress was the harmonious link between the aristocrats (human body) and nature.

RANK OFFICES OF MEN

Only the highest offices of rank have been discussed in this text because of their complex nature. Brief descriptions of the top five ranks are presented here:

Chancellor Often this rank was left vacant unless a man could be found of outstanding character. In short, he was the role model for the Emperor. He was the highest and grandest of all the Ministers of State. Known as Daijo Daijin.

Minister of the Left Next and most powerful of the ministers. Known as Sadaijin.

Minister of the Right Substitutes for Sadaijin, and at times even has more power than him, depending on his ties with certain political and family factions. Known as Udajin.

The Palace Minister Has considerably less power than the top three positions. This post is normally occupied by a much younger person, perhaps in his early thirties. Known as Naidaijin.

Major Counselors Mostly of the Fujiwara family, but occasionally a Minamoto family member, usually in their fifties or sixties. An elite group who was second to the Ministers of State. Known as Dainagon.

Middle Counselors Had to be of suitable birth, and have served in lower positions. Normally a post for a young man in his twenties. Known as Chunagon.

SUMMARY OF HEIAN COURT HARMONY

Color harmony is responsible for the arrangement of color relationships, by which we are able to develop specific themes. As we know from the previous reading, aristocrats created elaborate themes from specific color harmonies. These accords were created to match the mood of the particular season or event being celebrated. The following is a summary example of seasonal color harmonies:

Late Summer (early autumn) Color Harmony

One typical color harmony of late summer, or more accurately early autumn, is seen in the reading section, "Dress Code and Types of Gowns for Women":

> That evening, the ladies-in-waiting assembled before her in all their finery. Princess Teishi wore a coat in *fallen-leaf* colors over aster robes. Kenshi was a white figure, her two or three robes matched by her complexion.

The aster was a combination of various light purples with green lining, purple with a brown or dark orange lining, or brown (dark orange) with a yellow-green lining. Early autumn colors were evident by the correlation to the season. Some leaves of various brown/orange colors were falling, while other leaves of green and yellow-green remained on the tree. The fabric worn by the aristocrats

was in perfect color harmony with the surrounding seasonal elements. Even careful attention was given to the colors of the inner linings so that they would carefully harmonize with the skin color. Everything had to be in perfect harmony—color, imagery, and celebration.

Early Spring Color Harmony

One of the most elaborate events cited in this particular study was "The Picture Contest," from the previous reading section, "The Story of Affinity Within the Japanese Aristocracy" (refer to that section for the story).

Consider once again, the color harmonies of "The Picture Contest":

1. Boxes of *red sandalwood* on sapponwood stands.
2. *Purple Chinese brocades* under stands.
3. Little girls wore *red robes*.
4. Jackets of *white lined with red*.
5. *Red and lavender* peeped from under the jackets.
6. Lady Oborozukiyo dressed the same as the little girls.

1. *Heavy aloes* and boxes on lighter aloes stands.
2. *Green Korean brocades* covered stands.
3. Little girls wore *green robes*.
4. Jackets of *white lined with green*.
5. *Grayish-green* lined with *yellow*.
6. Lady Kokiden dressed the same as the little girls.

Figure 6-67 Yugiri—Yugiri Reads the Letter from his Lover's Mother Miyasu-dokoro, and his Wife Kumoi-no-Kari Tries to Take it from Him.

CHAPTER SEVEN

Figure 7-1 Performance of Red Giraffes—Trafalgar Square, London.

7

COLOR
EXPRESSION

INTRODUCTION TO COLOR
EXPRESSION: MOOD AND
EMOTIONAL ATTRIBUTES

By color expression, we are more specifically referring to the mood that a given color is able to transmit to the viewer. It is the inner or spiritual essence of color, or the feeling of red, orange, yellow, green, blue, or violet. Red, for example, is a very warm color and conveys moods such as sensuality and anger. Orange is very passionate and full of energy, whereas yellow is celebratory or happy. Green and blue are typically calm and tranquil, and the deep color of violet is somber and sometimes a bit depressing in mood.

Expression can be registered in several different ways. On the following pages, the physical *outer* (representational) reality, which can be seen, for example, in body language or facial expressions (Figure 7-2), contrasted with the emotional or psychological realms of the *inner* expression, manifested through physical forms such as non-objective color choreographed responses (Figure 7-3). Figure 7-3 also can be interpreted as the mood created by Figure 7-2. The lighthearted delight of a young child can be manifested as pure mood in Figure 7-3. *Emotional responses* are usually brought about suddenly, and are generated by one's association to specific images or occurrences, which creates a given physical expression. Emotional situations are evidenced by *physical* manifestations, or that which is **seen** by the viewer. Mood development occurs somewhat more slowly, and is often the long-term result of emotional response. Mood cannot always be detected as easily, yet makes a critical difference in the *actions* of one's self. The psychological nuances or tones in *mood development* are therefore **felt** by the viewer. Our supreme example of color expression can easily be seen and felt through the color choreography process, which is an emotional response by the choreographer (painter) and then *felt* by the viewer.

INTRODUCTION TO COLOR EXPRESSION: MOOD AND EMOTIONAL ATTRIBUTES

By color expression, we are more specifically referring to the mood that a given color is able to transmit to the viewer. It is the inner, or spiritual essence of color, or the feeling of red, orange, yellow, green, blue, or violet. Red, for example is a very warm color and conveys moods such as sensuality and anger. Orange if very passionate and full of energy, while yellow is celebratory or happy. Green and blue are typically calm and tranquil, and the deep color of violet is somber and sometimes a bit depressing in mood.

Expression can be registered in several different ways. The physical outer (representational) reality, which can been seen for example, in body language or facial expressions (Figure 7-2), can be contrasted with the emotional or psychological realms of the inner expression, can be manifested through physical forms such as non-objective color choreographed responses (Figure 7-3). Figure 7-3 can also be interpreted as the mood created by Figure 7-2. The lighthearted delight of a young child can be manifested as pure mood in Figure 7-3. Emotional responses

Figure 7-2 Emotional Responses: Gina in Lampang, Thailand.

Figure 7-3 SHIJO, *Mood Development: Color Choreograph.*

Figure 7-4 Alan Burner and Debbie Tomaguchi Perform *Pearl,* from the movie sound track *"Pearl Harbor."*

Figure 7-5 Detail of Live Performance.

are usually brought about suddenly, and are generated by one's association to specific images or occurrences, which creates a given physical expression. Emotional situations are evidenced by physical manifestations, or that which is seen by the viewer. Mood development occurs somewhat more slowly, and is often the long term result of emotional response. Mood cannot always be detected as easily, yet makes a critical difference in the actions of one's self. The psychological nuances or tones in mood development are therefore, felt by the viewer. Our supreme example of color expression, can easily be seen and felt through the color choreography process, which is an emotional response by the choreographer (painter) and then felt by the viewer.

Mood and Emotional Attributes in Color Choreography Expression

In a live performance of *Color Choreography* (Figures 7-4 and 7-5), the emotions created by music selections from the soundtrack of the movie sensation *Pearl Harbor* are rendered in pure nonobjective forms. Color then creates the mood of two people's love for one another as they

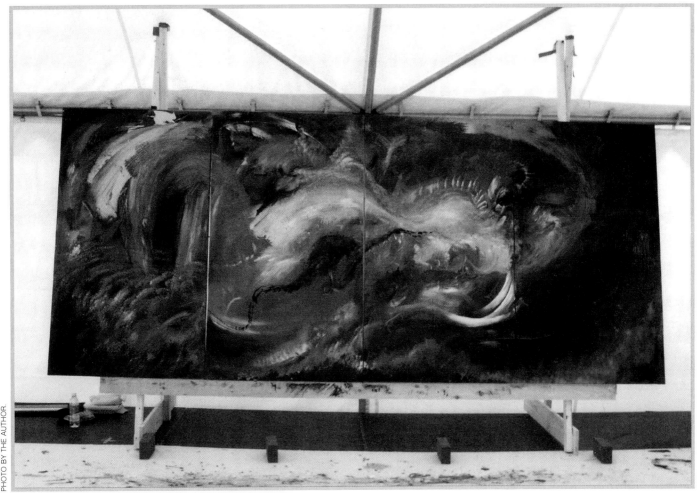

Figure 7-6 Alan Burner and Debbie Tomaguchi, ***Pearl: Color Choreography***, 70" 3 190".

are separated by war, and the fierceness of the infamous bombing of Pearl Harbor. The nontangible energy of the music has been translated into a physical image of emotion mood variances, which allows the performers to translate the music into visual harmony. The viewer then, begins to feel the mood of this situation in Pearl Harbor, as the finished painting (Figure 7-6) demonstrates both the moods *love* (love story), and *hate* (war story).

Color Expression in Performance

Typically, a performance or theatrical event involves both music and dance components. Choreography in any given performance has a central goal: the *core element* of the piece is that dance translates the music, which is unseen, into visual harmonious forms. The same occurs with color choreography. Consider the several forms of this expression process:

- *Concertos* are experienced differently, in that visuals only exist in the musician's movement. There is minimal distraction from listening to the pure mood of the composition. The music and colors created for each individual are subjectively perceived. The physical arrangement of colors and the colors of lights also are a factor in many operas. For most, color is subtle yet vital, because music ultimately is heard, *seen,* and felt.

- *Opera* involves choreography and music, such as *Romeo and Juliet* (Figure 7-12) or *Phantom of the Opera* (Figure 7-10), and translates music into sentiment and visual harmony, which simply interprets the mood. The colors of lighting are a vital element that assist the music in creating the ultimate mood enhancement. Color expression is only effective when these elements are well understood by the production crew.

- *Motion picture* production relies on the moods created by the music and color in cinematography. A great producer realizes the importance of color contrasts and specialized colors of light for the ultimate expressive potential in a film. Music alone is only part of the equation; it is the color elements within a given set, whether out of doors or inside.

To understand the importance of color is to appreciate its chief attribute, which is the ability to communicate specific mood variances to the viewer. Color choreography is one of several elaborate methodologies to demonstrate this, and certainly is an effective way to actually see that which often is so elusive and spiritual in nature. However, it is of commensurable significance that we explore some of the other forms of color expression as well. In order to fully understand color's elements, it is necessary to continue examining various forms of expression. Let's take a brief look at these areas for a more comprehensive understanding of color's demonstrative abilities through different forms as it relates to emotional and mood appeal. We will launch a brief study of emotion and mood concepts as it further relates to music, with a brief investigation into the symphony and the opera.

Mood and Emotional Attributes in Music

The Symphony

Originally, the symphony in the seventeenth century consisted of varied forms. They included short compositions but with few participants, which were to be thought of in terms of parts of a larger whole, but not as *the* opera itself. At the end of the eighteenth century, this system grew to include more instrumentation with a standard *four-part* movement. The normal form of the symphony (as is the current average structure) consisted of four movements, beginning with a *fast* movement, typically in sonata form, while the second and third movements were *slower* such as a minuet or sonata (etc.), and ending with a *fast* movement in sonata or rondo form.

As we noted, symphonies originally involved fewer instruments than we see today, and were separate from opera and much shorter movements. Over time, the symphony became more complex, with anywhere from a single movement to six. At some point the movements became more multilayered in structure, with varied placements of slow and fast movements in the form of sonatas, rondos, minuets, ternary (dance), and variation forms.

The symphony originally was and oftentimes just an introduction to the opera. As time passed, the uncomplicated nature of the symphony evolved to a more complex and sophisticated structure until the *symphony* became more closely involved with the *orchestra*, and the orchestra to the *opera*. The symphony today is a beautiful harmony of vastly different instruments that is capable of producing a complexity of mood variances throughout the performance.

BOWATER/MIRA.COM/DRR.NET.

Figure 7-7

JOHN HARRISON AND ULSTER ORCHESTRA SOCIETY.

Figure 7-8 Thierry Fisher Conductor Ulster Orchestra.

JOHN HARRISON AND ULSTER ORCHESTRA SOCIETY.

Figure 7-9

In like manner, color harmony and the emotional draw to create mood is much the same. The music creates specific moods, which are all connected to color; yellow is happy, orange is passionate and energized, red is angry or perhaps sensuous, blue is calm, green is tranquil, and violet is somber. The symphony is harmony, or instruments all in agreement with one another. Color harmony is symphonic color. It is the assemblage of colors in accord with one another, which then produces visual cadences in order to create mood.

The Opera

"Even passionate music fans may be forgiven for considering opera over-the-top. After all, how better to describe an art form that flaunts convoluted plots, incomprehensible lyrics, stormy orchestration, hyperbolic acting, exotic staging, and temperamental singers? Another word might be operatic."
—*Alan Riding and Leslie Dunton-Downer, May 2006*

Not too many events can exceed the visual excitement that music and performance can create at the opera. It is in effect music, theater, and dance, which originally came together in eighteenth-century Italy. Opera has the amazing ability to create very specific emotional appeals that transform people's emotions into serious moods. It creates an amazing adventure into the nontangible world of the

Figure 7-10 A billboard for the play *Phantom of the Opera* rests over the marquee of the Majestic Theater in Times Square.

human spirit. It is sometimes humorous or sad, celebration or disaster, angry or happy, ascetic or sensuous, and so forth. As the *stage undulates with the changing moods by colors* of lights, it can take our hearts and minds far away, through any number of journeys. Its strong correlation with *Color Choreography* sentiments can be seen by the physical expression of the inner emotions, or reactions to music.

La Traviata (Figure 7-11), the Italian opera, concerns a Paris courtesan by the name of Violetta (the real Traviata

Figure 7-11 Guiseppe Verdi's opera, *La Traviata,* had its premiere night August 7, 2005 at the world famous cultural Salzburg festival.

was Marie Duplessis) and her lover, Alfredo. His father manages to break the affair, but in the end Violetta and Alfredo reunite, if only for a short time. They fall into each other's arms and vow never to be apart again before she dies.

Shakespeare's **Romeo and Juliet** the French opera (Figure 7-12), is a passionate love story about two people who fall hopelessly in love. Their destiny is affected (as it was in La Traviata) by family interference and issues, in this case the feudal nature between the Capulet (Juliet) and Montague (Romeo) families. Juliet conspires with the friar to fake her death, so that her and Romeo could finally escape to live in harmony at an undisclosed destination. The message never gets to Romeo that it is a plot, and he returns thinking that she has genuinely died. Romeo cannot live without her, so he drinks a potion to end his life. As he is dying, she awakens to discover what has happened. As he slips near death, she ends her life with a dagger.

Romeo and Juliet, as well as *La Traviata,* demonstrates love and hate, passion and coldness, and disaster and success. These contrasts are played out through the opera, through the music, the actors response to the music, and the colors of stage lighting. Imagine that you have been assigned the task of deciding the colors of lighting in the various scenes of either opera. What color harmonies would you choose for the contrasting emotional elements of *Romeo and Juliet?* Perhaps in some situations you would use a dyadic harmony, others monochromatic? What types of contrasts would you set up with colors of light as well? Imagine the prowess in *color mood*

Figure 7-12 Nadezhda Gracheva and Yuri Klevtsov dancing in the Bolshoi Ballet production of **Romeo and Juliet.**

RCBBIE JACK/CORBIS.

how they affect the physical world. Let's look at a brief examination of the *outer* expression: the portrait.

Mood and Emotional Attributes in Individual Expression

Portraiture

When asked to color analyze a given color composition or setting, the beginning student of color will often confuse facial expression and body language with the pure expression of color. We say that color has no face, religion, culture, or ethnic group. Rather color has all faces, religions, cultures, and ethnic groups. Pure color itself is, therefore, not necessarily assigned to a specific form or shape. Paul Gauguin understood that grass did not necessarily have to be green, and often was a hindrance in creating the optimal mood. In *Jacob Wrestling the Angel,* he understood that the ground should be red inorder to create the intensity of the situation. Piet Mondrian reasoned that color itself, in his pure formless attempts to glorify color without form, was indeed beautiful and expressive in and of itself. Why do we need to assign yellow to a banana, red to a cherry, or blue to a blueberry? In his composition *Red, Yellow, and Blue* he did just that. He constructed a simple grid of red, yellow, and blue.

Thus far in the textbook we have established that color can create moods by its *independent* nature employing various saturations, intensities, values, contrasts, tints and shades, and harmonies. However, is the form commensurately independent of color? We know from Pablo Picasso's work that he was not chiefly a colorist, but rather a painter of form. His achromatic work did not need color to express the urgency and carnage of war, which he so effectively depicted in his work *Guernica* (Figure 7-54). He was indeed the master of form.

Vincent van Gogh (Figure 7-25) was a colorist who relied heavily on color to manipulate the viewer's moods. He was less concerned with form, and much more interested in establishing the emotional and mood component

effects that a good stage director, set designer, and costume designer must possess.

By now, we have a better understanding of the *inner* spiritual nature of color as it relates to music and performance, let's take a look at color and moods of hues and

Figure 7-13 SHIJO, **Remeo and Juliet,** 72″ x 168″. A physical color response to the moods interpreted from Shakespeare's foremost play.

PHOTO BY AUTHOR.

Figure 7-16 *Farmer,* Jalalabad, Afghanistan,1992.

The ***Farmer from Jalalabad, Afghanistan*** (Figure 7-16) presents us with quite a different mood altogether. The dark and light contrast brings the face to our immediate attention, and in reality the *background* and the *foreground* seem to become one. The background violet is so dark that it is barely perceived as color and is, therefore, forcing the viewer to focus completely on the foreground figure and its colors, as opposed to the previous portrait of the Xigaze girl. There is no other issue but for the expression of *mood* of the farmer's face, which is *exaggerated* by the warm yellow-oranges. The tenibristic value of this portrait allows us to focus without any other distraction, on the quiet dignity and confidence so apparent in his face. What first appears to be a monochromatic photo is on closer examination a dyadic color harmony of very dark blue-violets and yellow-oranges. The somber wisdom of this man's expression echose a very tranquil mood, which is partially responsible for the very approachable feeling sensed within the photograph. The addition of color harmony with its contrasting face against the background completes the mood scenario.

The ***Young Woman at a Horse Festival*** (Figure 7-17) is without a doubt the most upbeat in this series of six portraits. Once again, we see a dyadic color harmony,

only this time it is red and green. The best way to discuss color in this portrait is to identify the contrast element, that is, the character of color created by *saturation contrast,* demonstrated by the *dark shaded red* and the *saturated green.* It is the warm dark red ground that also lends additional vibrancy to the saturated red accessories of the girl's costume. Unlike the previous portrait, her figure races forward into the viewer's space, and gives it a much more confrontational character.

The playful and innocent mood emanating from this photograph creates a striking contrast in the viewer's emotional response to that of the previous two compositions. Normally, those who even so much as glance at the young woman will have a very optimistic reaction in terms of immediate mood response. This specific contrast of dyadic color harmony, accompanied by the girl's emotional appeal, will always create a powerful and stimulating effect.

The ***Nomad from Kham, Tibet*** (Figure 7-18) also has a red background, but in this composition it is a *cool red* instead of the previous warm red ground. The subtle difference in ground hues can make a monumental difference in the mood-generating character of a particular hue. If we were to make a comparision between the *Young Woman at a Horse Festival* and this photograph, we would have to

Figure 7-17 *Young Woman at a Horse Festival,* Tagong, Tibet, 1999.

Figure 7-18 *Nomad,* Kham, Tibet, 2004.

Figure 7-19 *Village Girl,* Band-e Amir, Afghanistan, 2002.

STEVE MCMURRY.

STEVE MCMURRY.

say that the warm red ground behind the "Young Woman" is energized and playful, as opposed to the "Nomad," which reflects a very serious and almost somber mood.

The facial expression is in perfect harmony with the color mood of the ground. Even the variances of blue, indigo, and violet hues create that very serious yet amiable mood setting. Her expression is forgiving and kind. She is a woman who has worked hard her entire life, having seen many hardships, and yet she is approachable and full of grace.

The cool violets and indigos of her clothing and hair are "pulled" into or influence the shades of the red ground to create a perfect analogous harmony of color (red-violet, violet, blue-violet, and blue).

The general attitude of *physical* and *color* expression projects a very thought-provoking intensity. The deep hues in this portraiture complement the longevity and wisdom that was so evident from the start.

The **Village Girl from Band-e Amir** (Figure 7-19) is not like any other portrait. The yellow, violet, orange, and blue forms a subtle tetradic harmony of colors, which is responsible for the dynamics of this somewhat confrontational gaze. Her demeanor leaves one with the immediate impression that she had been in deep thought when she then suddenly looks up at the viewer, but with no apparent surprise. The *ambivalent mood* is unmistakable, particularly in terms of facial expression; however, we need to see if the *physical* matches the *color mood* expression at this point.

One very important aspect about this portrait is that the saturated yellow yellow-orange background seems to launch the figure forward into this very confrontational space. The main attribute of color here is its ability to not just frame and contrast the figure, but additionally has the effect of projecting her persona almost beyond the picture limitations itself. The contrast of color—the extreme difference between the yellow ground and the violet head cover—create a conflict with the face as well. Saturated yellow is typically a color mood of celebration, yet here the emotional appeal is anything but that. In this case the use of yellow causes our mind's eye to focus ever more intently on the face, framed in deep violet.

The uncertainty and uneasiness created here is easily understood within the context of opposites on the color wheel. Even though there are four basic colors in the composition, the immediate reaction before looking carefully, is to see a dyad of yellow and violet. Their nature together as opposites are unstable in the sense that they are complements that are extreme of dark (violet) and light (yellow) color.

The portrait of the **Young Rinpoche** (Figure 7-20) monk is quite different than the Village Girl. Although the village girl projects a somber confrontational mood, the boy does not. His eyes do not make contact with the viewer, and they seem to be avoiding the possibility of confrontation, which provokes a very *conciliatory* mood. The young monk is neither happy nor sad, but even at

STEVE MCMURRY.

STEVE MCMURRY.

Figure 7-20 *Young Rinpoche,* Bylakuppe, India, 2001.

his young age, seems to implicate the Buddhist philosophy about non attachment to the cares of this world.

If we are to match the moods of the physical portrait with the expression of color, the first thing we would notice is the red robe's greater intensity compared to the deep blue-green ground itself. The rich red foreground effects the character of the blue-green, so as to imagine an even greater tranquility, almost sedating the viewer. In this situation, color and light creates a very focused attention on the boy's face, which is the outward example of his philosophical beliefs.

Conclusion of Color in Portraiture:

Whether there is *energy* or *tranquility, love* or *hate, anger* or *serenity, passion* or *apathy, sensual* or *spiritual, celebration* or *misery,* color-created moods are always powerful and persuasive. Our emotional response to portraiture depends on the color scenarios or harmony constructions that occur in a given work. In the case of recognizable imagery, color is the key element that adds the visual stimulus, intensifying the mood. The black and white version indicates that we recognize the mood, but hues of color are the crucial element that produces the inner feeling or felt mood.

in his work. Let's see what happens when we combine both accurate form and color together to create the ultimate mood response.

Color Expression in Architecture

Architecture also can be quite expressive, and contains two aspects: the physical structure and color. In previous chapters, we discussed the color effects seen on the *outside* of the Grand Palace in Bankok, Thailand, as opposed to the *interior* colors of the Gothic Notre Dame de Paris. But now, in Basil's Cathedral in Moscow (Figure 7-21), we are confronted with a completely different exterior than we are accustomed to seeing at this point.

The cathedral has been seen by some as playful and fanciful in appeal. To others, it is a sophisticated and charming monument to Christianity. One thing can be said; it is indeed one the greatest architectural exterior color displays in the world today. The combination of colors with the unusual architectural forms of *onion domes* create the emotional appeal, which is absolutely *the* paramount

STEVE BOURGEOIS/STOCK CONNECTION/DRR.NET.

IZZET KERIBAR/IML IMAGE GROUP/DRR.NET.

St. Basil's Cathedral in Moscow, Russia—Detail.

Figure 7-21 St. Basil's Cathedral in Moscow, Russia.

feature of this cathedral. It is both charming and thought provoking, but one thing every visitor remembers is the color exterior.

The color draw of the cathedral is unmistakable. It creates a beautiful color harmony in eight sections of onion domes, yet it is clearly the outside appeal that is the important issue, because the interior is quite simple by comparison.

Interior Design

Color expression is certainly an important concern for interior designers. An interior space can either produce an inviting character or not. Interiors can establish an emotional response on many different levels, creating the exact mood to suit the client. Whether coming home from an intense day of work, or creating a social event such as a dinner party, one's interior space can be vital to the emotional state. Few color expression functions are as important as creating the appropriate interior ambiance for a home or office.

Color harmony in the office space can create the ultimate productive environment for each worker. Color affects mood, and that translates into how efficient the workload is processed each day. At home, a relaxing and warm environment is often the choice of many, and color choices in the living space make for a more restful evening and a better day ahead.

Figure 7-23 GIAN LORENZO BERNINI, *The Ecstasy of Saint Teresa*, 1647-52.

SCALA/ART RESOURCE, NY.

Figure 7-22 Goreme, Cappadocia, Turkey, July 2005. Since Roman Times people have been cutting graves and home out of the soft tufo 'Fairy Chimney' rocks of Cappadocia.

FRITS MEYST/ADVENTURE4EVER.COM/DRR.NET.

The example of our Feng Shui kitchen (Figure 7-22) is a simple, but effective concept in design and color. There is a dyad (compliments) color harmony of wall space and furnishings in orange tones, contrasted against the cool blue hues of exterior architecture. The cool exterior creates an even warmer and cozier feeling, which is important for a creative culinary environment.

Color Expression in Sculpture

Let's use Bernini's sculpture *The Ecstasy of St. Teresa* (Figure 7-23) to separate and draw a comparison between *color expression* and *body language*. Just as we looked at the two components of expression in the portraits, we want to look in a similar fashion, but with a different approach. In St. Teresa's dream she is stabbed repeatedly by an angel of the Lord, and yet she recalls that there was a certain pleasure about the whole event. Certainly that is true according to her facial expression, as well as the angel's, which does not indicate any degree of suffering. In this form of sculpture, it is clear that body language is sufficient to create the energy and dynamic of the mood, and yet there are subtleties of color throughout. If we focus carefully, what would normally be thought of as a white stone sculpture is actually a combination of light yellow-orange tints, with lightest violet shades. The sculptural surface is reflecting the character of the yellow-orange bronze rays of light (rods) from behind. Often, this is why sculpture is not endowed with applied color. It is so blessed with dynamics, the addition of color

Figure 7-24 PHILIP HERMOGENES CALDERON, *Broken Vows*, 1856.

would be too extreme. This is about the *obvious* demonstration of *physical appearance*, and the *subtle* nuances of *color expression*. Put another way, it is the manifestation of physical mood, more than the spiritual nature of color itself. This is a subtle mood enhancement.

Color Expression in Painting

In Calderon's *Broken Vows* (Figure 7-24), we see that the facial expression in this painting is paramount to the entire composition. The face of the foreground figure illustrates a range of emotions. Her moods are apparent, as she has gone from the intense feeling of the probability that her suspicions have been correct, to the transformation of painful disappointment. The *expression form* focuses directly on her face, as the directional light illuminates the most important aspect of this painting. Typically we rely on this type of painting to give us the obvious information about the mood of any given painting. The examples of architecture, sculpture, and painting are particularly obvious when creating an expression, which translates into the

Figure 7-25 VINCENT VAN GOGH, *Street in Saintes-Maries,* 1888.

PRIVATE COLLECTION. CHRISTIE'S AUCTION. NEW YORK, 19.5.1981.

Arles, the town of van Gogh's favorite memories, was painted repeatedly, as if he was reliving his most memorable and pleasant days vicariously through his paintings (Figure 7-25). This is color expression in its finest moment, where color is not dependent on form or shape. Even though we understand there are structures and foliage, we also know the painting does not depend on the realistic nature of imagery for expression. It is rather the saturated and intensified nature of colors that set the mood in this painting. His color expressions are energized fields of vibrant warm and cool hues, which give the viewer a perspective on his emotional state as well as how fond he is of the area.

Color does not depend on form or recognizable shapes. Color is completely independent upon any other element of art or design. Color is expressive in and of itself, and needs no additional supportive element. Some say that color depends on form, but in reality it can even escape those boundaries, as we will see more clearly in Chapter 7. It is color expression can single-handedly create emotional content, and the moods associated with it. Franz Marc's *The Fate of the Animals* (below) speaks volumes about the effects of impending war on innocence. Color speaks loud and clear as it dominates the composition, creating a mood of terror. It is only after color has affected its emotional debut that line direction and abstracted animal forms begin to aid color in its total outcome. Marc was part of a popular art movement in the early part of the twentieth century aptly known as *German Expressionism.*

emotional factors of a composition. However, we do want to take a look at the less obvious, and most suggestive and authoritative elements of expression, which is color itself.

In the beginning of this book, we discussed van Gogh, but it bears repeating in this chapter, because he was one of history's most magnificent purveyors of *color expression.*

Figure 7-26 MARC FRANZ, *Fate of the Animals,* 1913.

ART RESOURCE, NY.

Color Connection in Prose

A story of integrity and passion, Romeo falls in love with Juliet, and their feuding families hamper their efforts to marry. The Montague family (Romeo's) and the Capulets (Juliet's), are enemies constantly at war with each other. It is a story filled with the highest degree of passion, a prototype for the quintessential love story, filled with high emotion and conflict.

Romeo only is interested in love; he is the lover who immediately becomes infatuated with a beautiful woman. When Juliet appears on the scene, it is Rosaline who has been holding Romeo's attention, but in spite of his romantic advances, Rosaline remains indifferent toward him. Suddenly, he is in love again, but this time the woman of his desire holds him in a love grip, such as he has never before experienced. She is intoxicating to the degree that he completely forgets about Rosaline.

To this point in Romeo's life, his concept of love is quite superficial, and certainly his ideas of love are skewed to say the least. He has been obsessed with the idea of love rather than the reality of it. When Juliet comes into his life, he seems to learn what love actually is, as evidenced by his stunning and passionate love poems.

Romeo's personality is impulsive, passionate, energetic, and immoderate. He is extreme.

Juliet, on the other hand, is clear-headed, determined, strong, loyal, and somewhat naïve.

She is from the aristocracy, which does not give her the broad freedom Romeo enjoys. So it is that one night, he sneaks into the courtyard of the Capulet family, his own family's sworn enemy, and ultimately up to Juliet's room to consummate their marriage, which had been kept a secret.

Figure 7-31 Philip Hermogenes Calderon, *Juliet*, 1888.

Juliet's parents finally reveal their intention for her to marry their choice, whose name is Paris. Juliet is unable to reveal that she is secretly married to Romeo, and so she conspires with her nurse to drink a potion that would make her appear to be dead. When she is finally put in the family crypt, the potion would wear off, after which time Romeo would come to her aid, and they would be able to live happily ever after without their family's reproach.

The night arrives when she takes the temporary poison, after which a messenger would fetch Romeo to let him know the plot. The problem is that the messenger is detained, and Romeo never hears of the plot, only that she is dead. He hurries off to her tomb, reaching it only to find (as he believes) that she is dead. Torn with grief and despair, and unable to face life without her, he commits suicide and falls at her side dead. Just then, Juliet's potion wears off and she discovers his dead body next to her. Juliet, unable to continue her life without him, puts a dagger to her chest, and falls dead on Romeo's body:

> Yea noise? Then I'll be brief. Oh happy dagger.
> This is thy sheath-there rust and let me die.
> (Juliet, Act 5, Scene 3)

Emotional Transference to Color Expression in Romeo and Juliet

Here, two people so desperately in love, a passion and joy so rarely experienced, turns to agony and tragedy. This is a story of love expression, so how could we translate the expression of emotion or mood content into abstract color expression?

The tragedy of *Romeo and Juliet* is *prose* expression, which easily converts into color expression. The life of Romeo and his persona is quite different from that of Juliet, and yet their goals are the same. There is, in fact, a spectrum of expression as the story unfolds. The intensity by which Romeo is able to love seems unparalleled in Shakespeare's plays. Romeo's epithet is that of being skilled at love, or being a lover. This is all brought into focus when Juliet appears, and he becomes so star-struck, he all but forgets Rosaline. Juliet loves Romeo with equal energy, yet she is more level-headed in most of her approaches whereas Romeo is mostly spontaneous.

Try to imagine in your mind's eye that Juliet's character and reactions to Romeo are strong, level-headed, and loyal, and her love is without compromise. Her nature, as the entire play reads, seems to imply hues of deep blues, indigos, and rich violets, as they pulse through the composition. Romeo's temperament, on the other hand, creates an environment of highly intense and charged colors. Orange, the color of energy, and the yellow of joy and celebration juxtapose and dance across the composition to contrast with their complements.

Later in the story, it is elucidated by various hues of red to dark red, which begin to permeate the picture plane. Finally, the tragedy creates the darkest of violets, reds, and even orange hues. The story becomes the spectrum of expression, or color.

Color Expression in Nature

The *Valley Curtain* (Figure 7-32) signifies just how important the role of color expression can be. The reasonably saturated orange curtain creates a powerful and ominous state of being as it contrasts against the complementary blue sky. The saturated contrast of orange against the dull greens and tinted blues of the ground surfaces create an abrupt and threatening wall as one drives down the road toward it. The sheer scale of the saturated orange wall allows one to imagine how cautious and apprehensive one could actually feel, driving towards this gigantic curtain. The *expression of orange* is energized and almost overwhelming to the point of trepidation.

Finally, we take a look at Christo and Jeanne-Claude's blue umbrellas (Figure 7-33) in Japan, and the yellow umbrellas (Figure 7-34) in California. It is significant to note that the umbrellas in Japan are more densely packed together, whereas the California landscape is peppered with umbrellas far and wide. It is much like the two soci-

eties, in that Japan's people and architecture are more closely crowded together, whereas in California comparatively, there is more space per person. One of the most interesting aspects of the work is the color ramifications. Anyone who has spent time in Japan can tell you that water is not a scarcity. Because the annual rainfall in Japan is about 60 inches, we could naturally conclude then that the umbrellas would represent the perceived notion of an abundance of *blue water.* In contrast, California is very dry with very little rainfall or water, accompanied by frequent sunny days. The yellow umbrellas seem to mirror the yellow, yellow-orange grasses that typically coat the hills in Southern California, as well as its source of dryness—the sun. This expression of color is very symbolical in the natural disposition of these two lands. The prevailing and saturated cool blues clustered through the Japanese fields lies tranquil with the saturated green rice paddies. The blue carries the eye through the fields quickly, while the warm saturated yellow umbrellas lead the eye more slowly and harmoniously through the hills

Figure 7-33 CHRISTO AND JEANNE-CLAUDE, **The Umbrellas**, Japan, 1984–91.

Figure 7-34 CHRISTO AND JEANNE-CLAUDE, **The Umbrellas**, California, 1984–91.

Figure 7-39 Shijo, *Libera Me Domine.*

if to feel emotionally the temperament of that color, and react to it accordingly.

In Shijo's *Libera Me Domine* (Figure 7-39), we must first acknowledge the style. We will refer to the work as contemporary Gothic painted constructions. The painting incorporates fragments of Renaissance concerns, as well as expressionist surface treatments. The more free-spirited application of red and yellow hues in the background is seen here as a more expressionist approach. The remainder of the painting, with its gilded framework, statuary, and the pulpit alludes to Gothic, Greek, and Romanesque attitudes. The deep red hues are contrasted with the intensities of yellow and yellow-oranges, which complete a very somber and perhaps fearful mood as the day of judgment materializes. The gray façade acts as a buffer or neutralizing zone transitioning into blue. Taken from the Requiem Mass, the occasional Latin phrases, and the blue tints and shades of the statuary add some degree of stability, calmness, and hope about the outcome. Observe the difference between the achromatic version and the chromatic. It is easy to see just how important color (color expression) is to establish the severity of the message, regardless of the form. It is of utmost importance to understand that color is the absolute authority to create this very serious emotional statement.

Color Expression in Performance/ Stage Lighting

The lights are turned down, the candles lit and set in place, and Aiko waits for Akihiko's return (Figure 7-40). The setting is somewhat obvious as to her intent, as she

waits for her husband. The hues range from intense yellow to deep red-oranges, and then to deepest red-orange in the background. There is warmth generated not only from the candles, but every color in the frame is warm and inviting. The intense yellow of the candles creates enough light to enhance the figure of Aiko, which in this very dim and soft red-orange light, becomes very sensuous and alluring. Any other harmony combinations of color expression would simply not work. Imagine her on stage as the lighting technicians change the colors of the stage to blues and blue-greens, or perhaps cool violets to warm violet. The mood would not have the same appeal, the emotional ambiance would be more cold and calculating, or perhaps just too calm.

Setting the appropriate mood is paramount in stage lighting design. A well-orchestrated performance is solidly based in *color,* usually enhanced by special lighting techniques, which take the audience through specific emotional expeditions. Lighting technicians have prior knowledge of the script's contents, and spend a considerable

Figure 7-40 Shijo, *Aiko Prepares for Akihiko's Return* (Video Still).

of stage lighting. The levitated figure creates an immediate calm, though somewhat rigid, first by virtue of the *horizontal relaxed* line of her body, but more importantly, by the high contrasting monochromatic composition of red-orange. The high color contrast is also about dark and light, which creates a very mysterious composition. It is mood expressive of calm, yet with a bit of an *edgy* ambiance.

Color expression in the vertical film composition (Figure 7-42) is perceived differently than *The Dreamscape*. Certainly she is relaxed, but more tranquil. Her body language, facial expression, and the secondary triad color harmonies help to create a more upbeat and casual feeling. There is a lack of mystery without the dark and light hues, and the colors are fairly saturated. There is a vertical stability that the other film clip does not have, but it is the color which is the main influence in mood here. The strength and stability of the standing vertical figure is reinforced by the strongest, yet least intense color in the spectrum, which is violet.

PICASSO, COLOR EXPRESSION AND ABSTRACTION

A study of Pablo Picasso's work (beginning on Page 340, Figure 7-43) at this point will help us to determine the nature of color expression from a different perspective. We will study both the artist and his work at some length, in order to further understand the nature of expression in art

amount of time planning and incorporating the exact color sequences into the duration of the performance. This is a vital function that serves to manipulate specific mood responses. The all-important aspects of performances, opera, musicals, and so on depend on color to *enhance* and in most cases *create* the mood. A *cool stage* (green, blue, violet) will create calm and even tranquil *moods*, whereas a warm stage (yellow, orange, red) generates a charged and energized presence.

The Dreamscape (Figure 7-41) presents us with a different color expression. The figure is calm as is a tranquil horizon. *The Dreamscape* is another example of the effects

Figure 7-41 Shijo, *Preparation for the Ceremony: The Dreamscape* (Video Still).

Figure 7-42 SHIJO, *Amy Relaxes Between Film Sequences on Stage.*

Figure 7-43 PABLO PICASSO, *Woman with Pigeons*, 1930.

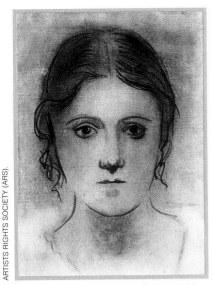

Figure 7-44 PABLO PICASSO, *Sad Olga*, 1923.

Figure 7-45 PABLO PICASSO, *Olga Apprehensive.*

Figure 7-46 PABLO PICASSO, *Olga Hurt.*

and design itself, and then to learn how to apply color to amplify the emotional and mood capacities of the work. Pablo Picasso, one of the twentieth century's most successful artists, will be the focus for the remainder of the color expression discussion. Actually, he was one of the wealthiest and most successful artists in recorded history.

Picasso was what we refer to as a "form" artist as opposed to a "colorist." That is to say, even though he incorporated color into much of his work, it was his prowess with shape and form that we know him by best. Abstract form, simple form, large and small forms, juxtaposed forms fragmented in space—all were about his style. Some of these forms involved color; some did not. At times he would use a full color palette; other times only a wash of color would complement the forms in the composition. The use of color as expression depended on his own life experiences. His work was about the man himself, which basically narrows down to his various relationships with women.

Still, Picasso knew the importance of color expression quite well. After all, he was usually the source of upset with the women in his life. Look at *Sad Olga* (Figure 7-44) to see his use of somber washes of color throughout the composition, which corresponds to the expression on her face. *Olga Apprehensive* (Figure 7-45) is endowed with considerably more color hues, and the colors are more specifically located in the painting. The red-orange tones seem to create some degree of tension, and thereby supporting the idea that there is a fair degree of apprehension about Olga's face. *Olga Hurt* (Figure 7-46), on the other hand, seems to have lost any emotional ability to holdup her facial expression. That is to say, the color has drained from the composition, only to leave deep shaded red to orange tones. The limited monochromatic nature of this portrait seems to express more fully a deeper sadness and hurt.

These color-enhanced portraits continued to change as the representational aspects become continuously more abstracted, and the shapes distorted.

Picasso no doubt knew he could be more expressive of his emotions toward his subject matter, if nothing more than to fragment, destroy, and then reinvent their form.

Figure 7-47 PABLO PICASSO, *Portrait of Dora Maar,* 1937.

Picasso's extramarital affairs took their toll on his wives and he became increasingly more distraught about his relationships. His compositions of fragmented planes and shapes—simple contour line drawings without color—began to express the condition of his emotional state.

It is most certainly color expression that portrays the mood of this portrait of Dora Maar (Figure 7-47)). Everything else about the composition is subservient to color, and it is this hexadic harmony of primary and secondary saturated complements that tell us of his strong emotional attachment to Dora. In this case, it is the destruction of typical

*From Picasso, *My Grandfather by Marinqa Picasso,* Riverhead Books, 2001.

tion of typical or conventional color that is replaced by unconventional color to translate the emotion.

Picasso exclaimed many times, in slightly different sentences, "Every act of creation is first of all an act of destruction" or "To paint is to destroy." Picasso knew full well about the *act of destruction*, he was after all the grand purveyor of this sentiment and action. He not only destroyed the lives of his lovers and wives, but that of his own children as well. Picasso's infidelity was the reason for the pain and suffering of his family, lovers, and himself. Everyone in his life, especially those close to him, gave repeatedly of their energies, until they had nothing left to give. Picasso would then move on to the next victim, stolen energies unrequited. His own granddaughter writes concerning his accomplishments as a human being, rather than his success as an artist:

Isolated inside Notre-Dame-de-Vie, he died in the same way as he had lived: alone, which is how he had wanted to be. He had made this cruel statement: When I die, it will be a shipwreck. When a large ship goes down many people in the vicinity are swept into the whirlpool."

It's true, many people were swept into the whirlpool. Pablito, my inseparable brother, committed suicide two days after our grandfather was buried at Vauvenargues. My father, the frail giant, died two years later feeling desperately orphaned. Marie-Therese Walter, the inconsolable muse, hanged herself from the ceiling of her garage in Juan-les-Pins. Jacqueline, the companion of his last days, also committed suicide with a bullet in her temple. Later, Dora Maar died in poverty surrounded by the Picasso paintings she had refused to sell, so she could preserve for herself the presence of the man whom she idolized.

I was meant to be one of the victims as well. If I'm still around, I owe it to a lust for life and struggle, which I inherited from a grandfather I dreamed about. And who wasn't there.*

Picasso left a path of destruction everywhere he tread. As he continued painting, he destroyed images, planes, and peoples' lives, all for the sake of his art. He continued to destroy, rearranging his expression of life with his women. He reinvents the form over and over in order to fit his own expressive needs.

In May of 1937, Picasso turned his attention to one of his greatest works ever produced. This time it was not about his own personal destructions as much as it was about the destruction of a town called *Guernica*. On April 26, 1937, German Nazi warplanes began their surprise attack on the town of Guernica. The headlines read *"Mille bombes incendiaries lancees par les avions de Hitler et de Mussolini reduisent en cendres la ville de Guernica"* (A Thousand Firebombs dropped by Hitler and Mussolini's Planes Reduce the Town of Guernica to Ashes).

The entire city of Guernica was destroyed in a matter of a few hours. Many reports said that the town glowed an eerie deep red-orange—not unlike dying embers in a camp fire—the evening after the destruction of Guernica. It was total carnage and chaos upon an innocent, unsuspecting civilian town. The German war machine had prevailed without a struggle.

Picasso labored with many sketches, working and reworking his plan to show the world the calamity in his native Spain. The painting itself is somewhat of an enigma, and so we will explore briefly the two interpretations that are most obvious. One could declare what is reasonably

The following color expression categories serve to illustrate the various forms by which color is involved with when creating effective emotional or mood appeals:

Typical Applications that Apply to Color Expression

TONAL VARIATIONS	SYMBOLIC	EMOTION/MOOD
Light (pale)	Important (noble)	Celebration (happy)
Bright (tints) {Intensity]	Winter	Hate
Vivid (purity) [Saturation]	Spring	Love
Deep (shades) [Value]	Summer	Peace/Tranquility
Dark	Autumn	Chaos
Dull	Cold/Cool	Depressing
Grayish [Light to grayish category will demonstrate variances of 10% to 100% densities]	Hot/Warm	Sensuous
Transparent	Sophistication	Passionate
Dense (Opacity)	Cultural	Quiet

This chart is a sample of color expression categories or elements that can be used either separately or in a formulaic manner to create effective emotional (mood) appeals.

obvious in that the painting is about the destruction of Guernica. All of the figurative forms have been through the extreme agony of a bomb attack because of the Nazi forces, and so the destruction of buildings, a couple of animals, and human forms indicate that the painting is purely about the physical destruction of the town. There are four women, one male, a baby, a horse and a bull, which dominate the figurative element. The people and horse are all in death's grip, as the agony prevails. The bull, it is said by many, is the Nazi General Franco of Spain, surveying his path of destruction. There is however another interpretation, or at least another opinion of the content in the mural.

Another approach to the mural is seen in light of Picasso's real life, considering the many spiritual destructions symbolized on this canvas. The figures represent women who have been emotionally and spiritually shattered. The horse also represents women, in either interpretation, which is generally agreed upon. In the bullfight, the horse saps the strength from the bull, which is Picasso himself. Picasso then surveys his own path of destruction. The faces in the composition all seem to turn in the direction of the bull, and he looks back on the destruction to survey the consequences of his life.

The Reading Compliment by Judi Freeman (page 348) documents much of the development of Guernica through a discourse about "Weeping Women," which are seen in his sketches and paintings in preparation for Guernica.

SUMMARY

A modest sampling of art and design categories of the various *color expression* components, such as the emotional and mood attributes in each of the following limited categories, have been examined:

1. Color Choreography
2. Music
3. Portraiture Photography
4. Architecture
5. Interior Design
6. Sculpture
7. Painting: Representational
8. Painting: Abstract and Nonobjective
9. Poetry
10. Nature
11. Stage Lighting

Thus far, we understand that color expression functions by the incorporation of emotional, mood, and symbolism components. We know that **warm colors** are typically *passionate, energized,* and *seductive,* as well as *subversive and agitated, while* **cool colors** are typically *quiet, tranquil,* and *composed,* as well as *loyal and calm.*

We have studied the difference between tangible expression and intangible expression, and the applicable scenarios to create the ultimate color expressive capabilities.

DYNAMICS OF COLOR EMOTION

Interestingly enough, we are going to execute color judgments about an achromatic mural. Picasso poured out his emotions onto the canvas, and so we shall attempt to do the same, yet with *color expression* rather than his grayscale painting approach.

At this point in your color investigations, we have learned about the importance of color expression to measure emotional responses. We are going to face a new challenge in this project by recreating *Guernica* in full color. Please remember, this project is cumulative in terms of the elements of color. The student will incorporate the use of color seen in previous chapter, such as saturation, intensity, tints and shades (values), contrast, and harmony. These color properties should be demonstrated in the mural itself.

We want to find out if we can enhance the mood of *Guernica* by using particular color harmonies. The painting is quite effective in illustrating the emotional factors of war. Picasso was tremendously successful at shape and form expression, but we want to find out if we can manipulate color to fit the mood of this composition. Remember to incorporate **mood of carnage** when selecting your color harmonies.

The Project

This project can be done as an individual, group, or a class. The proposal here will incorporate teams of four people per *Guernica* mural (Figure 7-52).

1. Make teams of four students each.
2. Divide the *Guernica* composition into four equal parts (as shown on the following *Guernica* example). Each student should then select the section they will render.

Each student's quadrant will be a 12" section of the *Guernica* composition.

3. Before painting the team mural, make a watercolor paper test tile replicating a smaller section of your quadrant, which best represents your opinion of carnage. Perhaps a 10" square portion of that quadrant will be sufficient in order to show your other team members what you have in mind.
4. After presenting your "test tile" to the group, and everyone is satisfied with the results, it will be time to begin the actual painting. Suggested size is 21 1/2 × 48 (Your instructor may want to give you a different size). Be sure you don't use a board that is more than 3/8" thick, or it will be too heavy. Plywood, particle board, etc., are suggested and can be cut to size at your lumber center.
5. Lightly sand the edges and give your board a coat of white or gesso to neutralize the surface.
6. Project the image (slide with slide projector for example) onto the board surface, and then trace the entire image of *Guernica* onto the board.
7. Now, you are ready to render the color onto the shapes of *Guernica*. At this point, you need to consult with your other team members as to what exactly your intentions are. You will need to determine color choices, texture, tints and shades, as well as contrast, saturation, intensity, and value issues.
8. Although each quadrant is side by side, make sure there is no line between which would indicate four different people worked on the project. It should have a variance of color harmonies throughout, but the shapes and forms must be juxtaposed where each quadrant begins and ends.

Figure 7-48 PABLO PICASSO, *Guernica* (Detail).

Figure 7-49 STUDENT TEAM PROJECT, *Guernica* (Detail I).

Figure 7-54 PABLO PICASSO, *Guernica*, 1937.

PICASSO AND THE WEEPING WOMEN: THE YEARS OF MARIE-TERESE WALTER AND DORA MAAR

by Judi Freeman

". . . Picasso sends us our death notice . . ."

To take up a pen, line up words as if they could add anything to Picasso's *Guernica*, is the most useless of undertakings. In the black-and-white rectangle of ancient tragedy, Picasso sends us our death notice: everything we love is going to die, and that is why right now it is important to die, and that is why right now it is important that everything we love be summed up into something unforgettably beautiful, like the shedding of so many tears of farewell.

—MICHEL LEIRIS, 1937

On January 8, 1937, Picasso began etching his *Dream and Lie of Franco*. Each of the two prints was divided, comic-strip style, into three rows of three scenes. Picasso worked on them from left to right, but as printed they read from right to left. He completed all but four of the eighteen scenes by the end of the next day. In the first scene (Figure 7-53, upper right) Franco appears as a composite scarecrow/jellyfish with enormous tentacles and an elephantine head. He is astride a disemboweled horse. Next he has dismounted and exposes his hairy scrotum and an enormous penis. In the third frame he raises a pickax to a female bust. In the fourth, he stands in the foreground, clad in a traditional Spanish mantilla and comb and holding a fan,

Figure 7-55 PABLO PICASSO, *Dream and Life of Franco* (scenes 1–9), 8 January 1937 (with aquatint added 25 May 1937). Etching and aquatint on paper 12 3/8 3 16 5/8 in. (31.4 3 42.1 cm).

Figure 7-56 PABLO PICASSO, *Dream and Life of Franco* (scenes 10–18) 8 January 1937 (with aquatint added 25 May 1937 and final four panels added 7 June 1937) Etching and aquatint on paper 12 3/8 3 16 5/8 in. (31.4 3 42.1 cm).

with a city on the distant horizon. A bull, symbolizing Spain generally and the Spanish Popular Front's resistance specifically, attacks him in the fifth scene. Kneeling at a makeshift altar surrounded by barbed wire, Franco prays in the sixth frame. In the seventh he gives birth to an array of snakes and disembodied heads. He strangles and lances his horse in the next scene, so that by the ninth he no longer rides astride an animal but has been metamorphosed into half-monster, half-pig. In the tenth scene, beginning in the second plate (Figure 7-54), Franco devours his dead horse's innards. The remnants of battle appear in the next two frames: a wounded woman lies on the ground amid burning buildings in scene eleven, while a dead warrior and horse dominate scene twelve.

Scene thirteen is a bust-length portrait. Franco, no longer the clean-shaven monster of panels one through ten, now is scruffy and hairy, an even more grotesque specter. He resembles a flayed animal or a caricature of Ubu Roi, the protagonist of Alfred Jarry's eponymous play, and is not dissimilar to Dora Maar's 1936 close-up photograph that she titled *Portrait of Ubu*. Both Picasso

and Maar were fascinated by the story of Ubu Roi, and he makes several appearances in Picasso's oeuvre (see Figure 7-54, middle right for example). Here Franco comes face to face with the head of a bull. In the next frame Franco's head (not mostly shaven) is appended to the body of a disemboweled horse, and he is confronted by the angry bull. This scene contains the densest and most violent activity on the second plate. Picasso completed the final four frames five months later, on June 7. Dramatically different from the previous fourteen, these last scenes contain victims of Franco's wartime atrocities. Frame fifteen (Figure 7-56) depicts a weeping woman, hands reaching upward and hair disheveled, with burning phallic forms in the distance. A wailing mother holds her dead child as she flees from a burning house in frame sixteen. Frame seventeen is a closeup of a fallen couple—the dead warrior from scene twelve and the female bust from scene three—caught in an embrace. Scene eighteen is an elaborated version of sixteen. Here two terrified children cling to their distraught mother as she stands before her fallen husband.

Figure 7-57 DORA MAAR, *Portrait of Ubu,* 1936.

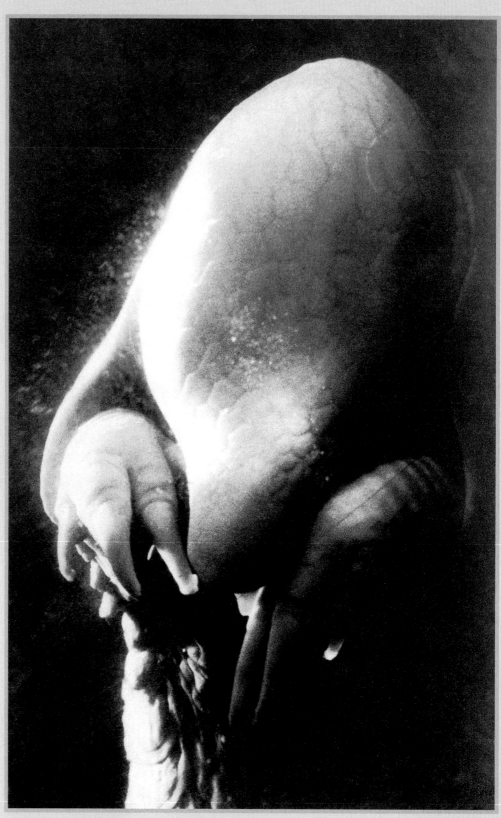

The prose poem by Picasso accompanying the two prints in the published folio vividly evokes images that underscore the horrors of the attacks of Franco and his forces: "swords of ill-omened octopuses dishrag of hairs from tonsures standing in the middle of the frying pan," writes Picasso at the beginning of his text. His images become increasingly grotesque: "beauty products from the garbage truck—rape of the ladies-in-waiting in tears and in large tears—on shoulders the coffin stuffed with sausages and mouths…lantern of lice where the dog lies knot of rats hiding place of the palace of old rags—the flags that fry in the frying pan writhe in the black of the sauce of the ink spilled in the drops of blood that shoot him." Sounds reach a crescendo:

Figure 7-58 PABLO PICASSO, *Scene 15 of Dream and Lie of Franco* (Detail).

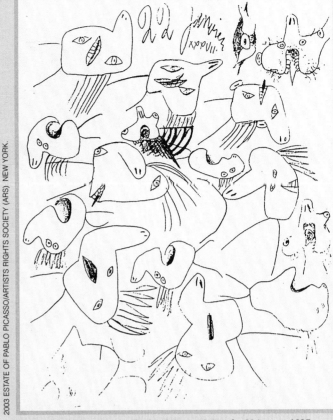

Figure 7-59 PABLO PICASSO, *Study of Women's Heads,* 22 January 1937.
Pencil on blue paper 10 5/8 3 8 1/4 in. (27 3 21 cm).

*cries of children cries of women
cries of birds cries of flowers cries
of wood and of stones cries of
bricks cries of furniture of beds of chairs
of curtains of pans of cats
and of papers cries of odors that scratch
themselves cries of smoke
pecking at the neck of the cries that boil
in the cauldron and of the rain
of birds that floods the sea.*

Clearly Picasso's preoccupation with *gritos*—cries, screams, howls, shrieks—increased between January and June. He obsessively wrote in his notebook nearly every day beginning January 25 and continuing through the month of February. The texts are laced with powerful sensory allusions: the odors of flowers or perfume, the textures of liquids, the colors of things, the inflections of music. A verbal permutation introduces his entry of February 20: "raging toothache in the eyes of the sun pique—pique raging sun-ache of the teeth in the eyes—eyes in the teeth pique of raging sun-ache pique eyes in the teeth of toothache—of the sun pique of raging eyes flower."

Just as this entry explores different combinations of the same elements, so too does his study of female heads (Figure 7-59). He captures these misshapen faces in various configurations. Within each head floats a pair of eyes, almond-shaped slivers punctured by circles filled with dots. Many of the heads have snouts in place of noses, chunky, bulging projections of flesh. All have nostrils reduced to short strokes. Most have mouths; some of these mouths consist of elongated ovals, while others are gaping orifices. Some are filled with teeth, usually square but occasionally rounded. From between several sets of teeth, knifelike tongues protrude.

These women are clearly related to the weeping women. None has tears, but all have other features that will be quoted in the weeping women images. All allude to women contorted by violence and horrific pain. On the very same day, January 22, Picasso drew an extremely graphic rape scene on a similar scale (Figure 7-60). The intensity of emotion contained in the weeping women could easily be excerpted from a violent scene of this nature. The rapist has a gnarled, monstrous, animal-like head, identical to the one on the upper right of the sheet of women's heads. The victim's face is that of an animal in agony. Her mouth is a large oval, a dark hole from which presumably a piercing scream of astonishing intensity emanates, with circumferential teeth pointing toward the center.

Tears and cries of pain, as features of the face, were not exploited by Picasso alone. His preoccupations were shared by his contemporaries as well as by previous generations

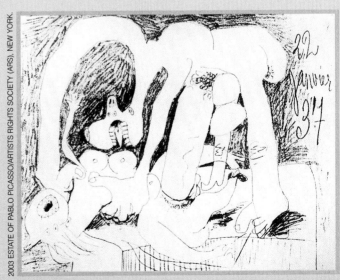

Figure 7-60 PABLO PICASSO, *Rape,* 22 January 1937. Pencil on paper 8 1/2 3 10 7/8 in. (21.5 3 27.5 cm).

PICASSO AND THE WEEPING WOMEN: THE YEARS OF MARIE-TERESE WALTER

Figure 7-61 JOAN MIRÓ, *Persons Haunted by a Bird*, 1938. Gouache, crayon, watercolor and charcoal on paper 16 1/8 3 13 in. (41 3 33 cm).

of Spanish artists. A tradition of weeping women exists in Spanish religious sculpture, particularly in statues of the Virgin Mary. The *mater dolorosa* was a favored theme with sixteenth-and seventeenth-century Spanish painters.

Among contemporary artists there is an unmistakable stylistic echo of Picasso's verses for *Dream and Lie of Franco* (and his subsequent notebook jottings) in the 1937 poetry of Joan Miró:

> *The flaming tree of the peacock's tail that bites the snouts of bats smiling before the charred corpse of my grandmother who was buried by a dance of transparent glass nightingales with rocket wings who dance the* sardana *around the phosphorescent carcass while pecking with the gold of their pincers the metal seeds of silver cypresses rushing down in waterfalls from the grandmother's big toe.*

Miró wrote this on October 2, 1937, using phrases reminiscent in both style and substance of Picasso's "raging toothache in the eyes of the sun pique." Miró drew a sheet of heads (Figure 7-61) that sit atop bodies comparable to those in Picasso's *Rape*; they open their mouths to scream, they crane their necks to see, they gape in amazement. Such abbreviated, organically inspired forms also appear in the work of fellow Spaniard Julio González; his *Head* of 1935 (Figure 7-62) is an iron arc interrupted by short strands of hair at the very top, a gaping mouth with shardlike teeth at the bottom, and a looming eye with long lashes at the center. This reductive sculpture contains a pathos akin to any of Picasso's studies on the sheet of women's heads.

The *Rape* and *Study of Women's Heads* mark an unusually intense involvement with violent imagery during January 1937. Picasso's predilection for the subjects of these drawings was a fitting preparation for the invitation that he received in January from a representative of the Spanish republican government to design a large mural for the Spanish pavilion at the International Exposition in Paris that summer. His sympathies for the Spanish republican cause were clear in the equally violent *Dream and Lie of Franco*. Early in February he returned to the scarecrow-like figures from *Dream*. Now devoid of Franco's menacing features, these were transformed into bathers (Figure 7-63). In his effort to find an allegorical theme to explore for the Spanish pavilion, Picasso incorporated characteristics of these

Figure 7-62 JULIO GONZALEZ, *Head*, 1935. Wrought Iron. 17 3/4 3 15 1/4 3 15 1/4".

bathers into a series of works he embarked on in April depicting the artist and his model in the studio. On April 18–19, he drew at least fourteen sketches, trying to work out the compositional elements. The most revelatory was the sixth in the group (Figure 7-64), in which two reclining nudes are contorted and elongated, their heads wrapped within their arms. This drawing—with its highly detailed and exaggerated studies of individual body parts—holds the greatest suggestion of tension and violence of any in the series. Along the left side of the sheet Picasso lavished great detail on certain key body parts; an eyeball; a pointed tongue protruding between jagged teeth and a pair of lips; twisted fingers seen from the side, front, and back; a nose with pronounced nostrils; an erect nipple and its aureole.

By May 1, Picasso had abandoned his initial theme—artist and model—in favor of an allegorical encounter between bull and horse. Later he coyly observed, "My work is not symbolic...only the Guernica mural is symbolic. But in the case of the mural, that is allegoric. That's the reason I've used the horse, the bull, and so on. The mural is for the definite expression and solution of a problem and that is why I used symbolism." His six initial sketches, all created that Saturday, May 1, are experiments in different arrangements of the two animals. The third sketch (Figure 7-61) features several humans as well, including a woman holding a lamp and a standing, distraught form at the center right of the sheet. This figure, head tilted back and toothy mouth slightly open, is the first

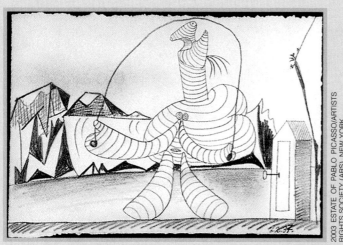

Figure 7-63 PABLO PICASSO, ***Bather by a Cabana Skipping Rope,*** 6 February 1937. Pencil on Paper 6 7/8 3 10 1/4 in. (17.5 3 26 cm).

indication that Picasso was interested in depicting states of intense emotion in his mural.

Three sketches of horses made the next day confirm his intention. One of them (Figure 7-65) shows an animal in agony, its tongue a sharp wedge thrust upward. The head is tilted back, the mouth is thrown open, and the massive teeth sit like stubs on the gums. In another of the sketches the teeth are neatly aligned. In this one and the third they seem about to fall out as they sit precariously on the edge of the muzzle.

One week later, on May 8, Picasso's thoughts about the composition took a dramatic turn. New to his concept for the mural was a mother carrying the body of her wounded or dead child (Figure 7-65). This figure was almost certainly inspired by the news coverage of the violent events in Guernica (in the northern Basque region of Spain) that had appeared in Paris newspapers during the previous week. On Monday, April 26, German planes from the Condor Legion acting in support of Franco's forces bombed central Guernica repeatedly. Toward the close of market day the town was overrun by fire and for the most part leveled.

Paris learned the news the following day; *L'Humanité's* headline read: "Mille bombes incendiaries lancées par les avions de Hitler et de Mussolini réduisent en cendres la ville de Guernica" (A thousand firebombs dropped by Hitler's and Mussolini's planes reduce the town of Guernica to ashes). While other newspapers initially covered and then abandoned the story, *L'Humanité* vigorously pursued it. On April 29 it published a vivid account of the carnage (translated from the preceding day's London *Times*) by a British correspondent in Bilbao who had been to Guernica the day after the bombing:

> At 2 a.m. to-day when I visited the town the whole of it was a horrible sight, flaming from end to end. The reflection of the flames could be seen in the clouds of smoke above the mountains from ten miles away.

Figure 7-64 PABLO PICASSO, ***The Studio VI,*** 18 April 1937. Pencil on paper 7 1/8 3 11 in. (18 3 28 cm).

Figure 7-65 PABLO PICASSO, *Guernica: Study for Composition*, 1 May 1937. (III) Pencil on paper 10 5/8 3 8 1/4 in. (27 3 21 cm).

Figure 7-66 PABLO PICASSO, *Head of a Horse*, 2 May 1937. (I) Oil on canvas 25 5/8 3 36 1/4 in. (65 3 92 cm).

Figure 7-67 PABLO PICASSO, *Guernica: Study for Composition*, 8 May 1937. (I) Pencil on paper 9 1/2 3 17 7/8 in. (24 3 45.5 cm).

PICASSO AND THE WEEPING WOMEN: THE YEARS OF MARIE-TERESE WALTER

Throughout the night houses were falling until the streets became long heaps of red impenetrable debris. Many of the civilian survivors took the long trek from Guernica to Bilbao in antique solid-wheeled Basque farmcarts drawn by oxen. Carts piled high with such household possessions as could be saved from the conflagration clogged the roads all night. Other survivors were evacuated in Government lorries, but many were forced to remain round the burning town lying on mattresses or looking for lost relatives and children, while units of the fire brigades and the Basque motorized police...continued rescue work till dawn.

The president of the Basque region, José Antonio Aguirre, issued a statement reprinted in many papers:

Before God and before history that will judge us I swear that for three-and-one-half hours German planes bombed with

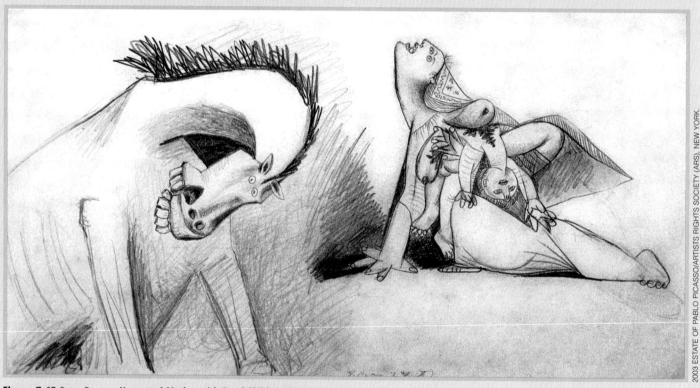

Figure 7-68 PABLO PICASSO, *Horse and Mother with Dead Child*, 8 May 1937, Pencil on paper.

Figure 7-69 PABLO PICASSO, *Mother with Dead Child*, 9 May 1937. (I) Ink on paper 9 1/2 3 17 7/8 in. (24 3 45.5 cm).

inconceivable destruction the undefended civil population of Guernica, reducing the celebrated city to cinders. They pursued with machine-gun fire the women and children who were frantically fleeing.

The accounts of these horrific events ignited the passions of Popular Front activists in France. The traditional May Day celebration in Paris brought out more than a million demonstrators, who marched from the Place de la République to the Bastille to express their outrage and appeal for aid to the victims.

May Day was Picasso's first day of concerted work on the Guernica mural. He initially expressed his reaction to the events in Spain by using his preferred symbolic combatants: the bull and the horse. By May 8 accounts of the individual human tragedies in Guernica had clearly permeated his thinking. The inclusion of the mother and child (and their consistent appearance henceforth in his scheme for the picture) demonstrates this. In Figure 7-67 the mother has an extended trunk for a neck that protrudes from one long mass of flesh encircling the body of a limp child. Her cast-back head, shown in profile, is composed of an open, toothless mouth, a slight protrusion for a nose, and two dotted ovals for eyes. Picasso drew her head in a single rapid stroke, then added lines to alter the neck slightly. This quick, self-assured gesture indicates his certainty about the face, the pose, and the emotional tone.

The motif is further elaborated in a second drawing done that day (Figure 7-68); a shawl, draped around the mother's head and shoulders, serves to cover the child. The child's blood stains the mother's breast and hand. She looks upward. Her face conveys the intensity of the horror. Her teeth, lips, and tongue are defined in exquisite detail; her nose is now further developed, thanks to comma-shaped nostrils; her eyes now have eyebrows. Her mouth is slightly open; she is speaking, screaming, wailing.

The next day's drawing, an ink close up of the mother and child, provides further infor-mation (Figure 7-69). As Picasso lavishes greater attention on the mother, the child becomes increasingly doll-like, with abbreviated, caricatured features. The mother's mouth is open wider; her eyelids appear for the first time and define her expression; her brows are bushier and pinched together. She appears shocked but not helpless, angered but not enraged, whereas her predecessor seems dazed and distraught. Picasso was of course aware of the ways in which his most minor graphic decisions would alter the viewer's perception of his subject's emotions. Placed on a ladder (Figure 7-70), the mother looks like a recumbent dinosaur turned upright. Her head is thrown back 180 degrees. Several strokes of ink define the tears falling from her eyes. Her tongue, now rounded, dangles in her open mouth, while her teeth are studs on her lips. Her hair forms a clipped cap of strands that, like the tongue, creates an angular protrusion. All of these elements contribute, along with the extremely contorted poses of the two figures, to a sense of their physical and mental agony.

Later that day, May 9, Picasso drew a study (Figure 7-69) for the mural's overall composition into which he inte-

grated the mother with dead child. She kneels at the lower right, the child in her arms, her head is tilted backward. Her profile is minimally detailed, much like the mother in Figure 7-65. Two other women appear in this scene. The first is an embellished version of the woman holding the lamp in Figure 11. Now she holds a candle and stares with amazement. Her lips are parted, but she appears speechless. Her wide-open eyes and arched brows communicate her horror. The second appears at the far left, framed by a doorway. Her jagged profile and elongated neck-body resemble those of the mother with dead child at the right. The concept for all three women originated in Picasso's earlier sketches for the mother with dead child, which in turn had their origins in his many drawings of women's heads. There is a clear lineage, then, back to January 1937 (and even earlier) for these ideogrammatic women-signs.

Figure 6-70 PABLO PICASSO, *Mother with Dead Child on Ladder,* 9 May 1937. (III) Pencil on paper 17 7/8 3 9 1/2 in. (45.5 3 24 cm).

Figure 7-71 PABLO PICASSO, ***Guernica: Study for Composition,*** 9 May 1937. (II) Pencil on paper 17 7/8 3 9 5/8 in. (45.5 3 24.5 cm).

Most of the following day, May 10, was devoted to studies of the bull and horse, with the exception of one sketch, *Mother with Dead Child on Ladder* (v) (Figure 7-72). This drawing is the first colored version of the theme, and its hues are vibrant. The mother is wide-eyed and aghast. Her mouth is a dark, gaping orifice. Her nose is less rounded and more angular than in Figure 7-71, and her mass of hair is framed by thickly applied green crayon. Surrounded by saturated, intense color, she embodies a heightened, macabre violence.

On May 11 Picasso began drawing the mural itself. He translated the minute sketches of the previous weeks onto a canvas of enormous scale—more than 11 feet high by 25 feet wide. He must have changed some elements in the process of applying them to the canvas because the differences between his most recent compositional study (Figure 7-71) and the first version of the actual work (Figure 7-73) (photographed by Maar in his Grands Augustins studio) were dramatic. The stage set defined by Picasso in his May 9 study—with a flaming building on the right and a doorway on the left—is now somewhat reduced in size. The doorway at the far left has disappeared. The bust-length wailing woman previously situated there has been replaced by a mother with dead child, resembling the pair that appeared in the first May 8 study. Another wailing woman, this one without a child, appears with raised arms at the far right of the canvas. The many lines running through her suggest that Picasso debated about how he would configure her. Three other women appear. One lies dead along the bottom right edge of the canvas. Another appears to kneel at center right, holding the dead woman. Her face resembles the mother in Figure 7-69, but she looks plaintive rather than distraught or agitated. Above her is the

woman holding the candle, who plays such an essential role in the final mural. The latter two are witnesses rather than emotional participants in the scene.

Over the next six days, a period of intense work, Picasso filled in sections of the canvas. He began to define its dark and light areas. He added a large round sun above the wounded horse and filled the fist (which first appeared in an April 19 drawing on the theme of the artist and his model) with a sheaf of wheat. This fist would disappear when he revised the mural several days later. He slightly refined the horse's position and shifted the placement of its teeth. These were minimal changes, but within the next several days Picasso completely redrew the horse's head, inverting it. Save the addition of hands to the woman at the lower right, who now appears to be running or fleeing, Picasso left the women essentially unchanged.

On May 20 he turned his attention to the animals in the scene, completing four studies of the heads of the horse and the bull. In one (Figure 7-74) he drew numerous eyes: eyes like butterflies, insects, birds, goblets, flames. At this moment it is clear that he was considering which of these to use as the eyes of the bull, but later that day he incorporated two of them into his sketch of a woman (Figure 7-73). This is very probably a study for the figure at the far left of the mural as it was then conceived: the mother holding the dead child. Her eyes are connected teardrop shapes. One contains a butterflylike form. Her brows are two intersecting wedges, considerably more minimal than those used in previous figures. The lack of physiognomical detail in this area makes it difficult to read her expression and attitude.

Picasso provides considerably more articulation in the mouth area. Her lips are shaped and modeled, her teeth are drawn in three dimensions, and her tongue is a spike.

Figure 7-72 PABLO PICASSO, ***Mother with Dead Child on Ladder,*** 10 May 1937. (v) Pencil and crayon on paper 17 7/8 3 9 5/8 in. (45.5 3 24.5 cm).

Figure 7-73 DORA MAAR, **Guernica, State I.** Photographed on 11 May 1937 from Judi Freeman, "Picasso Sends Us Our Death Notice," *Picasso and the Weeping Women: The Years of Marie Thérèse & Dora Maar*, 1994, PP. 24–61.

Figure 7-74 PABLO PICASSO, **Head of a Bull with Studies of Eyes**, 20 May 1937. Pencil and gouache on paper 11 3/8 3 9 in. (29 3 23 cm).

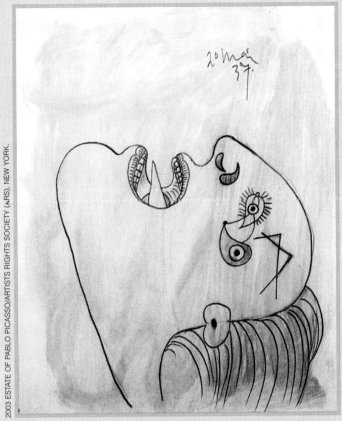

Figure 7-75 PABLO PICASSO, **Head of a Woman**, 20 May 1937. Pencil and gouache on paper 11 3/8 3 9 in. (29 3 23 cm).

The form Picasso gives to the mouth is highly erotic. Its lips are labia, its tongue a sharpened clitoris. None of Picasso's *Guernica*-related women up to this point had mouths on which so much attention had been lavished. Her nostrils are bulbous, shaded commas, and her single ear is an enlarged version of the simplified eyes found in his January studies. Her hair is now a series of thin, dangling lines.

Whatever Picasso was attempting in this drawing, he did not immediately incorporate it into his mural, as demonstrated by the photograph Maar took no later than May 24 (Figure 7-76). Much of Picasso's energy thus far had been devoted to the arrangement of the bull and the horse. The bull, with its human eyes based on the May 20 study, is turned around and now faces the woman with dead child. Picasso's completion of the dark and light areas of the canvas emphasizes the blade of the horse's tongue and the teeth standing, as they seem to, on their roots. The horse's mouth is much more menacing than the woman's in Figure 7-75; there is clearly a different threshold for anger and violence among animals than humans. Picasso focused considerably more attention on the female figures during this phase of *Guernica*'s evolution. The hands of the figure below have been completely repositioned; one remains up, the other is now down. The neck has become highly contorted. The bulbous commas of her eye are filled with enlarged pupils. Picasso also clothed the fleeing woman at the lower right by applying collage elements to

Figure 7-76 DORA MAAR, **Guernica, State IV.** Photographed between 20 and 24 May 1937 from Judi Freeman, "Picasso Sends Us Our Death Notice," *Picasso and the Weeping Women: The Years of Marie Thérèse & Dora Maar*, 1994, PP. 24–61.

mimic a kerchief and a floral dress. In subsequent revisions of the mural these additions were removed.

Two heads of May 24 (Figures 7-77, 7-78, and 7-79) suggest that Picasso was continuing to explore alternatives, although these visages never appeared in the final mural. These are the first weeping heads among the preparatory drawings and paintings created for *Guernica*. Their tears are like splayed multipronged rakes. In the first (Figure 7-77), tears drop from each eye. Her eye sockets resemble cells with cilia; one contains a bow tie, the other a wrapped bonbon. She has dark eyebrows and a furrowed forehead. Picasso drew the contour of her face in two rapid strokes. The texture of the mouth receives considerable description; the tongue is scaled and the palate is ridged. The teeth are neatly aligned and rounded. She wears makeup, or so the circular lines on her cheek suggest.

Within a single day Picasso's approach toward representing the weeping women took a new direction. In the second version of May 24 (Figure 7-79) the irregularly shaped face is more a mask than an observed head. It is surrounded by a mass of dark, unruly hair. Set beneath thick eyebrows, her teardrop-shaped eyes fall to either side of her face and appear to contain elaborately wrapped candies. Her tears trace random paths across her cheeks, in contrast to their more controlled formation in Figure 7-77. Her lashes are clusters of spiky leaves. Her bulbous enlarged nostrils are joined to form a snout. Picasso experimented with rapidly scribbled patches of line on her cheeks, between her eyes, and around her mouth, whose fleshy lips form a gaping hole containing jagged teeth and a knifelike tongue.

A third weeping woman (Figure 7-77), drawn May 27, is also disheveled, the result of lines rapidly scribbled on virtually all her features. Such hasty gestures indicate the certainty with which Picasso executed these figures; he labored over the elements he had yet to finalize and rapidly sketched those with which he was less obsessed. Her eyes now come together on one side of her face, and

Figure 7-77 PABLO PICASSO, *Weeping Woman (I),* 24 May 1937. Pencil and gouache on paper 11 3/8 3 9 in. (29 3 23 cm).

Figure 7-78 PABLO PICASSO, *Weeping Woman (II)*, 24 May 1937. Pencil and gouache on paper 11 3/8 3 9 in. (29 3 23 cm).

her eyebrows are two prominent angles retraced several times. Her right ear is presented as two overlapping ovals on the side of her head, while another ear is visible at the top. A quickly executed series of teeth and the texture of her lips are the result of several looping strokes. Her tears both fall and rise, defying gravity, and her hair, as in the previous drawing, is a mass of scribbles. Evidently Picasso was considering the question of clothing: these three women wear, respectively, a dotted V-neck collar, a striped crew-neck shirt, and a checkered blouse.

The women's heads of May 20 and 24 (Figures 7-74) and those of May 24 and 27 (Figures 7-76 and 7-77) indicate two degrees of emotional distress Picasso considered in developing the figure of the falling woman at the right of *Guernica*. He appears to have been willing to explore extreme states in his studies, but in the evolving mural he adopted relatively toned-down expressions for his figures. When his work on the mural was recorded on

the 27th (Figure 7-78), the visage of the falling woman, like the face of the mother with dead child at the left side of the canvas, most closely resembled the May 20 drawing. Picasso once again altered the position of her arms, now resolutely having them point upward, with open hands desperately reaching for something to hold on to. Although he had considered replacing her with a weeping man and rapidly sketched one that day (Figure 7-81), he evidently rejected changing the figure's gender and retained the concept of two women framing the composition.

The following morning, May 28, Picasso resumed sketching the mother and dead child. For the first time the mother weeps. In his first study of the day (Figure 7-82) he endowed her with the teeth of the rearing horse of May 2 (Figure 7-65). Her teardrop-shaped eyes are weighted by their pupils, with pronged eyelashes attached to each. She has no ears, and her nostrils are darts, a motif appearing here for the first time in the studies for *Guernica*. Her

Figure 7-79 PABLO PICASSO, ***Weeping Woman (III)***, 27 May 1937. Pencil and gouache on paper 9 3 11 5/8 in. (23 3 29.5 cm).

Figure 7-80 DORA MAAR, ***Guernica,*** State V. Photographed around 27 May 1937 from Judi Freeman, "Picasso Sends Us Our Death Notice," *Picasso and the Weeping Women: The Years of Marie Thérèse & Dora Maar,* 1994, PP. 24–61.

Figure 7-81 PABLO PICASSO, *Falling Man,* 27 May 1937. Pencil and gouache on paper 9 3 11 5/8 in. (23 3 29.5 cm).

Figure 7-82 PABLO PICASSO, *Mother with Dead Child (II),* 28 May 1937. Pencil, crayon, and gouache on paper 9 3 11 3/4 in. (23 3 30 cm).

general configuration is essentially unchanged from the one already painted on the mural; what Picasso endeavored to resolve was her facial expression.

His approach in the second drawing of the day (Figure 7-83) was far more experimental. Here, Picasso applied actual tangled hair to the mother's head. She now looks upward, her head tilted back at the same 90-degree angle that Picasso had used in the falling woman. This drawing is a marked rethinking of the entire left side of the composition, from the architecture (Picasso now considered placing a burning building there) to the woman's pose (it mirrors that of the fleeing woman at the canvas's

Figure 7-83 PABLO PICASSO, **Mother with Dead Child (III)**, 28 May 1937. Pencil, crayon, gouache, and hair on paper 9 3 11 3/8 in. (23 3 29 cm).

lower right). The mother is now in a state of frenzy—and for good reason. A lance runs prominently through the child's body, yet the child, arm upraised and mouth open, appears to be still alive, though barely. The scene is one of utter terror. The mother simultaneously flees, shields, and reaches for help. Her tongue and teeth jut out of her wideopen mouth; her eyes roll back in her head, while tears stream from them.

That Picasso elected not to incorporate such a violent image into the mural is significant. Once more he chose the more restrained approach, with suggestive but not blatant figures. He resolved to let the figures' faces convey the emotion of the scene, believing that these images, read in the aggregate, would effectively express his anti-Franco, pro-republic message. He now devoted his energies to refining the motif. His color study of a weeping woman from the same day (Figure 7-84) is a compromise between the more restrained versions (Figures 7-75, 7-77 and 7-82) and the more radical solutions (Figures 7-77, 7-78, and 7-83) of the previous week. The scribbled hair last seen the day before (Figure 7-77) and the sprouting

lashes first appearing on May 24 (Figure 7-78) adorn a head of simplified contour. There is an ear at the top of the face and another where the head meets the neck. Tears flow in long arcs downward along the cheeks; the comma-shaped nostrils seem to be tears of another sort. Picasso labored over the mouth, carefully drawing each tooth, describing the upper and lower palates, and shaping the lips. These weathered lips and rotten teeth are suggestive of the peasant population of Guernica. They underscore the likely metaphorical relationship between Guernica's inhabitants and the weeping women Picasso had planned for the mural. The application of orange to the tears strangely animates the face, in a macabre reference to the "made-up" ladies of Paris—initially seen in the artist-and-model studies—that Picasso had eliminated from his monochromatic mural.

Picasso did not work during the last weekend of May. Most likely he spent part of his time visiting Walter and their daughter Maya at Ambroise Vollard's house in Tremblay-sur-Mauldre. A single sheet drawn the following Monday, May 31 (Figure 7-85), contains several images. A weeping head is superimposed on a burning building and a large hand. The head is crossed by a swath of yellow flame, or smoke, emanating from the building. The juxtaposition suggests that this study, like the May 28 sketches, is related to the falling woman. The reappearance of the burning building demonstrates that a suggestion of the devastation that prompted the women's weeping was essential to Picasso's underlying concept. The eyes have become thickly outlined mollusks encircled in blue; the lashes still sprout in clusters, but the eyebrows look like stalks of wheat. The nostrils are darts again, now encircled. We see every tooth and its root. The woman has several strands of tentacle-like hair at the nape of her neck in addition to thin hairs elsewhere. Her tears consist of thin, orange rivulets; the drops at the ends are echoed by thick, vertical streaks of blue and green. The increased intricacy of this drawing indicates that Picasso was now fully immersed in the question of how best to express grief and despair. He was actively articulating each feature in a manner previously unexplored, and his addition of color now cast the entire head in an eerie glow.

Despite these explorations, however, the painted portions of the mural itself had not changed significantly by the time it was photographed around June 1. He added several collage elements of wallpaper, but the figures remained unchanged. It is likely that Picasso visited the pavilion sometime during the first week of June, and that he assessed the location and environmental situation of the mural. José Lluis Sert, one of the pavilion's architects, probably visited Picasso in his Grands Augustins studio at this time to ascertain his progress. There was considerable concern among the pavilion's organizers that the mural would not be ready in time for the opening.

Though Picasso would remove the pieces of wallpaper from the canvas in the next several days, the painting was very close to its final form. Nevertheless, he continued to make sketches related to the weeping woman and the dead warrior. Three extraordinary weeping heads date from June 3. One (Figure 7-86) is a slightly modified version of Figure 7-83. Extraneous detail is eliminated and individual features are sharpened. The eyes are still mollusks, but their lashes are minimal; the eyebrows are

Figure 7-84 PABLO PICASSO, *Weeping Woman,* 28 May 1937. Pencil, crayon, and gouache on paper 9 3 11 5/8 in. (23 3 29.5 cm).

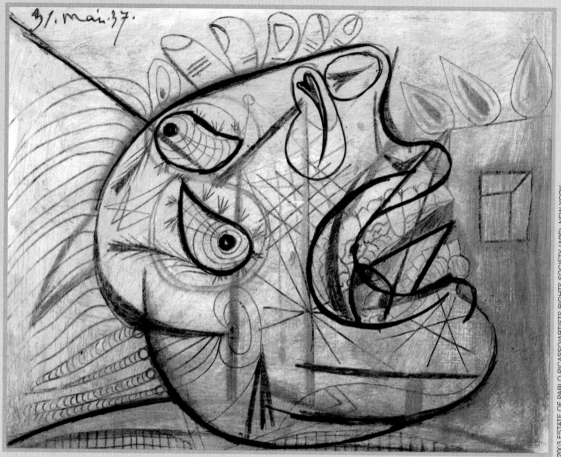

Figure 7-85 PABLO PICASSO, *Weeping Woman (IV)*, 31 May 1937. Pencil, crayon, and gouache on paper 9 3 11 5/8 in. (23 3 29.5 cm).

Figure 7-86 PABLO PICASSO, *Weeping Woman (V)*, 3 June 1937. Pencil, crayon, and gouache on paper 9 3 11 5/8 in. (23 3 29.5 cm).

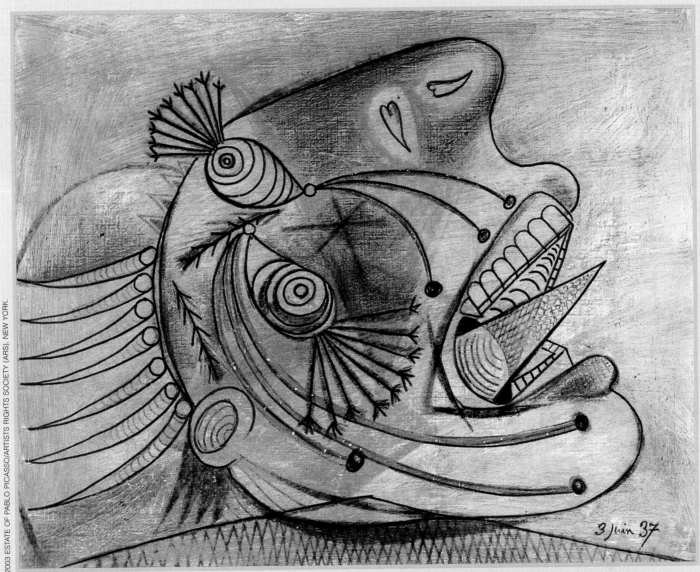

Figure 7-87 PABLO PICASSO, **Weeping Woman (VI)**, 3 June 1937. Pencil, crayon, and gouache on paper 9 1/4 3 11 1/2 in. (23.5 3 29.2 cm).

clearly defined stalks of wheat. Tears now stream only from tear ducts, marked by stars. The nostrils are darts transformed into elongated hearts with halos. The mouth is less crowded, though there are far too many teeth lined up along the lower palate and six large teeth along the upper. The tongue is an unadorned triangle; the lips are modeled with six short curving lines. The ear is now crescent-shaped, and its auditory function is conveyed by the diverging lines emanating from it. The hair consists solely of tentacles. Patches of color enliven the forms but do not add substantive detail.

In Picasso's second pass at the theme that day (Figure 7-86) planes of blue, red, and yellow intersect on the face, and the head, topped by small, triangular flames, is set in front of a field of green. This woman has long, thick lashes, and her tears amplify the contours of her face. Her ear is hollow, like the mouth of a horn. Her teeth are neatly aligned, and her tongue is now richly textured. Picasso in fact reversed the placement of the textures on the upper surface of the tongue so that what is most visible on the tip of an actual tongue is, on the tongue of this woman, furthest from the tip. Picasso's attention to such minute

anatomical detail indicates how very thorough was his experimentation with these figures. The third drawing of the day (Figure 7-87) is the most chaotic. The tentacular hairs are falling over. The tears run in serpentine patterns along her ill-defined cheek. The precise contour of this head is difficult to discern where it disappears along the hairline. Her mollusk eyes now contain several concentric circles, and lashes extend from them like dangling wires. The teeth have multiplied, and the wedge of the tongue has been softened. Her ear has become a frame with sound waves visualized inside it.

Beginning with the May 31 drawing (Figure 7-85), his renderings of the weeping women depart from previous versions. They are more readable as monstrous masks than as expressive faces. Picasso did not use any of them in *Guernica*. The very fact that he was preoccupied with them—indeed with nothing but them—in the closing days of completing the mural suggests that he was considering last-minute options to alter aspects of the painting. With the aid of sketches made during the week of May 31 he continued to make changes to the fallen warrior and to other small areas, but essentially he was concluding his

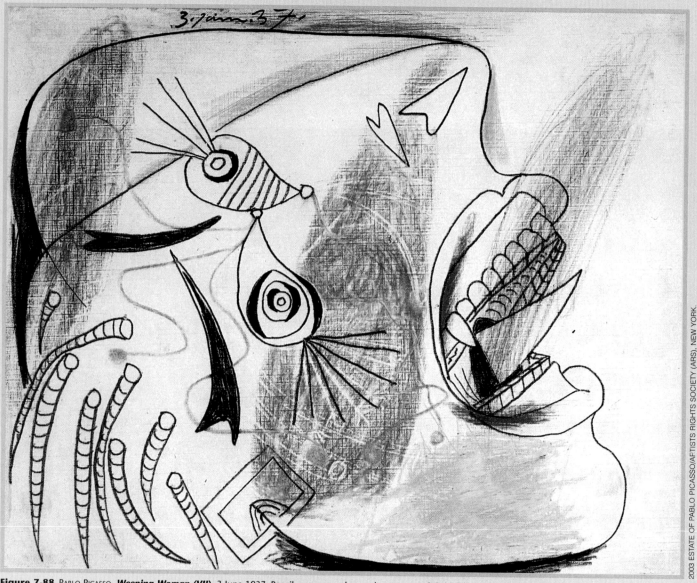

Figure 7-88 PABLO PICASSO, **Weeping Woman (VII)**, 3 June 1937. Pencil, crayon, and gouache on paper 9 3 11 5/8 in. (23 3 29.5 cm).

work. Maar's final photograph prior to the completion of the canvas was taken around June 4, and the painting was delivered to the pavilion a week or so later.

"In the panel on which I am working, which I shall call *Guernica*," wrote Picasso, "and in all my recent works of art, I clearly express my abhorrence of the military caste which has sunk Spain in an ocean of pain and death." This ocean of pain and death consumed him. He continued to consider alterations throughout the day that the canvas departed his studio. Although the mural arrived at the pavilion in mid-June, the architects thought Picasso would continue to work on it until the inauguration on July 12, which he apparently did not. Picasso told Sert: "I don't know when I will finish it. Maybe never. You had better come and take it whenever you need it."

"It was necessary for the pictorial expression to be horrible, for the outlines to weep, for the discolored color to be one of sadness, for the whole to be a penetrating clamor—tenacious, strident, and eternal," observed Jaime Sabartés, Picasso's secretary and confidant. Picasso's absorption in each individual feature of the women's faces and his repeated reworking of those features was the key to his effort to attain this clamor. Films made of Picasso's *Guernica* contain footage where the camera creeps along the surface of the canvas, slowly taking in every minute detail and nuance. This was Picasso's desired effect, and his studies attest to his methodical search for the most suitable motif for each figure. Picasso unleashed his *Guernica* (Figure 7-54) for the world to share in the town's—and the artist's—tragedy. With the painting's departure from his studio Picasso abandoned for a time the themes of the mother with dead child and the fallen warrior. The one motif he could not relinquish was that of the weeping woman. Her visage haunted him. He drew her frequently, almost obsessively, for the next several months. She was the metaphor for his own private agonies.

COLOR EXPRESSION/HARMONY MOOD PORTFOLIO

The Project

This project incorporates the use of a digital camera, in order to document your understanding of color harmony, by identifying how color harmonies create particular moods. You will use your own self-portrait image to demonstrate this. Each week you will make appropriate choices of hues to create the most effective composition, according to the assigned color harmony of the week.

Three photographs will be due each week; one portrait, one torso and one full image of yourself. All six harmonies will be assigned; one harmony per week for six weeks for a total of 18 Mood / Harmony compositions.

Illustrate the Following Harmonies:

Week One: Monochromatic—Three Compositions
Week Two: Dyad—Three Compositions
Week Three: Triad—Three Compositions
Week Four: Tetrad—Three Compositions
Week Five: Hexad
Week Six: Analogous

Every object including the background in the photographic composition should be the colors of the specified harmony. Any color in the composition that is not a part of that color harmony invalidates the photograph. Be creative; your skin tone, clothing, objects and background must demonstrate the selected harmony. You may use colored lights and filters, but do not color edit the compositions digitally.

Your body language (expression) and *color expression* should be compatible with and enhance one another. Both should emphasize your prowess with color harmony and the use of color to create mood.

Install your photographs in a portfolio. Photos should be matted and attached to black pages for optimal presentation.

Specifications:

4" × 6" Ultra-brilliant gloss photo paper
5" × 7" Mat behind the photo
8" × 10" Pages and cover
Label each photo with harmony type, mood, and colors
Facing pages: Label / Photograph
Sample open portfolio layout:

Monochromatic here is nothing more than various values of blue, which even has a suggestion of blue tint on the skin tones, creates a calm elegance.

In this dyad harmony of orange and blue, the orange is deep and sedate, which energizes and complements the appropriate percentage of blue hues. The absence of the green hue seen in the next photo, allows only the two colors to react with each other, without the conflict of a third color. The harmony and facial expression create a very passive mood.

This tetrad color harmony creates a tranquil ambiance because all of the hues create a balance. That is to say, there is a very passionate display of saturation, seen in the blue head covering and the red background. The blue covering creates a barrier between the calmer and more peaceful hues of her dress and skin tones.

This secondary triad composition of orange, green, and violet demonstrates a certain agitation that is mostly created by the green tints of light. Additionally, the mood is enhanced by t he body language and facial expression. Orange creates a certain negative energy that is necessary to complete this very powerful composition.

Analogous is a family of colors, all side by side on the color circle. Here, warm colors of saturated red and orange produce a more playful mood, which complements her body language.

Saturated hexad harmonies are very energized, but the tints and shades in these six hues seduce the eyes into a very meditative mood. Again, body language is paired with the appropriate harmony to generate the proper emotional response.

CHAPTER EIGHT

Figure 8-1 Coco Lee, China's Premier Pop Singer; the Quintessential Mood Expression.

8

ADVANCED COLOR
EXPRESSION
ONE STEP BEYOND

ONE STEP BEYOND THE EXPRESSION OF COLOR: TRANSITIONS OF THE INTANGIBLE TO THE PHYSICAL

Introduction to Advanced Color Expression

Coco Lee's *dynamic* in her performances is the embodiment of this chapter's emphasis. The context of *advanced color expression* for example, is to bring the intangible unseen qualities of emotion and mood (created by music in this case), into physical and visual existence. Emotional responses from music are interpreted by her body language, or the dance. The unseen attributes of mood in music is literally translated. Color enhances and brings to life the music. Taken one step beyond, and color becomes the literal translation of mood, whether a recognizable form, or not. The music and body language of Coco, as well as the dyad color harmony of this composition, reflect not only the character of the music, but the energy of Coco Lee's personality.

In order to understand advanced forms of color expression, one must first take *One Step Beyond,* that is to say, realize the importance of the spiritual nature of humankind. The term spiritual often is misunderstood regarding the impact of color on the spirit. The subject is complex by nature because we are dealing with the unseen or intangible. This subject is a step beyond the *expression of color,* in that it can function separately from the material world and has no particular required shape or form. It is at times somewhat ethereal, whereas at other times it is nothing more than sensation waiting for a physical manifestation. Wassily Kandinsky, one of the art world's great intellects of the twentieth century, referred to the Greeks and Romans and their preoccupation of expressing external realities. Kandinsky was inferring that the Greeks and Romans were not dealing with the spiritual as we define it, but only the superficial layer of human life. Kandinsky refers to this distinction as "The Spiritual in Art."

There actually is a connection between how the Greeks envisioned themselves and the spiritual; it has a lot to do with the human body and the gods of the Greek culture. However, when we discuss the term spiritual, we are referring more to a total inner being and a person's responses in all aspects. The spiritual dimension should not be confused with the "religious" aspect of

Figure 8-2 SANDRO BOTTICELLI, *The Birth of Venus,* 1486—Detail.

SCALA / ART RESOURCE. NY.

Figure 8-3 WILLEM DE KOONING, *Woman and Bicycle,* 1952–1953.

THE WILLEM DE KOONING FOUNDATION / ARTISTS RIGHTS SOCIETY (ARS), NEW YORK.

the inner person, because that is but one category. Rather we are looking at the inner being in its entirety, and not so much the individual characteristics and responses to a particular aspect of spiritual functions.

It was the Greeks who brought us *idealism,* which attempted to represent or recreate the human figure within a framework of perfection. They were obsessed with the concept that humankind could be "super-perfect," as they sculpted the figure to appear much better than humanly possible. The Romans then adopted the Greeks' sensibility about physical perfection in their artwork as well.

After the Greeks, the Roman Empire began to copy the styles of sculpture and architecture. Soon enough, the Roman Empire fell, which ushered in the *Middle Ages,* whereby Greek and Roman influences vanished. A thousand years later, during the Renaissance (rebirth of the classical Greek/Roman arts), people such as Michelangelo, Raphael, Botticelli (Figure 8-2) and Leonardo da Vinci began faithful studies of the old Classical forms. The Renaissance painters were careful to study Greek classicism, because they wanted to paint exactly as the outward world appeared. This period mostly addressed the exterior, or appearance, of the outward shell of a person and their environment. In the twentieth century everything changed. Artists such as Willem de Kooning (Figure 8-3) dealt very deeply with the inner person. Through the physical

Figure 8-4 Nisei Week Celebration in Little Tokyo, Los Angeles 2004. Energized expression is body language and color.

Figure 8-5 SHIJO, ***Ode to the Greeks: Visions of Quarks.*** Abstract color responses to the forces within the atom, whereby energy sources can be felt inwardly and interpreted by outward physical reactions. Even the contents of an atom can be felt and produce certain mood color responses.

medium of paint, Kooning demonstrated that there were some serious psychological ramifications to his attitudes concerning women. He had done just the opposite of the Greek and Romans by actually destroying, or tearing the figure apart, perhaps attempting to show the "imperfection" rather than the "idealism" in humankind.

And last but not least, we remember that it was the Greeks (Chapter 1) who hypothesized early in history about the atom. The paintings on the previous page illustrate a transition of the *spiritually perceived* energies within the atom into physical color. These paintings are a concept of these normally unseen forces.

Spiritual Persuasions

Kandinsky, an artist/intellectual from the Bauhaus, said, "The relationships in art are not necessarily ones of outward form, but are founded on inner sympathy of meaning." It was Kandinsky who laid a solid foundation that color could and should not be limited to recognized forms. The artist Mondrian had stated earlier that color must be "liberated" from the confines of standard forms. Representation should therefore be more about the **inner spirit** rather than an outer representation. Take for example the portrait. One can either execute the outer appearance of the person, or the inner spiritual essence. Obviously, the physical result will be quite different. Although the *outer image* or portrait will be obvious to the viewer, one may not recognize the demonstration of a pure *spiritual color* rendition of the inner, or spiritual, essence of the person. This concept

Figure 8-7 PABLO PICASSO, *Dora Maar Seated,* 1937.

Figure 8-6 PABLO PICASSO, *Portrait of Dora Maar.*

Figure 8-8 Paul Gauguin, *Yellow Christ*, 1889.

ERICH LESSING/ART RESOURCE, NY.

begins to be seen by the tempestuous nature of Picasso's relationship with Dora Maar (Figures 8-6 and 8-7).

When we presume to render or print a person's portrait, we are actually attempting to capture the essence of the person, as well as the physical likeness. There are numerous issues when attempting to capture the essence of who that person is, because we are limited by the exterior physical reality. When we paint the likeness of the outer representation of the person, we are basically saying "What you see is what you get," because there is no other information about the subject available.

In the first *Portrait of Dora Maar* (Figure 8-6), we really are not seeing exactly "who" Dora Maar is, or how Picasso feels about her entirely, because we only see his

outward representational expression of her. Although there is a certain mood captured in the drawing, we are still very limited as to what conclusions we can assume about her. In the painting of *Dora Maar Seated 1937* (Figure 8-7), we can see quite a difference. Her image has been abstracted down to the simplest gestures. The primary colors of red, blue, and yellow highlight her facial tones, as well as the composition itself. There is an ambiance of casual tranquility and bliss about her portrait, which tends to indicate that his relationship with her *at this point* was not as turbulent as it often was reported to be. The portrait seems to have a more spiritual direction, as it would indicate *his emotional response* to who she is, or *her inner actual self,* and has little or nothing to do with outer physical representation.

Figure 8-9 SALVADOR DALI, *Metamorphosis of Narcissus*, 1937.

Looking to a different artist, we turn to the French painter Paul Gauguin, who indicates that he is very much in tune with the spiritual aspects of color.

Gauguin creates a certain separation between the actual reality of Christ crucified on the cross (Figure 8-8), and his own whimsical vision of himself crucified, as the painting seems to become more of a visual autobiography. The actual biblical report tells us that Mary the mother of Jesus, Mary the wife of Cleophas, and Mary Magdalene sat at the feet of Christ. Instead, Gauguin paints three peasant women who take the place of the three Marys. The painting has much to do with color expression, and more importantly, alludes to spiritual qualities of color. Here, the dominant yellow in the composition is in serious contrast to the dark thundering sky reported at the time of Jesus Christ's death. The yellow is very harsh, and does not seem to reflect its usual upbeat and celebratory nature. The mood of the crucified Christ is in serious conflict with the usual character of yellow and psychologically alters one's perception of both the event and the color. Gauguin typically simplifies his forms toward the spiritual arena of color, albeit not to the point of pure spiritual expression.

Turning to Salvador Dali's *The Metamorphosis of Narcissus* (Figure 8-9), with its very symbolic imagery, reminds us of the dream world that we all have experienced during our lifetime.

Dali's work helps to open the window into the spiritual world in order to better understand the more ethereal world of dreams. Dreams are part of the spiritual world, as opposed to the tangible existence of the physical world.

Oftentimes, the spiritual expression of color relates to the dream world, where colors are sometimes unlimited in form and shape, and are often difficult to define, or perhaps vague as to their existence. In the physical world forms and shapes are well defined, and in fact color is usually relegated to the parameters of those areas, such as a red apple or a yellow lemon. These forms have assigned colors because the color belongs to that object. The lemon is validated by its color, whereas conversely the color of yellow does not need an object to validate its own existence. In this case, the lemon confines color to its own form, and yellow cannot extend beyond those required boundaries. In the spiritual or nontangible existence such as a dream, color cannot be limited to those conditions. Yellow can exist without limitations. The spiritual part of the human being, whether awake or in a dream state, can imagine or see color without limitations, as color travels beyond any form or peripheral vision.

Another aspect by which we can observe the function of the *spiritual expression* of color is to look at various words. *Love,* for example, can be a very emotional aspect of human experiences, and extends deep into the spiritual or nontangible world. Love seems limitless until we attempt to express it physically. There are a number of complexities interpreting love into an accurate *measurable* expression in the tangible physical form. We know that there are limited physical expressions that indicate love, but to what *degree* becomes quite another issue.

The use of color in the *spiritual context* is much the same. The limitations are nonexistent until we attempt to discern. Unlike the previous images, color is now the most important expression of the composition with its very saturated ambiance. Rather than seeing imagery first and foremost, the most immediate attribute of this painting is color and line. Color is now being freed from its bondage and allowed to express itself with less dependence on form. The color here seems to be undulating in a type of controlled chaos. It is now creating movement with line and is no longer stable. Color now begins to work its way towards the spiritual or non-tangible expression in its abstraction. Still, Kandinsky continues to wrestle with the idea that color and line can be abstracted to the non-objective composition—where color projects the concept of the limitless expression of the spiritual realm even though there is a physical end to the boundaries of the canvas. Somehow that boundary seems less limiting.

Improvisation 11 (Figure 8-13)has reached its purest state in the spiritual representation of color. Without the representation of specific form, we can imagine that the vibrant colors are continuing far beyond the edge of the canvas—almost infinite as the moods of these colors take us on a journey far beyond the composition itself. Without the representation of forms, we understand that color itself is not limited to the physical properties of the

materials. The etherealness of the imagination or the non-tangible allows us to experience and "improvise" our own experience with this work. Recognizable objects tend to belong within the boundaries because there is a physical understanding about the limitations of our tangible world. It is, however; the nature of unrestrained color that is no longer bound by representation and is allowed to *roam* freely.

Kandinsky exclaimed that "the canvas is my enemy," giving reference to the difficulties of imparting spiritual creativity, or rendering of the *spiritual into the physical world.* Our emotions and concepts are of a spiritual, non-tangible nature, while the canvas is a physical limitation. The emotional issues and content of the story lay locked in the soul until paint is applied to the canvas surface. The tangible product—the canvas—becomes a tool to express what is being felt by the artist; yet, it is an imperfect vehicle.

In the chronology of change, from the physical to the spiritual emphasis, we have briefly examined Pablo Picasso, Paul Gauguin, and Wassily Kandinsky. Picasso worked passionately to systematically and rationally destroy the image as we know it, by dividing and reconstructing from his inner self, responding to his emotional state. Picasso said

Figure 8-14 PAUL GAUGUIN, *Vision After the Sermon, Jacob Wrestling with the Angel,* 1888.

he painted what he knew, not what he necessarily could see. He applied what he observed in the physical world, but with a more emotional or spiritual connection.

The French artist Paul Gauguin was, however, one of the most faithful painters dealing with the spiritual connection of color, and this concept is more fully realized as we continue to examine his work.

In *Vision After the Sermon* (Figure 8-14), Gauguin examines the emotional aspects of the *passion* with which Jacob wrestles the angel (background), more than his concern for any realistic form or perspective space. In reality, the composition is very flat, as the red background seems to advance into the viewer's space. Dealing with the spiritual responses was not about green grass, or dark shaded orange soil, but saturated red, which represents the *spiritual struggle*. The agony and passion with which Jacob wrestles the angel through the night is felt by the emotion brought forth in the saturated red hues. Again, he was not at all concerned with physical representation of the world that he saw, but the spiritual reality of the inner person that he knew.

At this point, we would like to examine more of Kandinsky's philosophy about color and the pure spiritual, where only the forms of color and directional line exist. The subject matter or content may oftentimes only be known by the lyrical emphasis of poetic or musical motions within the canvas, or merely by the title of the work. His compositions must be felt, experienced, and carefully considered as only the colors of spiritual responses can record.

The subject of the spiritual in art merits further investigation in order to fully understand all of its ramifications. Let's take a look at how music factors into the visual art of color.

COLOR AND MUSIC RELATIONSHIPS

Continuing from where we left off in Chapter 7, let's continue our deeper journey into the heart of color expression through music relationships. There is a relationship between visual color and music that is undeniable. In fact, Kandinsky elaborates extensively on the relationship of the spiritual between color and music. His canvases often reflect a type of symphony in color, titling some of his most important works as though they were musical "compositions."

Although there are differences in some comparisons in general, the use of terms and their connection to color are often strikingly similar. It is important to make a connection both in spiritual terms and vocabulary. Please observe some of the similarities between vocabularies of music and color theory:

The next page is a page from one of the earliest and best examples of illuminated Gothic choir books. *The Gradual from St. Katharinenthal* (Figure 8-15) is basically a book of choir responses, sung alternately by two groups during church services. The words and the musical notes on the page have their origins from the spiritual inspiration of the inner person. The page then represents the spiritual, as *physical* responses in the form of musical notes and text. These are then sung as chants by the monastic population in the great Gothic cathedrals of Europe. The page, then, is the physical evidence of the nontangible spiritual existence.

There are some very similar functions between color and music (below). Some are not quite the same, yet there still remains a certain relationship between the two definitions. *Music* is the audible component, and *color* is often the visual interpretation of a musical piece. It is very common for a color painter to listen to his or her preferred

MUSIC THEORY	COLOR THEORY
Pitch: Do, Re, Mi, Fa, So, La, Ti [Musical alphabet of seven].	**Spectrum of Colors:** Red, Orange, Yellow, Green, Blue, Indigo, and Violet.
Modes: Seven Scales-Organization of a sequence of pitches into an articulate arrangement.	**Tone:** Mixing gray into a specific hue in successive steps from light to dark.
Chromatic Scales: (consecutive pitches) [All twelve notes in octave arrangement upward and downward].	**Color Circles:** Made up of primary, secondary, and intermediate color (12 hues total).
Key Signature: Sharps and flats that appear at the beginning of a staff, which indicates the key of a musical work (sharp and flat notes).	**High Key and Low Key Colors:** Designates the tonal intensity or dullness (composition's character of lightness or darkness).
Chords: Major triad and minor triad (Simultaneous sounds of three or more notes).	**Color Chords:** Harmonies of color created by primary and secondary color triads, as well as dyads, tetrads, hexads, analogous, etc.
Harmony: Is a arrangement of simultaneous tones.	**Harmony:** Methodical color relationships that are made up of specific color chords, which create a basic structure for a composition.
Four-Part Harmony: Basically, functional harmony is comprised of triads. When the root of a triad is doubled, it becomes a four-part harmony.	**Tetradic Color Harmony:** Four colors that are indicated by intersecting lines of either a square or rectangle drawn inside of the color circle.

Figure 8-19 Taiko Performers in Nisei Week Parade, Los Angeles 2004.

creates bone-chilling moods, just as color itself can do. That is to say: the reds, oranges, and yellows are, of course, commensurate to the energetic sounds of the Taiko drums. One is audible, and one is visual, but they both create a certain emotion. Put another way, the paintings very animated, multi-directional color explosion seems to replicate the extreme dynamic of a Taiko performance.

Taiko and color are always in league with one another. Red and black costumes replicate the contrasts found in the extreme tonal qualities of Taiko. At times the sound of color was black, heavy and slow. Other times along the parade route, the sound of red was more aggressive, fast, and even angry.

Notice that the colors of the performance stage of Taiko is well thought out. In two of the examples, a fairly saturated red is incorporated with the Taiko performance. We remember that the power, thunder, and intensity of energy is very indicative of the nature of red. The spirit of Japan is embodied within the sound of the drum and the energy of the performers, as well as the color red. Historically, Taiko has been associated with Shinto and Buddhism, as well as wartime drums to intimidate the enemy or as a method to drive off evil spirits. Today, the thundering rhythm of the drums create spiritual awe, in their stern and forceful command. It is conceivable that if Kandinsky had been at the Taiko performance, he may have perhaps been inspired to have painted the *Red Oval.* Looking at the photograph of the Taiko, we cannot see the movement firsthand, so obviously one is limited by the comparison between the painting and the Taiko images.

The spiritual connection of interpretational possibilities is certainly there. If the reader has attended a Taiko performance, then it is clear as to the focus of this comparison.

Encountering a professional Taiko performance is one of the most spiritually moving experiences one can have. It is the intangible sound that permeates the soul, reaches deep down spiritually, and inspires physical creativity. It is probably one of the most dynamic expressions of the spiritual part of humanity. It remains the challenge of the visual artist today, to be able to inspire and create that kind of emotional response through color.

Verdi's Requiem Mass

Another example of the spiritual effect is through the amazing work of Verdi's Requiem Mass. Few examples serve better to affect a visual emotional color response through music. The words to the Requiem *Lacrymosa* (Figure 8-20) are:

> Mournful shall be that day,
> When there shall arise from ashes
> Guilty man to be judged.
> Therefore spare them Lord,
> Good Lord Jesus,
> Grant them rest.

The lament is repeated as the tempo continues to control the mood, with its quiet and mournful timbre. The title of the piece and the first word "lachrymose"

Figure 8-20 *Section of the Musical Composition from Giuseppe Verdi's Requiem.* Whether you prefer digital or pigmented applications, practice interpreting the spirit of the above two compositions into pure color emotion.

(mournful) creates a somber tone of weeping and misery. Yet, there is hope for the redemption of the dead reflected in the construction of mood in this very spiritual music.

The Requiem begins very softly, and slowly builds into the sounds of hope, only to drop into mournful depression once again. The spiritual ambiance of the Requiem seems to alternate between the despair of losing someone to death, and the hope of their eternal salvation and rest. As one listens to the music, one understands the somber and weighty spirit of the music. Interpretations of the Requiem into color expressions could be seen through deep reds and deep warm violets, or perhaps darker blues. The spiritual rendition of color is relegated to very specific colors and values in order to maintain the mood integrity of the musical composition.

Continuing with the color assessment, it would be possible to intermittently see the deeper reds and warm violets transform into more saturated or intense colors of red, orange, or perhaps yellow. These would provide the enhancement of the composition's element of hope in the midst of despair.

In the case of the *Requiem composition,* it is most often experienced in a church or cathedral setting. The emotional variances of *sound* and *color* influence the mood of the worshipper, which in turn creates an atmosphere of awe, respect, and dignity. Kandinsky's canvas and his application of colors are very much like a musical composition, a concert, a poet's journal, or the performance of dancers with their expression of body gesture.

THE RELATIONSHIP OF COLOR CHOREOGRAPHY TO MOVEMENT/ DANCE AND SOUND

Once again, we are visiting the expression element of music and performance, in this case, dance. The precise interpretation of the emotional content felt in music can best be seen in the pure human form. Body language is the direct expression of the mood's setup in a given musical composition.

It is important to remember that all judgment of expressive elements is based on interpreting the human form, whether facial expression or body language. Its graceful lines and form are capable of interpreting physically the specific story and mood of a given opera, symphony, or musical arrangement.

As we seek to understand more clearly the translation of the more ethereal properties of color choreography, it is of great benefit to study the similar nature of the *audible sound* realized into *physical form.* Bach's concertos could easily take temporal possession of the three dancers, Figure 8-21 while the painted choreography (Figure 8-22) interprets the performer.

The color choreographed triptych (Figure 8-22) demonstrates the pure color expression of the three dancers (Figure 8-21). The *movement of color* is demonstrated in the choreography of their forms and the *colors of the mood* are rendered in response to the emotional elements produced by Bach's Concerto in C minor.

Figure 8-21 Pure form body gesture in dance demonstrates physical responses to mood influences or inspiration upon the spiritual or inner person in this *Dance of Life.*.

A compelling issue in this advanced color expression concept is the complexity of the human being itself. The body itself is a completely separate entity from the *real self,* the body being *thoroughly physical* and the inner self, *wholly spiritual.* The two are often at odds with each other. The corporeal deals with the "right now," or tends to be more *animal* in terms of its basic needs, while the spiritual conversely involves itself more with the "timeless," whose attributes are to be *insightful* and sensitive. It is the music that inspires and moves the spiritual forces from within, and the body then interprets by giving the intangible sound a physical form or representation. *It is important to remember that it is the same with revealing the nature of color. We are inspired from within and create from without.*

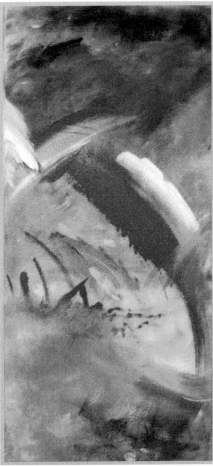

Figure 8-22 SHIJO, ***The Dance of Life,*** 2007. [Interpretation of the Dance-Color Choreography]. Music: Bach's Concerto for Violin, Strings, and Continuo—Hilary Hahn, Violin Los Angeles Chamber Orchestra—Jeffrey Kahane.

Figure 8-23 Body gesture is the pure form response to the spiritual or inner being of a person. Commensurately, the application of color is often the same, and is one of the purest expressions of mood.

There is always a continuous physical response to the inner emotional feeling. The spiritual energy is revealed by actual body movement. Since color can be translated from pure energy into physical form, how would you interpret this composition into a choreography of harmonious colors?

Dancers on stage are attempting to convey a story that until now has been lockedup tight in their souls. A performer chooses just how much of that story to reveal, while parts of it remain sealed behind the heart's door, just as the artist/designer creates the mood of the story with color.

Judging by the performance above (Figure 8-23), it is now easier to understand the concept of the spiritual. It also helps to identify the process of color abstraction, as abstraction leads the way toward the nonobjective. This figure illustrates such a strong presence, or suggestion of the ethereal, by its captured energy. In this case, if the physical world can help lead our eye to the spiritual connection of color, then we have mostly accomplished our task of understanding what Kandinsky refers to in his essay on "The Spiritual in Art."

COLOR EXPRESSION IN BODY LANGUAGE

We have studied how color represents expressions in paintings, music (audible) and dance (visual). We understand the relevance of color to facial and body expression, and their connection to musical responses. Indeed color

is life, and it is imperative that we understand this connection as designers and artists. As professionals in these varied careers in the creative world, we begin to excel in our work when we truly make the connection of real life and its experiences to the world of color.

There is a real attachment to color in the human experience, which many professionals often overlook. It seems obvious to us that dancers, painters, poets naturally understand color, and the importance of it. We walk into an old gothic church and connect with the idea of colored glass windows, or walk past a retail establishment with a fashion display of color splashes, but do we grasp the brevity and importance of color in all professional design applications? The color of life must be experienced with all peoples in careers involving color. Website designers, interior and industrial designers, fashion, animation, advertising, graphic designers and game art programmers are just some of many fields that need to know the power or authority that color has to transform their ideas into successful outcomes.

COLOR IN POETRY

Let's briefly consider color and poetic forms. Because we are using various art forms in order to express the nature of the spiritual use of color, *poetry* can be no less important. In Jozan's poem, there are two distinct words by which to focus—the *rain* and the *petals*.

Secondary words would be *red* and *white*. The life of a monk was to forsake the world as we know it and follow a

Figure 8-24 Color is Life. Color replicates the emotions and moods of life, and manipulates the senses of the viewer. If indeed color is life, then this woman is the epitome of that expression.

simple and uncomplicated way of living. Possessions were objects that weigh down the heart, or spirit, anchoring one to the world. Typically, the Japanese monks of old would take refuge in the forests, rejecting carnal ways. Contact with other people was, in some cases, rare. What normally drew attention to the average person became a monumental event in the life of Jozan. His life was so focused on the simple that a blossom petal falling prematurely from the force of the rain was an event.

The rain's hastening of falling flower petals disturbed the poet because he loved spring and the seasonal flowers. His concern became very spiritual, as he transformed into a butterfly, chasing after each petal. Whether he was concerned about saving the petal, or experiencing every last moment of the petal's glory, his desires about them were very real and emotional. Energetic orange hues and saturated violets seem to fill the imagination's composition. The mood of the environment is urgent, as the butterfly expends enormous amounts of energy to retrieve the petals. Turbulent fluttering, the energy of orange, and deep subdued concerns of violet emotion fill the night skies as Jozan is filled with anxiety about the whole event.

Night Rain—Worrying About the Flowers

I sigh on this rainy late spring night:
the reds and whites that filled the forest are falling to the dust!
Late at night, my soul in a dream becomes a butterfly
chasing after each falling petal as it flutters to earth.

ISHIKAWA JOZAN
(1583–1672)

Figure 8-25 Blossoms of Heian Shrine Garden.

Figure 8-26 Heian Shrine at Kyoto, Japan, Morning Rain on the Pond. Certainly Jozan would have appreciated the tranquility at the Heian Shrine pond in Kyoto. Rather than a heavy rain knocking petals to the earth, which distressed him in his earlier poem, a gentle rain splashes across the serene still waters of the pond. The perfect tranquility in this scene has a very spiritual ambiance, as green and violet hues generate a very specific mood nuance. The comfort of a cool and quiet rain on a hot summer's day can almost be felt.

Figure 8-27 PAUL GAUGUIN, *Where Do We Come From? What Are We? Where are We Going?*, 1897.

Kandinsky wrote that Gauguin's paintings were in reality "tragic or passionate poems."

Where Do We Come From? What Are We? Where Are We Going? (Figure 8-27) is evident of Gauguin's *color poetry*, as a specific story is told here. This very emotional composition, laced with blues, greens, and oranges, presents a somber poetic rhythm of spiritual responses. Gauguin's paintings, of course, present the idea that color is of primary concern, not perspective and figurative accuracy. The warm and cool contrasts setup in this painting are both *very* warm and *extremely* cool. The composition creates warm and sensuous moods, by virtue of the orange and red-orange hues, primarily in the background. Yet, the blues exude an almost icy distance from those in the foreground, particularly the yellow figures. Color was always Gauguin's most powerful ally to convey his extreme emotional state of mind while in Polynesia. Color, not realistic accuracy, was always at the heart of Paul Gauguin. Color as an expression, was one of his methods of dealing with the demons that seemed to haunt him so frequently in the south pacific.

Gauguin's painting is as spiritually full of feeling (poetic) as it is visually lyrical (poetry). The work reads much like a musical composition, with its visual and spiritual accomplices. It is a painting from the heart, mind, and soul of the artist himself, choreographed with warm and cool imagery, which seems to flow through the entire painting.

Moods of Color

Color is both fantasy and reality,
It is the master of desire and the evidence of the spirit.
An element supreme, free from influence
And in all respects an extension of the soul.
It dominates with harsh persuasion and gentle maneuvers.
People unknowingly expect this behavior,
And want to be persuaded.

SHIJO, 2000

Na fir-chlis

We end the last chapter in similar form as to the first with a brief investigation of the atom, quarks, and the colors of light. We are referring to the northern lights of the *Aurora Borealis,* which has been nature's ultimate thriller *light show* for centuries. Far transcending the rainbow or the colors of light from a Gothic stained-glass window, this overwhelming phenomena is striking in its ability to form mood scenarios. It is also compatible to our early discussions about the quark and primary RGB colors of light.

The *Northern lights* of the *Aurora Borealis* has its association with magnetic movement, which is produced by central plasma sheet electrons. In short, the process is about negatively charged electrons and positively charged protons—energized particles that are on a collision course with atoms of various gases. The results of this crash are emissions of colored light generated from atomic oxygen, creating the amazing and overwhelming Aurora Borealis. It is the ultimate in *color choreography.*

Interestingly enough, the inference of choreography in Scottish folklore employs the term **na fir-chlis** when referring to the Aurora Borealis, which translated means **"the merry dancers."** Legend reports that the *na fir-chlis* were a playful bunch, but inevitably their playfulness often ended in a horrendous fight. The morning after the appearance of the Aurora Borealis, little children will go out into the field, and if they stumble upon stones with reddish lichens, then that is indeed confirmation of the injuries acquired by *the merry dancers.*

The Aurora Borealis, in effect, is the color choreographed version of the merry dancers; the lichens are the confirmation that they were indeed there. It is nature's color choreography extraordinaire, a display of physical choreographed colors put to the music of folklore.he creation of emotional appeal and mood effect.

Figure 8-29 Alaska: Aurora Borealis

Figure 8-28 Scenic view of green and red northern lights in the Aurora Borealis display over the silhouettes of trees. Tongass National Forest, Inside Passage, Alaska.

CHAPTER SUMMARY—ADDITIONAL HIGHLIGHTS

Far away, atop a mountain in the Northern Thailand province of Chiang Rai, a temple environment utilizes color *harmonies* and *contrasts* to create emotional responses. The spiritual nature (Buddhist philosophy) is reflected by the warm and cool tranquil moods evoked by this *color expression in nature.*

Before a day's work, near a Chiang Mai elephant camp, dozens of quick abstract leaf drawings are rendered in order to capture the mood-inducing colors of nature in the area. Part of color studies in a given area is aways carefully researched. One needs to know which colors are to be rendered *accurately,* and which hues to *exaggerate* to generate the best emotional response for the optimal mood. This method is not confined to expression in nature, but is an important consideration when choreographing color for architecture, interior design, graphic design, or any number of fields when color response is required.

PHOTO BY THE AUTHOR.

Figure 8-32 Thai Temple in Chiang Rai.

PHOTO BY THE AUTHOR.

Figure 8-30 Temple Grounds in Chiang Rai.

Figure 8-31 Environmental Mood Color Studies, Chiang Mai, Thailand.

PHOTO BY THE AUTHOR.

SUMMARY

Advanced Color Expression and the Spiritual Component in Color

Salvador Dali's painting will serve for our closing discourse on the spiritual aspects of color. Exactly how do we perceive the spiritual connection to color? What comes first, the inner inspiration or the outer? Is the dream inspired or created at the inner spiritual point, or is it the outer influences in life that inspire the content of a dream? One thing that does seem apparent is that normally dreams are influenced by forces in the physical world.

Salvador Dali tells us about his dream via the painting, which was originally inspired by a hanging pomegranate with a bee flying around it (Figure 8-33). The dream was then caused by external stimuli, the dream was built around the pomegranate alone, and then abridged by the artist in the form of a physical painting. What began in the physical world grew into the spiritual world and then recorded back into the physical existence again.

The Pomegranate Dream—The Painting

Gala, Dali's companion, lay suspended over a concrete or rock slab. The whole event should be rather terrifying, and yet it seems somewhat calm by nature. Out of the pomegranate springs a harsh figured fish, which in turn spews a tiger from its mouth, after which yet another tiger leaps from the previous mouth. Just before the tigers are able to sink their claws into her, the sting of the rifle's bayonet (bee sting) awakens her.

The composition is that of extreme contrasts. Gala hovers so peacefully over the slab, and yet the tigers are fiercely attacking. There is an emotional suggestion of terror by way of the contrasting figures, and yet it is very calm and peaceful. The slab, Gala herself, the horizon, and tigers are all horizontally located, which further enhances the tranquil environment. The quiet mood of blues and violets further confuse the intended urgency of the imagery in the composition, and the painting then becomes as a true spiritual representation in the physical world, albeit the limitations of size and realistic images.

The aspects of the *spiritual dimension of color* cannot be understated. No matter what the student's career objectives are, a thorough knowledge of how color's character affects the inner dimension is necessary. We have seen where the spiritual dimension is influenced by the physical world (i.e., dreams), or where the spiritual inspires the physical responses. Fine artists, graphic designers, interior designers, animators, and Web designers to name a few, must be able to fully comprehend and develop flawless color skills. One of the most important keys to a successful career as designers and artists is to be color proficient in all aspects.

Figure 8-33 SALVADOR DALI, ***Dream Caused by the Flight of a Bumblebee Around a Pomegranate a Second Before Awakening,*** 1944.

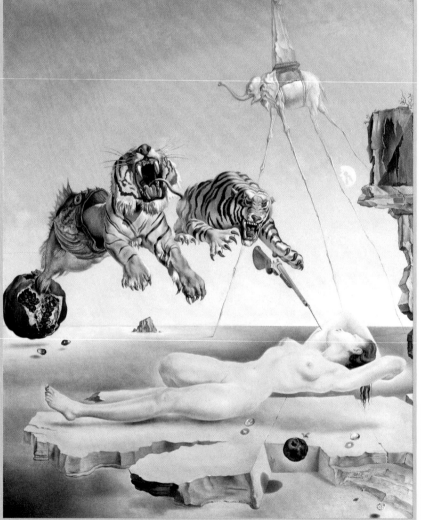

NIMATALLAH/ART RESOURCE, NY.

THE SPIRITUAL DIMENSION OF COLOR

An Exercise in Image Conversion to Pure Expressive Color

Much of Kandinsky's art career, especially after the Bauhaus, was spent in pursuit of the psychological effects of color. Kandinsky, a master colorist, believed that color was a spiritual matter and like Mondrian thought that color should be liberated from the conventions of the form. Because human emotion is a spiritual function, it cannot be confined to any particular representation or physical shape. As we have discovered, the single most important characteristic of color is the expression of emotional states, or the mood element by which it generates. Kandinsky illustrated

that human passions such as love and hate were shapeless. Additionally, just as music does not have physical form, we have seen that it can construct various types of emotional responses into the physical world through dance and various dramatic expressions. We therefore have also learned that all human emotions can be interpreted through the color vehicle into a tangible form.

Kandinsky proclaimed that the canvas was his "enemy" as he struggled to translate true spiritual emotion by means of physical color pigments. He captured the energy created

AFP/GETTY IMAGES.

Figure 8-34 Michelle Qwan.

by the music, using it to render the paint onto the canvas in abstracted or nonobjective forms. This was the liberation of the spectrum from its usual confines of traditional form.

Project Proposal with Subtractive Color: RYB

This can be accomplished in many ways. What we will be attempting to do is create an abstract or nonobjective painting from a realistic or representational photograph, using acrylic or watercolor mediums. Your instructor may want to select a particular image for you to interpret, or you may be instructed to interpret the *Michelle Qwan* (Figure 8-34) portrait, as the student examples reflect.

- Working from a photograph, or image assigned to you, recreate that representational image, translating it into a spiritual expression of nonobjective color (see *note*).

- If you are assigned the *Michelle Qwan* image on the previous page, try to interpret the energy, expression, and mood of the image.

- This often works well when selecting the appropriate music to match the image. Audio inspiration, in addition to visual inspiration, is always better. Remember that your selections are totally subjective, as long as you can *validate* your solution.

- See the following student examples:

Note: *This project can be done with a photograph, poem, musical composition, or all three. Rather than a photograph, one could simply interpret a musical composition (intangible) into a physical representation (tangible) of the mood, which the music creates. The same can be said of a poem as well. Using all three in symphony is a bit more complex, but enhances the student's mood sensitivity, as well as critical thinking skills.*

Student Examples

The following is a composite of student responses to a photograph (referred to as the *original*) seen on the previous page of the Project Proposal titled: *Michelle Qwan*.

Students were asked to respond to the nuances of the portrait: What is her portrayed personality? What emotions and moods are projected? Is it energetic, calm, angry, etc.?

They also were asked to select the appropriate music, which they felt would relate to the image, as well as their painting itself. All works were executed with acrylic paints.

Figure 8-35 Student Example #1.

Student Example #1

This student's composition interpreted the photograph in a very "Kandinsky esque" rendering. Although it is reasonably successful, try to break away from doing the same thing that Kandinsky did, and use your creative imagination. After all, these compositions should be straight from *your* inner response, not an exterior copy of familiar technique.

Student Example #2

This student example was accomplished with the airbrush technique. In this composition there are figures that materialize in the composition, which are abstracted rather than non-objectified. With this technique, the lines are not as harsh and rigid as the previous example.

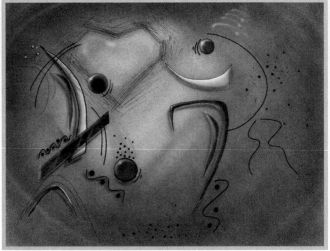

Figure 8-36 Student Example #2.

PHOTO BY THE AUTHOR.

Figure 8-37 Student Example #3.

PHOTO BY THE AUTHOR.

Figure 8-39 Student Example #5.

PHOTO BY THE AUTHOR.

Figure 8-38 Student Example #4.

Student Example #3

This example is more minimalist than the previous. The figures have been de-objectified so that only the essence or spiritualness can be revealed. The combination of line to background mood seems to be accomplishing the passionate and energetic quality of the original photo.

Student Example #4

This example has incorporated hard-edged solid stationary shapes, and contrasted them against the high tempo brushstrokes. The contrast of saturated blue and then red of shapes conflict with more intensified lighter background hues.

Student Example #5

This student's work has an odd tranquility about it, even though there is a contrast in terms of directional line. There seems to have been a type of explosion from the center of the composition. There is movement and dynamic, which addresses the energy in the original photograph, but the dominance of light blue controls just how much energy can be interpreted here. This composition is exemplary of the student's general nature, which is calm and one who loves inner peace. She has succeeded in transforming her spiritual character onto a tangible surface, as well as interpreting the energy of the photograph.

APPENDIX A

BRIEF INTRODUCTION TO DIGITAL COLOR: RGB AND CMYK

DIGITAL COLOR: RGB AND CMYK

We will now briefly introduce digital color, which typically applies to specific color applications such as Photoshop, Illustrator, Quark, and InDesign. The subject matter then requires extensive training in a computer lab situation with its own related and specific materials and text. The purpose of this introduction is to simply acquaint the student with the function of the RGB and CMYK process.

You will remember that we discussed the nature of subtractive and additive color in the beginning of this text. It is important at this point, as many students will begin to work with digital color more often, to identify more carefully just how additive and subtractive color relates specifically to the digital processes.

We are no longer dealing with pigments in the sense of oil, acrylic, watercolor, or other fine art mediums, but rather the process of color reproduction and color correction. In this case the ultimate goal is to reproduce a perfect color corrected composition via printed inks.

Although we know that the primary subtractive *pigments* mixed equal black (RYB), we also know from earlier discussion that the combination of all colors of *light* equal white. The RGB or primary colors of light are additive and consist of red, green, and blue (Remembering back to the beginning of the text, we discovered that there were bundles of quarks located in protons and neutrons. Each bundle of three quarks contain one red, one green, and one blue quark, which combined produced white light). The CMYK, or the primary colors of pigments (inks), are subtractive and they are known as cyan, magenta, and yellow. Because cyan, magenta, and yellow inks do not mix to an accurate black, there is no other choice but to add black proper. The "K" in CMYK refers to "key," which basically separates it from blue ("B"). An example of the CMYK subtractive process is to look at specific color combinations. It is important to note that the CMY to RGB are different in some ways than we have previously studied concerning the color circle. Here is the difference: cyan's complement is red, magenta's complement is green, and yellow's complement is blue. So therefore, the *additive RGB* has a *subtractive complement* of CMYK.

Computer monitor colors are generated by white light, but the printed inks of the same images are subtractive color. What this means is that the imagery that you print from the monitor onto the paper is going to yield much different results. A designer can never hope to have the same luminous results on paper as seen on the screen. Color processing and editing will always be essential to a process, whereby RGB is converted to CMYK. The quality and type of paper that is used will often exaggerate the lack of appropriate colors as well.

In terms of the complementary colors, that is, of the RGB and CYMK, we find that we have to think about them differently. As white light shines onto the surface of yellow ink, for example, it is the yellow ink that absorbs or subtracts all of the blue light, and produces a mixture of red and green light, which we see as yellow. Cyan absorbs red light and reflects green and blue, and magenta then absorbs green light, which then reflects red and blue. The student may recognize that the mixing of lights is explained very differently than we discussed in the first and second chapters. Before we were mixing physical pigments and applying them to a paper or canvas surface. The process was different, because the application of wet pigment does not change significantly from wet to dry state (depending on the paper), whereas RGB additive colors are quite different when printed in subtractive CMYK inks.

Remembering back to Chapter 4, we learned about rods and cones at the back of the eye, and their special function. We know that *rods* are sensitive to intensity or brightness, whereas *cones* are exclusive to color ranges, such as the RGB light. Rods and cones function differently according to, for example, what type of day it may be. On a very foggy day rods would be the dominant functioning element of the two, because rods deal with brightness more than cone's role of color. Imagery on digital equipment is going to assign different tasks to *rods than to cones*, as it does viewing an acrylic painting, or the printed CMYK composition.

Please see CMYK and RGB Color Sampler Charts immediately following the Project Proposal.

PROJECT PROPOSAL WITH DIGITAL COLOR: RGB TO CMYK

A s with the previous project, create a composition translating mood and emotion into a nonobjective color response. This time you are creating the color composition with the RGB or additive colors of light, typically seen on your computer monitor, for example, in Photoshop, Illustrator, Quark, or InDesign. Your RGB composition will then be translated into the CMYK for producing subtractive color prints.

- Produce three compositions that replicate a perceived mood within a given picture, such as the previous project proposal. Your instructor will give you the appropriate image to interpret.

  (Some find that this project is more challenging in terms of inspiration.)

- As you will be experiencing color difference between the screen product that you produce and the printed copy, it will be important to do adequate color corrections in order for the mood, or spiritual, component to function. Many students find this even more of a challenge, because the computer program alienates the designer somewhat from the inner person. Try not to allow technology to interfere in the process of interpreting the project.

- Be sure to use high-quality gloss paper.
- Leave a white border around the compositions.

Note: Because CMYK color spaces are normally smaller than RGB, be sure to store your finished images in RGB for as long as possible, because you will be discarding valuable color information as soon as you make the conversion to CMYK.

Student Examples

The following three compositions are various responses to the same original photograph, but each composition belongs to a different musical arrangement. These examples are a student's nonobjective response to the energy and spirit of the portrait of *Samurai Chick*.

Try to determine the emphasis of line and shape as they relate to color emotion. What mood do you feel and why? Is it color, line, or both that supports your evaluation? What exactly is happening between the relationship of line and color? How do they function together, or is one independent from the other in the function of the composition?

Student Composition #1.

Student Composition #2.

Student Composition #3.

RGB/CMYK Color Sampler Charts

The following graphic arts guide is a re-creation of one that was originally produced to assist the user in the selection of colors on Xerox color printers. It is also useful to the student of this text in order to determine accuracy and appropriate selections of color and color harmonies, as well as a guide for tints and shades, values, etc. Additionally, it serves to assist in the further understanding of the color charts and project proposals in Chapters 1 and 2 in terms of saturations and intensities, and is a good reference guide as to the properties of each hue. The RGB (first set of charts) and CMYK (second set of charts) Color Samplers indicate under each color patch the constituents of cyan, magenta, yellow, and black of that particular hue.

RGB Color Sampler

R 255 G 255 B 255

R 255 G 255 B 255

R 255 G 255 B 255

R 255 G 255 B 255

R 255 G 255 B 255

R 255 G 255 B 255

R 255 G 255 B 255

R 255 G 255 B 255

R 255 G 128 B 0

R 255 G 0 B 0

R 255 G 0 B 255

R 128 G 0 B 255

R 0 G 128 B 255

R 0 G 255 B 255

R 0 G 255 B 128

R 128 G 255 B 0

R 255 G 128 B 0
R 255 G 0 B 0
R 255 G 0 B 255
R 128 G 0 B 255
R 0 G 128 B 255
R 0 G 255 B 255
R 0 G 255 B 128
R 128 G 255 B 0

R 0 G 0 B 0
R 0 G 0 B 0
R 0 G 0 B 0
R 0 G 0 B 0
R 0 G 0 B 0
R 0 G 0 B 0
R 0 G 0 B 0
R 0 G 0 B 0

R 0 G 0 B 255

R 0 G 255 B 0

R 0 G 0 B 255

R 255 G 0 B 0

R 0 G 255 B 0

R 255 G 0 B 0

R 0 G 255 B 255

R 0 G 255 B 255

R 255 G 0 B 255

R 255 G 0 B 255

R 255 G 255 B 0

R 255 G 255 B 0

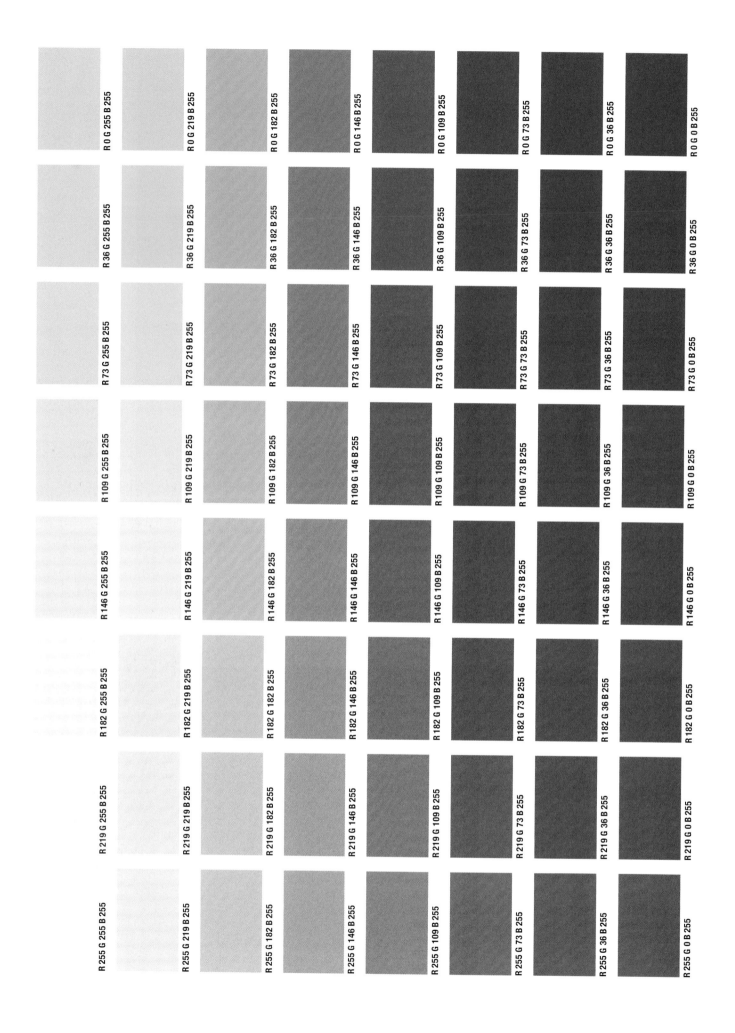

R 0 G 255 B 255 | R 0 G 219 B 255 | R 0 G 182 B 255 | R 0 G 146 B 255 | R 0 G 109 B 255 | R 0 G 73 B 255 | R 0 G 36 B 255 | R 0 G 0 B 255

R 36 G 255 B 255 | R 36 G 219 B 255 | R 36 G 182 B 255 | R 36 G 146 B 255 | R 36 G 109 B 255 | R 36 G 73 B 255 | R 36 G 36 B 255 | R 36 G 0 B 255

R 73 G 255 B 255 | R 73 G 219 B 255 | R 73 G 182 B 255 | R 73 G 146 B 255 | R 73 G 109 B 255 | R 73 G 73 B 255 | R 73 G 36 B 255 | R 73 G 0 B 255

R 109 G 255 B 255 | R 109 G 219 B 255 | R 109 G 182 B 255 | R 109 G 146 B 255 | R 109 G 109 B 255 | R 109 G 73 B 255 | R 109 G 36 B 255 | R 109 G 0 B 255

R 146 G 255 B 255 | R 146 G 219 B 255 | R 146 G 182 B 255 | R 146 G 146 B 255 | R 146 G 109 B 255 | R 146 G 73 B 255 | R 146 G 36 B 255 | R 146 G 0 B 255

R 182 G 255 B 255 | R 182 G 219 B 255 | R 182 G 182 B 255 | R 182 G 146 B 255 | R 182 G 109 B 255 | R 182 G 73 B 255 | R 182 G 36 B 255 | R 182 G 0 B 255

R 219 G 255 B 255 | R 219 G 219 B 255 | R 219 G 182 B 255 | R 219 G 146 B 255 | R 219 G 109 B 255 | R 219 G 73 B 255 | R 219 G 36 B 255 | R 219 G 0 B 255

R 255 G 255 B 255 | R 255 G 219 B 255 | R 255 G 182 B 255 | R 255 G 146 B 255 | R 255 G 109 B 255 | R 255 G 73 B 255 | R 255 G 36 B 255 | R 255 G 0 B 255

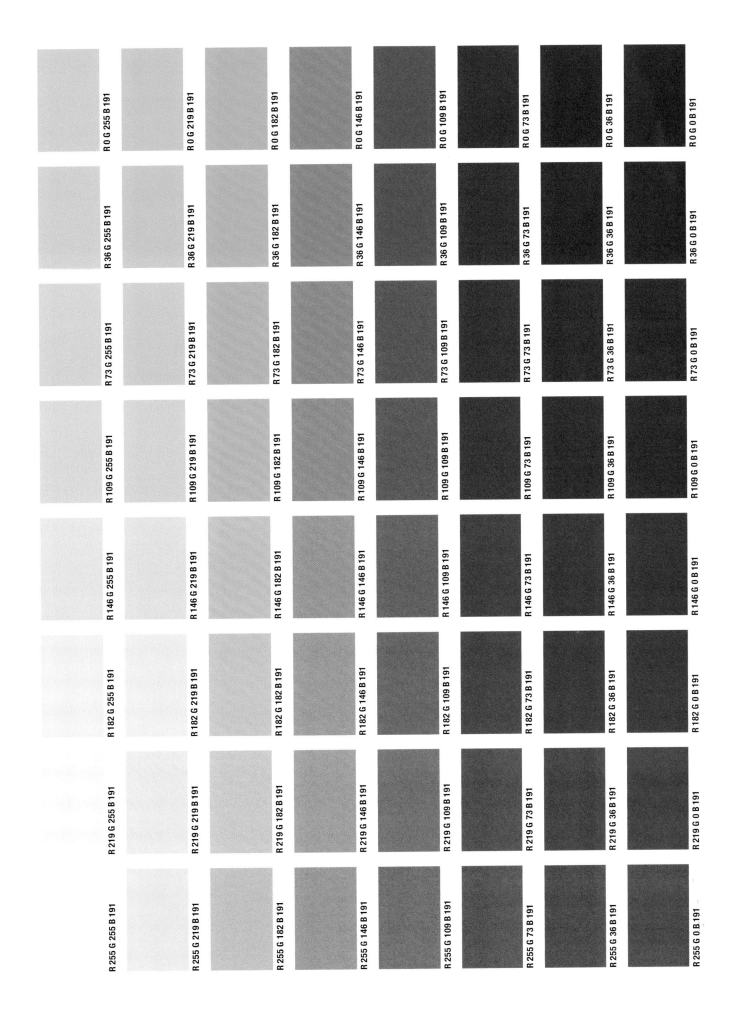

R 0 G 255 B 191 · R 0 G 219 B 191 · R 0 G 182 B 191 · R 0 G 146 B 191 · R 0 G 109 B 191 · R 0 G 73 B 191 · R 0 G 36 B 191 · R 0 G 0 B 191

R 36 G 255 B 191 · R 36 G 219 B 191 · R 36 G 182 B 191 · R 36 G 146 B 191 · R 36 G 109 B 191 · R 36 G 73 B 191 · R 36 G 36 B 191 · R 36 G 0 B 191

R 73 G 255 B 191 · R 73 G 219 B 191 · R 73 G 182 B 191 · R 73 G 146 B 191 · R 73 G 109 B 191 · R 73 G 73 B 191 · R 73 G 36 B 191 · R 73 G 0 B 191

R 109 G 255 B 191 · R 109 G 219 B 191 · R 109 G 182 B 191 · R 109 G 146 B 191 · R 109 G 109 B 191 · R 109 G 73 B 191 · R 109 G 36 B 191 · R 109 G 0 B 191

R 146 G 255 B 191 · R 146 G 219 B 191 · R 146 G 182 B 191 · R 146 G 146 B 191 · R 146 G 109 B 191 · R 146 G 73 B 191 · R 146 G 36 B 191 · R 146 G 0 B 191

R 182 G 255 B 191 · R 182 G 219 B 191 · R 182 G 182 B 191 · R 182 G 146 B 191 · R 182 G 109 B 191 · R 182 G 73 B 191 · R 182 G 36 B 191 · R 182 G 0 B 191

R 219 G 255 B 191 · R 219 G 219 B 191 · R 219 G 182 B 191 · R 219 G 146 B 191 · R 219 G 109 B 191 · R 219 G 73 B 191 · R 219 G 36 B 191 · R 219 G 0 B 191

R 255 G 255 B 191 · R 255 G 219 B 191 · R 255 G 182 B 191 · R 255 G 146 B 191 · R 255 G 109 B 191 · R 255 G 73 B 191 · R 255 G 36 B 191 · R 255 G 0 B 191

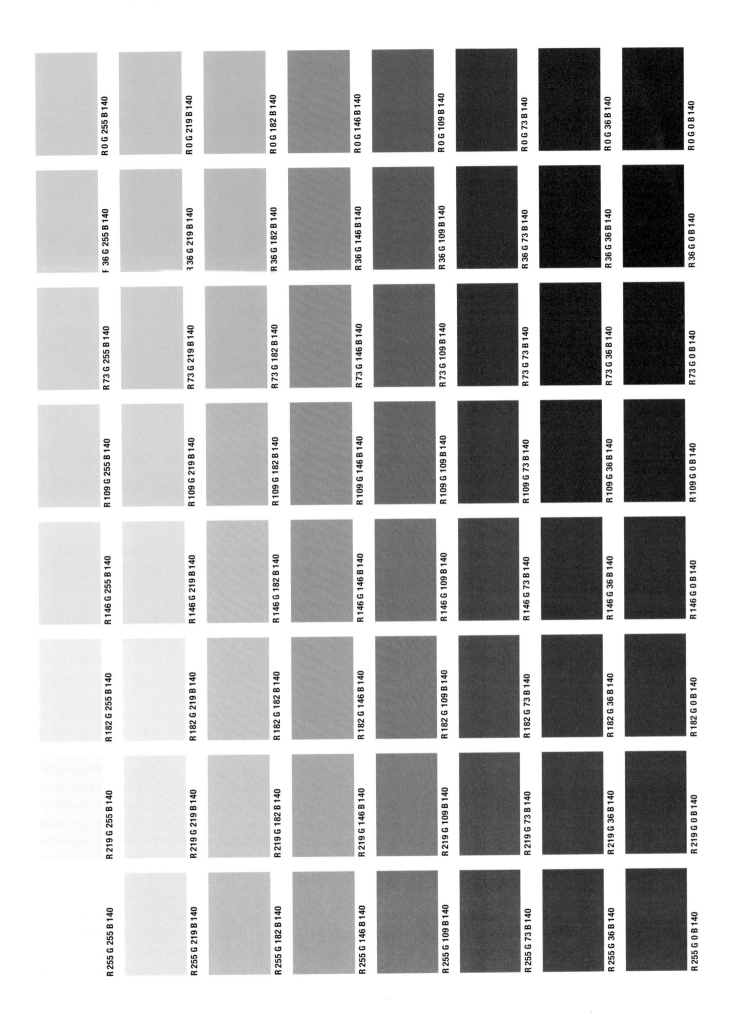

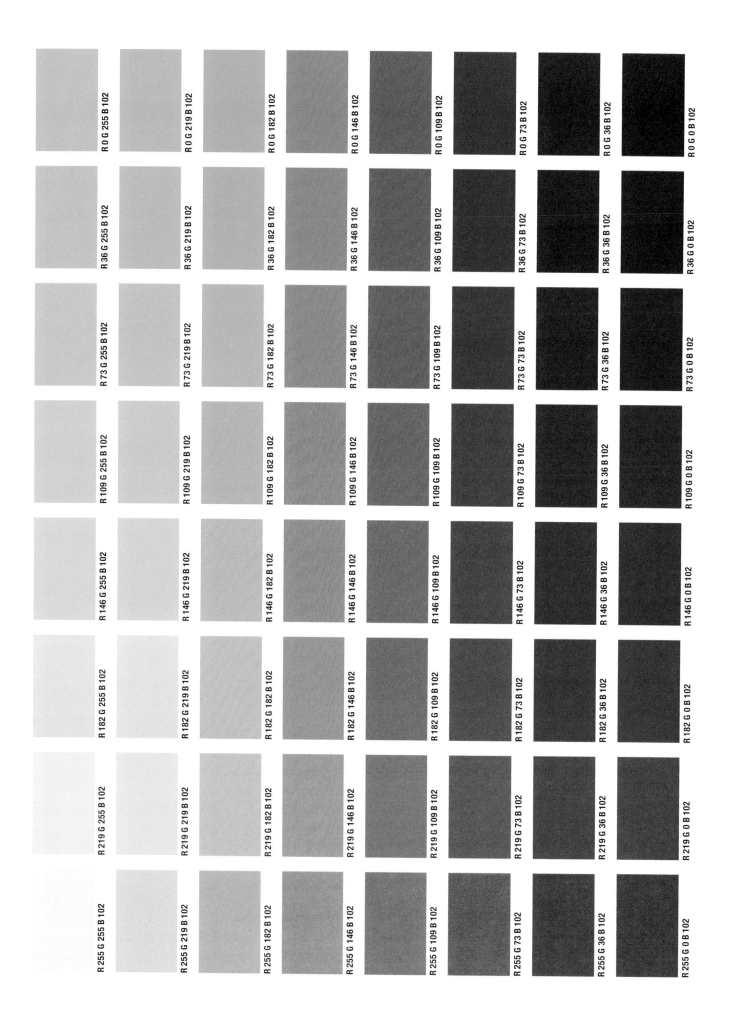

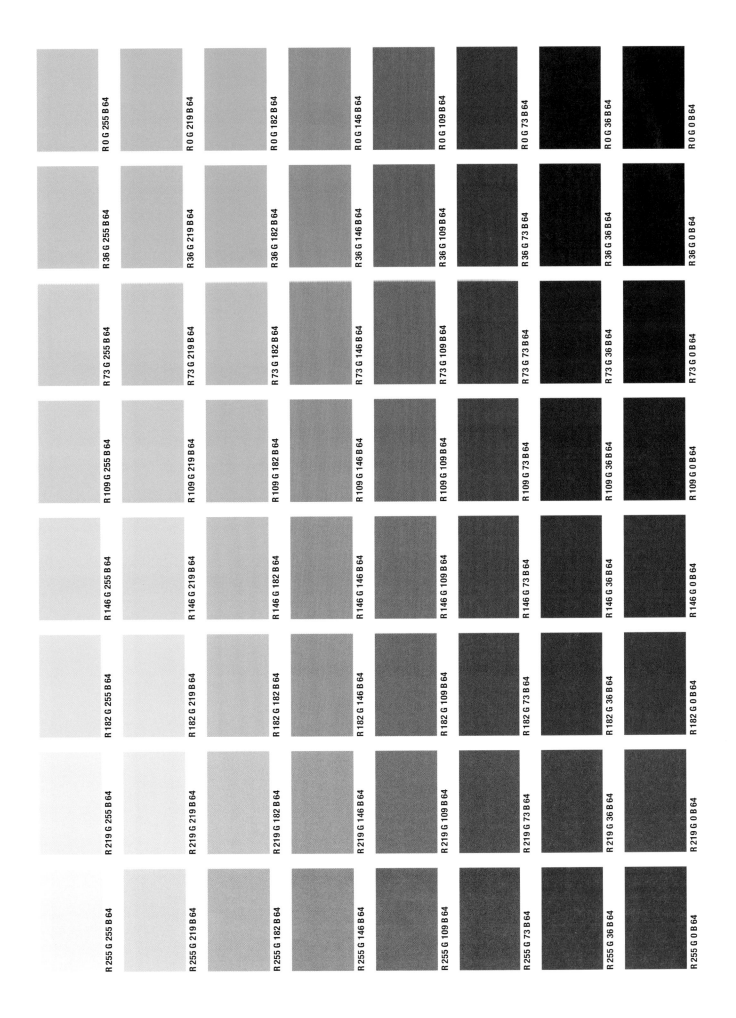

R 0 G 255 B 64
R 0 G 219 B 64
R 0 G 182 B 64
R 0 G 146 B 64
R 0 G 109 B 64
R 0 G 73 B 64
R 0 G 36 B 64
R 0 G 0 B 64

R 36 G 255 B 64
R 36 G 219 B 64
R 36 G 182 B 64
R 36 G 146 B 64
R 36 G 109 B 64
R 36 G 73 B 64
R 36 G 36 B 64
R 36 G 0 B 64

R 73 G 255 B 64
R 73 G 219 B 64
R 73 G 182 B 64
R 73 G 146 B 64
R 73 G 109 B 64
R 73 G 73 B 64
R 73 G 36 B 64
R 73 G 0 B 64

R 109 G 255 B 64
R 109 G 219 B 64
R 109 G 182 B 64
R 109 G 146 B 64
R 109 G 109 B 64
R 109 G 73 B 64
R 109 G 36 B 64
R 109 G 0 B 64

R 146 G 255 B 64
R 146 G 219 B 64
R 146 G 182 B 64
R 146 G 146 B 64
R 146 G 109 B 64
R 146 G 73 B 64
R 146 G 36 B 64
R 146 G 0 B 64

R 182 G 255 B 64
R 182 G 219 B 64
R 182 G 182 B 64
R 182 G 146 B 64
R 182 G 109 B 64
R 182 G 73 B 64
R 182 G 36 B 64
R 182 G 0 B 64

R 219 G 255 B 64
R 219 G 219 B 64
R 219 G 182 B 64
R 219 G 146 B 64
R 219 G 109 B 64
R 219 G 73 B 64
R 219 G 36 B 64
R 219 G 0 B 64

R 255 G 255 B 64
R 255 G 219 B 64
R 255 G 182 B 64
R 255 G 146 B 64
R 255 G 109 B 64
R 255 G 73 B 64
R 255 G 36 B 64
R 255 G 0 B 64

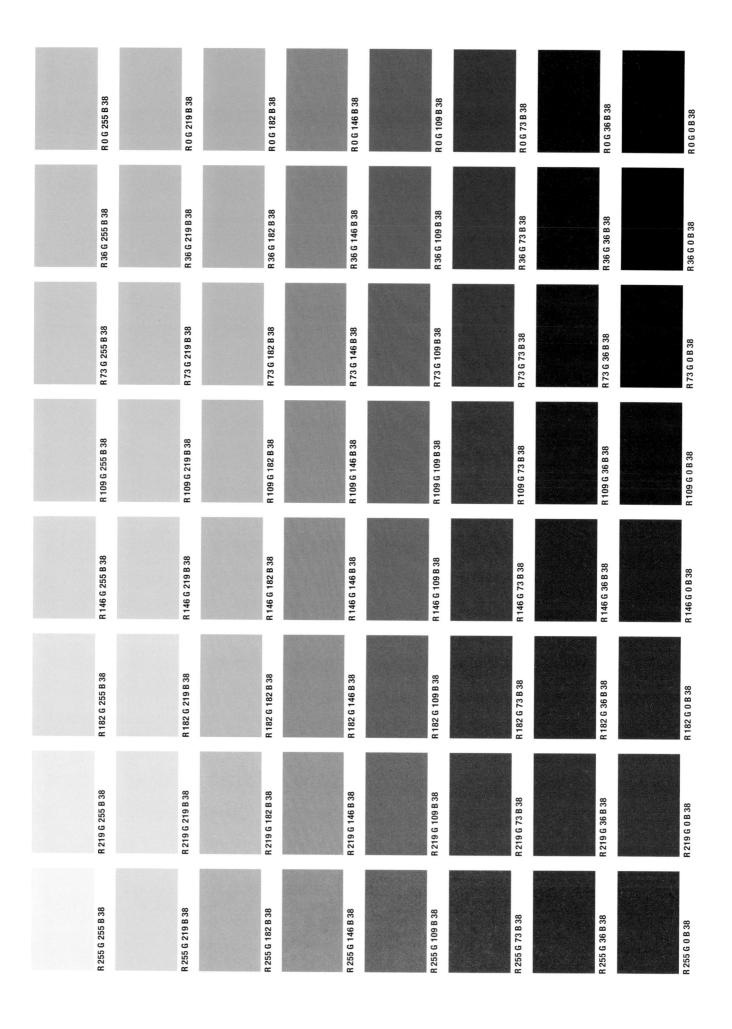

R 0 G 255 B 38   R 0 G 219 B 38   R 0 G 182 B 38   R 0 G 146 B 38   R 0 G 109 B 38   R 0 G 73 B 38   R 0 G 36 B 38   R 0 G 0 B 38

R 36 G 255 B 38   R 36 G 219 B 38   R 36 G 182 B 38   R 36 G 146 B 38   R 36 G 109 B 38   R 36 G 73 B 38   R 36 G 36 B 38   R 36 G 0 B 38

R 73 G 255 B 38   R 73 G 219 B 38   R 73 G 182 B 38   R 73 G 146 B 38   R 73 G 109 B 38   R 73 G 73 B 38   R 73 G 36 B 38   R 73 G 0 B 38

R 109 G 255 B 38   R 109 G 219 B 38   R 109 G 182 B 38   R 109 G 146 B 38   R 109 G 109 B 38   R 109 G 73 B 38   R 109 G 36 B 38   R 109 G 0 B 38

R 146 G 255 B 38   R 146 G 219 B 38   R 146 G 182 B 38   R 146 G 146 B 38   R 146 G 109 B 38   R 146 G 73 B 38   R 146 G 36 B 38   R 146 G 0 B 38

R 182 G 255 B 38   R 182 G 219 B 38   R 182 G 182 B 38   R 182 G 146 B 38   R 182 G 109 B 38   R 182 G 73 B 38   R 182 G 36 B 38   R 182 G 0 B 38

R 219 G 255 B 38   R 219 G 219 B 38   R 219 G 182 B 38   R 219 G 146 B 38   R 219 G 109 B 38   R 219 G 73 B 38   R 219 G 36 B 38   R 219 G 0 B 38

R 255 G 255 B 38   R 255 G 219 B 38   R 255 G 182 B 38   R 255 G 146 B 38   R 255 G 109 B 38   R 255 G 73 B 38   R 255 G 36 B 38   R 255 G 0 B 38

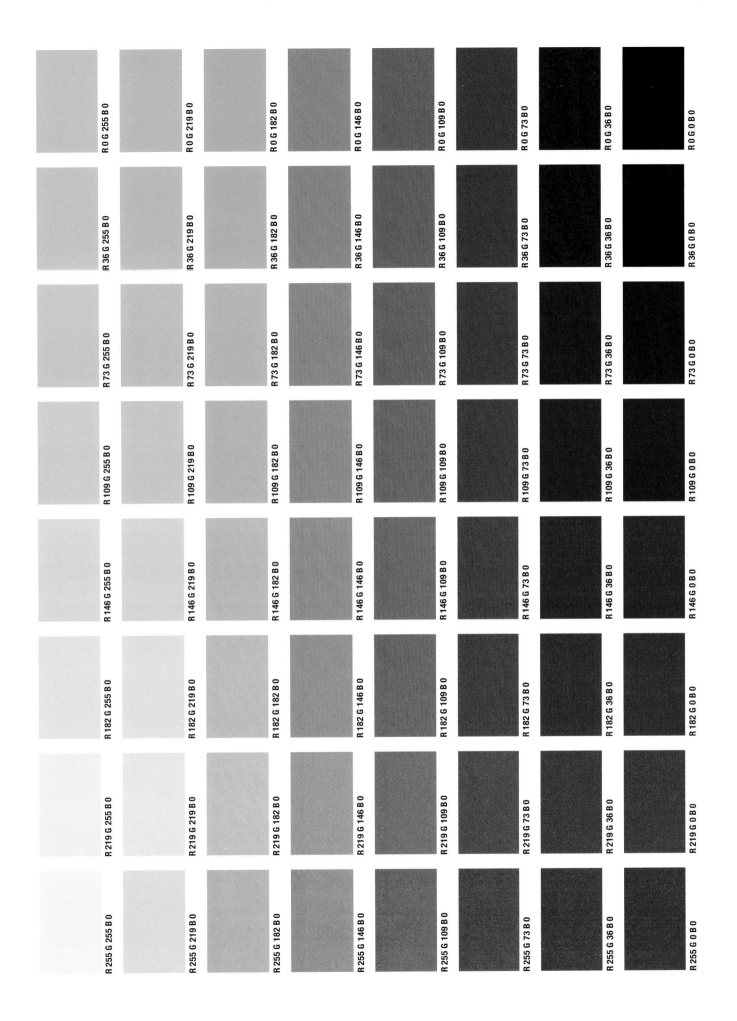

CMYK Color Sampler

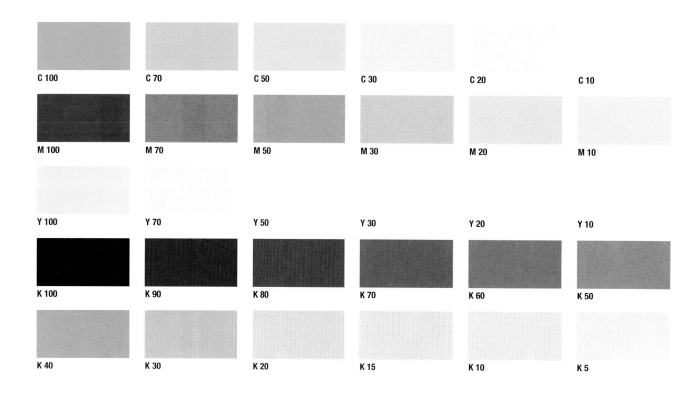

C 100   C 70   C 50   C 30   C 20   C 10

M 100   M 70   M 50   M 30   M 20   M 10

Y 100   Y 70   Y 50   Y 30   Y 20   Y 10

K 100   K 90   K 80   K 70   K 60   K 50

K 40   K 30   K 20   K 15   K 10   K 5

C 100   C 100 M 100

C 100   C 100 Y 100

M 100   C 100 M 100

M 100   M 100 Y 100

Y 100   C 100 Y 100

Y 100   M 100 Y 100

Y 100

M 50 Y 100

M 100 Y 100

M 100

C 50 M 100

C 100 M 100

C 100 M 50

C 100

C 100 Y 50

C 100 Y 100

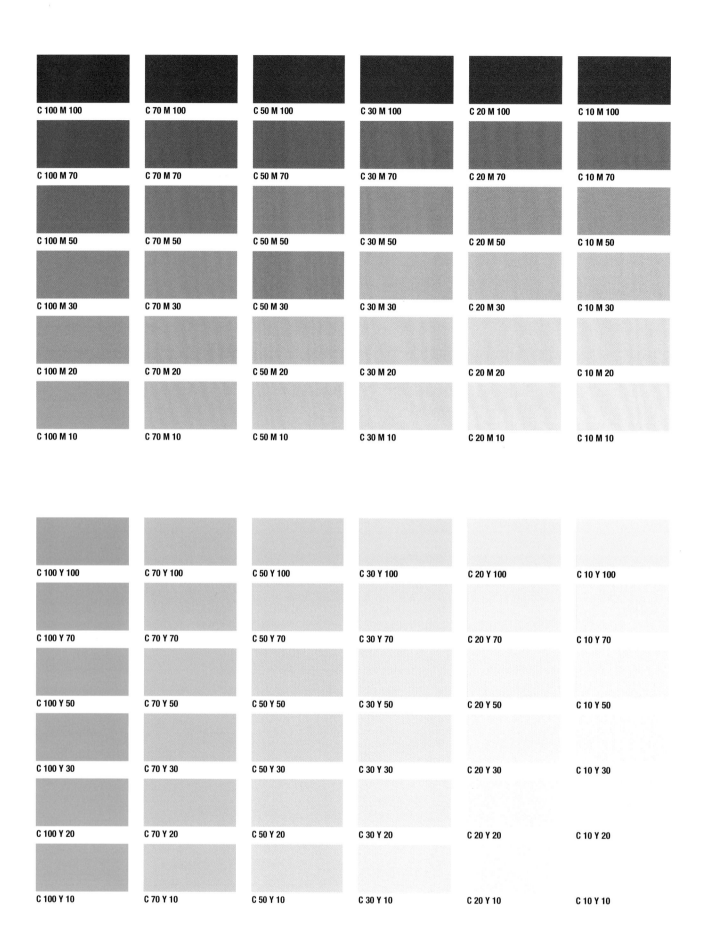

C 100 M 100   C 70 M 100   C 50 M 100   C 30 M 100   C 20 M 100   C 10 M 100

C 100 M 70   C 70 M 70   C 50 M 70   C 30 M 70   C 20 M 70   C 10 M 70

C 100 M 50   C 70 M 50   C 50 M 50   C 30 M 50   C 20 M 50   C 10 M 50

C 100 M 30   C 70 M 30   C 50 M 30   C 30 M 30   C 20 M 30   C 10 M 30

C 100 M 20   C 70 M 20   C 50 M 20   C 30 M 20   C 20 M 20   C 10 M 20

C 100 M 10   C 70 M 10   C 50 M 10   C 30 M 10   C 20 M 10   C 10 M 10

C 100 Y 100   C 70 Y 100   C 50 Y 100   C 30 Y 100   C 20 Y 100   C 10 Y 100

C 100 Y 70   C 70 Y 70   C 50 Y 70   C 30 Y 70   C 20 Y 70   C 10 Y 70

C 100 Y 50   C 70 Y 50   C 50 Y 50   C 30 Y 50   C 20 Y 50   C 10 Y 50

C 100 Y 30   C 70 Y 30   C 50 Y 30   C 30 Y 30   C 20 Y 30   C 10 Y 30

C 100 Y 20   C 70 Y 20   C 50 Y 20   C 30 Y 20   C 20 Y 20   C 10 Y 20

C 100 Y 10   C 70 Y 10   C 50 Y 10   C 30 Y 10   C 20 Y 10   C 10 Y 10

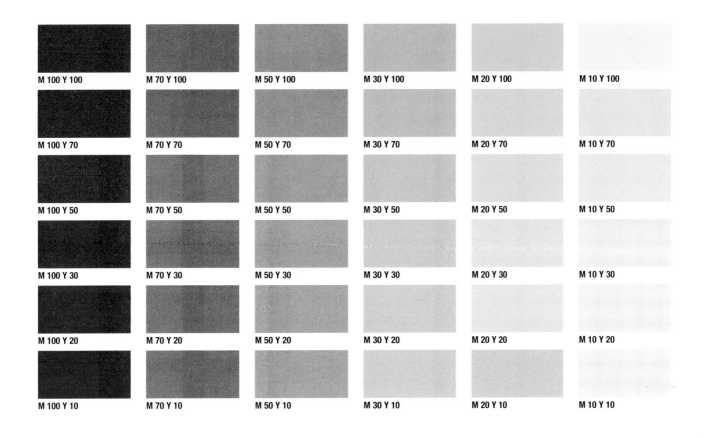

M 100 Y 100   M 70 Y 100   M 50 Y 100   M 30 Y 100   M 20 Y 100   M 10 Y 100

M 100 Y 70   M 70 Y 70   M 50 Y 70   M 30 Y 70   M 20 Y 70   M 10 Y 70

M 100 Y 50   M 70 Y 50   M 50 Y 50   M 30 Y 50   M 20 Y 50   M 10 Y 50

M 100 Y 30   M 70 Y 30   M 50 Y 30   M 30 Y 30   M 20 Y 30   M 10 Y 30

M 100 Y 20   M 70 Y 20   M 50 Y 20   M 30 Y 20   M 20 Y 20   M 10 Y 20

M 100 Y 10   M 70 Y 10   M 50 Y 10   M 30 Y 10   M 20 Y 10   M 10 Y 10

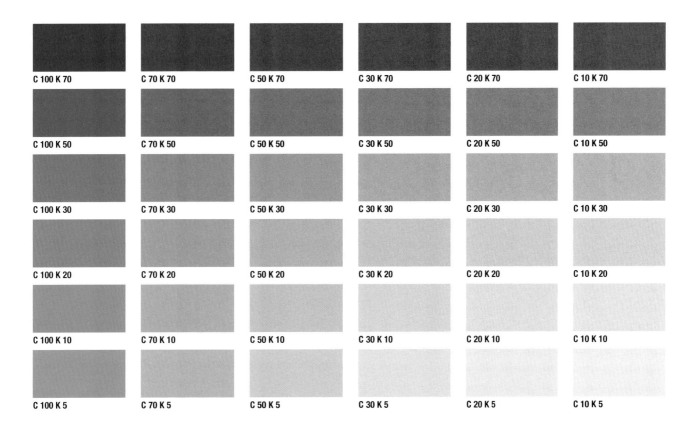

C 100 K 70   C 70 K 70   C 50 K 70   C 30 K 70   C 20 K 70   C 10 K 70

C 100 K 50   C 70 K 50   C 50 K 50   C 30 K 50   C 20 K 50   C 10 K 50

C 100 K 30   C 70 K 30   C 50 K 30   C 30 K 30   C 20 K 30   C 10 K 30

C 100 K 20   C 70 K 20   C 50 K 20   C 30 K 20   C 20 K 20   C 10 K 20

C 100 K 10   C 70 K 10   C 50 K 10   C 30 K 10   C 20 K 10   C 10 K 10

C 100 K 5   C 70 K 5   C 50 K 5   C 30 K 5   C 20 K 5   C 10 K 5

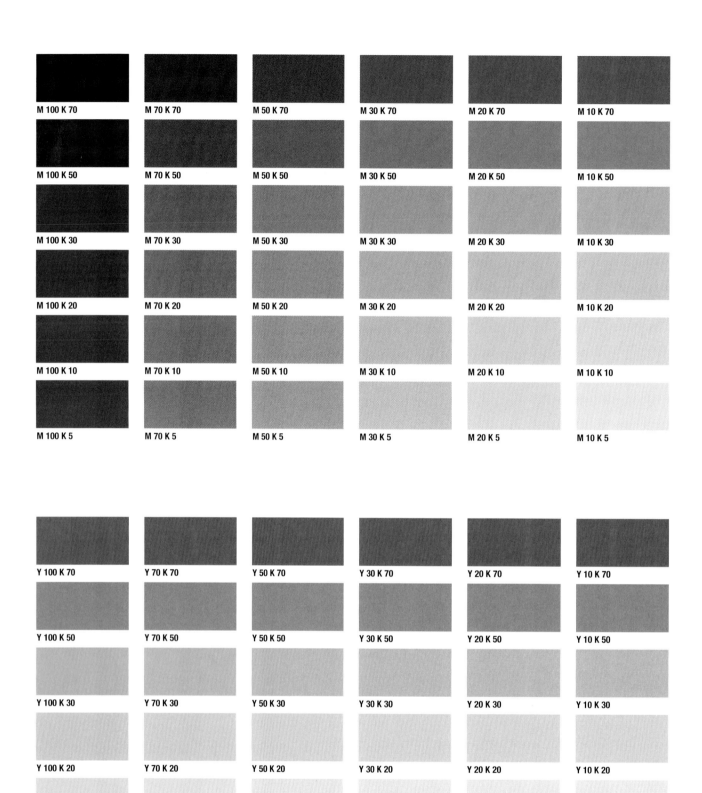

M 100 K 70	M 70 K 70	M 50 K 70	M 30 K 70	M 20 K 70	M 10 K 70
M 100 K 50	M 70 K 50	M 50 K 50	M 30 K 50	M 20 K 50	M 10 K 50
M 100 K 30	M 70 K 30	M 50 K 30	M 30 K 30	M 20 K 30	M 10 K 30
M 100 K 20	M 70 K 20	M 50 K 20	M 30 K 20	M 20 K 20	M 10 K 20
M 100 K 10	M 70 K 10	M 50 K 10	M 30 K 10	M 20 K 10	M 10 K 10
M 100 K 5	M 70 K 5	M 50 K 5	M 30 K 5	M 20 K 5	M 10 K 5

Y 100 K 70	Y 70 K 70	Y 50 K 70	Y 30 K 70	Y 20 K 70	Y 10 K 70
Y 100 K 50	Y 70 K 50	Y 50 K 50	Y 30 K 50	Y 20 K 50	Y 10 K 50
Y 100 K 30	Y 70 K 30	Y 50 K 30	Y 30 K 30	Y 20 K 30	Y 10 K 30
Y 100 K 20	Y 70 K 20	Y 50 K 20	Y 30 K 20	Y 20 K 20	Y 10 K 20
Y 100 K 10	Y 70 K 10	Y 50 K 10	Y 30 K 10	Y 20 K 10	Y 10 K 10
Y 100 K 5	Y 70 K 5	Y 50 K 5	Y 30 K 5	Y 20 K 5	Y 10 K 5

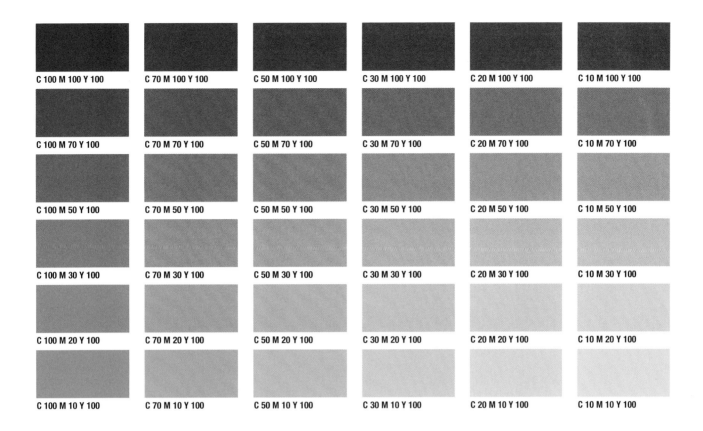

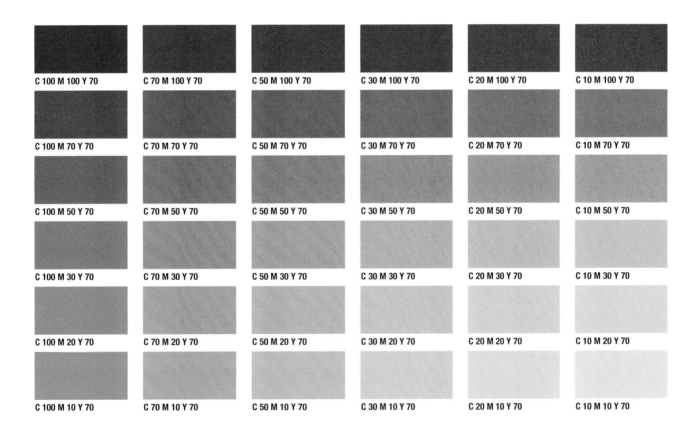

C 100 M 100 Y 50   C 70 M 100 Y 50   C 50 M 100 Y 50   C 30 M 100 Y 50   C 20 M 100 Y 50   C 10 M 100 Y 50

C 100 M 70 Y 50   C 70 M 70 Y 50   C 50 M 70 Y 50   C 30 M 70 Y 50   C 20 M 70 Y 50   C 10 M 70 Y 50

C 100 M 50 Y 50   C 70 M 50 Y 50   C 50 M 50 Y 50   C 30 M 50 Y 50   C 20 M 50 Y 50   C 10 M 50 Y 50

C 100 M 30 Y 50   C 70 M 30 Y 50   C 50 M 30 Y 50   C 30 M 30 Y 50   C 20 M 30 Y 50   C 10 M 30 Y 50

C 100 M 20 Y 50   C 70 M 20 Y 50   C 50 M 20 Y 50   C 30 M 20 Y 50   C 20 M 20 Y 50   C 10 M 20 Y 50

C 100 M 10 Y 50   C 70 M 10 Y 50   C 50 M 10 Y 50   C 30 M 10 Y 50   C 20 M 10 Y 50   C 10 M 10 Y 50

C 100 M 100 Y 30   C 70 M 100 Y 30   C 50 M 100 Y 30   C 30 M 100 Y 30   C 20 M 100 Y 30   C 10 M 100 Y 30

C 100 M 70 Y 30   C 70 M 70 Y 30   C 50 M 70 Y 30   C 30 M 70 Y 30   C 20 M 70 Y 30   C 10 M 70 Y 30

C 100 M 50 Y 30   C 70 M 50 Y 30   C 50 M 50 Y 30   C 30 M 50 Y 30   C 20 M 50 Y 30   C 10 M 50 Y 30

C 100 M 30 Y 30   C 70 M 30 Y 30   C 50 M 30 Y 30   C 30 M 30 Y 30   C 20 M 30 Y 30   C 10 M 30 Y 30

C 100 M 20 Y 30   C 70 M 20 Y 30   C 50 M 20 Y 30   C 30 M 20 Y 30   C 20 M 20 Y 30   C 10 M 20 Y 30

C 100 M 10 Y 30   C 70 M 10 Y 30   C 50 M 10 Y 30   C 30 M 10 Y 30   C 20 M 10 Y 30   C 10 M 10 Y 30

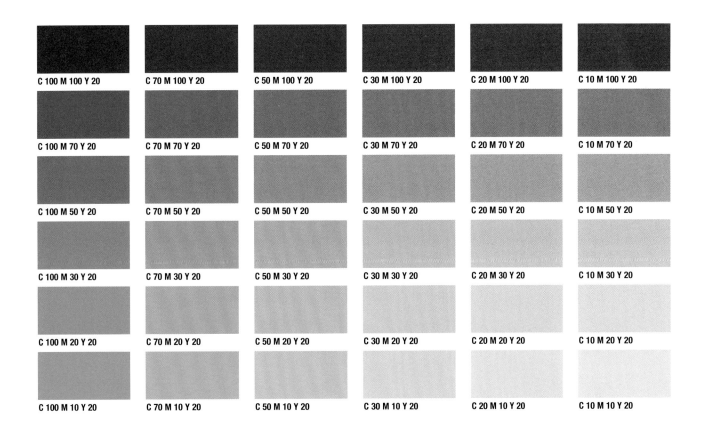

C 100 M 100 Y 20   C 70 M 100 Y 20   C 50 M 100 Y 20   C 30 M 100 Y 20   C 20 M 100 Y 20   C 10 M 100 Y 20

C 100 M 70 Y 20   C 70 M 70 Y 20   C 50 M 70 Y 20   C 30 M 70 Y 20   C 20 M 70 Y 20   C 10 M 70 Y 20

C 100 M 50 Y 20   C 70 M 50 Y 20   C 50 M 50 Y 20   C 30 M 50 Y 20   C 20 M 50 Y 20   C 10 M 50 Y 20

C 100 M 30 Y 20   C 70 M 30 Y 20   C 50 M 30 Y 20   C 30 M 30 Y 20   C 20 M 30 Y 20   C 10 M 30 Y 20

C 100 M 20 Y 20   C 70 M 20 Y 20   C 50 M 20 Y 20   C 30 M 20 Y 20   C 20 M 20 Y 20   C 10 M 20 Y 20

C 100 M 10 Y 20   C 70 M 10 Y 20   C 50 M 10 Y 20   C 30 M 10 Y 20   C 20 M 10 Y 20   C 10 M 10 Y 20

C 100 M 100 Y 10   C 70 M 100 Y 10   C 50 M 100 Y 10   C 30 M 100 Y 10   C 20 M 100 Y 10   C 10 M 100 Y 10

C 100 M 70 Y 10   C 70 M 70 Y 10   C 50 M 70 Y 10   C 30 M 70 Y 10   C 20 M 70 Y 10   C 10 M 70 Y 10

C 100 M 50 Y 10   C 70 M 50 Y 10   C 50 M 50 Y 10   C 30 M 50 Y 10   C 20 M 50 Y 10   C 10 M 50 Y 10

C 100 M 30 Y 10   C 70 M 30 Y 10   C 50 M 30 Y 10   C 30 M 30 Y 10   C 20 M 30 Y 10   C 10 M 30 Y 10

C 100 M 20 Y 10   C 70 M 20 Y 10   C 50 M 20 Y 10   C 30 M 20 Y 10   C 20 M 20 Y 10   C 10 M 20 Y 10

C 100 M 10 Y 10   C 70 M 10 Y 10   C 50 M 10 Y 10   C 30 M 10 Y 10   C 20 M 10 Y 10   C 10 M 10 Y 10

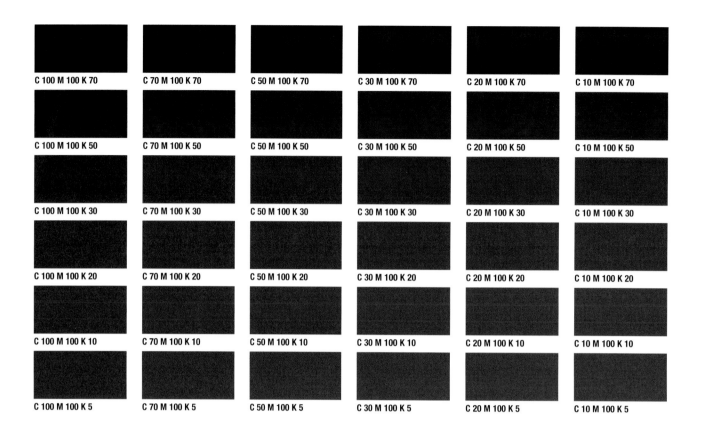

C 100 M 100 K 70   C 70 M 100 K 70   C 50 M 100 K 70   C 30 M 100 K 70   C 20 M 100 K 70   C 10 M 100 K 70

C 100 M 100 K 50   C 70 M 100 K 50   C 50 M 100 K 50   C 30 M 100 K 50   C 20 M 100 K 50   C 10 M 100 K 50

C 100 M 100 K 30   C 70 M 100 K 30   C 50 M 100 K 30   C 30 M 100 K 30   C 20 M 100 K 30   C 10 M 100 K 30

C 100 M 100 K 20   C 70 M 100 K 20   C 50 M 100 K 20   C 30 M 100 K 20   C 20 M 100 K 20   C 10 M 100 K 20

C 100 M 100 K 10   C 70 M 100 K 10   C 50 M 100 K 10   C 30 M 100 K 10   C 20 M 100 K 10   C 10 M 100 K 10

C 100 M 100 K 5   C 70 M 100 K 5   C 50 M 100 K 5   C 30 M 100 K 5   C 20 M 100 K 5   C 10 M 100 K 5

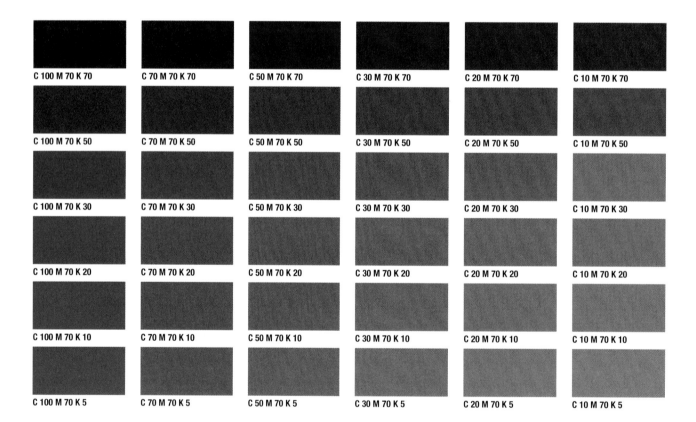

C 100 M 70 K 70   C 70 M 70 K 70   C 50 M 70 K 70   C 30 M 70 K 70   C 20 M 70 K 70   C 10 M 70 K 70

C 100 M 70 K 50   C 70 M 70 K 50   C 50 M 70 K 50   C 30 M 70 K 50   C 20 M 70 K 50   C 10 M 70 K 50

C 100 M 70 K 30   C 70 M 70 K 30   C 50 M 70 K 30   C 30 M 70 K 30   C 20 M 70 K 30   C 10 M 70 K 30

C 100 M 70 K 20   C 70 M 70 K 20   C 50 M 70 K 20   C 30 M 70 K 20   C 20 M 70 K 20   C 10 M 70 K 20

C 100 M 70 K 10   C 70 M 70 K 10   C 50 M 70 K 10   C 30 M 70 K 10   C 20 M 70 K 10   C 10 M 70 K 10

C 100 M 70 K 5   C 70 M 70 K 5   C 50 M 70 K 5   C 30 M 70 K 5   C 20 M 70 K 5   C 10 M 70 K 5

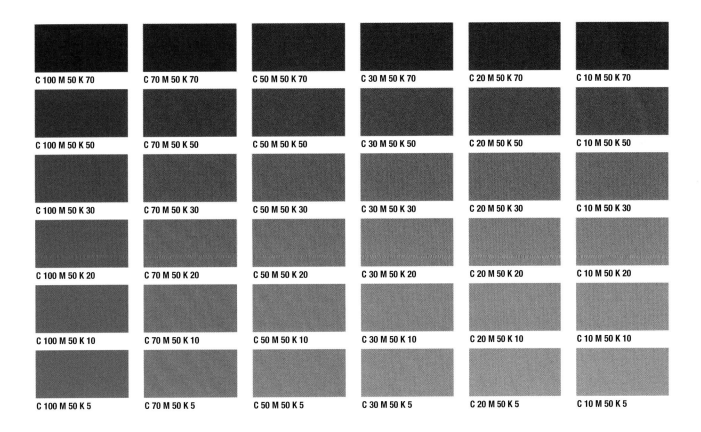

C 100 M 50 K 70 | C 70 M 50 K 70 | C 50 M 50 K 70 | C 30 M 50 K 70 | C 20 M 50 K 70 | C 10 M 50 K 70

C 100 M 50 K 50 | C 70 M 50 K 50 | C 50 M 50 K 50 | C 30 M 50 K 50 | C 20 M 50 K 50 | C 10 M 50 K 50

C 100 M 50 K 30 | C 70 M 50 K 30 | C 50 M 50 K 30 | C 30 M 50 K 30 | C 20 M 50 K 30 | C 10 M 50 K 30

C 100 M 50 K 20 | C 70 M 50 K 20 | C 50 M 50 K 20 | C 30 M 50 K 20 | C 20 M 50 K 20 | C 10 M 50 K 20

C 100 M 50 K 10 | C 70 M 50 K 10 | C 50 M 50 K 10 | C 30 M 50 K 10 | C 20 M 50 K 10 | C 10 M 50 K 10

C 100 M 50 K 5 | C 70 M 50 K 5 | C 50 M 50 K 5 | C 30 M 50 K 5 | C 20 M 50 K 5 | C 10 M 50 K 5

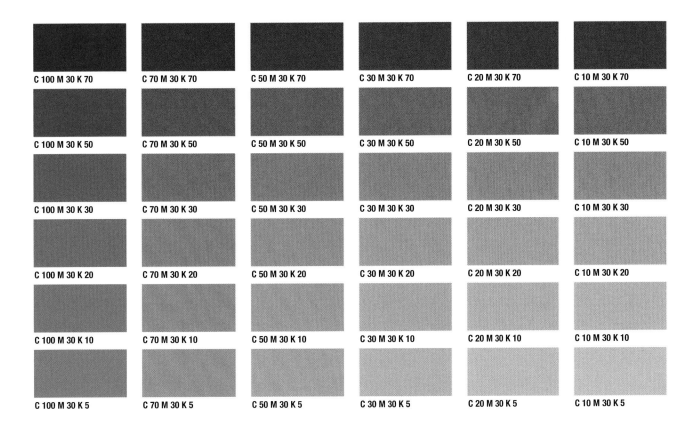

C 100 M 30 K 70 | C 70 M 30 K 70 | C 50 M 30 K 70 | C 30 M 30 K 70 | C 20 M 30 K 70 | C 10 M 30 K 70

C 100 M 30 K 50 | C 70 M 30 K 50 | C 50 M 30 K 50 | C 30 M 30 K 50 | C 20 M 30 K 50 | C 10 M 30 K 50

C 100 M 30 K 30 | C 70 M 30 K 30 | C 50 M 30 K 30 | C 30 M 30 K 30 | C 20 M 30 K 30 | C 10 M 30 K 30

C 100 M 30 K 20 | C 70 M 30 K 20 | C 50 M 30 K 20 | C 30 M 30 K 20 | C 20 M 30 K 20 | C 10 M 30 K 20

C 100 M 30 K 10 | C 70 M 30 K 10 | C 50 M 30 K 10 | C 30 M 30 K 10 | C 20 M 30 K 10 | C 10 M 30 K 10

C 100 M 30 K 5 | C 70 M 30 K 5 | C 50 M 30 K 5 | C 30 M 30 K 5 | C 20 M 30 K 5 | C 10 M 30 K 5

C 100 M 20 K 70	C 70 M 20 K 70	C 50 M 20 K 70	C 30 M 20 K 70	C 20 M 20 K 70	C 10 M 20 K 70
C 100 M 20 K 50	C 70 M 20 K 50	C 50 M 20 K 50	C 30 M 20 K 50	C 20 M 20 K 50	C 10 M 20 K 50
C 100 M 20 K 30	C 70 M 20 K 30	C 50 M 20 K 30	C 30 M 20 K 30	C 20 M 20 K 30	C 10 M 20 K 30
C 100 M 20 K 20	C 70 M 20 K 20	C 50 M 20 K 20	C 30 M 20 K 20	C 20 M 20 K 20	C 10 M 20 K 20
C 100 M 20 K 10	C 70 M 20 K 10	C 50 M 20 K 10	C 30 M 20 K 10	C 20 M 20 K 10	C 10 M 20 K 10
C 100 M 20 K 5	C 70 M 20 K 5	C 50 M 20 K 5	C 30 M 20 K 5	C 20 M 20 K 5	C 10 M 20 K 5

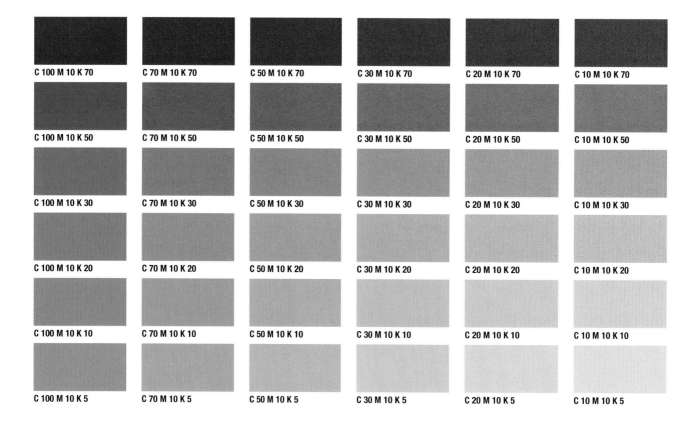

C 100 M 10 K 70	C 70 M 10 K 70	C 50 M 10 K 70	C 30 M 10 K 70	C 20 M 10 K 70	C 10 M 10 K 70
C 100 M 10 K 50	C 70 M 10 K 50	C 50 M 10 K 50	C 30 M 10 K 50	C 20 M 10 K 50	C 10 M 10 K 50
C 100 M 10 K 30	C 70 M 10 K 30	C 50 M 10 K 30	C 30 M 10 K 30	C 20 M 10 K 30	C 10 M 10 K 30
C 100 M 10 K 20	C 70 M 10 K 20	C 50 M 10 K 20	C 30 M 10 K 20	C 20 M 10 K 20	C 10 M 10 K 20
C 100 M 10 K 10	C 70 M 10 K 10	C 50 M 10 K 10	C 30 M 10 K 10	C 20 M 10 K 10	C 10 M 10 K 10
C 100 M 10 K 5	C 70 M 10 K 5	C 50 M 10 K 5	C 30 M 10 K 5	C 20 M 10 K 5	C 10 M 10 K 5

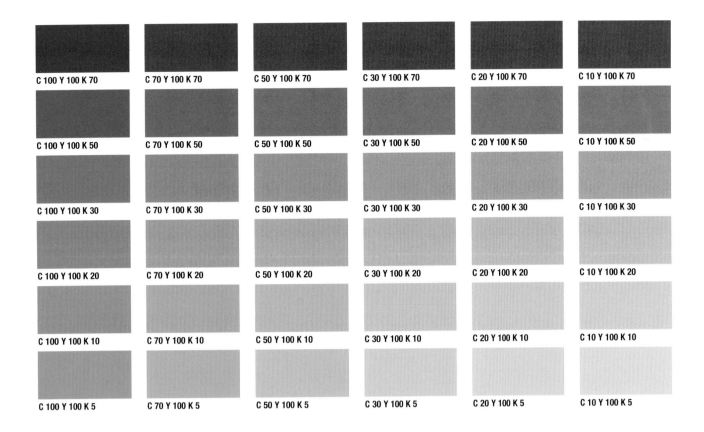

C 100 Y 100 K 70   C 70 Y 100 K 70   C 50 Y 100 K 70   C 30 Y 100 K 70   C 20 Y 100 K 70   C 10 Y 100 K 70

C 100 Y 100 K 50   C 70 Y 100 K 50   C 50 Y 100 K 50   C 30 Y 100 K 50   C 20 Y 100 K 50   C 10 Y 100 K 50

C 100 Y 100 K 30   C 70 Y 100 K 30   C 50 Y 100 K 30   C 30 Y 100 K 30   C 20 Y 100 K 30   C 10 Y 100 K 30

C 100 Y 100 K 20   C 70 Y 100 K 20   C 50 Y 100 K 20   C 30 Y 100 K 20   C 20 Y 100 K 20   C 10 Y 100 K 20

C 100 Y 100 K 10   C 70 Y 100 K 10   C 50 Y 100 K 10   C 30 Y 100 K 10   C 20 Y 100 K 10   C 10 Y 100 K 10

C 100 Y 100 K 5   C 70 Y 100 K 5   C 50 Y 100 K 5   C 30 Y 100 K 5   C 20 Y 100 K 5   C 10 Y 100 K 5

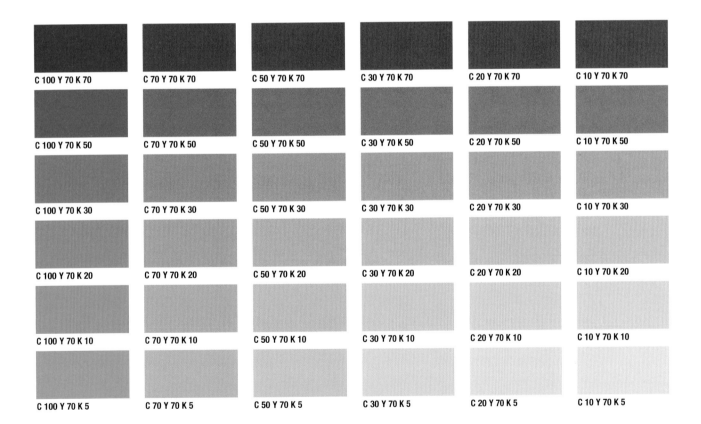

C 100 Y 70 K 70   C 70 Y 70 K 70   C 50 Y 70 K 70   C 30 Y 70 K 70   C 20 Y 70 K 70   C 10 Y 70 K 70

C 100 Y 70 K 50   C 70 Y 70 K 50   C 50 Y 70 K 50   C 30 Y 70 K 50   C 20 Y 70 K 50   C 10 Y 70 K 50

C 100 Y 70 K 30   C 70 Y 70 K 30   C 50 Y 70 K 30   C 30 Y 70 K 30   C 20 Y 70 K 30   C 10 Y 70 K 30

C 100 Y 70 K 20   C 70 Y 70 K 20   C 50 Y 70 K 20   C 30 Y 70 K 20   C 20 Y 70 K 20   C 10 Y 70 K 20

C 100 Y 70 K 10   C 70 Y 70 K 10   C 50 Y 70 K 10   C 30 Y 70 K 10   C 20 Y 70 K 10   C 10 Y 70 K 10

C 100 Y 70 K 5   C 70 Y 70 K 5   C 50 Y 70 K 5   C 30 Y 70 K 5   C 20 Y 70 K 5   C 10 Y 70 K 5

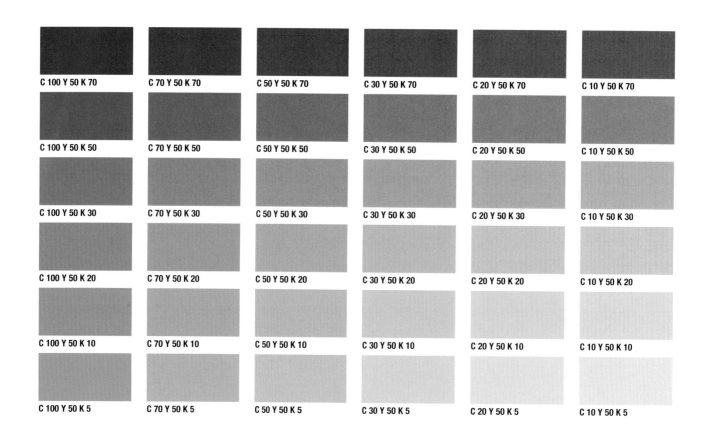

C 100 Y 50 K 70   C 70 Y 50 K 70   C 50 Y 50 K 70   C 30 Y 50 K 70   C 20 Y 50 K 70   C 10 Y 50 K 70

C 100 Y 50 K 50   C 70 Y 50 K 50   C 50 Y 50 K 50   C 30 Y 50 K 50   C 20 Y 50 K 50   C 10 Y 50 K 50

C 100 Y 50 K 30   C 70 Y 50 K 30   C 50 Y 50 K 30   C 30 Y 50 K 30   C 20 Y 50 K 30   C 10 Y 50 K 30

C 100 Y 50 K 20   C 70 Y 50 K 20   C 50 Y 50 K 20   C 30 Y 50 K 20   C 20 Y 50 K 20   C 10 Y 50 K 20

C 100 Y 50 K 10   C 70 Y 50 K 10   C 50 Y 50 K 10   C 30 Y 50 K 10   C 20 Y 50 K 10   C 10 Y 50 K 10

C 100 Y 50 K 5   C 70 Y 50 K 5   C 50 Y 50 K 5   C 30 Y 50 K 5   C 20 Y 50 K 5   C 10 Y 50 K 5

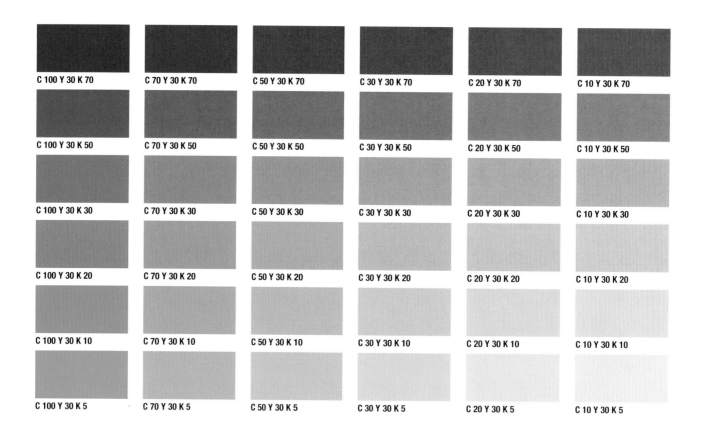

C 100 Y 30 K 70   C 70 Y 30 K 70   C 50 Y 30 K 70   C 30 Y 30 K 70   C 20 Y 30 K 70   C 10 Y 30 K 70

C 100 Y 30 K 50   C 70 Y 30 K 50   C 50 Y 30 K 50   C 30 Y 30 K 50   C 20 Y 30 K 50   C 10 Y 30 K 50

C 100 Y 30 K 30   C 70 Y 30 K 30   C 50 Y 30 K 30   C 30 Y 30 K 30   C 20 Y 30 K 30   C 10 Y 30 K 30

C 100 Y 30 K 20   C 70 Y 30 K 20   C 50 Y 30 K 20   C 30 Y 30 K 20   C 20 Y 30 K 20   C 10 Y 30 K 20

C 100 Y 30 K 10   C 70 Y 30 K 10   C 50 Y 30 K 10   C 30 Y 30 K 10   C 20 Y 30 K 10   C 10 Y 30 K 10

C 100 Y 30 K 5   C 70 Y 30 K 5   C 50 Y 30 K 5   C 30 Y 30 K 5   C 20 Y 30 K 5   C 10 Y 30 K 5

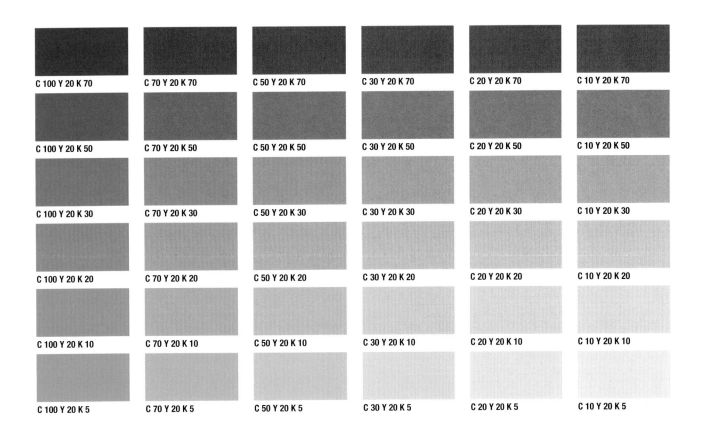

C 100 Y 20 K 70   C 70 Y 20 K 70   C 50 Y 20 K 70   C 30 Y 20 K 70   C 20 Y 20 K 70   C 10 Y 20 K 70

C 100 Y 20 K 50   C 70 Y 20 K 50   C 50 Y 20 K 50   C 30 Y 20 K 50   C 20 Y 20 K 50   C 10 Y 20 K 50

C 100 Y 20 K 30   C 70 Y 20 K 30   C 50 Y 20 K 30   C 30 Y 20 K 30   C 20 Y 20 K 30   C 10 Y 20 K 30

C 100 Y 20 K 20   C 70 Y 20 K 20   C 50 Y 20 K 20   C 30 Y 20 K 20   C 20 Y 20 K 20   C 10 Y 20 K 20

C 100 Y 20 K 10   C 70 Y 20 K 10   C 50 Y 20 K 10   C 30 Y 20 K 10   C 20 Y 20 K 10   C 10 Y 20 K 10

C 100 Y 20 K 5   C 70 Y 20 K 5   C 50 Y 20 K 5   C 30 Y 20 K 5   C 20 Y 20 K 5   C 10 Y 20 K 5

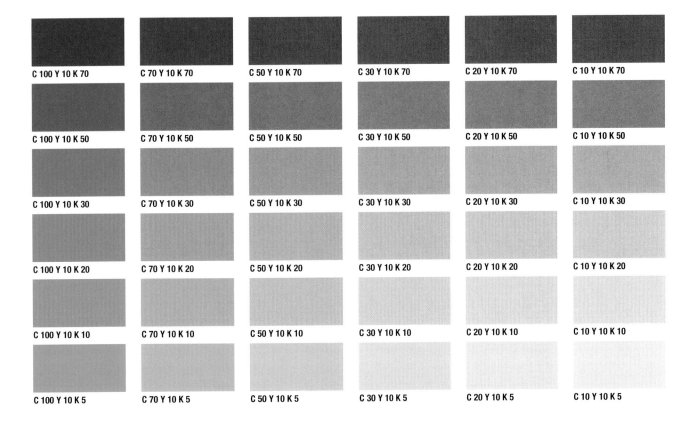

C 100 Y 10 K 70   C 70 Y 10 K 70   C 50 Y 10 K 70   C 30 Y 10 K 70   C 20 Y 10 K 70   C 10 Y 10 K 70

C 100 Y 10 K 50   C 70 Y 10 K 50   C 50 Y 10 K 50   C 30 Y 10 K 50   C 20 Y 10 K 50   C 10 Y 10 K 50

C 100 Y 10 K 30   C 70 Y 10 K 30   C 50 Y 10 K 30   C 30 Y 10 K 30   C 20 Y 10 K 30   C 10 Y 10 K 30

C 100 Y 10 K 20   C 70 Y 10 K 20   C 50 Y 10 K 20   C 30 Y 10 K 20   C 20 Y 10 K 20   C 10 Y 10 K 20

C 100 Y 10 K 10   C 70 Y 10 K 10   C 50 Y 10 K 10   C 30 Y 10 K 10   C 20 Y 10 K 10   C 10 Y 10 K 10

C 100 Y 10 K 5   C 70 Y 10 K 5   C 50 Y 10 K 5   C 30 Y 10 K 5   C 20 Y 10 K 5   C 10 Y 10 K 5

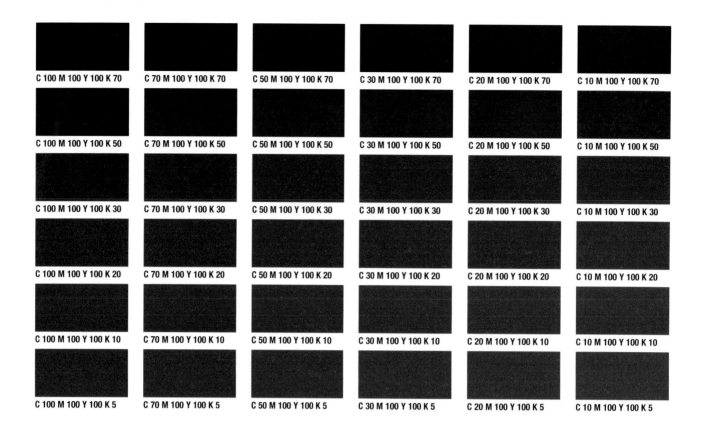

C 100 M 100 Y 100 K 70 | C 70 M 100 Y 100 K 70 | C 50 M 100 Y 100 K 70 | C 30 M 100 Y 100 K 70 | C 20 M 100 Y 100 K 70 | C 10 M 100 Y 100 K 70

C 100 M 100 Y 100 K 50 | C 70 M 100 Y 100 K 50 | C 50 M 100 Y 100 K 50 | C 30 M 100 Y 100 K 50 | C 20 M 100 Y 100 K 50 | C 10 M 100 Y 100 K 50

C 100 M 100 Y 100 K 30 | C 70 M 100 Y 100 K 30 | C 50 M 100 Y 100 K 30 | C 30 M 100 Y 100 K 30 | C 20 M 100 Y 100 K 30 | C 10 M 100 Y 100 K 30

C 100 M 100 Y 100 K 20 | C 70 M 100 Y 100 K 20 | C 50 M 100 Y 100 K 20 | C 30 M 100 Y 100 K 20 | C 20 M 100 Y 100 K 20 | C 10 M 100 Y 100 K 20

C 100 M 100 Y 100 K 10 | C 70 M 100 Y 100 K 10 | C 50 M 100 Y 100 K 10 | C 30 M 100 Y 100 K 10 | C 20 M 100 Y 100 K 10 | C 10 M 100 Y 100 K 10

C 100 M 100 Y 100 K 5 | C 70 M 100 Y 100 K 5 | C 50 M 100 Y 100 K 5 | C 30 M 100 Y 100 K 5 | C 20 M 100 Y 100 K 5 | C 10 M 100 Y 100 K 5

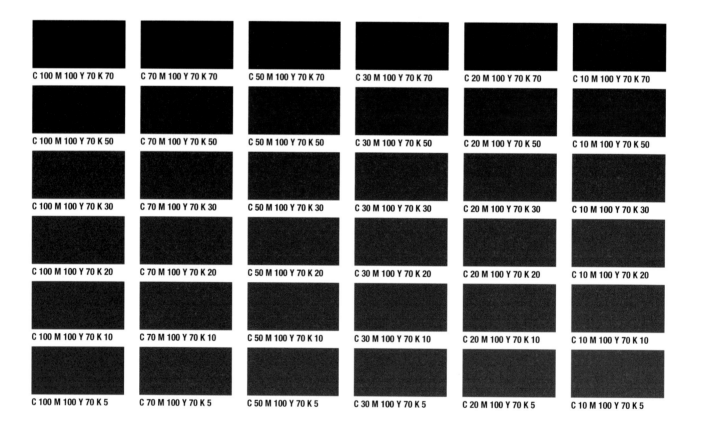

C 100 M 100 Y 70 K 70 | C 70 M 100 Y 70 K 70 | C 50 M 100 Y 70 K 70 | C 30 M 100 Y 70 K 70 | C 20 M 100 Y 70 K 70 | C 10 M 100 Y 70 K 70

C 100 M 100 Y 70 K 50 | C 70 M 100 Y 70 K 50 | C 50 M 100 Y 70 K 50 | C 30 M 100 Y 70 K 50 | C 20 M 100 Y 70 K 50 | C 10 M 100 Y 70 K 50

C 100 M 100 Y 70 K 30 | C 70 M 100 Y 70 K 30 | C 50 M 100 Y 70 K 30 | C 30 M 100 Y 70 K 30 | C 20 M 100 Y 70 K 30 | C 10 M 100 Y 70 K 30

C 100 M 100 Y 70 K 20 | C 70 M 100 Y 70 K 20 | C 50 M 100 Y 70 K 20 | C 30 M 100 Y 70 K 20 | C 20 M 100 Y 70 K 20 | C 10 M 100 Y 70 K 20

C 100 M 100 Y 70 K 10 | C 70 M 100 Y 70 K 10 | C 50 M 100 Y 70 K 10 | C 30 M 100 Y 70 K 10 | C 20 M 100 Y 70 K 10 | C 10 M 100 Y 70 K 10

C 100 M 100 Y 70 K 5 | C 70 M 100 Y 70 K 5 | C 50 M 100 Y 70 K 5 | C 30 M 100 Y 70 K 5 | C 20 M 100 Y 70 K 5 | C 10 M 100 Y 70 K 5

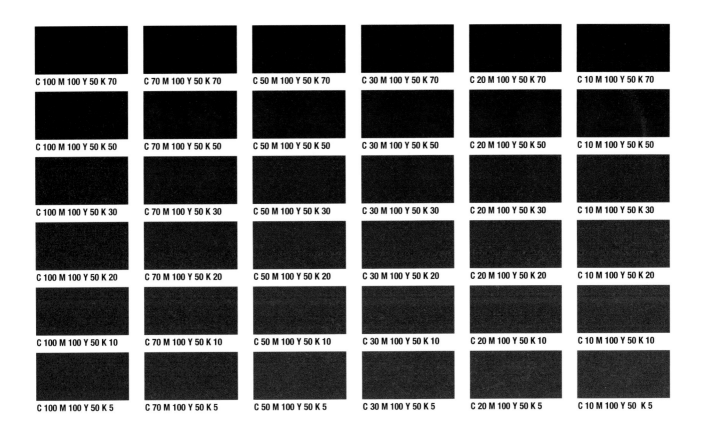

C 100 M 100 Y 50 K 70	C 70 M 100 Y 50 K 70	C 50 M 100 Y 50 K 70	C 30 M 100 Y 50 K 70	C 20 M 100 Y 50 K 70	C 10 M 100 Y 50 K 70
C 100 M 100 Y 50 K 50	C 70 M 100 Y 50 K 50	C 50 M 100 Y 50 K 50	C 30 M 100 Y 50 K 50	C 20 M 100 Y 50 K 50	C 10 M 100 Y 50 K 50
C 100 M 100 Y 50 K 30	C 70 M 100 Y 50 K 30	C 50 M 100 Y 50 K 30	C 30 M 100 Y 50 K 30	C 20 M 100 Y 50 K 30	C 10 M 100 Y 50 K 30
C 100 M 100 Y 50 K 20	C 70 M 100 Y 50 K 20	C 50 M 100 Y 50 K 20	C 30 M 100 Y 50 K 20	C 20 M 100 Y 50 K 20	C 10 M 100 Y 50 K 20
C 100 M 100 Y 50 K 10	C 70 M 100 Y 50 K 10	C 50 M 100 Y 50 K 10	C 30 M 100 Y 50 K 10	C 20 M 100 Y 50 K 10	C 10 M 100 Y 50 K 10
C 100 M 100 Y 50 K 5	C 70 M 100 Y 50 K 5	C 50 M 100 Y 50 K 5	C 30 M 100 Y 50 K 5	C 20 M 100 Y 50 K 5	C 10 M 100 Y 50 K 5

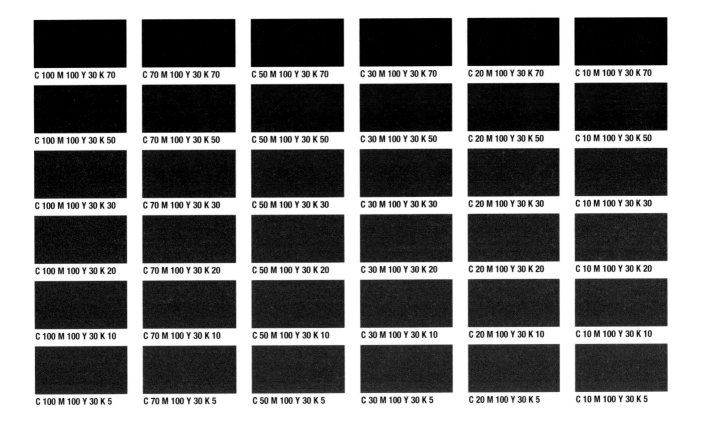

C 100 M 100 Y 30 K 70	C 70 M 100 Y 30 K 70	C 50 M 100 Y 30 K 70	C 30 M 100 Y 30 K 70	C 20 M 100 Y 30 K 70	C 10 M 100 Y 30 K 70
C 100 M 100 Y 30 K 50	C 70 M 100 Y 30 K 50	C 50 M 100 Y 30 K 50	C 30 M 100 Y 30 K 50	C 20 M 100 Y 30 K 50	C 10 M 100 Y 30 K 50
C 100 M 100 Y 30 K 30	C 70 M 100 Y 30 K 30	C 50 M 100 Y 30 K 30	C 30 M 100 Y 30 K 30	C 20 M 100 Y 30 K 30	C 10 M 100 Y 30 K 30
C 100 M 100 Y 30 K 20	C 70 M 100 Y 30 K 20	C 50 M 100 Y 30 K 20	C 30 M 100 Y 30 K 20	C 20 M 100 Y 30 K 20	C 10 M 100 Y 30 K 20
C 100 M 100 Y 30 K 10	C 70 M 100 Y 30 K 10	C 50 M 100 Y 30 K 10	C 30 M 100 Y 30 K 10	C 20 M 100 Y 30 K 10	C 10 M 100 Y 30 K 10
C 100 M 100 Y 30 K 5	C 70 M 100 Y 30 K 5	C 50 M 100 Y 30 K 5	C 30 M 100 Y 30 K 5	C 20 M 100 Y 30 K 5	C 10 M 100 Y 30 K 5

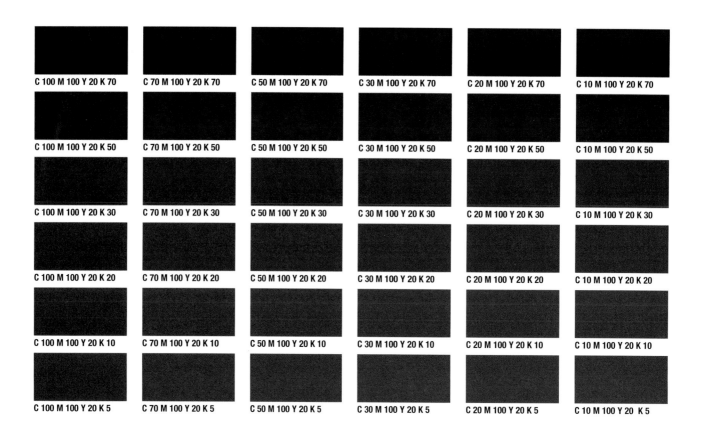

C 100 M 100 Y 20 K 70   C 70 M 100 Y 20 K 70   C 50 M 100 Y 20 K 70   C 30 M 100 Y 20 K 70   C 20 M 100 Y 20 K 70   C 10 M 100 Y 20 K 70

C 100 M 100 Y 20 K 50   C 70 M 100 Y 20 K 50   C 50 M 100 Y 20 K 50   C 30 M 100 Y 20 K 50   C 20 M 100 Y 20 K 50   C 10 M 100 Y 20 K 50

C 100 M 100 Y 20 K 30   C 70 M 100 Y 20 K 30   C 50 M 100 Y 20 K 30   C 30 M 100 Y 20 K 30   C 20 M 100 Y 20 K 30   C 10 M 100 Y 20 K 30

C 100 M 100 Y 20 K 20   C 70 M 100 Y 20 K 20   C 50 M 100 Y 20 K 20   C 30 M 100 Y 20 K 20   C 20 M 100 Y 20 K 20   C 10 M 100 Y 20 K 20

C 100 M 100 Y 20 K 10   C 70 M 100 Y 20 K 10   C 50 M 100 Y 20 K 10   C 30 M 100 Y 20 K 10   C 20 M 100 Y 20 K 10   C 10 M 100 Y 20 K 10

C 100 M 100 Y 20 K 5   C 70 M 100 Y 20 K 5   C 50 M 100 Y 20 K 5   C 30 M 100 Y 20 K 5   C 20 M 100 Y 20 K 5   C 10 M 100 Y 20 K 5

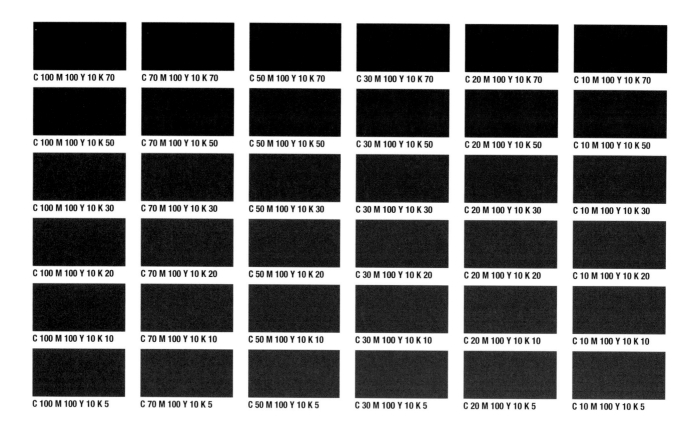

C 100 M 100 Y 10 K 70   C 70 M 100 Y 10 K 70   C 50 M 100 Y 10 K 70   C 30 M 100 Y 10 K 70   C 20 M 100 Y 10 K 70   C 10 M 100 Y 10 K 70

C 100 M 100 Y 10 K 50   C 70 M 100 Y 10 K 50   C 50 M 100 Y 10 K 50   C 30 M 100 Y 10 K 50   C 20 M 100 Y 10 K 50   C 10 M 100 Y 10 K 50

C 100 M 100 Y 10 K 30   C 70 M 100 Y 10 K 30   C 50 M 100 Y 10 K 30   C 30 M 100 Y 10 K 30   C 20 M 100 Y 10 K 30   C 10 M 100 Y 10 K 30

C 100 M 100 Y 10 K 20   C 70 M 100 Y 10 K 20   C 50 M 100 Y 10 K 20   C 30 M 100 Y 10 K 20   C 20 M 100 Y 10 K 20   C 10 M 100 Y 10 K 20

C 100 M 100 Y 10 K 10   C 70 M 100 Y 10 K 10   C 50 M 100 Y 10 K 10   C 30 M 100 Y 10 K 10   C 20 M 100 Y 10 K 10   C 10 M 100 Y 10 K 10

C 100 M 100 Y 10 K 5   C 70 M 100 Y 10 K 5   C 50 M 100 Y 10 K 5   C 30 M 100 Y 10 K 5   C 20 M 100 Y 10 K 5   C 10 M 100 Y 10 K 5

COLOR VOCABULARY

Achromatic. The total absence of color: Comprised only of black, gray, and white values.

Additive color. Color created by mixing the rays of white light, from which all color is derived. The spectrum of color exists within the rays of white light. Superimposing the three *additive* primaries (RGB), which when reversed will create white light.

Analogous Colors that are closely related in hue. They are side by side on the color circle, and cannot be broken in their sequential order. Three to five is the normal variance of side-by-side hues, with a maximum of six. They are *basically* a family of hues.

Atom. The smallest particle of an element that still retains the properties of any given element. The atom is the *mother ship* with a cargo of smaller particles and units, including the all-important color quark.

Brilliance. Same as the word intensity, which refers to the change in lightness in any given hue.

Chroma/Chromatic. Pertains specifically to the presence of color. The opposite of achromatic.

Chiaroscuro. The average gradation of values from light to dark. A type of tonal shifting across a curved or variable surface, which is responsible for creating volume and mass. The skilled use of chiaroscuro is to create believable space, or the illusion of form, on a flat surface.

Color. Color is the visually revealed component of light. Color possesses certain physiological factors, which are accompanied by various psychological ramifications and symbolical elements. The symbolical and psychological aspects of color are at variance, because they are determined by specific cultural perceptions.

Color Dyad. A color harmony consisting of two opposing colors on the color circle. Another definition for dyads is a *complementary* color scheme (see first page of Chapter 1).

Color Hexad. A color harmony comprised of six colors. A hexagon within the color circle determines specific color orders. The color order is designated by the points where each line meets. A hexad is made up of three complementary pairs (see first page of Chapter 1).

Color Tetrad. A color harmony comprised of four colors. A tetrad can exist in two forms. The first is a perfect square inscribed within the color circle. Each point where lines connect will determine the harmony color order. The second form of a tetrad harmony can be determined by inscribing a rectangle in the color circle. The same method determines the color order as before. Tetrads contain two primary colors

and their complements, or a complementary pair of intermediates (see first page of Chapter 1).

Color Triad. A color harmony containing three colors. A triad is an equilateral triangle inscribed within the color circle. Color harmony is determined by the point where each line meets. Primary and secondary triads are the most common (see first page of Chapter 1).

Color Quarks. Contained within the atom are *baryon* particles, each one containing three quarks. Each baryon bundle of three quarks contains one red, one green, and one blue quark. Together, these constitute the additive *primary* colors. Constantly colliding, these quarks form white light, the sum of all colors. *Mesons* by comparison, carry a colored quark and a antiquark, which consist of *complementary* colors.

CMYK. An acronym for digital color: cyan, magenta, yellow, and black. They are the subtractive colors of inks in a printer.
　　Color while on the monitor is referred to as RGB *additive* color, but when printed, it becomes CMYK *subtractive* color.

Complementary Color. Two colors directly opposite of each other on the color circle.
　　The three basic complements are comprised of one primary and one secondary, such as red and green, yellow and violet, and blue and orange.

Electromagnetic Spectrum. A chart representing every possible radiation emitted from high-energy gamma rays (shortest waves) to low-energy radio waves (longest waves). *Visible light,* which equates to the spectrum of colors, is located in the center of the spectral chart between the gamma and radio waves spectrum.

Hue. Hue is the common *name* of a color and indicates its position in the spectrum or color circle. Hue is determined by the specific wavelength of the color in a ray of white light.

Intensity. Intensity is the degree or amount of saturation strength, or purity in any particular hue. Intensity also refers to brightness, whereas its cousin, which is *saturation,* refers to purity. Intensity then, refers to a certain level of brightness in a given hue, as well as its amount strength of purity in a given color.

Intermediate Color. A color produced by the mixture of one primary and one secondary color. In the color circle, it is located between any single primary and secondary color. It is also referred to as *tertiary* color. (See tertiary).

Key Color. Ordinarily, there are two basic keys: high and low key in the art and design world. The film industry, however, refers to medium key (such as on a set) as well. High key is very *intense or bright* with optimal clarity. Low key is the less intense, or *dull state of colors,* which reveal much less of the imagery, often in relative darkness. Medium key is that state that lies between bright and dull. It is the *clear saturated color* with a normal condition of lighting.

Light. The revealed *source* of component colors within the electromagnetic system of wavelengths, known as the visible spectrum of color.

Local Color. Local, or objective, color is the perceived notion about the color we see. It is what we *think we see,* as opposed to what the eye actually sees.

Monochromatic. Having only one hue with a complete range of values. So, a monochromatic blue composition will have a range or variable of values from light to dark blues.

Neutrals. 1. The inclusion of all color wavelengths will produce white, and the absence of any wavelengths will be perceived as black. With neutrals, no single color is noticed—only a sense of light and dark, or the range from white through gray to black. 2. A color altered by the addition of its complement, so that the original sensation of hues is lost or grayed.

Neutralized Color. A color that has been grayed or reduced in intensity by being mixed with any of the neutrals or with a complementary color.

Optical Color. A type of additive color when two or more colors are closely juxtaposed. When viewed from a distance these combinations of colors appear to blend optically to produce colors other than those seen as *local colors.* When positioned closely together, they are perceived as a new color. Optical color is what your eye *actually perceives,* as opposed to what you think you see.

Pigment. Physical color substances, both natural and synthetic, that can be mixed to cover another tangible surface. Pigments are added to liquid vehicles, such as egg yolk or linseed oils to produce paints or inks, and are considered *subtractive* color. See *Sennelier Pigments* list of Pigment Properties in Chapter 2.

Primary Color. The preliminary hues that cannot be broken down in order to make other component colors. The basic hues in any *subtractive* color system that in theory may be used to mix all other colors (red, yellow, and blue). In theory, all colors of subtractive pigments mixed together produce black. *Additive primary* colors are the primaries of light (red, green, and blue). All colors of the additive primary lights mixed produce white (light).

Reflected Color. The absolute truest color of any particular object is revealed by reflected color. Its true color is separated from the other spectral colors when the remaining colors are absorbed into that object's surface. A red apple appears to be red because the red is reflected back into the viewer's eyes, while the remaining spectrum of colors are absorbed into the apple's surface. Basically, the molecular constitution of the apple's surface recognizes the ray of red light only.

Refracted Light. The bending of light as it travels from one transparent medium to another, such as when light travels through two pieces of glass, through a white diamond, or when light travels from air to water.

Saturation. In pigment, it is the absolute purity of a given hue. It is total freedom from black, gray, or white; it is the pure state of a color, or full strength. In additive color or prismatic hues, it is the color spectrum, which possesses the maximum saturation of a hue.

Secondary Color. A color produced by a mixture of two primary colors on the color circle, which are Orange, Green and Violet.

Shade. The addition of black to a given hue. Shading gradates from white to gray on the value scale, in that order.

Simultaneous Contrast. When two different colors such as complements, come into direct contact with one another, they create a neutral gray zone between. The contrast intensifies the difference between the two, and in many cases a thin gray line will appear at the point where the colors come together. This is particularly true when saturated red is joined to its complement of green, which will produce a very obvious gray line between them. The two complements have visually cancelled each other at that juncture. Basically, the eye mixes the two complements, and cancels (neutralizes) them between.

Split Complements. One specific color plus the two colors that exist on either side of its complement. An example would be yellow and its complement of violet. One half of violet would be added to red, producing a warm violet, and the other half of the violet would then be added to blue, which produces a cool violet. Therefore, the split complement is comprised of yellow, red-violet, and blue-violet. It is in effect a non-equilateral triangle of three colors. (See first page of Chapter 1.)

Subjective Color. Color resulting from the mind, which demonstrates a personal viewpoint, particular bias, mood, or emotion. Color combinations that tend to produce creative or original results.

Subtractive Color. The sensations of color that are produced by wavelengths of light, which are reflected back to the viewer's eyes after all other colors have been absorbed by the object. For example, the surface of a green leaf has a particular molecular constitution that is only recognized by green in the spectrum of visual light. All other colors are not accepted, and are absorbed into the leaf rather than reflected back to the eye.

Temperature. The colors of the spectrum, which are observed in their warm to cool and cool to warm order. Warm colors are red, orange, and yellow.

Cool colors are green, blue, indigo, and violet. Violet can be either warm or cool, depending on whether it is closer to the red side of the color wheel or the blue side, respectively.

Tertiary Color. Most refer to this as interchangeable with the word *intermediate.*

Tint. The addition of white to a given hue. Tinting is a gradient from gray to white on the value scale, in that order. Tinting tends to brighten a color.

Tone. Tone is often difficult to define, because it is related so closely to *value* and *tints and shades.* Often, the tone of a composition is used to refer to the overall sameness of dullness, grayness, or intensity throughout the picture plane. Another way to address the definition is to understand that tone is a *modification of a color* or hue in various ways. One could transform a hue with another, such as red with yellow, or the addition of black white to change a saturated color, or gray can be added to mute a given hue. Most use the phrase *to tone-down* a color, meaning to take away its intensity or saturation, but that usually does not apply to intensifying a color. Even with that there are some loopholes. There is no one completely satisfactory definition, in and of itself.

Value. The relative degree of lightness or darkness, or light to dark gradations, which can be seen on a gray scale. *Chiaroscuro* is much the same in this respect.

Visible Spectrum. A band of seven individual colors that results when a beam of white light is broken into its component wavelengths, which we can identify as particular hues (for example, from the sun's white light). Located in the center of the electromagnetic spectrum in the form of *red, orange, yellow, green, blue, indigo (blue-green), and violet.*

INDEX

successive contrast, 263
Surrealism, 54–55
Suzumushi I, 290
Swing, The, 36–37
symphonic opera, 321
Symphonic Sculpture, 113–115
symphony, 318
systems, color. *See* color systems

T
Tahitian Landscape, 170
Taiko performance, 388–389
Takehawa II, 288
Tale of Genji, The, 280–283, 289–293
tempera, 18, 25
temperature
    absolute, 142
    defined, 438–439
    warm/cool contrast, 175–180
Temple du Lac Bratan, 187
temples
    Temple du Lac Bratan, 187
    Thailand, 100–102
tenebrism value system, 221, 231–232
terracotta calyx-krater, 13
tertiary colors, 439. *See also* intermediate colors
tesserae mosaic tile, 17
tetradic color harmonies, 270–272, 386, 437
tetrahedrons, 81
Thailand, 100–102
Theory of Colors, 71–72
thermodynamics, first law of, 141
thermosphere, 69
third firing, 12–13
Third-Class Carriage, 168–169
Thomson, Joseph, 76–77, 142
tints and shades
    in animation, 223–224
    in classical world, 218
    in Contemporary art, 222–223
    defined, 439
    in early American Realism, 221
    key color, 224–227
    mass and deep space project, 256–258
    in Middle Ages, 219
    in Modern art, 222–223
    overview, 217
    in Renaissance Age, 220
    value systems
        chiaroscuro, 230–231
        sfumato, 227–230
        tenebrism, 231–232
titanium white, 148
Titian, 30–31
Tivoli, xvi–xvii
Tokyo, 279
Tolkowsky, Marcel, 81
Tomaguchi, Debbie, 316–317
tonal color, 30
tone
    color theory, 386
    defined, 439
topaz, 22
Toreador fresco, 10–11
Tori Gate, 277
Torricelli, Evangelista, 132
Tour, Georges de la, 182–183
Trattato della pi, 233
Trevi Fountain, 176

triadic color harmonies
    defined, 437
    overview, 265–269
    split complementary, 268–269
troposphere, 69
twelve–part color circle, 61–64
twentieth-century painting, 48–49
Two Nudes, 264

U
Ulster Orchestra, 318
ultramarine blues, 152
ultramarine violet, 153
Umbrellas, The, 334–335
underpainting, 34
Untitled (Rothko, Mark), 57
Untitled (Yellow Table on Green), 335

V
Valley Curtain, 334
value, 94–96, 439. *See also* tints and shades
value star, 105
Van Der Weyden, Rogier, 24, 94
Van Dongen, 95
Van Dyck brown, 149
Van Eyck, Jan
    Arnolfini Wedding, The, 27
    Marriage of Giovanni Arnolfini and Giovanna Cenami, The, 27, 173
Van Gogh, Vincent
    Café Terrace by Night, 187–188
    Four Cut Sunflowers, 46–47
    Harvest Landscape, xviii
    Haystacks in Provence, 46–47
    overview, xviii
    Red Vineyard at Arles, The, xxiii–xxv
    Starry Night, 187–188
    Street in Saintes-Maries, 330
vegetable colors, 204–208
Venetian glass, 31
Venetian red, 150
Venus of Urbino, 30–31
Verdi, 389–390
Vermeer, Jan, 34–35, 332
Veronese green, 151
Village Church in Riegsee, Bavaria, 189
Village Girl from Band-e Amir, 325
Violet Catastrophe, 143
violets, 153
Virgin and Child with Two Saints, 19
visible color spectrum, 65–66, 386, 439
Vision After the Sermon, Jacob Wrestling with the Angel, 179–180, 320, 385–386
Voices of Spring, 335
Von Helmholtz, Hermann Ludwig Ferdinand, 141

W
warm and cool contrast, 175–180
warm illumination, 256
warm stage, 338
Washington National Cathedral, xxviii, 88, 90, 92
Wat Rongkun, 216
water
    sensations of color in, 193–201
    waves, 135
Watt, James, 141
wavelengths, 67
Weeping Woman , 362–364, 367–370
weld, 34